Martin Guardado
Discourse, Ideology and Heritage Language Socialization

Contributions to the Sociology of Language

Edited by
Ofelia García
Francis M. Hult

Founding editor
Joshua A. Fishman

Volume 104

Martin Guardado
Discourse, Ideology and Heritage Language Socialization

―

Micro and Macro Perspectives

ISBN 978-1-5015-1941-3
e-ISBN (PDF) 978-1-61451-384-1
e-ISBN (EPUB) 978-1-5015-0073-2
ISSN 1861-0676

Library of Congress Control Number: 2018934539

Bibliographic information published by the Deutsche Nationalbibliothek
The Deutsche Nationalbibliothek lists this publication in the Deutsche Nationalbibliografie;
detailed bibliographic data are available on the Internet at http://dnb.dnb.de.

© 2019 Walter de Gruyter Inc., Boston/Berlin
This volume is text- and page-identical with the hardback published in 2018.
Cover image: sculpies/shutterstock
Typesetting: Integra Software Services Pvt. Ltd.
Printing and binding: CPI books GmbH, Leck
♾ Printed on acid-free paper
Printed in Germany

www.degruyter.com

Preface

I have been involved in research surrounding heritage languages since the year 2000. One thing that became clear to me early on was the wide range of aspects that make up this topic. This made me realize that in order to attempt to understand the workings of heritage language socialization, one would need varied sources of data and multiple tools of analysis. I also found, however, that these are not straightforward decisions given the debates taking place, even in fields that are only vaguely relevant to heritage language studies. In a book chapter published in 1979 by Elinor Ochs, *Transcription as Theory*, she drew attention to an old controversy in linguistics about what constitutes appropriate data for proposing linguistic norms. It is well known that Noam Chomsky, a theoretical linguist, has argued for decades that actual language use is not only unnecessary but useless for conducting linguistic analyses. Others, such as Dell Hymes, William Labov, and Michael Halliday—who view language from cultural, social, and functional standpoints respectively—take the contrary position that the way speakers use language is what really matters in any analysis of language. In other words, rather than working with an idealized system, language scholars ought to observe and examine what language users actually produce. In essence, this is an ontological debate of whether our understandings of what constitutes language and language use should be based on what speakers *do* or on what they *say*—or think—they do. Both of these approaches—what speakers do and what they say they do—have been applied to heritage language development research.

The two perspectives taken in this book, though not identical to the ones described above, do exhibit some parallels of sorts. In analyzing and theorizing heritage language socialization, development, and maintenance, I draw on what families and children say they feel, think, and do in relation to the languages in their lives. At the same time, I observe, record, and transcribe actual language behaviour between children and adult caregivers in a variety of daily life situations. These two forms of data represent a self-reported (even idealized) position as well as the observed enactment of these accounts. I analyze both types of data through various techniques, such as thematic analysis, on one hand, and tools borrowed from the ethnography of communication and conversation analysis on the other. Significant qualitative research in heritage language development privileges the first perspective. That is, the arguments and explanations are largely drawn from families' "opining" about heritage language development and their linguistic practices. This book attempts to take a balanced approach by drawing on both paradigms and analyzing the data from micro and macro perspectives. It is my hope that this combination of approaches will result in productive ways of advancing this critical research area.

My main motivation for engaging in this project largely stems from my interest over the last two decades in bringing these perspectives together in one book. I will have to admit, however, that the multifaceted nature of the topic I referred to earlier has been found to be more profound than I initially realized. Undertaking this project, then, became much more challenging and took much longer than I had anticipated. As a result, the list of people I am indebted to also became longer than expected.

This book has been in the making for close to two decades as I have formally worked on heritage and minority language issues. During this time, I have read extensively and learned from both academic and non-academic literature while working on several projects with ethnolinguistic minorities examining different aspects of heritage language socialization. I have also learned through presentations, courses, and by unwittingly listening in on public conversations as well as by engaging in formal and casual discussions with mentors, students, peers, and colleagues. Many others have fed my thinking through casual interactions, including my children, an assortment of family members, and strangers. Most of all, I have lived—heritage languages are an intimate part of life for linguistic minorities. I have lived more than half of my life as a linguistic minority and in some ways this project is an extension of my life. Thus, each of the above activities and interactions has informed and shaped my thinking around the topics that I address in this book. I owe a great debt to all of the above people as I realize that in writing this book I have depended on so many of them, most of whom will never read these words—or know that I have written a book that is partly theirs. I would like to sincerely acknowledge all of those who have contributed directly or indirectly to this project.

First of all, I would like to acknowledge the participants in all of the studies that have informed the content of the book, and in particular, the three focal families and three grassroots groups that generously opened their doors so that I could conduct my ethnographic work in Vancouver, Canada. I am deeply thankful to the late Joshua Fishman who founded and co-edited with Ofelia García the book series *Contributions to the Sociology of Language* at De Gruyter Mouton at the time this book project was undertaken. I am profoundly grateful to them for believing that this book would be a valuable contribution to heritage language socialization and to the sociology of language more broadly. Their encouragement and guidance from the initial proposal made a tremendous difference. Their constructive comments throughout the project, along with those of the anonymous reviewers, strongly contributed to the quality of the final product and I am particularly grateful for their support. I also thank Lara Wysong at De Gruyter Mouton for her incredible patience during the several years that took me to complete the project.

I would like to express my sincere appreciation to my mentors at the University of British Columbia who guided me through much of the research I draw on, particularly Drs. Patsy Duff, Margaret Early, Jim Anderson, Lee Gunderson, Geoff Williams, Steven Talmy, Bonny Norton, and John Willinsky. I thank my UBC peers, Sandra Zappa-Hollman, Jérémie Séror, Lyndsay Moffat, and Diane Potts for being such a valuable source of support in many aspects of the work reported in the book. I have many people to thank at the University of Alberta. In particular, I am grateful to Dean Katy Campbell for her encouragement and support and to Anne Merritt for her assistance with parts of the final version. Last but not least, I am indebted to my amazing research assistant, Ava Becker, who became involved in this project early on and played a key role at many stages of development.

I would like to acknowledge the funders whose generous support made the various research projects possible: Social Sciences and Humanities Research Council of Canada (both a Doctoral Fellowship as well as a Standard Research Grant), the Faculty of Education Graduate Student Research Grant (UBC), the Joseph Katz Memorial Award for Multicultural Education (UBC), and the Faculty of Extension Research Grant (University of Alberta).

Contents

1	**Introduction** —— 1	
1.1	Why heritage language studies? —— 3	
1.2	Reconsidering the first language maintenance construct —— 5	
1.3	Research methods in heritage language studies —— 6	
1.4	Sources of data —— 9	
1.4.1	2001 case studies —— 10	
1.4.2	2005–2007 ethnography —— 10	
1.4.2.1	Access, settings and participants —— 12	
1.4.2.2	Data collection —— 13	
1.4.2.3	Data analysis —— 13	
1.5	Organization of the book —— 14	
1.6	Chapter summary —— 15	

Part I: Setting the stage

2	**Overview of heritage language studies** —— 19	
2.1	Introduction —— 19	
2.2	A historical overview —— 19	
2.2.1	The contributions of Joshua A. Fishman —— 20	
2.3	Heritage language development: A progress report card —— 22	
2.3.1	Language beliefs and attitudes —— 22	
2.3.1.1	Forces against heritage language development —— 23	
2.3.2	Three key factors in heritage language development —— 25	
2.3.2.1	The role of schools —— 25	
2.3.2.2	Affiliation to ethnic group —— 27	
2.3.2.3	Intergenerational communication and family unity —— 28	
2.3.3	Agnes He's hypotheses —— 30	
2.4	Chapter summary —— 32	

3	**Language socialization** —— 34	
3.1	Introduction —— 34	
3.2	Defining language socialization —— 34	
3.2.1	Language socialization: Theory and methods —— 35	
3.3	The evolution of language socialization —— 37	
3.3.1	Language socialization across contexts —— 39	

3.3.1.1	Second language socialization —— 39	
3.3.1.2	Language socialization in multilingual contexts —— 43	
3.4	Heritage language socialization —— 46	
3.4.1	Heritage language socialization in interlingual families —— 49	
3.5	Evolving conceptualizations and issues —— 51	
3.6	Chapter summary —— 53	

4 Language ideologies —— 55
- 4.1 Introduction —— 55
- 4.2 Defining language ideologies —— 55
- 4.3 Ideologies and heritage language development —— 57
- 4.3.1 Ideologies that devalue languages —— 59
- 4.3.2 Language ideologies and an emerging body of research —— 61
- 4.3.3 Socializing language ideologies —— 62
- 4.3.3.1 Language ideology socialization, accommodation and resistance —— 63
- 4.3.3.2 Reproducing dominant language ideologies —— 64
- 4.3.4 Is there an ideological paradox? —— 66
- 4.4 Chapter summary —— 68

5 What is discourse? —— 70
- 5.1 Introduction —— 70
- 5.2 Defining discourse —— 70
- 5.3 Origin, development and perspectives —— 71
- 5.3.1 Michel Foucault's contributions —— 73
- 5.3.2 Critical discourse analysis and critical discourse studies —— 74
- 5.3.3 The dialectics of discourse —— 75
- 5.3.4 Discourse, critique and power across disciplines —— 75
- 5.4 Discourse and ideology —— 77
- 5.5 Chapter summary —— 78

Part II: The discursive construction of heritage language development

6 Discourses of heritage language development I: A preliminary typology —— 81
- 6.1 Introduction —— 81
- 6.2 Thematic analysis of data —— 81
- 6.3 The discourses of Spanish as a heritage language —— 83
- 6.3.1 Utility —— 83

6.3.2	Cohesiveness —— 84	
6.3.3	Identity —— 85	
6.3.4	Affect —— 86	
6.3.5	Aesthetics —— 88	
6.3.6	Validation —— 89	
6.3.7	Correctness —— 91	
6.3.8	Opposition —— 92	
6.3.9	Access —— 94	
6.3.10	Cosmopolitanism —— 96	
6.4	Chapter summary —— 98	

7 Discourses II: Mapping the literature —— 101
7.1   Introduction —— 101
7.2   Testing the typology —— 101
7.3   Selection of studies —— 101
7.4   Identifying discourses within studies —— 102
7.5   Discourses in the research literature —— 105
7.5.1   Discourses of cohesiveness —— 106
7.5.2   Discourses of identity —— 108
7.5.3   Less frequently found discourses —— 109
7.5.4   Least representative discourses —— 111
7.6   Chapter summary —— 113

8 Discourses III: Problematizing the discourse typology —— 115
8.1   Introduction —— 115
8.2   Rationalizing a discursive approach to heritage language studies —— 115
8.3   Overlapping discourses of heritage language development —— 116
8.3.1   Interconnected constellations of discourses and their attributes —— 116
8.4   Implications of typologizing discourses —— 119
8.4.1   Theoretical implications —— 119
8.4.2   Empirical implications —— 120
8.4.3   Dialectical implications —— 120
8.5   Chapter summary —— 120

Part III: Socializing strategies and metapragmatic practices

9 The role of community —— 125
9.1   Introduction —— 125

9.2	Why are communities relevant? — 125	
9.2.1	Introducing the role of community through sense of community — 126	
9.2.2	The therapeutic role of churches in Black communities — 127	
9.2.3	Hispanic familism — 128	
9.2.4	The role of grassroots community groups in HL development: British Columbia — 128	
9.2.4.1	El Grupo Scout Vistas — 129	
9.2.4.2	El Centro de Cultura — 131	
9.2.4.3	La Casa Amistad — 132	
9.2.5	The role of grassroots community groups in HL development: Alberta — 134	
9.2.5.1	The Co-Op — 134	
9.2.5.2	REPARA — 135	
9.2.6	Motivations for starting the groups — 135	
9.2.7	Motivations for group participation — 137	
9.2.8	Interpreting the role of the grassroots groups — 137	
9.2.8.1	Creating language and cultural spaces — 137	
9.2.8.2	Linguistic and cultural validation — 140	
9.2.8.3	Social relations — 141	
9.3	Parallels across communities — 143	
9.4	Grassroots groups as primary communities — 144	
9.5	Chapter summary — 145	
10	**Family language and literacy practices — 147**	
10.1	Introduction — 147	
10.2	The home context and heritage language development — 147	
10.2.1	A mother's lonely struggle — 148	
10.2.2	The role of family intimacy — 150	
10.2.3	"Language injections" — 152	
10.2.4	Family literacy and the role of transnationalism — 156	
10.2.5	Engaging in critical family literacy — 159	
10.3	How do the above practices fare? — 162	
10.4	Chapter summary — 164	
11	**Family language policy and language regulation — 166**	
11.1	Introduction — 166	
11.2	Family language planning and management — 166	
11.3	Metadiscursive reports of language regulation — 167	
11.4	The linguistic interactional picture — 170	

11.5	Heritage language socialization and conversation analysis —— 173	
11.6	Conversation analysis —— 174	
11.6.1	A few words on transcription —— 176	
11.7	Concepts associated with language regulation —— 180	
11.7.1	Self-repair —— 180	
11.7.2	Corrective feedback —— 181	
11.7.3	Recasts —— 183	
11.7.4	Cross-code recasts —— 183	
11.7.5	Clarification requests —— 184	
11.7.6	Lectures —— 185	
11.8	Chapter summary —— 185	
12	**Heritage language regulation —— 187**	
12.1	Introduction —— 187	
12.2	Lectures as a defensive language socialization practice —— 188	
12.3	Cross-code recasts and conversational expansions —— 191	
12.4	Requests and negotiation —— 193	
12.5	Clarification requests and conversational closings —— 195	
12.6	Commands, resistance and sequence closings —— 197	
12.7	Implications of the analyses —— 199	
12.8	Chapter summary —— 202	

Part IV: Family, community and education in global perspective

13	**A cosmopolitan turn in heritage language studies? —— 205**	
13.1	Introduction —— 205	
13.2	Generation 1.5 and Third Culture Kids —— 205	
13.3	Cosmopolitanism —— 206	
13.4	Growing up ethnic or pan-ethnic? —— 208	
13.5	Growing up around other languages and cultures —— 209	
13.6	Growing up with a broader vision of the world —— 212	
13.7	Growing up cosmopolitan —— 213	
13.8	Implications of a cosmopolitan turn —— 216	
13.9	Chapter summary —— 218	
14	**From multiculturalism to cosmopolitanism —— 220**	
14.1	Introduction —— 220	

14.2	The global race to "be" global —— **220**	
14.3	Transnationalism, cosmopolitanism and global citizenship —— **221**	
14.4	Cosmopolitanism and education —— **223**	
14.4.1	Higher education —— **223**	
14.4.2	Language education —— **224**	
14.4.3	Canadian K-12 curricula —— **224**	
14.5	From multiculturalism to cosmopolitanism —— **226**	
14.6	Cosmopolitanism in educational practice —— **227**	
14.7	Cosmopolitanism and Canadian identity —— **227**	
14.8	Chapter summary —— **228**	
15	**Final reflections and ways forward —— 230**	
15.1	Introduction —— **230**	
15.2	Signposting to new conversations —— **230**	
15.3	Research directions —— **236**	
15.4	In closing —— **237**	

References —— 239
A note on the texts —— 262
Subject index —— 263

1 Introduction

I am my language. Until I can take pride in my language, I cannot take pride in myself.
(Anzaldúa 1987: 59)

Language is central to human life. It is intricately interknitted in culture and in how people see themselves in the world. Language is the main vehicle of cultural values and meanings and therefore plays a key role in shaping the worldview of individuals and communities. At the local level, language is the primary means by which families help young children become members of a cultural community. If language is essential to a wide range of human endeavours for all groups, fostering the heritage language is a critical necessity for linguistic-minority families living in multilingual settings. Their language is the means through which they can more successfully socialize their children into the beliefs, values, ideologies, and discursive practices as well as into their conceptions of the world. This process of socialization also involves the shaping of children's particular identities, drawing them to identify with a community of speakers, and expecting them to interact competently and appropriately with the broader society. Heritage language development, then, is not a trivial matter for linguistic-minority families. Rather than viewing language development and maintenance as a narrow pursuit, inspired by a "backward" and nostalgic stance based on families' intractable wish to cling to their past through their heritage language, it should be seen as an essential component of their adjustment, integration, and overall well-being.

As an interdisciplinary project, this book takes both micro and macro perspectives on heritage language development and draws on three interrelated theoretical and conceptual perspectives as organizing principles and analytical lenses, namely, discourse, language ideologies and socialization. I take a macro perspective that draws on critical discourse studies in order to analyze the ways in which language development and maintenance is "talked about" in popular and academic circles. I draw on ethnographic data to construct a typology of discourses of heritage language development and maintenance and then apply it to a selection of the research literature, which becomes the catalyst for engaging in a critical examination of the research area and of the typology itself.

The broad perspective taken in the book also includes a close examination of the interaction between issues of heritage language development and the macro socio-politico-cultural structures in society. These interactions are indelibly implicated in relations of power, which are critically confronted throughout the book. At the micro level, I discuss the patterns of communication between children and caregivers in multilingual settings. This discussion is facilitated via analyses of day-to-day interactions in homes and community groups. Using analytic tools borrowed mainly from the conversation analysis (CA) tradition, I describe the linguistic strategies that adults employ in attempts to regulate the language use of children. Taking a critical stance, I demonstrate how certain strategies have a positive effect on family interactions, potentially expanding the conversations, while other strategies act negatively by ending communicative sequences.

Concerns have emerged recently within the linguistic anthropology of education research about the usefulness of the micro/macro scale as a heuristic. In particular, questions have been raised regarding the perceived narrow, deterministic, and potentially misleading nature of this scale (Wortham 2012). While acknowledging these as valid critiques, a decision was made to apply this heuristic in the present book for several reasons. First of all, while much research has been conducted within education from micro and macro perspectives, significantly informing the field through nuanced analyses of agency and structure, the study of HLs has not yet benefited from such analyses at the micro and macro levels. Indeed, leading scholars in this and related research areas continue to utilize this framing fairly productively (e.g., Lanza 2001, Piller and Takahashi 2006, Lanza 2007, Talmy 2010, Fogle 2013, Fogle and King 2013). Therefore, it is argued that HL socialization is not yet at the stage of moving beyond this social scale and into a more fluid consideration of, for instance, contingent emergence and enduring constraints (Wortham 2012). It is expected that once these more traditional scales have been sufficiently explained, HL socialization may also outlive a micro/macro distinction and perhaps benefit from currently emerging models that draw on different spatial and temporal scales. In this regard, Wortham (2012) discusses the concept of "enduring struggles" used by Holland and Lave (2001) in their work on practice theory, from among several possibilities. Finally, Wortham acknowledges several problems with approaches that attempt to move beyond the micro and macro distinction as obstacles for fully implementing them in the linguistic anthropology of education and in other fields, positing that these need to be fully articulated to be useful. The time may come, but it is not yet here, for HL socialization to draw on appropriate approaches that can take the field further in this regard.

Throughout the book, language socialization is used as the theoretical lens that facilitates the analyses at both the micro and broader scales, productively connecting the two. The language ideology concept is used throughout the book as the critical thread that interweaves all issues and perspectives. Thus, at the microlinguistic level, it frames discussions related to the adults' views of different languages and how they should be used in their daily interactions. It also helps illuminate how children are socialized into language practices and views of the world. Therefore, provocative conceptualizations of heritage language development and maintenance are put forward as a result of the synergistic interaction of discourse, ideologies, and language socialization.

Dell Hymes stated in 1974 that a multidisciplinary approach was indispensible for studying language, positing that just as linguistics was obviously needed in this endeavour, so were anthropology, sociology, education, and other fields. Hymes' words have perhaps never been truer than they are today, as evidenced by the multidisciplinary developments in language-related areas of research, but especially in relation to the study of heritage languages. In this book, I attempt to heed Hymes' call and take the position that the scholarly study of heritage language development and maintenance is a necessarily interdisciplinary endeavour. It is a highly complex phenomenon that plays out at micro and macro levels, both for individuals and communities and thus is connected to several fields and research areas. As a result, it has been investigated from various disciplinary perspectives combining different methods. Some of the fields from which heritage language development and maintenance has been examined include, but are not limited to, linguistics, applied linguistics, ethnolinguistics, sociolinguistics, anthro-political linguistics, education, early childhood education, and speech-language pathology. Perhaps partly due to the diversity of scholarly backgrounds involved in heritage language studies, the terms used in heritage language scholarship have also been varied. The perspective more closely associated with this book falls within the scope of linguistic anthropology, sociolinguistics, and the sociology of language. In the next chapter, I discuss the sociology of language and sociolinguistics more specifically as a way of setting up the body of the book. In most chapters, a variety of linguistic anthropological focal points are also foregrounded.

1.1 Why heritage language studies?

A pressing research issue in societies with local linguistic minorities (including aboriginal groups) and immigrant receiving societies is the need to better understand how families, communities, and governments deal with minority languages and cultures. As the world becomes more interconnected and the mobility of people intensifies globally, language contact also increases, individuals continue to add new languages to their repertoires, and more children are born and raised among several languages. In this rapidly evolving living environment, parents invariably wonder what the best child-rearing practices are in relation to language, they want to know what to do with the languages in their lives and how these affect their parenting styles and outcomes. Many questions emerge among parents about how these languages relate to them as families, to their children as individuals, to who they are, and to how they can see themselves in their communities. They continue to wonder whether to keep or abandon their languages, and if so, how. They nervously speculate about whether their actions hinder or enable their children's futures. They ask themselves and their friends what other families in similar situations do and what their experiences are. Many would like to know what language experts think and know about these concerns and what advice they can get from them.

Policy-makers and educators would like to know how to better cater to their increasingly multilingual classrooms in a culturally and multilingually sensitive manner that is pedagogically sound. It is important for them to access research findings concerning the language and literacy attitudes, goals, and practices of families in order to design curricula that is consonant with families' efforts in supporting their children's schooling and work cooperatively in pursuing common educational goals. Indeed, research on heritage language attitudes and home practices can provide critical insights for educators to better understand the experiences and characteristics of families who face differing circumstances (e.g., in relation to educational background) and possible differing educational goals (e.g., literacy, biliteracy, monolingualism, multilingualism). By identifying such goals and circumstances and designing programs that take these issues into consideration and offering more flexible, culturally responsive, and effective programs (DeBruin-Parecki and Paris 1997), stakeholders may be able to more successfully address the education desires and goals of differently advantaged families. Relatedly, it is essential for governments to know what appropriate and fair language policies are and what programs to support and how. The future is increasingly multilingual and societies need to be prepared for this reality and learn how to capitalize on such resources.

All of the above questions, concerns, and issues are often talked about in academic, family, community, and other circles in various ways. These ways of talking—discourses—are of course prompted by particular ideologies, situations, and contextual realities. One of the key arguments that I make in this book, following Michel Foucault and others, is that discourses are not only produced by, but also producers of, "the subjects and the worlds of which they speak" (Lessa 2006: 285). Thus, engaging theoretically and empirically with such talk is a fruitful direction as it has the potential of contributing to enacting heritage language development in the new generations. This book addresses these and related areas and attempts to move the conversation further into as of yet unexplored directions.

Finally, as part of the process of building this emerging area of research (heritage language studies), the book attempts to expand HL socialization theorization across increasingly complex settings, social scales (micro and macro), drawing on a variety of concepts borrowed from neighbouring disciplines, research methodologies, and analytical techniques. The unifying thread in this book is its broad—and yet deep—treatment of a large set of relevant characteristics of heritage language socialization. The centeredness of ideology and discourse in this process is salient in relation to issues of identity, power, agency, negotiation, and resistance. All of these features are intertwined and, as such, are addressed separately and in relation to one another throughout the book.

1.2 Reconsidering the first language maintenance construct

An array of themes and processes are investigated across disciplines in connection with the terms *language maintenance* and *loss*, including *language shift, language attrition, language forgetting, language obsolescence, multilingual development,* and *heritage language development*. Although the term *language maintenance* is arguably more widely known and understood, and it is the term that leading scholars originally used to launch this and related areas of study (see, e.g., Fishman 1965), in this book I mostly[1] use *heritage language development and maintenance* in order to emphasize *development*, and not just keeping an already-developed level of language ability, as the term language maintenance seems to suggest. Adding the word heritage to the term also helps to bring attention to the fact that the minority language might never have been the child's dominant (native) language, and indeed only have been spoken by the parents, with the children having mere receptive abilities in the language.

Furthermore, the term *first language (L1) maintenance,* and its variations (e.g., mother tongue maintenance, heritage language maintenance), has been used widely in applied linguistics scholarship. However, so far the exact meaning of the term has not been fully fleshed out. In general, although *L1 maintenance* also entails complex socialization processes of cultural continuation and the development of particular identities, it may create the impression that it is an autonomous, amorphous, linear, and unproblematic phenomenon. Additionally, though *maintenance* connotes something that is already present, for second-generation linguistic-minority children this is generally not the case as they need sufficient exposure to the family language in order to acquire it. Moreover, their socialization experiences tend to be much more complicated; outside the home, they are often socialized through a societal language that is usually different from

---

[1] In certain cases, when citing the work of others I use *language maintenance, language loss,* and similar terms in order to more closely retain the authors' terminology preferences and the contextual reality.

that of their parents or through a mixture of languages or language varieties. In the home, these children may be socialized through their parents' languages, through the societal language (in the case of language shift at home), or also through a combination of languages or language varieties.

Even if this is not the central focus, the discussions in this book underscore such complexity and highlight the need to reconceptualize *L1 maintenance* as a multifaceted, contested, and socially situated process whose meaning goes beyond retaining something concrete that is already in one's possession (i.e., language ability). Rather, language maintenance comprises fostering, developing, and using both a repertoire of language/literacy knowledge and practices *and* a particular cultural orientation in individuals in childhood and beyond. More than *maintaining*, to be successful this process entails a more active and deliberate transmission of linguistic ideologies and cultural connections to younger generations. The families may already share these ideologies and connections, but the final "product" of socialization may be a symbiotic blend of the families' histories, beliefs, and practices in relation to language and culture and those of the milieus in which these children interact, which may be rather different from what their parents experienced in their own primary and subsequent socialization. The detailed descriptions and analyses in which I engage in this book, from various angles, provide a nuanced understanding of this phenomenon and draw attention to the limited explanatory power and thus the inadequacy of the construct *L1 maintenance*, attempting to make a contribution to the reconceptualization of its use and to the unpacking of its multiple meanings. These meanings, for instance, might refer to maintaining a linguistic knowledge base and set of traditions across generations vs. developing the linguistic repertoire in new generations, possibly to higher levels of proficiency (e.g., across a wider range of oral/written genres and registers) than even the parents' generation. Thus, future development of this scholarly line needs to more fully account for the intricacy and textured nature of the factors implicated in minority and heritage language socialization.

1.3 Research methods in heritage language studies

Most of the work related to heritage language development conducted in past decades utilized a quantitative approach (Silva-Corvalán 1991, Lambert and Taylor 1996, Landry, Allard and Henry 1996) or mixed methods (Merino 1983, Waas 1997). Nevertheless, recently there has been an increase in the use of qualitatively oriented approaches such as ethnographic case studies (Schecter and Bayley 1997) and oral histories (Kouritzin 1999). The quantitative studies that were dominant in the 1960s, 1970s and 1980s provided essential foundational work for the research that would be conducted in future decades. Fishman's (1966) research with several ethnolinguistic groups in the United States focused on the rationales, efforts, and successes in language maintenance from the perspective of community leaders. His research with Puerto Rican intellectuals in New York's *Barrio* (Fishman et al. 1968) examined the sociolinguistic norms that existed in that community. Given Fishman's seminal and extensive contributions to the development and expansion of related fields and areas of study, it is not surprising that he was involved in most of the research on relevant areas in this formative period of time. In Northern Ireland, Milroy's (1980: 36) study used what she referred to as "a modified participant observation technique" for quantitatively analyzing linguistic data in the study of the relationship between social networks and language maintenance in a Belfast community. She found that cohesive communities are a strong mechanism for language maintenance in the face of dominant status-oriented language use norms in a society.

Merino (1983) conducted a two-part mixed methods longitudinal study (two years apart) with Spanish-speaking elementary school children about the experience of growing up bilingual in the United States. She reportedly found more language loss than bilingualism among her participants and blamed the government, educators, politicians, and parents for their sole concern with the prompt integration of ethnolinguistic minority children in the school system (and their subsequent success in society in general). Also relying on mixed methods, Waas (1993, 1997) investigated a group of speakers of German who moved to Australia after the age of 16. She found that they had suffered considerable L1 loss after living in Australia for 20 years. Studies on closely related topics (e.g., language attrition) also draw on a range of methodologies and data analysis techniques, such as the cases reported in Seliger and Vago's (1991) edited collection.

Arguably, an article published by Wong Fillmore in 1991, which painted a bleak picture for minority children learning English in the United States, represents a major milestone along the road toward increasing awareness of the role of L1 maintenance or loss in families. Hers was a large-scale mixed methods study with families who spoke minority languages whose children had attended preschool programs in the United States. Many children, particularly those who started learning English before the age of five, were already losing their first language and parents were troubled because that change was already affecting communication at home. She discovered that many of the children had given up their first languages yet they had not mastered the second either. This is a serious effect, because as Wong Fillmore (1991: 343) writes, "what is lost is no less than the means by which parents socialize their children: when parents are unable to talk to their children, they cannot easily convey to them their values, beliefs, understandings, or wisdom about how to cope with their experiences."

Wong Fillmore's study is not only a classic in HL development, maintenance, and loss, but also methodologically, it is an exemplar of the power of using multiple methods in investigations of this complex research area.

Although there has been no shortage of quantitatively oriented or mixed methods research in HL development in the past decade, including my own (e.g., Guardado 2013b), there has been a clear surge in phenomenologically and ethnographically oriented studies in the past two decades. This new generation of studies has provided much more nuanced accounts of a wide range of contextual factors related to HL development. For instance, a seminal study conducted by Fishman, Cooper and Ma (1971) in New York's Puerto Rican *Barrio* uncovered how language use in bilinguals is usually compartmentalized as they tend to use the L1 in some domains, but the community dominant language in others[2]. Following in Heath's (1983) research tradition (briefly reviewed in Chapter 3), Zentella (1997) also completed an influential ethnographic study. Zentella's 14-year ethnography has become a classic for its comprehensive analysis of code switching across three generations in New York's Puerto Rican *Barrio*, although in relation to Fishman's research in the same context, she found the opposite to be true. In Zentella's study, neither the usual Spanish domains nor the English ones were impenetrable, as most of the community members were able and willing to code switch[3] across contexts. Among many possible explanations, one thing such a discrepancy may underscore is the complexity and situated nature of language practices, even in communities that are seemingly similar. Of more relevance to this section, it also points to the need to draw on multiple methodologies and time-spans when investigating heritage language issues. This point is clearly exemplified also through the ethnography conducted by Schecter and Bayley (1997), which consisted of intensive case studies of four Mexican descent families—two from California and two from Texas. Schecter and Bayley assert that their work can be interpreted as a response to Zentella's (1996) call for efforts toward better understanding the diversity of the Spanish-speaking community. Their ethnography effectively demonstrates that such a linguistic group is in no way homogeneous and that although their participants had the same national origin, their diversity was undeniable.

To conclude this section, I should point out that much of the work cited above is treated in more detail in later chapters. For now, suffice to say that these works

---

2 That is not necessarily a negative practice, as that would seem one way of retaining both languages.
3 In this book, code-switching is defined as the practice of alternating between two languages in a conversation.

provide a glimpse into the evolution of heritage language research methodologies and into how different methodological designs facilitate the generation of insights about different aspects of HL development, and by extension, the ability to draw more nuanced and complementary conclusions. Most of the contributions that this book makes are informed by phenomenological interpretivist paradigms, and in the next section, I provide a brief overview of the two main datasets on which I draw.

1.4 Sources of data

The book is organized around key theoretical and conceptual propositions. Insights for the development of the content and the formulation of these propositions were drawn from a variety of sources. For instance, Chapter 14 is partially based on the outcomes of a thematic analysis of the K-12 curriculum documents for social studies and language programs in the ten provinces and three territories of Canada, as well as from examinations of the visions and academic plans of selected Canadian universities.[4] In order to develop the discourse typology presented in Section II of this book, empirically illustrate issues, and in some cases, exemplify their discursive deployment or actual interactional realization in daily communication, data were drawn from several studies. These include case studies conducted in Metro Vancouver, Canada, in 2001, as well as an ethnography conducted between 2005 and 2007, also in Metro Vancouver. Many other analyses presented were based on the research and theoretical literature. In the sections that follow, I describe the main studies in more detail, but still at a broad enough level in order to avoid excessive repetition later in the book. This is because the different types of data that form the basis for the arguments advanced in the book are introduced and described in significant detail as I prepare to present the analyses in each of the book sections. At times, the data collection techniques and significant context are presented along with the text that introduces the data, including the particular approach taken in the analysis. In the case of Chapters 11 and 12, where much of the micro-level interactional analyses are conducted, significant space is devoted to introducing the theory behind transcription along with a description of the transcription notation used. In those chapters I also provide a succinct—but hopefully sufficient—overview of conversation analysis with a particular focus on the constructs of key relevance to the analyses presented. I deemed this "online" approach of introducing the data, analytical tools,

---

[4] The rationale for selection was the availability of their strategic plans online.

theoretical, and conceptual angles, as well as other indispensable information a useful one in order to establish the relevant background—and provide the heuristic tools as it were—for actively engaging with the arguments. Hence, the reader is kindly invited to view the following methodological descriptions as unfinished starting points rather than comprehensive research design delineations.

1.4.1 2001 case studies

The work of Wong Fillmore, particularly her seminal 1991 article, touched me deeply at personal and scholarly levels, leaving a lasting impression on me at that early phase of my academic path. Both motivated and troubled by Wong Fillmore's striking findings and poignant reflections, in 2001 I set out to understand firsthand the extraordinarily complex linguistic lives of immigrant families through a qualitative study in Metro Vancouver, Canada under the supervision of Professor Margaret Early at the University of British Columbia. Given the dearth of research focusing on HL development issues with Hispanic populations in Canada at that time, this project was decidedly exploratory. Conducted as part of a Master's degree program, my intention was to cast a broad net with the following research questions:

1. What do parents perceive to be the causes of Spanish language loss among their Hispanic children?
2. What do parents perceive to be the factors that facilitate the development and maintenance of Spanish?
3. How do Spanish-speaking parents feel about their children's loss or maintenance of Spanish?

In order to examine these questions, I decided to recruit four families: two with at least one child over the age of six who was fluent in English and showing considerable deficiency in Spanish and/or reluctance to speak it, and two families with at least one child in the same age range who was fluent in both languages. Two of the participating families are profiled in Chapter 10 and the extended case study reports can be found in Guardado (2002, 2006). Semi-structured interviews averaging about an hour in length were conducted with each family in combination with informal observations.

1.4.2 2005–2007 ethnography

Although I have incorporated material from several sources, the backbone of this book is built on the dataset generated from an ethnography also conducted in Metro Vancouver, between 2005 and 2007. This project, directly building on the 2001 exploratory case studies, sought to examine the following question: What are the contextual factors and ideologies that impact the heritage language socialization of immigrant Hispanic families and their children in home, school, and community settings in Metro Vancouver?

I chose an ethnographic approach because my theoretical framework, language socialization, is solidly grounded in ethnography (Garrett and Baquedano-López 2002). Indeed, ethnographic interviews and participant observation with Hispanic families in various settings provided me with an opportunity to conduct an in-depth investigation of the complex nature of heritage language socialization in these families. Through these observations and interviews, I examined the processes and outcomes of the implicit and explicit language socialization that the child participants experienced at home and in the community as well as the effects of these processes on their multilingual development. As argued by several scholars (e.g., Garrett and Baquedano-López 2002, Bronson and Watson-Gegeo 2008), a combination of linguistic tools and social theory allows researchers to connect micro processes to the macro context. Through these combined perspectives, I conducted close analyses of the data while connecting the emerging issues to the broader sociopolitical/sociocultural context. Thus, I was able to conduct a more empirically grounded analysis of the issues related to heritage language and cultural development and maintenance, reproduction, and transformation (Garrett and Baquedano-López 2002). An ethnographic approach, then, was deemed the most suitable method for the specific research questions I addressed. I believed that an analysis of the micro- and macro-level factors affecting the families' heritage language socialization would provide a more holistic—and arguably more truthful—depiction of this process than by analyzing only one of these domains independently of the others.

Doing ethnography is often seen as a synonym of doing fieldwork, the heart of ethnography. Ethnographers spend considerable time in a particular setting engaging in participant observation, participating in local daily life (Duranti 1997), taking notes in order to describe, explain, and interpret the everyday as well as the distinctive practices of the culture of that setting. Several academic traditions have increasingly embraced ethnography as a research methodology because of its robustness. In this vein, as posited by Duff (1995: 507), "representing a range of possible techniques, levels of analysis, and domains of inquiry, ethnography offers a holistic, grounded, and participant-informed perspective ..." This versatility of techniques, types of analysis, and areas of research in which they can be applied make ethnography an appealing methodology, particularly in the social sciences, enabling researchers to provide a more complex, richer portrait of a group or phenomenon from an *emic* as well as *etic* perspective.

A specific type of ethnographic work, the ethnography of communication, has now been established as a viable method of inquiry in a variety of speech communities, which are often monolingual, but not necessarily mono-dialectal. Although this line of work has been highly influential in monolingual communities (see e.g., Heath 1983), following the advent of the ethnography of communication there has been an increased interest in multilingual speech communities as well in order to locate the patterns of language usage of the group members. I discuss the ethnography of communication in more detail in Chapter 3 as it is intricately linked to language socialization.

1.4.2.1 Access, settings and participants
Thirty four families from 10 national origins were recruited through a combination of purposive sampling (Patton 1990) and snowball sampling. Palys (1997: 137) states that "all sampling is purposive to some degree, since identifying a target population invariably expresses the researcher's interests and objectives." Thus, participants were recruited through various contacts, including: community organizations; non-governmental organizations that provide services to the general population, including recent Hispanic immigrants; Vancouver School Board Hispanic multicultural workers; interviews in Spanish language radio programs; and acquaintances. Potential participating families were sought who had at least one child of school age, preferably attending elementary school. It is largely acknowledged that the most influential language socialization milieu for immigrant children in terms of HL development, maintenance or shift outside the home is the school environment. Therefore, studying school-age children was a strategic decision in this investigation. In order to work with a somewhat comparable group of participants, an effort was made to only recruit those families who had arrived as landed immigrants, excluding refugee claimants. The rationale for excluding this demographic was that refugees might present additional post-traumatic-related issues and barriers to their integration. Other forms of diversity were desired and sought in recruiting study participants, such as length of residence, national background, socioeconomic status, and family situation. It is noteworthy that the majority of the families that volunteered to participate were middle-class. To sum up, criteria for recruiting participating families for the ethnography included:
- national origin: variety of origins
- length of residence in Canada: broad range
- children's ages: school age
- family status: one-parent and two-parent families
- immigration status: Canadian citizens and permanent residents
- socioeconomic background: broad range

1.4.2.2 Data collection

This was a multi-site ethnographic study. The initial phase of the study consisted of in-depth interviews with families. These interviews generally took place in the families' homes, but in some cases, the families chose a setting that was more convenient to them (e.g., workplace). Three focal families and three grassroots groups[5] in which they participated were selected for in-depth ethnographic study. Although the broader pool of participating families exhibited significant diversity across all recruitment criteria, all of the families in these grassroots groups were university-educated, middle-class families. Participant observation and other forms of ethnographic data collection took place in the three families' homes and in the three grassroots groups. The homes and the groups were located in three different municipalities of Metro Vancouver. Data generation was accomplished through a variety of strategies, including demographic and language use questionnaires; multiple interviews with parents, children, and other relatives; participant observation in homes and grassroots groups; parents' written reflections; fieldnotes; fieldwork journal; and audio-recorded reflective memos. These strategies were applied in two main phases over a period of 18–24 months, generating a rich dataset.

1.4.2.3 Data analysis

Data analysis was an ongoing process that involved four main interrelated and recurring stages. It began with the generation of data and ended with the writing of this book. However, the different stages were revisited numerous times throughout the entire process. Both transcribed and untranscribed data were organized in different groupings chronologically, but also by other criteria such as research stage, data collection method, grassroots group, and type of data. Interview data were coded and organized in categories from which themes emerged. The procedures for conducting the thematic analysis of formal interviews are described in Chapter 6. Naturally ocurring interactions were transcribed in detail (i.e., noting overlaps and pauses) and grouped by activity. The procedures for the discourse analysis of natural interactions are described in Chapters 11 and 12 where most of this analysis is presented.

In the above sections I provided a broad overview of the methodology and the main sources of data informing the arguments advanced in this book. As I stated, these are only partial descriptions of the main studies given that more details are provided in key chapters and sections of the book as these become relevant. If detailed methodological design descriptions are desired, the reader is referred to the full reports of the main studies (e.g., Guardado 2002, 2006, 2008a, 2012).

---

5 The groups were *El Grupo Scout Vistas, El Centro de Cultura,* and *La Casa Amistad*. These groups are discussed in detail in Chapter 9.

1.5 Organization of the book

The book is arranged in four parts and 15 chapters. In Part I, Chapter 2 begins to set the stage by providing an overview of the heritage language development and maintenance research area. In Chapters 3, 4, and 5, I define and exemplify the overarching theories and concepts utilized throughout the book: language socialization, language ideologies, and discourse. I first undertake a detailed review of the language socialization paradigm, as it is the central theory that frames the arguments in the book. Language socialization is to be understood as the process through which children are taught to use language—and thus acquire language. This process also includes learning the culture of the community. Therefore, it is a dual process of language learning and culture learning that enables individuals to become competent members of their communities. The concept of language ideologies, the focus of Chapter 4, refers to the attitudes and beliefs held by individuals and communities about the value of their languages as well as about how these languages ought to be used in their social lives. Language ideologies are developed and transmitted in the socialization process. Chapter 5 is concerned with the meanings of discourse. This notion has been used in a variety of ways and is considered a highly elusive term. Current conceptualizations vary depending on many factors, including whether the analytic perspective is strongly linguistic or strongly social. The critical perspective taken in the book, which is presented and discussed in Chapter 5, is that discourse is a social practice.

The three chapters in Part II deal with the discursive construction of heritage language development. Drawing on the notion of discourse outlined in Chapter 5, Chapter 6 proposes a typology of discourses of heritage language development and maintenance. To this end, I present data generated in the ethnography briefly described above, on which a typology of ten discourses is developed. In Chapter 7, I summarize an analysis of 24 published studies from the research literature. These are examined through the typology proposed in the previous chapter. The goal of Chapter 8 is to problematize the discourse typology. Although the discourse-based model proved useful when applied to the broader literature, in this chapter I intend to make its complexity explicit.

Part III of the book deals with the strategies found in families and communities, as well as their metapragmatic practices, all intended to foster the development and maintenance of the heritage language in the new generations. This part begins with an overview of the role that communities play in the lives of various social groups and describes the three grassroots groups mentioned in the previous section, as well as their activities, which were uncovered as part of the ethnography conducted in Vancouver between 2005 and 2007. Chapter 10 zooms in on the homes of the participants. It presents five case studies from the two main studies and discusses a range of family initiatives implemented with the goal of supporting their children's language and literacy development. Chapter 11 drills even further into the home practices. This chapter provides a detailed analysis of the linguistic devices utilized in families with the goal of regulating their children's language use. Chapter 12 builds on this description and delves into a critical analysis and discussion of the positive as well as negative consequences of using particular linguistic tools for socializing the children. Furthermore, in this chapter I argue that certain linguistic practices that are commonplace in some families can inadvertently silence children.

Part IV zooms back out into the broader realm of heritage language development and maintenance. This time, however, the focus is directed at both the national and the global spheres. Chapter 13 proposes a reconceptualization of heritage language development from the perspective of cosmopolitanism and posits this relationship as a potentially fruitful scholarly path to follow. Chapter 14 ends the body of the book with a discussion of heritage language development and maintenance in relation to educational and multicultural policies in the context of a rapidly globalizing international community. Finally, Chapter 15 closes the book by recapping a selection of key points, reflecting on salient features, and attempting to stimulate a new round of conversation on heritage language studies.

1.6 Chapter summary

Recognizing the existence of numerous approaches to and conceptualizations of heritage language development and its significance to individuals, families, and societies, my intention in writing this introductory chapter was to make explicit my particular stance on fundamental concepts surrounding the development of heritage languages, as what follows is written from this perspective. To summarize, then, if language is taken to be the carrier of cultural values and meaning, heritage languages must not be reduced to frivolous and nostalgic barriers to integration. Rather, these must be recognized for their indispensability as tools for language minority parents to socialize their children into their value systems, which subsequently aid in their integration insofar as a family united by a common language and culture is more resilient in times of challenge or adversity.

Due to the complex nature of HL development, I found that an interdisciplinary approach to understanding this phenomenon was best. Indeed, as is evidenced by the plethora of terms mentioned above which are variously used to describe this process, interpretive diversity in heritage language studies occurs even at the terminological level. To a growing list I have added *HL development*, which seeks to capture the mutable process of language maintenance, instead of treating heritage language maintenance as a monolithic given in which the child is presumed to already have some competence. In order to do justice to the evident inderdisciplinarity of HL development, I feel that it is necessary to examine its macro- and micro-level manifestations and implications. Through an examination of these, I hope that a clearer and fuller picture of HL development is allowed to emerge, enabling scholars to look at new facets of the phenomenon with a critical lens, thereby bringing about a more nuanced understanding of HL development factors and processes in general. Because I take discourse to be not only a social practice, but also a constructive one, in this book I suggest how the discourses surrounding HL development have potential practical implications for its success or failure.

An underlying goal in writing this book was to encourage the reader to think critically about the role of HL development in the lives of language minorities, and to inquire about what this process means for individuals, families, communities, and the larger society at local and global levels. It was also my hope that the reader would be tempted to inquire further about some of the issues raised here, especially those that have received little academic attention as of yet.

Part I: **Setting the stage**

2 Overview of heritage language studies

2.1 Introduction

The present chapter offers a selective but foundational review of heritage language development and maintenance research, focusing on central features of this growing body of knowledge. In the first half of the chapter I provide an overview of what I see as the most relevant aspects of the pioneering work that Joshua A. Fishman conducted over six decades. I then introduce some of the thematic trends within heritage language research, which will likely be familiar territory for most readers, but which will perhaps help others become acquainted with this interdisciplinary area. I then focus on issues connected to the HL development phenomenon and factors affecting its outcomes. Many of these factors arise from schools and family as well as form the common threads found in the literature. Therefore, in this chapter I introduce the key concepts and concerns in the area of heritage language development and maintenance research and as a result, the chapter becomes the subject matter backdrop against which the discussions in the rest of the book are conducted.

2.2 A historical overview

Heritage language development, maintenance, and loss together form a field that had been largely neglected by applied linguists until the early 1980s according to several scholars (Oxford 1982, Merino 1983, Pan and Berko-Gleason 1986, Wong Fillmore 1991). However, in the last three decades, there has been an increased interest in investigating this important area. In fact, a new generation of researchers working in a variety of interconnected fields such as linguistics (Wong Fillmore 1991, Thomas and Cao 1999), applied linguistics (Kouritzin 1999, Sakamoto 2001, Tannenbaum and Howie 2002, Tannenbaum 2005, de Courcy 2007, Suarez 2007), ethnolinguistics and sociolinguistics (Schecter and Bayley 2002), anthro-political linguistics (Zentella 1997), education (Torres 2006), and even speech-language pathology (Schiff-Myers 1992) have completed insightful inquiries combining a variety of research methods, but largely relying on qualitative approaches. These projects have contributed to new understandings of heritage language development, maintenance, and loss, providing the basis for growing investigations in various directions. To understand the genesis of HL development—and heritage language socialization for that matter—I find it necessary to return to the work of a scholar who is arguably the most responsible for the emergence of what some scholars refer to as a sub-field of sociolinguistics.

2.2.1 The contributions of Joshua A. Fishman

Some of the most important insights into this area in the last 60 years come from sociolinguistics mainly through the work of Joshua A. Fishman. Although relevant research published prior to Fishman's seminal scholarship may be seen as early precursors to what has come to be known as HL development, arguably, it was Fishman's work in the 1940s, 1950s, and 1960s that marked the beginning of heritage language studies. Due to his pioneering and lifelong dedication to a vast array of aspects around language and society, with a particular commitment to linguistic minorities both as a scholar and activist, Fishman has been called a teacher, a leader, a visionary, and even an intellectual prophet.

Fairly early on, Fishman conceptualized his brand of sociolinguistics as the sociology of language, rightfully earning him the title of father of the Sociology of Language (see García and Schiffman 2006). He helped establish this field with the publication of an edited collection of over 40 chapters, *Readings in the Sociology of Language*, published by Mouton in 1968. Therein he brought together many of the leading scholars whose work informed this new field, including Halliday, Labov, Hymes, Gumperz, Erwin-Tripp, Bernstein, Haugen, Berry, and dozens of other major contributors to the development of congruent disciplines. Later on he updated this emergent field with a two-volume collection entitled *Advances in the Sociology of Language* (Fishman 1971, 1972), also published by Mouton. Although both of these volumes were edited collections, half of the content of Volume I was written by Fishman himself (the final chapter). In it, he meticulously delineated his vision for the sociology of language as an interdisciplinary enterprise focusing on the effects of language on social patterns and behaviours as well as the developments and challenges that led to its conceptualization. Together, these three volumes became instrumental in establishing a type of sociolinguistics that investigates the effect of language on society—downplaying the linguistic aspect of this process and emphasizing its social and cultural dimensions.

One of the challenges this new field faced from the start was its fuzzy distinction from sociolinguistics. Sociolinguistics is concerned with the effect of a variety of societal factors on how language is used, whereas the sociology of language studies the effect of language attitudes and behaviours on society. Although both fields are devoted to understanding the relationship between language and society, the crucial distinction is that while sociolinguistics stresses the linguistic, the sociology of language emphasizes the social. Given this difference, the research conducted by sociolinguists is necessarily narrower in focus as it often deals with questions of language variation (e.g., based on region, class, gender) and dialects. Scholars working from a sociology of language perspective, on the other hand, have a macro focus as they are concerned with questions of national language loyalty, policy, planning, ideologies, and other broader-level topics. Therefore, this scholarship is most evidently exemplified by the title of Fishman's seminal publication in 1965, *Who Speaks What Language to Whom and When?*, subsequently reproduced in several other collections (e.g., Gumperz and Hymes 1986, Wei 2000). In other words, the sociology of language is profoundly concerned with fundamental social and cultural questions with which Fishman deals in this article. For instance, he engages with issues of linguistic identity, both at the individual and community level, delineating factors that often determine who has the right to use a particular language or language variety, who the interactants might or should be, under what circumstances these things should occur, and so on. This new area was officially launched with the *International Journal of the Sociology of Language*, which Fishman founded in 1974 and continued to co-edit with Ofelia García until his passing in 2015. This journal is published by De Gruyter Mouton, also the publisher of the present book, *Discourse, Ideology and heritage language socialization*. The present book is part of De Gruyter Mouton's Series *Contributions to the Sociology of Language*, also founded by Joshua A. Fishman and co-edited with Ofelia García until 2015.

One of the points of making the connection between the present book, the *International Journal of the Sociology of Language*, and the legacy of Joshua A. Fishman's work is to explicitly locate the work I present in this book within the field of the sociology of language. In fact, in the introduction to *Volume I* that I referenced above (Fishman 1971), as well as in many other works, he clearly placed language maintenance and related areas as central to the sociology of language:

> Rather than emphasize the ethnography of communication as an end in and of itself, *the sociology of language* would hope to utilize the ethnography of communication, as it would utilize sociolinguistics and social science more generally, in order to more fully explain variation in societally patterned behaviors pertaining to language maintenance and language shift, language nationalism and language planning, etc. (italics in original) (9).

In various ways, I attempt to follow Fishman's vision in drawing on a variety of disciplines, theoretical orientations, and methods. Indeed, the data analyses, arguments, and conceptual propositions contained in the present book have benefited greatly from much interdisciplinary work and research methodologies, including the ethnography of communication, as Fishman pointed out in the above quote. It is my intention to contribute in a small way to the understanding of heritage language development and maintenance and related interests to which Fishman's vast scholarship has provided a strong foundation and development over six decades.

2.3 Heritage language development: A progress report card

2.3.1 Language beliefs and attitudes

The extant scholarship on HL development has uncovered a constellation of interconnected issues. Described in general—and somewhat reductionist—terms, some of these studies have addressed families' rationales for HL development (Schecter, Sharken-Taboada and Bayley 1996, Dagenais and Berron 2001, Guardado 2002, Nesteruk 2010), factors influencing heritage language, development, maintenance, and loss (Guardado 2002, Kouritzin 2006), the role of and effect HL development has on families (Wong Fillmore 1991, Thomas and Cao 1999, Tannenbaum and Berkovich 2005, Nicholas 2009, Xie 2010), activities and strategies used by families (Bayley, Schecter and Torres-Ayala 1996, Roca 2005, Li 2006, Guardado 2011), and the role of identity (Iqbal 2005, Sodhi 2007, Comanaru and Noels 2009, Bale 2010, Guardado 2010, Wright 2010, Brown 2011, Carreira and Rodríguez 2011, Cope 2011, Szecsi and Szilagyi 2012, Ferguson 2013), among others. A traditionally significant trend within this growing research area focuses on caretakers' perceptions, attitudes, beliefs, and opinions in relation to HL development (Chumak-Horbatsch 1999, Schecter and Bayley 2002, Tigchelaar 2003, Park and Sarkar 2007, Cho 2008, Guardado 2008a). In fact, language beliefs, attitudes, and behaviours have been the primary areas of focus in HL studies at least since Fishman's (1972) declaration that these are some of the elements found at the intersection of social behaviour and language use, for dominant and minority language speakers alike.

Yet, there are key epistemological and ontological differences in the studies on language attitudes that have dominated in different periods of time. Much of the scholarship on language attitudes, particularly Fishman's, between the 1960s and 1980s was the result of large-scale survey studies that attempted to present a broad view of an entire ethnolinguistic community. Examples of this work include Fishman's work with Puerto Ricans in New York's *Barrio* (Fishman et al. 1968). His later work on positive ethnolinguistic consciousness (1996a) could be considered mixed methods as it was based on participant self-reports collected over a long period of time as well as statistical descriptions of the data (presented in an appendix). This was Fishman's way of privileging the "insider views" on the topic. The 1990s saw a rise in studies on language maintenance/HL development attitudes that were methodologically different from those that dominated in previous decades. Although survey studies with larger groups were still common (e.g., Moin, Schwartz and Breitkopf 2011), many scholars designed and conducted studies that were more contextualized and used methods that allowed them to provide a more in-depth examination of a few cases. Ethnographic research, case-studies, narrative inquiry, oral histories, auto-ethnographically oriented approaches, among others, provided a richer, fuller, and more multifaceted understanding of these issues in individuals, families, and small groups.

Along these lines, many studies have reported that parents' attitudes about the HL are a significant factor related to its development and maintenance in their children. In a study with Chinese families in the United States, for example, Luo and Wiseman (2000) found that the parents' attitudes about the HL had a strong influence on the children's own attitudes about its use, a finding that is also intuitively expected, given children's language socialization processes (Schieffelin and Ochs 1986a). This connection, however, is far from guaranteed. In a study with Hispanic families in Canada (Guardado 2002), I found that both 'language maintenance' and 'language loss' families held positive and optimistic attitudes about the HL and its continuity in the family. However, other factors such as the nature and tone of discourse used by parents to encourage children to use it; cohesive family relations; and an active engagement in fostering ethnic identity, strongly influenced the families' success (or lack thereof) in their HL development efforts. Likewise, Schecter and Bayley (2002) found that maintenance attitudes alone did not result in HL transmission and maintenance in some of the participating California and Texas families in their ethnographic study.

An extension of the work on beliefs, attitudes, and identities can be found in my analysis of middle-class Hispanic families' constructions of HL development (Guardado 2010). The parents in the study endeavoured to inculcate in their children a sense of value for other cultures and languages, including English, in an explicit effort to add a hybridized, cosmopolitan layer to their children's identities. Therefore, Spanish HL development was seen as a tool that would socialize their children into a broader worldview. I argued that the participating parents constructed their children's HL development as a passport to a worldview that went beyond the limits posed by narrower and essentialist notions of identity, such as ethnic, nation-state, or pan-ethnic identities. I elaborate on these issues in several chapters in Parts II and III of the book. Arguably (see comments by Woolard and Schieffelin 1994, McGroarty 2010), aspects of the work on heritage language attitudes can be seen as related to the discussion on heritage language ideologies in which I engage in Chapter 4.

2.3.1.1 Forces against heritage language development

A growing body of research indicates that there are numerous barriers to HL development for most linguistic minority groups in immigrant contexts. Zentella (1997) posits, for example, that HL development and maintenance beyond basic skills requires much more than daily contact with a limited circle of two or three family members, even in cases where the child makes annual trips to the heritage culture. She argues that bilingual education is necessary in order to successfully foster bilingual skills, something that is unlikely to happen in most cases in Zentella's research context, given the policies on bilingual programs in the United States, which do not accommodate English-dominant bilinguals and continue to decline even for non English-dominant bilinguals. That hope becomes even more unlikely, given the tendency in many States to do away with such programs, rendering Hispanic children in such contexts further disenfranchised and, in Ofelia García's words referring to minority language loss, putting minorities in a situation that "sinks them even further into the silence of the oppressed" (García 1995: 144). However, motivated by various factors and life circumstances, some families do privilege the language loss path, a point discussed further in Chapter 4.

Some scholars point out that another common threat to heritage language development arises from immigrant parents' concern with their rapid integration into the host country (Merino 1983, Worthy and Rodríguez-Galindo 2006). This implies learning the dominant language as quickly as possible as a means of securing employment, fulfilling their daily needs, and establishing themselves as members of the community. It also implies encouraging their children to learn the dominant language quickly and well in order to succeed in school and in life (Cummins 2000, Howard 2008). Quite often, however, parents and children face unforeseen toil and adverse consequences in achieving this integration. This can be an elusive goal and sometimes minority families interpret the need to integrate as mutually exclusive with minority language development and maintenance. Often parents work extremely hard and still fail to acquire enough skills to attain adequate employment and consequently end up with low-level, low-paying jobs,[1] a fate immigrants cannot easily escape, even with sufficient English skills (Hondagneu-Sotelo 2001). Their children move along the language-learning path at a much faster rate due to their extended contact with the dominant language and frequently find themselves dealing with adult situations as their parents' interpreters at doctors' offices, government agencies, and other places. According to some accounts (e.g., Norton 2000), children are sometimes asked to assist their parents in such challenging tasks as job-hunting, putting the children in an awkward situation, often witnessing their parents' frustrations at repeatedly being refused employment. These circumstances may further strain parents and negatively impact their sense of 'adults in charge' and their self-esteem, to the detriment of the well-being of the family.

---

[1] Even a decade after immigrating to Canada, as many as 47% of immigrants are still living below the poverty line (35% across Canada, 40% in Vancouver and 47% in Montreal, according to Statistics Canada (2004).

Faulstich Orellana (2009), however, takes a radically different stance on this issue and claims that this system can function well in families. She posits that "[t]he allocation of parental power to a child is a natural arrangement in large families, in single-parent families, or in families where both parents work outside the home. The younger children are cared for and the parental child can develop responsibility, competence, and autonomy beyond his years" (10–11). She goes on to argue that the majority of child participants in her study said they either "didn't notice" translating for their parents, or were happy to help out. The parents in the study stated that the pride they felt at watching their children use English to help them was stronger than any embarrassment or loss of face they might have felt. The parents did not feel that their children's translation in different contexts undermined their parental authority or position. Regardless of how such experiences might affect parents and their children, however, it is essential to note that such perceived blessing—language acquisition ability—does not come without a cost for children and familial relationships. Even when the family as a whole benefits from their evolving language skills, in the process of learning the dominant language, their HL erodes gradually (Wong Fillmore 1991).

2.3.2 Three key factors in heritage language development

The development, maintenance, or loss of heritage languages is affected by a variety of factors, both from within and outside the family unit. Although family language practices are the most critical and decisive in this process, these do not emerge in a vacuum and are also influenced by multifarious forces that are largely out of the control of the families. Factors such as family and their aspirations and ideologies, the broader societal language ideologies, the role of schools and the community, and more broadly, the cultural, socioeconomic, and political context, are some of the most critical elements that have a bearing on home language practices. These practices are arguably some of the most influential in HL development or loss, which subsequently have important consequences for individuals and families in various aspects of their lives and throughout their lifetimes. Schools have a major role to play as it is in these settings where much socialization takes place, strongly contributing to the production and possible transformation of the linguistic ideologies of society.

2.3.2.1 The role of schools
Research shows that a powerful influence on heritage language development, maintenance, and loss is related to schools. In his incisive (1996b) article, *What Do You Lose When You Lose Your Language?*, Fishman posited and answered a

fundamental question about the role of schools: "'What are you going to do with the mother tongue before school, in school, out of school, and after school?' Because that determines its fate, whether it is going to become self-renewing" (81). And that is a broad set of school-related domains that cannot be underestimated. For example, soon after starting school, children often start speaking the dominant language to siblings and friends—and even to their monolingual or nearly monolingual parents. Sometimes in response to the tensions created by the experience of being a subordinated cultural and linguistic group, and also because of the various outside pressures, families adopt home language practices that favour the decline of the mother tongue, especially when a novel language brought from school begins to be "domesticated." There are several cases of this nature reported in the literature (see e.g., Kouritzin 1999) as well as informal accounts related by those who have had this experience. On other occasions parents and other adults in the family encourage the children to speak the dominant language at home, turning the children into resources from which to learn and with whom to practice.

However, frequently the influence of schools on home language practices goes well beyond the enthusiastic embracing of the second language (L2) by the children. Often, parents are encouraged by school personnel to speak the dominant language at home (Schecter and Bayley 1997, Kouritzin 1999, Schecter and Bayley 2002, Tsushima and Guardado in press), to the detriment of the heritage language, and when this happens, the primary means by which families and their children are socialized begins to crumble (Wong Fillmore 1991). Schecter and Bayley (1997, 2002) explain how the teachers of some of the children in their ethnographic study recommended to parents to speak only in English to their children in order to facilitate their integration into the schools, an issue that has repeatedly emerged in the literature (Rodríguez 1982, Wong Fillmore 1991, Chumak-Horbatsch 1999, Kouritzin 1999, Pacini-Ketchabaw, Bernhard and Freire 2001, Lawson and Sachdev 2004, Guardado 2008a). In this vein, Pacini-Ketchabaw et al. (2001) reported on an exploratory study as part of a larger project of 45 families from several different Spanish-speaking countries. The main focus of this study was on the influences of school on home language practices. Many of the parents had received specific instructions from school personnel to only speak English to their children. Moreover, whenever there was a deficiency in the performance of the children, school officials would often suggest that it was caused by the use of Spanish at home, thus still reflecting a deficit-model conceptualization of minority-language-as-problem (Ruiz 1984). Recently, Tsushima and Guardado (in press) conducted a study with Japanese mothers in Montreal (Province of Quebec, Canada) who had formed linguistically mixed families. When interacting with teachers in the K-12 school system, several of the mothers also received strong advice to change their linguistic practices with their children from Japanese to French, the official language in Quebec.

2.3.2.2 Affiliation to ethnic group

In relation to language acquisition in general, and particularly concerning the issue of HL development, it can be argued that people's social interactions largely shape their language growth or lack thereof. The relationship between identity and HL development and maintenance has been a recurrent theme in the research literature for decades, although recently it has become a more central concern in research on the topic conducted from a variety of disciplinary perspectives. It has been argued that cultural and ethnic identity gives families the potential to more actively pursue the preservation of their heritage—including their heritage languages—by consciously or unconsciously implementing language ideologies in the home (and enacting home language practices) that are more conducive to the multilingual and multiliterate development of their children. I posit that this heritage language socialization in turn strengthens the individual cultural identity, turning this process into a dialectical relationship with the potential for infinite iterations. The dialectical relationship between identity and HL development, for instance, is a point that has been gaining currency in recent years. It should not be surprising to learn that this link has also been strongly advanced across Fishman's scholarship with even an edited book on the topic (Fishman 1999). He has made the analogy, at least once, between his trousers and his handkerchief to illustrate the tight connection between identity and language (1996b). He stated that the role of language is much more substantive than that of a handkerchief that can be taken out of one's trousers and replaced by a new one. To Fishman, cultural identity cannot be separated from heritage language issues and further asserts that the connection is bi-directional (1996a).

This theme has been discussed by Schecter and Bayley (1997) who found that all the participants of their four focal families understood L1 loss as cultural identity loss. Although all the parents in the study reported having a strong Mexican cultural identity and were attempting to pass down their cultural roots to their children as a way of maintaining their heritage, not all the families succeeded. Likewise, Pacini-Ketchabaw et al. (2001) reported that the participating families saw HL development and maintenance as a way to foster Latino identity, among other goals. Sakamoto's (2000) findings suggest that cultural awareness and the connection of HL development and identity are also important factors, as the parents' understanding of this complex issue is one of the keys to success in HL development, coupled with the complete cultural, social, and economic capital (Bourdieu 1986) necessary to provide children with an enriching experience. In other studies, the HL has been seen as "a necessary social resource for maintaining cultural tradition and ethnic identity" (Schecter and Bayley 2002: 79). While the ability to successfully maintain the home language in a dominant language environment gives minority language speakers a stronger identity and sense of self, a strong HL identity has been identified as one of the most critical factors conducive to maintenance.

In this vein, children who do not develop a strong HL attachment may even be ambivalent about their identity and feel "shame about the home language and culture" (Cummins 1984: 119). If identity can be defined as "how the self conceives of itself, and labels itself" (Mathews 2000: 17), how does someone "label" themselves when there is a contradiction in how they 'perceive' themselves? If the "individual and culture are inseparable" (Cope and Kalantzis 2000: 203), how can they acknowledge and value who they are when they are ashamed of the language and culture expressed at home, for instance? This raises a myriad of questions about the study of HL development and loss, between the interests of different generations and how research can serve these interests.

In relation to forces supporting minority identities, it can be argued that ethnolinguistic and ethnocultural groups have unique characteristics that help shape the degree of success they can expect in HL development. For instance certain groups, like Japanese families in Canada, may have at their disposal a number of symbolic and material resources (i.e., Japanese Saturday School) (Bourdieu 1986) that enable them to pursue their goals more successfully (see e.g., Sakamoto 2001) than other groups that lack such resources, and therefore, are unable to operate such programs. Certainly, not only material resources play a crucial role in HL development, as some forms of cultural capital such as cultural and linguistic awareness (Guardado 2006), seem to also strengthen the likelihood of HL development in individuals. In the end, however, even for Japanese families the challenge of raising multilingual children is a formidable one (Tsushima and Guardado in press).

2.3.2.3 Intergenerational communication and family unity

The language use choices that parents and children make have a direct impact on intergenerational communication, most often between children and extended family including grandparents, aunts, uncles, and cousins (Wong Fillmore 1991, Kouritzin 1999, Thomas and Cao 1999, Guardado 2002, Schecter and Bayley 2002, Guardado 2008b, Farruggio 2010, Brown 2011, Hashimoto and Lee 2011, Kim 2011, Ferguson 2013). One of Fishman's mantras over several decades was that intergenerational communication within home and family are the basis for heritage language continuity (e.g., 1996b) and called this domain "the real secret weapon of reversing language shift" (2001: 459). Indeed, the majority of studies in the field echo this intuitive but crucial position from one viewpoint or another. For instance, an important goal in fostering Spanish reported by the participants in Schecter and Bayley's (1997) study was the promise of a connection with family and family history. Similarly, Li (1999) addressed the vital role that HL development has in ensuring familial unity and bridging generation gaps. In Pacini-Ketchabaw et al.'s (2001) study, among other findings, the families saw HL development as a way to cultivate family unity and Sakamoto (2001) emphasized that for her Japanese participants, family cohesion was the most important factor. The Japanese participants in Tsushima and Guardado's study cited family bonding as a major family motivation. In her qualitative study of adults who had experienced language loss in childhood, Kouritzin (1999) found that the great majority of participants reported many negative familial effects. Likewise, in a sociolinguistic study of a Chinese community in Britain, Wei (1994) detailed generational changes in language choice among Chinese immigrant families, a sign of language shift and loss in the younger generations.

A notable case illustrating intergenerational communication issues is provided by Thomas and Cao (1999). Among the documented findings, one of the most salient issues pointed to the frustrations of family members in communicating with one another in their daily lives. The children communicated with their parents with difficulty and only barely with grandparents, a situation that created a tense atmosphere in a home where different languages and cultures collided and where generation gaps exacerbated the circumstances of family members. All of the children had almost completely shifted to English, a language not mastered by the parents or grandparents. Thomas and Cao observed that parents could not even "know" their children or what kind of people they were. The parents felt that they had lost authority over their own children, especially being incapable of dealing with or even understand the different aspects of their children's schooling, and only being able to advise them to do what they thought was right while hoping for the best. It is clear from this study that in relation to the issue of parent-child distancing due to the lack of a shared language, HL development and maintenance is not only important based on nostalgic grounds, as is often stated or implied (Fishman 1991). Although nostalgia may play a role in the desire of minority groups to transmit the home language and culture to their children, family cohesion and harmony are jeopardized when the lack of a shared language in the family brings misunderstandings and frustrations to its members and they gradually choose to spend less time attempting to communicate or share experiences as a result. Parents and grandparents are also unable to succeed in the transmission of family traditions to their children or to help them understand and cope with their experiences as they are growing up. Thomas and Cao also provide an analysis of the repercussions of parents' inability to participate in their children's education and academic decision-making process as well as subsequent feelings of lack of control over their children's lives.

When the HL loss process is underway many "parents often feel that they are losing their children" (Skutnabb-Kangas 1999: 47) because they are no longer able to fully reach them in the language in which they are most competent. For the children, the nuances of the L1 are often lost in the messages. In connection to the issues discussed above, this situation presents obvious implications for identity and possibly a sense of alienation between children and their parents and grandparents. There is no doubt that as this process progresses, not only language is lost. Almost three decades ago, Wong Fillmore (1991: 343) notably stated:

> When parents are unable to talk to their children, they cannot easily convey to them their values, beliefs, understandings, or wisdom about how to cope with their experiences. They cannot teach them about the meaning of work, or about personal responsibility, or what it means to be a moral or ethical person in a world with too many choices and too few guideposts to follow. [...]. When parents lose the means for socializing and influencing their children, rifts develop and families lose the intimacy that comes from shared beliefs and understandings.

In the essay, *What Do You Lose When You Lose Your Language?*, Fishman (1996b), too, speaks eloquently and passionately about the tremendous role that intergenerational communication plays in HL development and suggests that although bilingual schools are extremely important for supporting the process at certain levels (gaining access to wider communities through literacy, increasing power in society for the HL), he emphasizes the need to direct the key efforts close to the family, home, and community as "that is where the mother tongue or vernacular is handed on" (78).

2.3.3 Agnes He's hypotheses

As alluded to earlier, the work of Agnes He has done much to move us forward as a field (2001, 2003, 2004, 2006, 2008, 2012, 2016) and is arguably considered the leading scholar in Chinese heritage language socialization and related studies. One of her most recent contributions is an elaborate set of hypotheses that attempt to predict whether a HL will be maintained or not, albeit in the Chinese speaking population (He 2006, 2012). He's hypotheses are part of her theory of identity and have been drawn from data collected over time in several studies with Chinese heritage language learners in the United States. The following is a summary of He's 10 hypotheses in which she outlines what she views as the key variables affecting HL development (adapted from He 2012: 595–597):

1. The rootedness hypothesis: The degree of success in HL development correlates positively with one's desire to be rooted in the heritage culture and to appreciate similarities with members of the HL community.
2. The benefits hypothesis: The degree of success in HL development correlates positively with one's perceived future benefits and rewards (e.g., economic).

3. The interaction hypothesis: The degree of success in HL development correlates positively with one's desire to communicate successfully in a moment-by-moment fashion.
4. The positive-stance hypothesis: The degree of success in HL development correlates positively with the positive stance the dominant language community has towards the HL.
5. The by-choice hypothesis: The degree of success in HL development correlates positively with the frequency with which one's family uses the HL by choice.
6. The diverse-input hypothesis: The degree of success in HL development correlates positively with the extent to which one has access to rich and diverse HL input.
7. The discourse-norms hypothesis: The degree of success in HL development correlates positively with the extent to which the discourse norms in HL contexts (home, classroom, or community) are sensitive to the discourse norms in the dominant language community.
8. The enrichment hypothesis: The degree of success in HL development correlates positively with the extent to which one has created a niche (linguistic, social, cultural) in the English-speaking community.
9. The multiplicity hypothesis: The degree of success in HL development correlates positively with the ease with which the learner is able to manage differences and discontinuities presented by multiple speech roles in multiple, intersecting communities.
10. The transformation hypothesis: As one negotiates with a variety of languages across contexts (family, peer groups, school institutions), one is engaged in a double process of socialization into given speech communities, a process that can also transform the HL community.

He's hypotheses were formulated based on a variety of datasets from HL learners of Chinese. Thus, they were worded specifically addressing Chinese heritage language (CHL) learners. For the purposes of this chapter, however, I have taken several liberties and have adapted He's original phrasing (significantly in some cases) by wording the hypotheses in a way that can be more generically applicable to any heritage language. Clearly, she did not intend for these to be applied to other HLs and it would be unfair to suggest that any perceived shortcomings of the hypotheses when applied to other heritage languages could be blamed on inherent weaknesses. However, I find He's work highly insightful and with broader potential than perhaps originally intended or anticipated. When substituting Chinese heritage language with HL in general, for instance, the value and usefulness of her hypotheses seem to be preserved. A useful example of this is found in Chapter 6 of the present book. As I show, at least the first four hypotheses seem to speak directly to the discourses produced by Hispanic families.

To conclude this chapter, all of the above scholars, whose work are referenced frequently throughout the book, have provided some of the most productive and informative insights in this recent area. Many newer generation scholars have already built on this important work and in some cases perhaps extended it. In the very recent HL development scholarship, and also more specifically addressing the individual and family domains that this book is concerned with, Agnes He has advanced the field in significant ways. Although her research is very specifically focused on Chinese populations, the research questions pursued and the insights provided are visibly relevant across ethnolinguistic minorities, including the Hispanic populations that have been the focus of my own work. Fishman's work encompasses both a broad range of scholarship areas at the societal and international level as well as discussions of issues at the familial and community level, with lesser coverage of the individual level. At various points in this book references are more frequently made at the individual level. However, since the book also aims to address the macro HL development picture, the arguments related to this aspect of the book benefit greatly from Fishman's macro level work.

2.4 Chapter summary

In this chapter, I provided an overview of heritage language development scholarship and suggested that this is a rapidly emerging area of research. Aside from a select group of scholars such as Joshua Fishman, heritage language development, loss, and maintenance received little attention from applied linguists and sociolinguists until the last few decades. Since the 1980s, however, much research has centered on factors contributing to HL development, including the role of families, identities, attitudes, and beliefs. Heritage language development strategies and practices in families, and more recently in community grassroots groups, have also become a productive avenue of inquiry in trying to arrive at a more nuanced understanding of HL development and related phenomena. Although in several cases positive language attitudes have been correlated with HL development, a growing body of research is beginning to show that positive language attitudes alone are not sufficient to develop and maintain a language. More recent studies are looking at how other kinds of progressive beliefs and worldviews, such as ideologies and cosmopolitanism, might provide a more fruitful point of entry to understanding successful cases of HL development in modern (post-globalization) families.

Two major forces against HL development that are increasingly attracting attention include the role of school and the push for assimilation of linguistic minorities. The school is the child's main point of immersed contact in the dominant language, which effectively reduces the number of daytime hours the child spends speaking the HL. Negative attitudes from teachers regarding HL development in the home can also be damaging to home language development. As many linguistic-minority immigrant parents are eager for their whole families to master the dominant language in society and thus gain some type of socioeconomic mobility, many parents welcome their children's use of the societal language in the home and seize the opportunity to practice this language themselves, thereby further reducing the child's exposure to the HL.

The lasting legacy of the father of the sociology of language, Joshua Fishman, was emphasized in this chapter. For him, language maintenance and language shift were at the heart of the sociology of language, and he viewed research methodologies such as the ethnography of communication as ideal tools for studying these phenomena. Fishman delved in discussions of language maintenance and shift in relation to, arguably, every factor and issue that is taken up in this book. He engaged with issues that he saw as core to this topic, such as the aspirations and ideologies of families and communities regarding the minority language; school and community support; the cultural, socioeconomic, and political context; as well as home practices and individual identities and attitudes. In tandem with an ethnic group's symbolic and material capital is the ability of the group to instill in their young a sense of identification with and pride in their culture. These are issues that we know have positive implications for HL development. These issues were consistently discussed in Fishman's work for decades. Many families point to family cohesion as the main reason for HL development. Indeed, HL loss can have the direst consequences for families, as a parent that is unable to communicate freely with their child (especially on important matters) is robbed of their ability to "know" their child, provide guidance, and socialize them into their value systems. Much of Fishman's work addressed this aspect of the research area with scholarly rigour and emotional commitment. Admittedly, in this chapter I only give a review of aspects of Fishman's work, but my intention was to provide a sampling of the issues he engaged with in relation to heritage languages and suggest that few aspects of this area were left untouched by his extensive scholarship.

3 Language socialization

3.1 Introduction

In this chapter, I introduce language socialization, a notion that originated in the 1970s as a result of research in several interrelated areas, but mainly in sociolinguistics and linguistic anthropology. Rooted in an ethnographic tradition, language socialization has evolved into a robust paradigm that supports the description, investigation, and interpretation of language acquisition and enculturation processes. These processes are made possible through interaction in social contexts. Context is to be understood as the entire set of relationships in which socialization takes place. After defining language socialization, I provide a brief synopsis of its evolution and subsequent expansion into a variety of settings and areas of focus. I then describe the genesis of second language socialization and its embracement in multilingual research, out of which HL socialization has recently emerged. The complexities found in these diverse contexts of investigation and the concomitant continuous theorization of language socialization are put forward.

3.2 Defining language socialization

The concept of language socialization addresses two major interdependent areas of social and cultural development: socialization *through* language use and socialization *into* language use. Alternatively, we may describe these two areas as language learning and culture learning. Thus, language socialization is the process by which people are socialized both to use the language of their community and to become members of that community. Although language socialization is a lifelong process that arguably begins even before birth and continues through life, by far, most research has focused on children. From this perspective, children's socialization into the cultural practices of their social group is mediated by language. Language, then, is the chief tool that members of the social group use in order to transmit their values and beliefs—their worldview—to the child. At the same time, the language itself codifies many social and cultural elements, such as hierarchical relations among members of groups, a process that helps form the child's emerging sense of self. It is through this process that the child learns to think and act appropriately—in harmony with the norms of the group. By the same token, through social interaction and "in the process of acquiring social knowledge, children acquire knowledge of language structure and use" (Schieffelin and Ochs 1986a: 163–164). Thus, children learn the language variety and the distinctive ways of speaking of their linguistic community.

3.2.1 Language socialization: Theory and methods

Language socialization may be seen as a three-way concept that refers to a *topic* of investigation, a *theory* of learning, and a *method* of analysis. Bronson and Watson-Gegeo (2008) argue that language socialization as topic is involved when studies only "touch on aspects of the LS [language socialization] process without necessarily embodying an LS approach or methods in the way the inquiry is actually conceived and conducted" (48). In such instances, they explain, researchers are using language socialization as topic, as opposed to language socialization as method. They argue that language socialization as method entails full-blown longitudinal ethnographies. From this perspective, these studies need to employ discourse analysis of social interaction and a consideration of the relevant micro and macro dimensions. While most language socialization studies are ethnographic, Bronson and Watson-Gegeo's canonical view of language socialization research is not widely shared by scholars in the field. Duff and Talmy (2011), for instance, regard attempts at clearly demarcating the boundaries of what counts as language socialization research as "premature and overly restrictive" (102). They explain that ideally language socialization research would follow an ethnographic approach that analyzes linguistic and other cultural practices based on naturally occurring interactional data. They caution, however, that such a stance could curtail promising new ways of conducting language socialization research and as a consequence, they seem to imply, arrest the further theorization and development of the paradigm.

Language socialization as theory endeavours to explain the processes of language and culture learning in a variety of contexts, from home, school, work, community, and other settings. It is the interpretive lens through which learning processes are understood. Language socialization as a theory of language learning rests comfortably on the key assumption that language and culture are intrinsically connected. Based on this premise, the process of language learning and culture learning (enculturation) are one and the same and happen simultaneously. Enculturation refers to the socialization process that takes place in a first culture context. Acculturation, a term related to, but not the same as enculturation, is the learning and adopting of the norms and ways of life of a new culture, as is the case of immigrants who settle in a new country. Just like L1 learning and enculturation are connected, the process of L2 learning and acculturation are also closely linked. Since language is an element of culture (Fishman 1994, Jandt 2006), then language and culture are learned simultaneously in the process of socialization. Thus, L2 learning, although linked to acculturation, is not the result of acculturation per se.

The language and culture learning process involves both social aspects of language as well as culture. When applied as a research method, language socialization becomes a versatile tool for investigating a variety of factors around linguistic interaction and social participation within particular speech communities. To be precise, language socialization enables researchers to investigate the microlinguistic processes and broader socio-cultural-ideological factors implicated in how individuals become competent members of their communities. Therefore, often (but not exclusively) this process is informed by ethnographic research and the ethnography of communication (Duff 1995). The ethnography of communication and language socialization as method are inseparable, and as such, are intimately linked to linguistics and anthropology. To better appreciate the function of language socialization as a research method, let us digress, albeit momentarily.

The object of ethnography as the quintessential research method of anthropology is to describe and interpret cultures. The object of linguistics is to study language codes. The ethnography of communication, as part of the field of sociolinguistics, pursues the goal of studying communication in different communities. Since language is inseparable from culture and language is one of the systems of culture, this ethnographic orientation provides methods for studying these linguistic norms. To this end, the ethnographer of communication requires the necessary tools for the task: linguistic knowledge and ethnographic techniques. In a specific research setting, the ethnographer of communication studies a multiplicity of issues related to language socialization and enculturation, social interaction, communicative events, communicative strategies, communicative functions, communicative patterns, communication behaviour, ways of speaking, routines and rituals, and other issues. In some settings, it may also be significant to focus on questions of code-switching and style-shifting, intercultural communication, cross-cultural communication and in general, the researcher would endeavour to provide an in-depth description and interpretation of how social meaning is conveyed and how it affects the speech community. Therefore, the ethnography of communication contains the mechanisms to study how language socialization occurs over a period of time, even throughout the lifespan (Duff 1995). The ethnography of communication requires in-depth observation, description, and interpretation of questions, issues as well as unknown phenomena posed by language socialization theory. While sociolinguistic research typically focuses on how language practice is organized within narrow settings, such as a neighborhood, a factory, or a school, a language socialization approach expands the researcher's gaze to the entire social and cultural milieu (Saville-Troike 2003).

3.3 The evolution of language socialization

In the 1960s and early 1970s, Dell Hymes was instrumental in establishing the interdisciplinary subfield of linguistic anthropology. He was also responsible for coining the term "ethnography of speaking," an early precursor to the ethnography of communication, which embodied what Hymes saw as the agenda for linguistic anthropology. With these disciplinary developments in anthropology and sociolinguistics as its backdrop, and informed by psycholinguistic work, the language socialization paradigm evolved out of the work in the 1970s of two key figures, the linguistic anthropologists Bambi B. Schieffelin and Elinor Ochs. The main studies—and many other related publications—that initiated the paradigm are represented by these two publications: (1) Elinor Ochs' (1988) *Culture and language development: Language acquisition and language socialization in a Samoan village* and (2) Bambi B. Schieffelin's (1990) *The give and take of everyday life: Language socialization of Kaluli children.* They conducted ethnographic work with a focus on the language acquisition of Kaluli children of Papua New Guinea between 1975 and 1977, and children in Samoa between 1978 and 1979, respectively. In their work, they used linguistic and ethnographic methods to collect and analyze children's spontaneous speech and to document their observations on sociocultural beliefs, ways of thinking, worldview, and behaviours, which organized their social order. This provided Schieffelin and Ochs with an in-depth understanding of how children become members of a community, learn to participate in the community's culture, and to use the community's language in socially appropriate ways (see Ochs and Schieffelin 2008, 2012 for recent accounts).

Ochs and Schieffelin reunited at the end of their fieldwork, and as a result they arrived at the understanding of how children's acquisition of language and their learning of culture are not separate processes, but tightly integrated into a single one. Their subsequent publications (particularly the seminal Schieffelin and Ochs 1986b) effectively laid out their compelling findings and solidly inducted language socialization as a theory and research paradigm in its own right. Around the time they completed their work, another seminal ethnography of communication was coming to a close: Shirley Brice Heath's now classic (1983) *Ways with Words.* In the linguistic anthropological tradition of Schieffelin and Ochs' work, Heath researched young children's socialization into language, literacy, and oral practices at home and school in two nearby communities in the Piedmont Carolinas of the United States. Roadville was a community of white-working class families and Trackton a black working-class community. Heath identified significant cultural differences between the two working-class groups and reported that the literacy practices of the two differed considerably. Additionally, she found that these ways with words also varied between the working-class families and the townspeople—the *mainstreamers*[1]—who subscribed to middle-class values. In Trackton, when there was a new born baby in the house "everyone talks *about* the baby, but rarely *to* the baby" (75), stated Heath, whereas in Roadville, everyone except young boys and some men acquaintances who are considered "awkward and 'ignorant 'bout babies'" (121) are expected to talk to them. Baby talk—talk that is especially modified and channeled for them—is used with babies. Overall, Heath's language socialization work underscored the finding that literacy orientations considered common in "mainstream" middle-class homes in the Western world are but only one type in a range of models found in different communities. Thus, Schieffelin and Ochs' and Heath's work became the key foundations that firmly established the language socialization paradigm in the 1980s.

As exemplified above, language socialization was originally conceptualized as the process through which "children are socialized through the use of language as well as how children are socialized to use language" (Schieffelin and Ochs 1986a: 184). Hence, it is not surprising that the traditional domains of language socialization have been monolingual settings, both in North America and elsewhere. Building on, and including, the above seminal studies, this line of research has focused on the culture specific aspects of day-to-day language use, in particular those speech acts that children are expected to acquire. These included prompting routines in Lesotho, Africa (Demuth 1986), affective competence and construction of social identity in Samoa (Ochs 1982, 1988, 1993), teasing and shaming in Hawaii (Schieffelin 1986, 1990), calling-out practices on the Solomon Islands (Watson-Gegeo and Gegeo 1986), the development of communicative style in Japan (Clancy 1986), gender socialization in Ecuador (Miles 1994), register variation in the United States (Andersen 1986), and children's socialization into language and literacy at home and at school, also in the United States (Heath 1983). Although the home context—as the locus of the process of apprenticeship—has traditionally been the main site of language socialization investigations, other settings have now become commonplace in this type of research. These include workplaces (Bell 2003, McAll 2003, Roy 2003), classrooms (Poole 1992, Duff 1995, 1996, Atkinson 2003, Cole and Zuengler 2003, Harklau 2003, He 2003, Lotherington 2003, Luykx 2003, Pon, Goldstein and Schecter 2003), extracurricular activities and community groups (Guardado 2008a, Guardado and Becker 2013), among others.

---

[1] Heath (1983) defines mainstreamers as those who "exist in societies around the world that rely on formal educational systems to prepare children for participation in settings involving literacy. Cross-national descriptions characterize these groups as literate, school-oriented, aspiring to upward mobility through success in formal institutions, and looking beyond the primary networks of family and community for behavioral models and value orientations" (398).

3.3.1 Language socialization across contexts

With increasing immigration and globalization evolving rapidly over the last decades (e.g., United States, Australia and Canada), more languages and cultures are coming into contact and populations are becoming more culturally and linguistically diverse than ever before. This state of affairs poses an important challenge to researchers who need ever more effective and sophisticated research approaches to address issues arising in a variety of contexts, including school, online, and ethnolinguistic communities. Expanding language socialization into multilingual, multicultural, and multimodal settings offers possibilities for investigating pertinent issues in such communities. Patricia A. Duff (2002), a leading second generation language socialization researcher who studied under Elinor Ochs, posits that the ethnography of communication (through a language socialization lens) offers advantages "as a culture- and- context-sensitive method for conducting research" (315). Therefore, both in and out of the classroom, on and offline, language socialization has been utilized as a suitable tool for carrying out interactional linguistic analyses. In combination with the ethnography of communication, a language socialization lens has provided the means for exploring, describing, and interpreting the beliefs and attitudes about language in speech communities, as well as the communication behaviours, strategies, and patterns of language usage that may reveal underlying relationships and power dynamics within these communities. In a nutshell, this paradigm has evolved in ways that make it a rather versatile set of tools for theorizing and empirically investigating the increasing complexity of the role of language in all aspects of human development across the lifespan.

3.3.1.1 Second language socialization

The notion of second language socialization is partly the result of developments in second language acquisition (SLA) over several decades. It draws on "sociological, anthropological, and psychological approaches to the study of social and linguistic competence within a social group" (Schieffelin and Ochs 1986a: 163), clearly situating language learning in general, and L2 learning in particular, in the social realm (Ochs and Schieffelin 1995, 2008). In effect, second language socialization research evolved in response to critiques to traditional conceptualizations of SLA theory, mainly because these traditional approaches tended to emphasize individual cognitive processes in language acquisition, rather than processes of participation and membership negotiation in social worlds. Scholars working from an L2 socialization perspective seek to fill this gap by incorporating social and cultural domains into analyses of L2 learning and highlighting the situated nature of the learning process in general, but more specifically in relation to L2 learning, and the socializing nature of linguistic interaction.

More specifically, a key distinction between SLA and L2 socialization is in focus and scope. While the former's interest lies in describing the discrete aspects of linguistic skill development, such as morphosyntaxis, phonology, and lexis, the latter aims to investigate not only language learning, but also at a broader level the learning of all types of knowledge that takes place through language (see also Schieffelin 1990, Duff and Talmy 2011). The oft-cited notion that this process involves socialization through language and into language use is the most succinct definition of language socialization available. The "through" aspect of this definition may be an even more complex one in L2 contexts as it involves a wide range of subjective forms of knowledge which are intertwined with all aspects of social life, including culture, identity, ideologies, and many other dimensions of learning. This may be especially complicated by the fact that these learners are "children or adults who already possess a repertoire of linguistic, discursive, and cultural traditions and community affiliations when encountering new ones" (Duff 2007c: 310) and are expected to simultaneously negotiate these intricate elements through a language into whose use they aspire to be socialized. Furthermore, Duff and Talmy describe how from a language socialization perspective, the definition of "language" itself is recast as a social practice. It is no longer seen as a set of discrete "morphemes, syntactic structures, lexis, and pragmatic norms" (96) with the function of neutrally transmitting information, but rather, as one of many social practices that are "in-flux, contested, and ever-changing" (Duff and Talmy 2011) and which form the core of speech communities.

A potential source of confusion for newcomers to social approaches to L2 learning may be found in relation to sociocultural theory. L2 socialization is in tune with sociocultural approaches to L2 learning in that both emphasize social interaction and the situatedness of language development. Accordingly, both approaches place interlocutors and other social participants at the centre of learning as they apprentice learners through this process (see Duff 2007c, for an extended discussion of the intersection between sociocultural theory and language socialization). While several commonalities between L2 socialization and sociocultural approaches to L2 learning may be found, there are some key differences. This is not surprising, given that sociocultural theory had its foundation in psychology (see Vygotsky 1978), and as a result is mainly concerned with higher cognitive processes. Sociocultural theory focuses on how external social interactions—one component of *mediation*, the central concept in this approach—are internalized, a process that leads to L2 learning. Having emerged from anthropology, L2 socialization is strongly concerned with how the macro context and local cultural orientations shape social interactions as individuals attempt to become competent members of the L2 community, a process that facilitates L2 learning.

Second language socialization drew its underlying theoretical tenets from first generation research (i.e., the founding language socialization studies), the most central of which is that language acquisition is facilitated by competent members of the target speech community in concert with other factors and features of the cultural environment. Building on the insights generated by the seminal language socialization work (Ochs 1982, Heath 1983, Schieffelin and Ochs 1986a, 1986b, Watson-Gegeo and Gegeo 1986, Ochs 1988, Schieffelin 1990), L2 socialization studies have investigated the relationship between L2 learning and the broader context in which it is expected to occur with an emphasis on how this context impacts the local interactions. Thus, L2 socialization is defined as the "process by which non-native speakers of a language, or people returning to a language they may have once understood or spoken but have since lost proficiency in, seek competence in the language and, typically, membership and the ability to participate in the practices of communities in which that language is spoken" (Duff 2012: 564). Although it shares many features with L1 socialization, L2 socialization deals with a series of added complexities. Duff points out that these additional complexities include the fact that the paradigm addresses the language learning processes of "learners who have already acquired or are still in the process of acquiring a primary language and the cultural knowledge and practices associated with that language" (Duff 2012: 569). Below I review selected studies addressing the multifaceted nature of some of this work, which has helped define L2 socialization as a research area in its own right.

Duff (1995) conducted an ethnography of communication in several English-medium history classes in post-Soviet-era Hungary. The focus of her research was on a particular traditional recitation routine (*felelés*), which was being replaced by less structured presentations and class discussions. During the time of her fieldwork in the schools, political changes at the national level and educational changes at the school level, particularly in the innovative immersion schools, were taking place. Duff found that students in the immersion (English-medium) classes placed a stronger value on what was seen as a Western interactional style, which was considered more desirable, and devalued the practices associated with the system that was on the decline. Duff's work is a clear example of how L2 socialization investigations can reveal ways in which macro forces impact on micro level discourse practices in terms of, in this case, L2 classroom interactions.

Willett's (1995) was an ethnographic study of four immigrant first-grade students (three girls and one boy) in a United States school. By examining the children's participation in the day-to-day classroom events over a year, she provided insights into how gender, class, ethnicity, and other social factors strongly affected their academic experiences. While the three girls in the group were rewarded by the teacher and praised by their peers for using certain participation strategies, such as collaborative work, the only boy in the class was socially penalized for attempting to engage in similar practices. Thus, she found that social identity factors shaped the expectations and interactions in the classroom, which benefitted the three female students and impeded access to language development and academic success to the only ESL boy in the classroom.

A recent study of L2 socialization that further illustrates how the paradigm informs language learning and interactional competence in instructed settings is Cekaite's (2007) ethnography in an immersion classroom in Sweden. Her study focused on a seven year old Kurdish girl, Fusi who, over one year, moved through three phases of interactional competence development in the classroom: silent, noisy and loud, and skillful. Cekaite explains that Fusi was mostly silent in the first phase, and made attempts to participate, although inappropriately, in the second phase (e.g., due to inexpert use of sequential turn-taking). In the third phase, however, she had attained mastery of the sequential organization of the classroom routines when engaging in different multi-party activities. In other words, Fusi had moved from a peripheral observer to a competent member of the classroom community in the course of a school year. This study, among many other important contributions, highlights the dynamic and changing nature of L2 socialization as well as the situatedness of this process and provides a concrete example of the unique trajectories of language socialization (Wortham 2005) that L2 learners may follow.

A sign of the widespread development and application of L2 socialization can be found in its increasing degree of specification. For instance, L2 socialization work at the post-secondary level has recently exploded into a wide range of areas, mainly focusing on particular aspects of L2 students' academic discourse socialization. An example of this rapidly growing line within the L2 socialization literature addresses L2 writing, such as Séror's (2008, 2009) ethnographic work examining Japanese undergraduate exchange students' experiences in content courses, uncovering, *inter alia*, the influential role of macro institutional factors on the L2 writing feedback practices of university instructors. Thus, many of the feedback practices in which instructors engaged were the result of the powerful institutional socializing forces in which these practices were embedded. Consequently, the students' academic literacy socialization experiences in Séror's study were also shaped by these forces through their instructors.

A closely related scholarly path addresses students' experiences with oral presentations, a pervasive aspect of academic work in Western higher education institutions, particularly (but not exclusively) at the graduate level. Some of this work includes research on individual oral presentations (Morita 2000, 2004, Zappa-Hollman 2007) and collaborative presentations (Kobayashi 2003). Also at the post-secondary level, but looking at language socialization from a slightly different angle, Kim (2008) examined the experiences of Generation 1.5 Korean-Canadian students as they negotiated academic discourses and investments in relation to their multiple identities and languages. Generation 1.5 is a term used to describe people who immigrate as children or teens to a new country, a term that is addressed in Chapter 13 as part of the analysis of heritage language socialization among Hispanic families in Canada. Kim provided a highly nuanced account of the paths of socialization that a small group of students followed. She highlighted, for instance, their linguistic ambivalence between Korean and English as well as insecurities with their English abilities, despite their secondary education through English. A line of research that has also grown recently in post-secondary settings is related to L2 socialization in online environments (Potts 2005, Yim 2011), pointing to the continuous development of applications of the language socialization paradigm.

With its origins in pioneering ethnographic work like Duff's (1995) in secondary schools in Hungary and Willet's (1995) examination of an elementary ESL classroom in the United States, L2 socialization has now expanded across various age groups as well as to formal and informal learning settings and aspects of this process. This work also includes that conducted in vocational (Duff, Wong and Early 2000), occupational (Goldstein 1997), and the educational settings reviewed in this section (see e.g., Duff 2007b, for a critical review of some of this work). Thus, in contrast to L1 socialization, L2 socialization frequently addresses the experiences of adolescents and adults (Duff 2012), a point that was evident in the brief overview conducted in this section.

3.3.1.2 Language socialization in multilingual contexts

In addition to the aforementioned research trends focusing on the intricacies of L2 socialization, recently also multilingual and multicultural populations have attracted much attention from researchers interested in the particularities of socialization processes (Garrett and Baquedano-López 2002, Fogle and King 2017). Some of the L2 socialization studies with multilingual and multicultural populations have often focused on one or combined home, school, and community and have taken up an array of issues. *Volume 8: Language Socialization* of the *Encyclopedia of Language and Education*, edited by Patricia A. Duff and Nancy Hornberger (2008) contains an impressive collection of 24 chapters with the empirical, theoretical, and methodological advances in language socialization scholarship in recent times, encompassing an equally wide selection of topics, populations, and settings. Some of the issues covered include language socialization in Canadian Indigenous communities (Pesco and Crago 2008), gendered L2 socialization (Gordon 2008), multimodality (Pahl 2008), and communication in online communities (Lam 2008), to mention but a few. These studies built on other influential work previously conducted in a variety of settings that included teasing (Eisenberg 1986), maternal teaching talk (Eisenberg 2002), explanatory emotion talk (Cervantes 2002), social identity in *doctrina* classes (Baquedano-Lopez 2000), cultural identity formation/maintenance and/or bilingual and multilingual socialization (Dagenais and Day 1999, He 2006), and attitudes toward L1 and L2 languages (Pease-Alvarez 2002, Patrick 2003, Pease-Alvarez 2003).

These studies illustrated some of the research possibilities in settings where two or more languages and language varieties are juxtaposed. Following in the tradition of Heath (and working under Heath's supervision), Zentella (1997) completed an ethnography of Puerto Rican children in a block community in New York's Spanish Harlem between 1977 and 1993. Unlike Heath's study, which was conducted in monolingual speech communities, the focus of Zentella's comprehensive research on bilingual usage among Puerto Ricans focused on the experiences of working class families raising, attempting to raise, or not succeeding in raising, bilingual children. Although this issue was not highlighted in her book, it is interesting to note that the participants in this study, much like Heath's Trackton participants, engaged in a particular style of child rearing, in which baby-talk by adults was avoided and the speech of children was not entirely valued and therefore not further expanded. This illustrates the transferability of language socialization theorizing across contexts and linguistic realities with its concomitant modifications. Zentella's 14-year language socialization study has become a classic for its comprehensive analysis and precise interpretation of how issues of (hybrid) language identities, socioeconomic status, family dynamics, and education influence one another. Her study covered a range of aspects of the participants' lives and the activities in which they engaged through language. For instance, it provided a detailed portrayal of how bilingualism is socially constructed in one of the most disadvantaged communities in the United States. It also presented a systematic picture of how the communication patterns of the participating children, and of the children's children, as well as the varieties of Spanish and English that they spoke, exemplified "Spanglish," which itself was devalued then and continues to be a devalued and stigmatized language variety in the United States today. In short, Zentella demonstrated that code-switching, the practice of alternating between two languages or language varieties within a conversation, was a normal—even desirable—aspect of bilingual language socialization for Puerto Ricans in New York's *El Barrio*.

Pease-Alvarez (2002) reports similar results, and posits that code-switching "is a normal language practice for bilingual youngsters who have the opportunity to draw on two different linguistic repertoires when speaking with other bilinguals" (126) although there seemed to be disagreement on this issue between some of the participating parents as well as the participating children. 34% of the parents and 63% of the children felt that code-switching was positive, normal, and acceptable. Yet, some parents expressed their rejection of code-switching as being incomprehensible and a marker of linguistic incompetence.

In the same way, Schecter and Bayley (1997) described how code-switching was a rather typical practice among the participating children in their study of Mexican-descent families in California and Texas. Some of the families engaged in this type of interaction as a normal practice, effectively socializing their children in the use of a mixture of English and Spanish as part of their daily home communication routine. More generally, Schecter and Bayley's (2002) study provided insights into the connection of language socialization practices and the dynamics of identity formation. Their study helped understand how members of speech communities use language to choose from different identities and also how language interacts in different ways with issues of ethnicity, gender, and class. Like Zentella, they addressed political issues of language in the United States context. This type of scholarship is important because there is a need to look at the larger sociopolitical contexts within which culturally situated communication takes place, as these contexts may determine features of communication in ways that are not evident from a narrow focus on communicative patterns alone. From its inception, an important feature in language socialization has been its emphasis on sociopolitical contexts and their intimate interdependence with patterns and styles of communication.

Clearly, many added complexities are presented by the language socialization of bilingual individuals (Luykx 2003). In their language socialization process, bilingual and multilingual individuals must assign meanings to their developing selves and negotiate their identities in multicultural homes, schools, communities, and other settings while attempting to find their place in society. This, of course, is further complicated by many other factors when immigrants are involved (see e.g., Duff, Wong and Early 2000). They may face the devaluing of their languages and cultures, contradictory language and culture ideologies within the families, and the clashing of cultural patterns between the home culture and the dominant culture, issues that are more fully addressed in the next chapter. The tensions generated by these issues may affect the languages spoken by family members or the degrees to which these languages are spoken within their families. Additionally, they may face linguistic, economic, social, and political difficulties in their quest for integration.

In the last two decades the language socialization paradigm has expanded and also become more specific. This movement is also increasingly impacting the HL area of research. The time seems appropriate for further developing this paradigm specifically from a HL perspective. Some of the complexities currently being addressed within HL studies were acknowledged in the original language socialization work, so it is timely to engage in work that provides more granularity to these issues. For instance, the agency of children in their socialization process is one of the areas that this book attempts to grapple with. Work on this and related issues will no doubt contribute to the further expansion and development of the language socialization framework overall. Therefore, throughout this book, agency, identity, power, ideologies, discourse, negotiation, and resistance are addressed, at times perhaps separately, but not far removed from the rest of these closely intertwined issues.

I would like to conclude this section by noting that language socialization research that focuses on the topics just discussed was previously subsumed under L2 socialization as a broader umbrella (see Duff 2003). Because the development and expansion of the language socialization paradigm had started in earnest in the late 1980s and early 1990s, research that involved anything other than L1 was grouped together (L2, foreign language, bilingual, multilingual, heritage, etc.). However, the 2000s saw a further specification of areas of focus and L2 socialization began to be conceptualized as a new area of language socialization research. Likewise, minority, bilingual, and multilingual socialization, often involving a minority language in an English dominant context, began to carve its own niche within language socialization studies. Two of the studies briefly summarized above (Zentella 1997, Schecter and Bayley 2002) focusing on the language socialization of linguistic minorities in the United States, specifically Spanish-speaking families, are now "modern classics" frequently cited in the literature that helped establish this line of research.

3.4 Heritage language socialization

In some ways resembling the way in which minority language socialization studies were loosely grouped under the L2 socialization umbrella in the past, some of the work reviewed in the previous section (*Language Socialization in Multilingual Contexts*) encompasses what is now beginning to emerge as a language socialization area in its own right—heritage language socialization. Studies addressing questions like the ones investigated in the works reviewed above have customarily been included in collections such as the volume edited by Duff and May (2017), Bayley and Schecter's (2003) *Language Socialization in Bilingual and Multilingual Societies,* and Zentella's (2005) *Building on Strength: Language and Literacy in Latino Families and Communities. The Handbook of Language Socialization,* edited by Duranti, Ochs and Schieffelin (2012), is a comprehensive and up to date collection of language socialization studies which organizes the chapters in the following five categories:

- Interactional Foundations
- Socialization Strategies
- Social Orientations
- Aesthetics and Imagination
- Language and Culture Contact

These five areas have direct or indirect relevance to the present book, but the last part, *Language and Culture Contact,* is at the core of Chapter 3 as it marks the foundational work that has recently led to the emergence of multilingual and heritage language socialization in the 2000s. An argument can be made that heritage language socialization research has been around for a while, in some shape or form, but it was not until recently that it started to be labeled this way. Agnes He, a pioneer in HL socialization research, has dedicated much of her recent work to "delineating the complexity" (594) along several dimensions of what she refers to as a "fledgling area" (587). Indeed, some of the early uses of the term are found in He (2008, 2012) (see also Guardado 2009, Tsushima and Guardado 2015). A Google Scholar search conducted at the beginning of 2014 while working on this chapter revealed that the term "heritage language socialization" was not used prior to 2008 in any publications indexed by this database. The first ever occurrence of the term was encountered in He's chapter focusing specifically on heritage language socialization as a separate type of socialization research, included in the *Encyclopedia of Language and Education* edited by Duff and Hornberger (2008). Other publications specifically using the term have appeared since (e.g., Avni 2008, Delgado 2009, Guardado 2013a, Guardado and Becker 2013, Minami 2013), a likely sign that the term is quickly catching on.

It has been amply demonstrated by work conducted by Duff (see e.g., 2002, 2003, 2012) and others (see e.g., Morita 2000, 2004) that L2 socialization offers many challenges and complexities not found in L1 socialization contexts. This point is further compounded in heritage language socialization, which includes features of L1 and L2 socialization, and even more so, given that the features of one (e.g., L1) or the other (e.g., L2) may be more salient in some contexts, families, individuals—and domains of use—than in others. As a result, attempting to develop a single model of HL socialization may not be a sensible objective. Yet, because of the growing recognition of the language socialization paradigm as a powerful and adaptable approach that is compatible with HL research questions, scholars interested in HL issues are increasingly adopting this framework in their work, and in the process, are contributing to the further expansion and conceptualization of language socialization more generally.

Indeed, HL socialization research is not only enriched by the growing sophistication in the theorization of language socialization, but it is also making important contributions of its own. As I discussed in the previous chapter, there is a significant body of literature indicating that cultural identity plays a key role in HL socialization, development, and maintenance. This is an area among many others—some of which are addressed in the final section of this chapter—that are contributing to this development. Pointedly, language socialization theory tells us that children develop a sense of who they are through the social interactions in which they engage in their daily lives (Schieffelin and Ochs 1986a). This point indicates that the process of language acquisition and language socialization are intertwined. Language acquisition concerns itself with the development of communicative skills, but does not account for the process of identity formation that language learning entails. Language socialization provides the missing piece of this puzzle by accounting for how novices and others are constructed as members of social communities and as particular kinds of people. Heritage language socialization also captures the processes of language learning, maintenance, and use while deeply scrutinizing the identity development and concomitant interactional complexity and conflict this often entails. Schieffelin and Ochs sum this up when they posit that "a twist in the interface of language learning and socialization into identity construction is the phenomenon of heritage language socialization, in which learners are expected to use the heritage code that displays them as suitable moral persons as envisioned by an idealized 'heritage culture'" (Ochs and Schieffelin 2012: 16–17).

Future chapters demonstrate that much is learned about HL socialization through analyses of day-to-day interactions and this focus is strongly emphasized in the book, although interpretive opportunities may be missed through a sole focus on the micro. Indeed, language socialization has traditionally emphasized the broader context within which interactions are embedded. While recognizing the emergence of possible alternative framings for the larger sociopolitical context and forces affecting culturally situated communication, it is also necessary to consider established macro heuristic models in the examination of factors impacting HL socialization. The case is made in the book for the need to conduct HL socialization research that considers narrow as well as broad vantage points.

According to Ochs and Schieffelin (2012), becoming a competent and recognized member of a community entails a very complex process. In heritage language socialization (and no doubt also in other multilingual language socialization settings), this means acquiring or at least to some pragmatic extent subscribing to the language ideologies that are valued in the group. These language ideologies contain the beliefs and values of community members about the worth of their languages and also about how, when, with whom, and in what contexts or circumstances these linguistic resources should be used (Fishman 1965). Heritage language socialization theory and research have shown that at the centre of this complex set of rules often lies the normative standard to use the heritage language for purposes such as expressing emotions, performing actions, displaying knowledge, constituting relationships, and so on. Additionally, HL socialization presents added complexities compared to monolingual socialization. These include the negative societal and individual attitudes—ideologies—related to their languages, which may be contested and contradictory, significantly affecting the family language policies and practices adopted by families. It is clear from the research literature that ideologies, policies, and practices are intricately related, and as a constellation of factors, strongly impact HL socialization outcomes. A topic that has not been significantly explored in contexts like Canada up to now relates to the experiences of families whose parents possess different mother tongues. As we see below, the role of emotions, constituting relationships, developing family language policies, and other issues may impact the contested and contradictory nature of socialization practices.

3.4.1 Heritage language socialization in interlingual families

Despite the increasing richness of knowledge in HL socialization, there is a relative lack of research with children who grow up in linguistically intermarried families with parents who have been raised in different ethnic communities and thus do not share the same native languages (Yamamoto 2001, Okita 2002, Jackson 2007, Braun and Cline 2014, Duff and Becker-Zayas 2017). Given the co-existence of two or more HLs and cultures in interlingual families, HL socialization becomes significantly more challenging compared to monolingual and even bilingual families (Blum Kulka 2008). These families face unique socialization challenges due to often competing and contradictory linguistic ideologies and cultural values at play. It is argued that these and other elements complicate their family dynamics, including metalinguistic negotiations, decision-making around family language policies, and the implementation of patterns of language use among all family members.

Families formed by individuals who marry outside of their ethnolinguistic group—linguistic exogamy—have been variously referred to in the research literature and associated scholarship as mixed unions (Statistics Canada 2011), linguistically intermarried couples (Piller 2001a, Jackson 2009), interlingual families (Yamamoto 2001, Jackson 2009), cross-linguistic and cross-cultural marriages (Constable 2005), and bilingual/multilingual couples (Piller and Takahashi 2006), among other terms in use. The terms I use most commonly are *interlingual* and *linguistically intermarried families* (see Guardado 2017). This definition differs somewhat from the usage sometimes found in the literature. For instance the typology of interlingual family proposed by Yamamoto (2001) includes parents who share a native language, but use their mother tongue or a third language for family communication. In her view, these families are interlingual in relation to the societal language.

The linguistic diversity of traditionally Anglophone countries is currently increasing in cities such as Sydney in Australia, London in the United Kingdom (UK), and New York in the United States (US). In Canada, the number of non-Anglophone speakers has grown steadily with each consecutive national census, and as of 2011, first generation Canadians (those who were born outside of Canada) and their children accounted for 39.4% of the total population, and this trend is likely to continue in the 2016 census (results unavailable at time of production). The growth of interlingual families globally has also been noted in relation to various countries, including Norway (Constable 2005), Japan (Yamamoto 2001), Australia (Oriyama 2010), and Canada (Minami 2013). In the latter, this type of exogamy has increased rapidly since at least the 1976 census (Castonguay 1982). The total number of married and common-law couples in mixed unions in Canada is 4.6% of the total population (Statistics Canada 2011). Although this is a relatively low number, striking differences are found across groups. For instance, out of the total of Japanese Canadian couples reported in this census, the group with the highest incidence of forming partnerships or marrying outside of their group, approximately 78.7% involved a spouse or partner who was not Japanese. Thus, there is a pressing need to examine the heritage language socialization processes of children who grow up in interlingual families.

The heritage language research with interlingual families using language socialization (Fogle 2012, Lanza 2001, 2007, Minami 2013) as well as other lenses (Yamamoto 2001, Okita 2002, Yamamoto 2005, Lanza 2007, Jackson 2009, Minami 2013), has demonstrated that this demographic exhibits more fluid language use patterns compared to other families. Indeed, this work has characterized the issues involved in these families as significantly intensified and embedded within added complications. For instance, language policies are often much more explicit and potentially problematic in interlingual families than in families where parents share a mother tongue. Indeed, for interlingual families the decision making process can be highly political (Liamputtong 1991, Piller 2001a, Jackson 2009), gendered (Lyon 1996, Pavlenko 2001, Minami 2013) and even emotional (Yamamoto 2001, Okita 2002). These decisions may be made consciously through discussion between parents (Tsushima and Guardado in press), the decision may be entrusted to the mother (Yamamoto 2001), the language used may by default be the language in which the couple originally began their relationship, or it may just emerge naturally (Okita 2002). Part of the emotional aspect of HL socialization with interlingual families is illustrated by Tsushima and Guardado's (in press) study with Japanese-descent mothers living in Montreal, Canada, who had formed partnerships with non-Japanese men. The mothers reported experiencing strong feelings of guilt and anxiety as a result of their status as the only native speakers of the HL in their families and therefore the sole linguistic resource, making HL socialization their responsibility.

Piller (2001a) explains that pervasive asymmetrical power relations in interlingual families on many dimensions can generate a variety of conflicts. Indeed, one of the parents is often positioned in an unfavourable position in the relationship, be it as non-native speaker, migrant, female, economically dependent, or other positionings based on national and cultural background, or all of the above. Gender power relations not only shape decisions around family language policy, but also HL socialization processes and outcomes. For instance, Lyon (1996) found that Welsh mothers accommodated the language of their husbands for family communication. Because mothers more directly impacted the language socialization of the children, this gender imbalance determined the fate of the children's heritage language development.

Given the uniquely political, gendered, and emotional heritage language socialization processes found in interlingual families, it is crucial to develop a more purposeful and systematic line of inquiry with a focus on their idiosyncratic experiences. Language socialization work and research using other lenses have started to build a solid foundation in this regard. However, it is argued that much more research needs to be undertaken which examines, documents, and theorizes the full range of ways in which interlingual parents negotiate the linguistic environments for their children and how the heritage language socialization experiences of these children are similar or different compared to children who grow up in more linguistically homogenous homes.

3.5 Evolving conceptualizations and issues

As a result of the diversity of scholarly work over the last three decades, language socialization has gradually evolved into a complex, multi-layered paradigm. I do not intend to propose that the multiplicity of layers of meaning and the diversity of interconnected and dialectical factors and agents that are part of the language socialization process were not recognized in earlier conceptualizations and applications of language socialization. As may be the case with any significant theoretical enterprise, development begins with attempts to understand the most immediate phenomena requiring examination. In the case of language socialization, this was found in the long-standing lack of attention to the role of social and cultural factors in language acquisition theory and research. More specifically, a need was identified to broaden our conception of language learning by redefining the role of language itself as more than a neutral transmitter of information, but also as the means through which individuals become competent members of their communities. While investigating the day-to-day speech routines through which children became socialized into the practices of their—mostly—L1 communities (Schieffelin and Ochs 1986a, Ochs 1988, Schieffelin 1990), the beginnings of the language socialization paradigm acknowledged some of the key characteristics that have been uncovered and emphasized in recent scholarship. This point may be particularly salient considering the expansion of language socialization focus areas to—arguably—more complex settings, such as the ones described in this chapter. These include—but are not limited to—L2 (notably, Duff, several publications) and multilingual and heritage communities (Zentella 1997, He 2001, Schecter and Bayley 2002, He 2012). This expanding focus and scope has targeted much unchartered research territory and exposed a great deal of complexity and many interconnected characteristics of the socialization process.

To be sure, one critique that language socialization has at times contended with was inherited from earlier "socialization" scholarship (e.g., Parsons and Bales 1956, as cited in Ochs and Schieffelin 2012). From this perspective, the process of socialization was viewed as unidirectional with parents socializing children in a progressive and unproblematic manner (Li 2008). This view shared much with the behaviouristic conditioning arguments (Duff 2007b) whose central tenets laid in repetition. Language socialization, while recognizing that parents and other adults are often the socializers of children, contends that the process of language socialization is fluid, contingent, multidirectional, and agentive. This conceptualization is especially the case in some of its more recent iterations of empirical and theoretical developments.

In the introductory chapter to *The Handbook of Language Socialization*, Ochs and Schieffelin (2012) outline how agency is clearly displayed in even the most seemingly mechanical and routinized performances. The fact that they selected agency as one of the few themes to highlight from the entire collection attests to the saliency of this particular feature of language socialization. This suggests that agency plays a direct role in language socialization studies across settings, areas of focus, types of participants, and other variables. Despite its centrality, children's agency in the language socialization process is not always apparent or recognized as such, but ever present and influential. This point has been shown even in the most mundane activities, as illustrated in Moore's (2012) research in Cameroon. Moore shows how repetition in speech, which on the surface may seem highly routinized, can be a site for children to exhibit their transformative role in their own socialization. Work of this nature further demonstrates how language socialization can enable the researcher to conduct analyses at various levels of depth even in relation to activities that may be considered mechanized and uncreative.

Although I do not gloss over a large set of characteristics of language socialization in this chapter, I do reiterate that most of these features are intertwined and, as such, are addressed separately and in relation to one another throughout the book. The centeredness of agency is salient in relation to issues of identity, power, ideologies, negotiation, and resistance. While language socialization has often been viewed as deterministic—children, learners, and other novices effortlessly attaining linguistic competence and community membership—(Duff 2007b, Ochs and Schieffelin 2012), the paradigm has now moved well beyond such criticisms. Indeed, language socialization is currently to be understood as a non-linear, dynamic, complex, and multidirectional process (Duff 2003, Cekaite 2007, Duff 2007b, 2007c, Duff and Hornberger 2008, Ochs and Schieffelin 2008, 2012, He 2016). Therefore, discussions of language socialization are often also discussions of the agentive, multidirectional, power-laden processes through which individuals and families socialize each other "into new domains of knowledge and cultural practice" (Bayley and Schecter 2003: 2).

As different sites, including a diversity of communities and participants, topics of interest and socialization issues, have been drawing researchers working from this perspective, the language socialization paradigm has been significantly expanded in terms of scope, focus, and depth. In essence, once L1 ceased to be the only domain of language socialization research, increasingly more sophisticated theorization as well as cross-pollination in terms of research methodologies and analytical tools have been undertaken. The result of this continuous multi-layered development is a considerable growth in the empirical applicability and theoretical explanatory power of language socialization across a very wide range of social activity.

3.6 Chapter summary

In this chapter, I have introduced language socialization, a concept that concerns a person's socialization *through* language and *into* language use within a community. I traced the development of language socialization from its origins based on the work of Ochs and Schieffelin who, using ethnographic methods, discovered that language learning and culture learning are in fact simultaneous processes. This early work revealed that children come to acquire a certain worldview *through* the language in which they are spoken to and which they learn to speak within a particular cultural framework of appropriateness. In other words, in learning to be competent speakers of a language, children also learn to become competent members of a society.

Although sometimes discussed as an unproblematic concept, language socialization is a multifaceted theory and framework of analysis. Given its explanatory and analytic robustness, it has evolved rapidly across a wide range of areas of research outside its original development in anthropology. Indeed, language socialization has been used to investigate a variety of issues in monolingual, second language, multilingual, deaf, online, and different ethnolinguistic communities. It has also helped to conduct research in a variety of formal and informal learning contexts such as elementary, secondary, post-secondary, workplace, apprenticeship, and others. This diversity of language socialization scholarship has helped advance its methodological development and theorization. Arguably, the most recent newcomers to this paradigm include heritage language socialization in families whose parents share a mother tongue as well as those whose native languages are different, such as interlingual families.

The rapid development referred to above has led scholars to expand and deepen their understanding of the language socialization process, which is now understood as a non-linear, dynamic, complex, and multidirectional process. For heritage language scholars, language socialization offers a convenient and principled way of studying beliefs, attitudes, and ideologies of language in speech communities, communication behaviour strategies in families, and patterns of language usage that may reveal relationships and power dynamics that impact HL development. It is generally accepted that language socialization processes in relation to heritage languages present many more complications to researchers than in groups where fewer languages—and possibly issues—are at play. Throughout the book, the language socialization lens is used to examine the processes involved in heritage language development, taking micro, meso, and macro perspectives in an attempt to create a balanced, nuanced, and holistic picture of this phenomenon.

4 Language ideologies

4.1 Introduction

Having studied the socialization of language, we now turn our attention to ideologies of language, one of the elements into which individuals are socialized from childhood and throughout life. In this chapter, I first trace the origins of language ideologies to early foundational work in associated disciplines, facilitating an engagement with this intricate concept in order to attempt the operationalization of a working definition. I also selectively examine the heritage language development and maintenance literature through a language ideology lens, and provide an exemplification of the socialization of language ideologies and their deployment in day-to-day interactions by drawing on ethnographic data. This analysis leads to a discussion of how particular ideologies that are prevalent in society are contested and reproduced in linguistic interactions. This in turn facilitates a critical discussion of the role of language ideologies for language socialization theory, research, and practice as well as their implications for heritage language socialization and maintenance. I end the chapter with a discussion of a particular feature of language ideologies—namely, their ubiquitous and web-like distribution—and propose this as a fundamental constituent of their contradictory nature.

4.2 Defining language ideologies

Language ideology is a line of scholarly inquiry that is concerned with critique and power—and closely associated with discourse studies, with which I engage in the next chapter. The first book length treatment of language ideologies ever published was *Language Ideologies: Practice and Theory*, edited by Bambi B. Schieffelin, Kathryn Woolard, and Paul Kroskrity (1998). In the introduction to that book, Woolard (1998) asserted that language ideology is an area that for much of the twentieth century had been dismissed in both anthropology and linguistics and often seen just as an interesting distraction. In the follow-up to that volume (*Regimes of Language: Ideologies, Polities, and Identities*), Kroskrity (2000b) proposed that one way of explaining the beginning of language ideology as an area of study and to "account for its relatively late arrival on the anthropological scene is to offer a language-ideological myth of origin" (5). Kroskrity explained that two neglected areas gave rise to the notion of language ideologies: the linguistic awareness of speakers and the non-referential functions of language. Not unlike Woolard, he contended that both of these areas were

https://doi.org/10.1515/9781614513841-004

dismissed by linguistics and anthropology, and argued that linguistics privileged a decontextualized form of language that did not see value in the speakers' own understanding of their language and usage[1], instead only valuing the perspective of experts. Kroskrity (2010) posited that although ideas related to this orientation had emerged in the past, as in the work of Benjamin Lee Whorf (1956, cited in Kroskrity 2010), language ideologies as an intellectual movement started with Silverstein's (1979) seminal work on the role of ideologies in shaping linguistic structures. Some of the bases for what came to be known as language ideologies were subsequently developed by scholars such as Dell Hymes and John Gumperz (Hymes 1974, Gumperz and Hymes 1986). Theorization of language ideologies—as a distinct area of inquiry—has more recently been enriched by the work of several contemporary researchers that, unsurprisingly, include Paul Kroskrity, Bambi B. Schieffelin and Kathryn Woolard (Woolard and Schieffelin 1994, Schieffelin, Woolard and Kroskrity 1998, Kroskrity 2000c, 2010).

Generally speaking, language ideologies are sets of beliefs about language (Silverstein 1979). Individuals and communities have values and beliefs about their languages and about how these languages should be used in their lives (Baquedano-Lopez and Kattan 2008). Ideologies also refer to what language *is* for a particular community and how its use is related to identity (Gal 1998). Although there is a multiplicity of definitions of language ideologies, these definitions imply at least two major dimensions. On one hand, language ideologies are closely connected to processes of social interaction. Thus, through microlinguistic analyses, people's language ideologies and identities are discoverable in their linguistic practices. I have examined this aspect of identity and language ideologies in the past and an excerpt from a previous publication (Guardado 2009) is analyzed later in this chapter in order to illustrate aspects of language ideologies and their socialization. Language ideologies also refer to people's local understandings, beliefs, and assumptions about the relationship between language and social life. Of relevance to the present book, these ideologies can refer to people's opinions about the relationship between HL development and cultural affiliations, a point to which Fishman (1966) alluded five decades ago. Also later in this chapter, I review relevant aspects of the HL development and maintenance research literature that

---

[1] The privileging of an idealized language as the focus of study to the detriment of local rationalizations of how the language is actually used in context is exemplified by Chomsky's transformational-generative grammar (Chomsky 1965). An alternative view, Halliday's Systemic Functional Linguistics (SFL), has highlighted context and construed language as a meaning-making resource (Halliday 1978, Halliday and Matthiessen 2004).

address the second dimension (i.e., beliefs and opinions). Many of the chapters that follow deal with a diversity of sub-topics also related to this second dimension.

4.3 Ideologies and heritage language development

Empirical work within language ideologies has been conducted across settings and with various foci, such as national language ideologies (e.g., Jaffe 1999, Bjornson 2007). For instance, Bjornson analyzed shifting ideologies of Dutch language in the Netherlands. Her work traced the shift from an ideology of Dutch as the basis for national identity to an ideology of 'language as commodity' in the newly implemented *burgering* program, which encapsulated a linguistic minority integration project. Jaffe's (1999) work on Corsica, a European language minority context, focused on how Corsican activists attempted to resist the dominance of French, particularly the processes involved in the shift from the heritage language, Corsican to French as a result of top-down language planning. Often closely related to the above foci, the work on language ideologies has investigated particular ethnolinguistic groups, revealing the impact of local and broader language ideologies on their language practices (Kroskrity 1992, Kulick 1992, Baquedano-Lopez 2000, Kroskrity 2000a, Fader 2001, Field 2001, Kroskrity 2010). A sub-theme within this line has examined shifting ideologies towards more powerful languages, sometimes motivated by the construction of these languages as more economically advantageous and thus more desirable (Hill 1985, Gal 1998, Field 2001, Meek 2007, Von Staden and Sterzuk 2017). Another thread, but again in a different ideological direction, is the role of ideologies in maintaining linguistic purism and ethnic cohesion. Kroskrity (1992), for instance, investigated the role that broader language ideologies played in the formation of particular multiethnic cultural identities among the Arizona Tewa, a North American Pueblo Indian group that left their traditional homeland in New Mexico to escape Spanish colonial oppression. Kroskrity explains that language ideology and use have contributed to the Arizona Tewa's maintenance of their ancestral language and distinct ethnic identity after 300 years of their migration to Hopi territory.

A focus on language ideologies becomes vital in studies of HL development and maintenance as these ideologies "envision and enact links of language to group and personal identity ..." (Woolard and Schieffelin 1994: 55–56), making them particularly explicit in multilingual contexts (Ochs and Schieffelin 1995). In these settings, the attitudes and beliefs of the community members about language are critical to their HL development success. These attitudes and beliefs evolve and change through the face-to-face interactions (Gibbons and Ramirez

2004), as well as indirect interactions, of the members of the minority community with in-group and out-group members. However, these local language ideologies do not operate in a vacuum as they are also subject to the considerable effect of the broader sociopolitical forces on all beliefs and attitudes that people have, including those about language (Zhang 2005, Worthy and Rodríguez-Galindo 2006) and the resulting behaviours (i.e., home language practices) (Morris and Jones 2008), which ultimately help facilitate or hinder HL development and maintenance. Thus, the linguistic ideologies of parents and children have a direct impact on HL acquisition and maintenance (Ochs and Schieffelin 1995, Howard 2008, Ochs and Schieffelin 2008).

Understanding how these preferred ideologies and communicative practices are socialized is central to elucidating the processes underlying HL development and maintenance. Through reflection, personal observation, and a diary study of herself and her Chinese-speaking 12 year old daughter while living in Hawaii, Li (1999) provided key insights into these issues, including the valuing of the L1 and L2, parental attitudes about L1 and L2 as well as associated cultures, and familial relationships. Li's study recognized that minority-languages are often marginalized in schools and in the larger community, causing those speakers to also feel marginalized. She declared that often "there is an invisible wall between the outside world and us" (116), a wall that—although not stated explicitly by Li—could well be sustained by a complex ideological framework. Her study also highlighted the value that minority language speakers should assign to their languages as an important prerequisite in heritage language socialization, a point also made by participants in other studies (e.g., Guardado 2002).

There are several recent developments related to language ideologies with Hispanic populations and with Spanish as a HL. Baquedano-Lopez (1997, 2000) researched the language socialization of Hispanic children into particular ideologies and religious identities. By analyzing teacher-student linguistic interactions in *doctrina* classes (Spanish catechism) in California, Baquedano-Lopez showed how these linguistic exchanges constructed a multiplicity of Mexican identities of the past and the present. In the Canadian context, Abdi (2011) examined linguistic interactions in a secondary school Spanish language class that included both HL and L2 learners in Metro Vancouver, Canada. One particular type of language ideology she analyzed was *displayed* speaking ability as a sign of language proficiency and heritage, revealing the impact of this overt ideology on the classroom dynamics. One of the HL students was reluctant to speak Spanish in class and was positioned as non-Hispanic as a result, equating willingness to speak with the right to ethnic inheritance, despite the student's strong Spanish literacy skills. Abdi's study provides insights into the complex identities of multilingual youth and the multiple—often-conflicting—language ideologies contributing to their formation. Relatedly, my recent work has looked at the socialization of language ideologies in Hispanic homes and grassroots groups (e.g., a Spanish-language Scout troop) in Western Canada (Guardado 2008a). Using a multi-site ethnographic approach, I found that the adults—and sometimes also the children—used admonitions in the home and in the community groups to force the children to avoid the use of English in favour of Spanish. Despite implicit and—often severe—explicit efforts to socialize the children into language ideologies that privileged Spanish, at times their actual language practices seemed to reproduce the dominance of English (Guardado 2009). I provide a glimpse into this particular incongruity later in the chapter.

4.3.1 Ideologies that devalue languages

Just as so-called "non-standard" varieties of English are devalued in the English-speaking world (e.g., African American and Appalachian English in the U.S.) (Tamura 1996, Wiley and Lukes 1996, Lanehart 1999), some varieties of Spanish are often held in low esteem in Spanish-speaking contexts and elsewhere, including the United States. Part of this hierarchization is historical and harks back to even before colonial times. Zentella (2005) reminds us that the Spanish varieties spoken in southern Spain, for instance, were devalorized compared to the variety spoken in Castile. Southern Spain settlers brought their Spanish variety to the Caribbean whereas settlers from Castile transported theirs to other Latin American regions. Many of these same language ideologies are produced and reproduced in the United States, Canada, and several other regions today as evidenced in research findings related to Spanish as a heritage language. In Schecter and Bayley's (1997, 2002) study, the participating parents reportedly felt that Spanish in general had no value in the community and that certain varieties of Spanish (e.g., Southwest Spanish) were devalued by speakers of "prestige" varieties (e.g., Standard Mexican Spanish). This points to a growing sense that many minority groups continue to devalue, or suppress at home (Howard 2008), "less desirable" varieties of their own language and in many cases, their own variety (see also Phillipson and Skutnabb-Kangas 1996). This unrelenting stance suggests that the hegemony of English and of standard colonial varieties (e.g., Continental Spanish) continues to have serious consequences for underprivileged groups in the United States (and quite possibly, in other English-speaking contexts), and as Schecter and Bayley argue, many of whom are convinced that English monolingualism and Americanization offer a fast track to success and the possibility of access to the *American Dream*, a hope that arguably continues to elude most members of minority groups.

While making important contributions to the literature and to the understanding of the field, some studies unfortunately do not emphasize important factors affecting the HL development process. These studies do not address the status of the participants' languages in relation to English within the community and fail to link the issues discussed to the larger sociopolitical context (e.g., Thomas and Cao 1999, Pacini-Ketchabaw, Bernhard and Freire 2001). As has been argued so far, these external forces have an important impact on the home language use patterns of linguistic minorities.

A recent study conducted in Toronto, Canada provides insights into the multilingual lives of recently arrived female Tibetan youth (MacPherson and Ghoso 2008). Having lived in various places outside Tibet before coming to Canada (e.g., India, Nepal, Bhutan), and consequently having had to negotiate multiple multicultural and nation-state contexts, these participants were highly multilingual, in some cases speaking up to five languages. Drawing on data from a questionnaire and observations, the researchers surveyed the participants' language practices across various contexts. Although they found strong home use of Tibetan, an evident sign of HL development and maintenance, they also identified many factors pointing to future language loss. Even though the participants were relative newcomers to Canada, Macpherson and Ghoso explain that their language use patterns exhibited characteristics of diglossia, selecting English for public use and relegating Tibetan to private settings, potentially leading to the reinforcement of negative Tibetan language ideologies. Despite this observation, they argue that the prognosis for the long-term maintenance and continued use of Tibetan among this community is optimistic, given three current conditions: high Tibetan language use at home, the continued replenishment of the community through new arrivals, and the Canadian ideology of multiculturalism. If anything, the fact that these newly arrived young women were already showing signs of language loss points to the fragile status of minority languages in the Canadian context, despite the promises of official multiculturalism.

Ideologies that devalue language varieties, particularly vernaculars, can be found in different settings, generations, and espoused by individuals that subscribe to a range of political leanings, a point that has often been made (Ruiz 1984, Fishman 1991, Galindo 1997, Fishman 1999, Ricento 2005, Alim 2010, McGroarty 2010). An excellent recent example can be found in Becker's (2013) qualitative study with the descendants of Chilean exiles in Edmonton, Alberta, Canada. Even though her main interest was in investigating the role that political ideologies played in the HL development and maintenance of a group of second generation adults, language ideologies were not only discoverable in her data, at times these appeared to be conspicuously central. Furthermore, the centrality of these ideologies also made it impossible not to notice the convoluted—and sometimes contradictory—nature of these. For instance, Victor, one of the focal participants classified as one of two "activists" in the study, spoke eloquently and fervently about his progressive views regarding local and global issues. His commitment and dedication to the cause of the oppressed and marginalized, no matter who they were, were unequivocal. Yet, when he spoke about different varieties of Spanish, such as the modern Chilean vernacular—particularly the distinctive working class variety—compared to the 1970s vernacular that he learned from his parents, as well as the standard Spanish he studied at university, he spoke in ways that seemed utterly at odds with his otherwise inclusivity-oriented, cosmopolitan, progressive worldview. Justifiably, Becker found it "surprising that Victor did not seem to be fully aware that to disparage a variety of a language is to disparage its speakers. Even though he clarified that he meant 'nothing bad about Lumpenproletariats,' his comments about their speech partly betray[ed] this intention. Indeed, ideologies that privilege certain varieties over others are pervasive and often go unnoticed, especially if they are confirmed at home" (Becker, 2013: 59). This example illustrates how individuals that would not otherwise produce oppressive discourses sometimes unwittingly espouse ideologies that devalue languages and language varieties.

4.3.2 Language ideologies and an emerging body of research

The interest in increasing our understanding of issues such as those discussed above is evident in the growing collection of studies with a focus on a variety of ethnolinguistic groups. In Canada, French undoubtedly enjoys a privileged position as an official language; outside Quebec, however, many Canadians who claim French-speaking ancestry still struggle to transmit the language to the next generation (Cartwright 1998, Iqbal 2005). Thus, research focusing on French–English bilingualism has dominated Canadian scholarship in this area. The few remaining First Nations languages are unquestionably another research priority in Canada (Pesco and Crago 2008). The loss of these languages and a shift to English continue relentlessly, owing to hegemonic language ideologies in society and conflicting ideologies in First Nations communities themselves (Shaw 2001). There has also been a surge in investigations that directly or indirectly touch on aspects of language ideology with a focus on Canadian immigrant linguistic minorities, such as speakers of Ukrainian (Chumak-Horbatsch 1999), Chinese (Xiao 1998), Tibetan (MacPherson and Ghoso 2008), and Spanish (Guardado 2008a, 2009, Abdi 2011, Becker 2013), as well as other languages (Kouritzin 1999, Slavik 2001, Sodhi 2007). A 10-year longitudinal study with

Ukrainian-speaking families in Toronto (Chumak-Horbatsch 1999) found that most children viewed themselves as English-dominant and expressed ambivalence about Ukrainian despite having been isolated from English in their preschool years, having attended a Ukrainian-only nursery school, and later, a Ukrainian secondary school. Although the reasons are unclear, the children may have resented the imposition of Ukrainian and their isolation from their English-speaking peers, which contributed to the development of hostile ideologies about their HL, which were possibly detrimental to its continued use. As Jaffe (Jaffe 1999) explains, drawing on her work in Corsica, what is imposed easily becomes a source of resistance, and it is not surprising to see this finding in Chumak-Horbatsch's research.

Often, families' desires for HL development and maintenance contrast with their actual practices, a point also made in Jaffe's study cited above. Along these lines, Cho (2008) found a mismatch between the attitudes and the behaviours of some of the Korean parents in her study, leading to language loss. As well, Slavik (2001) found that although most of the Maltese-Canadian parents in her study believed in the importance of Maltese HL development and maintenance, few of them actually spoke the language to their children or attempted to ensure that the children learned it in any other way. These examples clearly show that there can be a gap between explicit discourses about language use and actual socialization practices (Guardado 2008a, Howard 2008, Guardado 2009).

4.3.3 Socializing language ideologies

A concept that is of critical relevance when framing the present discussion is language socialization, which I addressed in detail in Chapter 3. In that chapter we claimed that it is through the process of language socialization that children and other individuals acquire values and beliefs and form their identities. These values and beliefs are central components of linguistic ideologies and are particularly explicit in multilingual contexts (Ochs and Schieffelin 1995). In these settings, the community members' language attitudes and beliefs are critical to their success in developing and maintaining the HL within the language socialization process, as their ideologies are transmitted to the new generations. As argued by Ochs and Schieffelin (1995, 2008), understanding language ideologies is a key move towards understanding the bilingual development of children as these have a strong effect on children's language socialization processes. In order to help illustrate these arguments more concretely grounded in data, in the following sections I analyze an excerpt from a naturally occurring interaction in my ethnographic dataset.

Thus far I have engaged with definitions of language ideologies, which is not an unambiguous task as these definitions are only our interpretations of the intersection between language and people in the social world (Woolard 1998). Life in the social world is largely shaped as language ideologies are formed, transmitted, contested, reproduced, and imposed in the socialization process. As such, language ideologies cannot be separated from the intricacies of language socialization—in fact, these ideologies are part of what makes language socialization such a complex phenomenon. During the process through which individuals acquire beliefs, attitudes, values, ways of thinking, and language structures and practices, they also internalize particular beliefs and attitudes about language. In effect, these are some of the constituents of ideology. In other words, language ideologies are one of the elements into which all individuals are socialized over the course of their lives.

4.3.3.1 Language ideology socialization, accommodation and resistance

An analysis of data drawn from my longitudinal ethnographic study (Guardado 2008a, 2009) helps illustrate aspects of the socialization of ideologies. The data came from the Grupo Scout Vistas, a Hispanic Scout troop in Metro Vancouver, Canada (Chapter 9 describes this group in more detail). The parents in this group displayed a variety of explicit and implicit practices designed to socialize their children into particular language ideologies, policies, and practices. At times they used explicit and implicit *directives* (instructions) and *recasts* (reformulations of utterances) as *corrective feedback* to directly or subtly guide children to follow Spanish-only rules. Less frequently, they used lectures to encourage children to maintain the habit of speaking Spanish, thus fostering positive Spanish language ideologies. Occasionally, children also *self-repaired* (corrected themselves) after having produced a *dispreferred* utterance (e.g., using English or mixing English and Spanish). In this way they displayed their nascent understanding of their parents' language ideologies. Examples and microlinguistic analyses of these families' strategies to socialize their children into particular language ideologies are found in Chapters 11 and 12.

The language socialization processes experienced by the children of the participating families, who were reportedly strongly committed to HL development and maintenance, were shown to be relatively complex. There was a variety of ways in which children were socialized into ideologies that valued Spanish and the children reacted in diverse ways by sometimes accommodating and other times resisting such socialization. Although Spanish-only policies have been previously mentioned in the research literature, there has been less discussion on how exactly these policies play out in the language socialization of the families and how these are interactionally enacted, negotiated, achieved, and resisted. For instance, parents used lectures, directives, and other tactics to remind their children to engage in Spanish-speaking behaviour, while children responded in various ways to these strategies. They complied and accommodated to these appeals, resisted them, and sometimes attempted to subvert their parents' rules. The children were at times able to act on their attitudes and modify the dynamics of the communicative situation, thus asserting their roles as agents in their own socialization. Clearly, parents endeavoured to transmit linguistic ideologies that valued Spanish, which could be theorized as resistance on the part of the parents toward the children's affiliation to English-speaking identities. The children's inclination to these identities could potentially become an important factor in socializing each other and their parents. Still, despite occasional resistance on the part of the children toward the language policies in the groups, no serious linguistic tensions were observed between the parents and the children. However, it is impossible to ignore the influence of the children on each other's linguistic behaviour, which collectively at times became an indication of the children's ambivalence, resistance, and even rejection of the identities being imposed on them. They perhaps resisted an imposed common identity and selected a self-forged, individual one that did not conform to their parents' heritage or to the dominant societal norms.

4.3.3.2 Reproducing dominant language ideologies

In the article referred to above (Guardado 2009), I looked at how these language ideologies operate and are discoverable in informal interactions and how these interactions may contribute to both reproducing and challenging dominant practices. In the following extract from the Grupo Scout Vistas, language ideologies, practices, and identities can be seen to interact in complex ways. Please refer to the section *A Few Words on Transcription* in Chapter 11 for transcription conventions (Mr. M=Mr. Maradiaga, Scout Leader):

```
[Excerpt 4.1]
  1  Mr. M:    ahora ustedes ustedes ustedes dos si quieren
  2            utiliza- ustedes váyanse allá a otro lugar
  3            ustedes si quieren utilizan la mesa la mesa lo
  4            van a esc- lo van a ordenar   e::[n
  5  Silvia:                                    [en inglés
  6  Mr. M:       en inglés
  7  Silvia: [o::::h ((half laughing))
  8  Diana:  [mmmmm?
  9  Diana:  en inglés es más fácil (xx) para yo
 10  Silvia: yo prefiero en español
 11  Mr. M:  en inglés pues allí viene la cuestión porque en
 12          inglés ese es el- en inglés esta en el libro en
 13          inglés esta en el libro- si ((the answer si
 14          could be in response to a non-verbal question))
```

```
Translation
1   Mr. M:    now you the two of you if you want you can
2             use-you go over there to a different place you
3             ((pl.)) if you want you can use the table you
4             ((pl.)) are going to wri- you are going to put
5             it in order i::[n
6   Silvia:                  [in English
7   Mr. M:    in English
8   Silvia:   [o::::h ((half laughing))
9   Diana:    [mmmmm?
10  Diana:    it's easier in English (xx) for me
11  Silvia:   I prefer in Spanish
12  Mr. M:    in English 'cause the thing is that in English
13            that's the- in the book it's in English in the
14            book it's in English- yes ((the answer 'yes'
15            could be in response to a non-verbal question))
```

While participating in Scout group activities, the children were constantly reminded to use Spanish at all times, and its importance was emphasized both implicitly (e.g., through the language of the instructions themselves) and explicitly (through directives). Thus, they were keenly aware of the local language policy in place, and in the above excerpt, Silvia might simply have been complying with these rules by stating her preference for Spanish. Alternatively, Silvia's utterance could be understood as an example of how children display the language ideologies to which they have been exposed. Interestingly, despite expressing surprise, none of the children questioned Mr. Maradiaga's language choice. Moreover, while in this excerpt Silvia privileged Spanish for conducting the activities, thus resisting (or, at least, failing to select) English, Mr. Maradiaga and Diana can be heard as reproducing the dominance of English.

It was unusual in the group for parents to instruct the children to work and complete an activity in English; in fact, this was the most substantial instance I observed. When I asked the group leaders why some children did the activity in English, they explained that the intention was to accommodate a child who had more difficulty with Spanish literacy, so it is also notable that an ideology of inclusiveness prevailed, perhaps an ideology with the power to override heritage language ideologies during certain occasions. Given that learning the pledge was a key principle for Scouts to follow (and necessary for 'investiture,' a ritual connected to becoming a Scout), they asserted, they wanted to ensure that the child learned it well. However, the implicit message the children might have received was that although Spanish was valuable, some things were too important to be done in Spanish—perhaps unwittingly socializing the children into a linguistic hierarchy that reaffirmed and endorsed the status of English as the language of power and the language of the international Scout movement. The children might have received a message that contributed to the reproduction of language ideologies that supported the hegemony of English, thus contributing to and participating in their own domination (Canagarajah 1993). This issue is reminiscent of what Kulick (1992) found in Gapun, Papua New Guinea, where the vernacular, Taiap, was strongly emphasized to children while parents used Tok Pisin, also implicitly socializing a positive evaluation of Tok Pisin as the language of power.

4.3.4 Is there an ideological paradox?

Jaffe's (1999) pioneering work on Corsica has powerfully demonstrated that people's language practices can unwittingly reproduce the very dominant language ideologies they are designed to challenge. Indeed, the studies summarized in this chapter have shown that the process of multilingual socialization can be fraught with complexities and paradoxes. On the one hand, the families in my ethnographic study were heavily invested in reproducing themselves, or aspects of themselves (their linguistic and cultural capital), in their children, and they attempted to do this through activities designed to model and showcase their linguistic and cultural ideologies and practices to their children, as well as engaging in explicit socialization activities. On the other hand, they participated in the continued dominance of English by privileging this language for certain activities within the group, and thus contributed to the socialization of ideologies that acknowledged and legitimized the status of English as the language of power (Pennycook 1994).

But is the incompatibility between ideology and practice really at odds with the very nature of language ideologies? Language ideologies are part of a larger and highly complex web of ideologies that are formed in the process of primary language socialization from childhood and which continue to be readjusted and molded during individuals' lifelong and lifewide experiences. As Gal (1998), McGroarty (2010) and others point out, ideologies of language are multiple and contentious, and are not only about language because they are part of what relates language to other social life dimensions. Ideologies are intimately linked to identity, which—as we have stated earlier in the book—are not fixed and unitary, but multiple and changing over time and space. To be sure, affiliations are not consistent everywhere, all the time, and in all circumstances, but are often fragmented and conflictual (Barvosa's 2008 work in this area is noteworthy). The adage "do as I say and not as I do" is a reflection of the fact that people not only do not always do as they say they do, but that they do not always act according to their beliefs. This expression, then, can be seen as a component of an analysis of ideology from a folk empiricism point of view. By definition, then, language ideologies are contradictory because they are tangled in broader ideological webs that are implicated in multiple relationships of power. Hill's (1998) work with Mexicano (Nahuatl) communities is an unambiguous example of conflicting language ideologies based on unequal gender relations.

Gramsci's (1971) conceptualization of hegemony, for instance, speaks to the political and cultural domination of the elite over the masses (*common sense* is an allied term). This domination, Gramsci asserts, is accomplished in complicity with the dominated, which also speaks to the ideological inconsistency found too often in minorities who see their heritage language—usually a vernacular—as worthless and useless in the dominant society in which they live and therefore, a language deserving of being forgotten.[2] This is made possible by powerful ideological work that renders the dominant language as the only essential and normal code in society. This kind of ideological domination has been strongly performed by the heavily funded English-only movement in the U.S. (Crawford 1992a, Wiley and Lukes 1996).

As seen in Becker's (2013) research on political ideologies and HL development in Canada, Victor's view of the vernacular spoken today in Chilean working class and marginalized communities was in disharmony with his openly progressive ideological stance that espoused a fervent solidarity with the underdog. However, such ideological disconnect may in fact also signal an attempt to construct an identity of an educated individual with command of standard Spanish, an index of sophistication and of membership in academia, and by extension an alignment with the interviewee, Becker, who in the speech event of the interview occupied the subject position of a member of academia.

McGroarty (2010) notes that ideologies are part of explicit and implicit systems that impact on language use, although their existence is sometimes only made visible through the decisions and actions occurring in social contexts. As we saw in the analysis of an excerpt during the Scout group activities, even though the declared ideologies as enacted in the language use goals and policies of the group pointed to ideologies that valued the heritage language, the decision of the leaders to conduct an important activity in English underscored a parallel ideology in relation to English. This decision, of course, was motivated by a seemingly complementary ideology that promoted the ideals of the Scouting

---

[2] Linguistic minorities often witness and experience the devaluing of their languages in implicit and explicit ways on a daily basis, so this is not a criticism towards their attitudes, but a recognition of the dominant forces they face.

movement. However, in doing so they also adhered to the mission of the movement that required participants to learn its philosophical principles, embodied in the Scout promise. In practice, then, these seemingly compatible ideologies were found to be at odds with each other. Thus, the paradox that surfaced was just another instantiation of the complex and contradictory nature of ideologies in general and the subset known as language ideologies in particular.

Although there exists a variety of definitions of ideology in general, a key element that is integral to understanding language ideologies and how this notion is threaded throughout the discussions in this book is discourse. Discourse is to be understood as a mediating element between our beliefs and values about language and language use itself. It is through language ideologies—encoded in discourse—that individuals make sense of their day-to-day linguistic interactions. Chapter 5 wraps up the introductory section of the book by attempting to define discourse.

4.4 Chapter summary

In this chapter, I have introduced the concept of *language ideology* and engaged with some of its complexity. Language ideologies are sets of beliefs, values, and feelings about languages that individuals and communities possess. As a relatively new concept, it has been used in investigations of a variety of topics and areas of inquiry, including language policy and planning, linguistic purism, literacy, language contact, and multilingualism. As regards to heritage languages, much of what is now seen as the purview of language ideologies has traditionally been discussed in the relevant bodies of literature under the names of beliefs and attitudes about language maintenance. In light of the current understandings of the notion of language ideologies generally, as discussed in this chapter, I propose that heritage language ideologies are somewhat fluid sets of understandings, justifications, beliefs, and judgments that linguistic minorities hold about their languages. These ideologies also include their desires and expectations regarding the relevance of these languages in their children's lives as well as when, where, how, and to what ends these languages should be used.

I have attempted to show in this chapter that language ideologies, as sets of beliefs about language, are identifiable through the examination of interactions and practices that involve language. Although the rest of the book addresses many of these issues related to language ideologies, I have begun to show in this chapter that language ideologies are interwoven with language socialization practices, identity development, and interpersonal relationships, to name but a few. Indeed, interactions and practices that reveal language ideologies can include the language choices of the speakers, the way speakers talk about their languages, the language policies and regulation strategies parents use in the home, among several other linguistic practices in daily life. In Chapters 11 and 12, I engage specifically with the metalinguistic strategies used by adult caregivers, which reveal a great deal about their language ideologies. It is also important to note the intimate relationship between language ideologies and language socialization, as well as the ways that language ideologies manifest themselves in language socialization processes, which help to better understand how families and societies interact to co-facilitate or inhibit HL development and maintenance.

Key notions that I have discussed in this chapter include the role of child agency in the processes of socialization and the ideological contradictions that are often discoverable in these processes. Just as parental language ideologies may influence their children's choice to use the heritage language, the children's language ideologies and subsequent language use can also influence intergenerational communication and the depth of their relationships with their parents and other family members. Additionally, as has been well documented in various studies, including my own, it is clear that people can hold counter-hegemonic language ideologies while inadvertently using language in ways that conform to hegemonic norms. If anything, this compelling point illustrates just how powerful and pervasive dominant language ideologies can be, and the real-world consequences of these. I return to many of these notions in the body of the book as I discuss HL development from a variety of perspectives.

5 What is discourse?

5.1 Introduction

In this chapter, I attempt to define one of the most elusive concepts in language studies: *discourse*. Book length treatises have been written on the meaning of discourse. Yet, few scholars use the term in exactly the same way. The object of this chapter, then, is to provide an operationalization of discourse as it is used for the purposes of this book. I begin by artificially and somewhat simplistically dividing definitions of discourse into two discrete categories, for the sake of practicality. I briefly trace the roots of the term, highlighting some of the most influential thinkers in the development of current understandings of discourse. I also gloss over some of the critical approaches to discourse analysis and discourse studies and their main exponents. In order to give the reader a feel for the kinds of work that are undertaken outside the central critical discourse domains, I touch on some of the topics that are commonly the object of critical discursive inquiry. Some of the key tenets of this tradition of analysis are highlighted throughout the chapter, namely, critique, power, and ideology. The chapter ends with a rationalization of what a discourse analytical approach can offer to heritage language studies.

5.2 Defining discourse

Norman Fairclough, one of the leading figures in critical discourse studies, refers to discourse as a "slippery" term (1992). Indeed, a multitude of competing definitions of discourse can be found in a variety of related scholarly traditions. This may be, at least in part, a direct consequence of the term discourse becoming "common currency in a variety of disciplines: critical theory, sociology, linguistics, philosophy, social psychology and many other fields" (Mills 2004: 1). Mills goes on to object to the term being used with the assumption that it is common knowledge and therefore left undefined. However, she claims that this term may have "the widest range of possible significations within literary and cultural theory" and possibly in the social sciences and the humanities. Its ambiguity may be given away by the number of books attempting to define it. Examples include: *Discourse: A Critical Introduction* (Blommaert 2005), *Discourse Analysis* (Brown and Yule 1983), *Discourse* (Cook 2004), *Discourse* (Howarth and Howarth 2000), and *Discourse: The New Critical Idiom* (Mills 2004). Therefore, attempting to unproblematically synthesize such conceptual complexity would most likely prove futile, particularly in the context of just a book chapter; as a result, the following is a simplified summary of the work of a selection of influential thinkers and discourse conceptualizations, which I hope facilitates the operationalization of the term, as it may be useful for understanding the discursive construction of HL development.

In general terms, discourse refers to extended text—that is, text beyond the sentence level—and is commonly understood to include oral and written language. While purely linguistic studies may see discourse only in linguistic terms as *language in use* while concerning themselves with the analysis of elements like syntactic structures, critical discourse analysis (CDA) and critical discourse studies (CDS) acknowledge the social nature of language and regard discourses as *social practice*. Additionally, it would be possible, given their diversity, to place conceptualizations of discourse on a continuum from narrowly to broadly defined, with branches starting at various points and moving in different directions while intertwiningly crisscrossing one another. For the purposes of this discussion, however, it may suffice to simply look at both ends of the continuum.

5.3 Origin, development and perspectives

Discourse can be viewed as mainly linguistic. Almost a century ago, the Swiss linguist Ferdinand de Saussure proposed his two-sided model of the *linguistic sign*, which contained a *signifier* (the word) and a *signified* (the object or idea referred to). He also made the distinction between *langue* (language as system) and *parole* (roughly equivalent to *speech*). To Saussure, *parole* was the external expression of language; a speaker's actual utterances. Today, we can generically define discourse as language in use, more or less in the Saussurean sense. Therefore, narrower views of discourse may refer to the classic understanding of discourse as "language above the sentence or clause" (Schiffrin 1994: 23). The focus of analysis from this perspective, then, is on the linguistic structure of linked speech or writing extended beyond the sentence (Savignon 1987). Given that in this book the central appeal of the notion of discourse is its interrelationship with the social, broader definitions are the main focus.

Gee (2005) distinguishes between two types of discourses: small "d" and big "D" Discourse. To him, small "d" discourse is language in use, in some ways as regarded in the classic notion, but in other ways going beyond structure itself. He defines this discourse as "how language is used 'on site' to enact activities and identities" (7), thus bridging small "d" with big "D" discourse through its functions. Gee goes on to explain how identities and activities are seldom enacted through language in isolation, so to him, when small "d" discourse is combined with what he calls "non-language 'stuff'" then "big D" Discourses are also at play.

Gee views language as more than a mere tool for the exchange of information. He argues that language is deeply political in the ways it is used to make visible who we are (identity) and what we do (practice) given that this performance does not only entail language. It is a process that involves valuing, thinking, acting, and interacting in ways that others can recognize as the specific kind of individual we are and the particular activity in which we are engaged. Gee's understanding of Discourse is much too broad for our purposes, but his emphasis on social practice as the site where Discourses are enacted is central to the present discussion.

The broad conceptualization of discourse as seen by Gee can be grouped under the discourse-as-social-practice umbrella. This view is more closely exemplified by scholars using interdisciplinary approaches within the CDA and CDS paradigms. Much of the work conducted from these perspectives has drawn on critical theory, mainly following a European intellectual tradition (Blommaert 2005). Specifically, critical discourse approaches have been influenced by the work of a long list of thinkers—many themselves influenced by Marxist thought—that include Mikhail Bakhtin, Michael Halliday, Jürgen Habermas, Pierre Bourdieu, Antonio Gramsci, and Michel Foucault. Gramsci, for instance, an Italian thinker who wrote from prison after being incarcerated by Mussolini's Fascist regime, contributed in several ways to aspects of what became CDS. His conceptualization of hegemony and other associated terms has become a key factor in critical discourse studies given its suitability for explaining how dominant groups maintain their positions of power—and thus other aspects of the *status quo*. Although violence and other forms of coercion are used for such purposes, control is largely maintained through ideological means—embodied in discourse—leading to the formation of a *common sense* whereby the masses see their own good as dependant on the good of the *bourgeoisie*, in Gramsci's (1971) terms. Given that this ideological work is embodied in discursive practices, it becomes of central importance to our understanding of discourse.

To conclude this section, then, we may see understandings of discourse from opposing vantage points. Pennycook (1994) argues that there are two distinct positions that emphasize different factors related to discourse. On the one hand, he argues, language can be seen as the larger concept and discourse only as an instance of language use. On the other hand, discourse can be seen as operating at a higher level and language use being only an instance of discourse. Therefore, I argue that it is possible to see discourse understandings on a multidimensional continuum. One end would contain linguistically based notions of discourse that are interested in how text is connected. The other end, after going through the entire gamut of conceptualizations and variations, would be occupied by notions that privilege the social realm and examine how inequalities are perpetuated through discourse. It should be obvious by now that the arguments advanced in this book take one position or the other at different times.

5.3.1 Michel Foucault's contributions

Arguably, the most influential scholar in this area is Michel Foucault, who saw discourse as social. Foucault was a French philosopher, social theorist, and historian of knowledge. He wrote on power, knowledge, and discourse, making foundational contributions to the conceptualization and development of discourse studies. Foucault was the most cited humanities scholar in 2007, according to the Web of Science. This is a testament to the enormous influence his work on discourse, knowledge, and power continues to have on the whole spectrum of disciplines in the social sciences and the humanities. Foucault's work focused on public institutions, such as mental hospitals and prisons, and pursued issues like the history of human sexuality. In his book *Madness and Civilization* (1965), Foucault goes all the way back to the Middle Ages to analyze how lepers and other individuals were excluded from society. Later on, when leprosy had largely disappeared, madness became a cause for social and physical exclusion—through institutionalization or banishment—the way leprosy had been in the past. In later works, Foucault became increasingly concerned with the relationship between knowledge and power, especially in *Discipline and Punish* (1975) and *The Archaeology of Knowledge* (1972). He conceptualized knowledge as power and often hyphenated both terms as *power-knowledge* as if they were one and the same. Foucault (e.g., 1980) also saw discourse and practice as the same thing, which is particularly meaningful for the subject of the present book. He acknowledged the fact that discourses are made of signs, but stressed the need to look beyond the linguistic sign. He explained that language does much more than designating things, making it necessary to direct our attention to everything else that discourses do.

Iara Lessa summarizes Foucault's definition of discourse as "... systems of thoughts composed of ideas, attitudes, courses of action, beliefs and practices that systematically construct the subjects and the worlds of which they speak" (2006: 285). In Foucault's view, social context, particularly institutions, determine the existence of discourse and at the same time, discourse makes possible the production and continuation of the social context (Mills 2004). Institutions are not only discursively produced, but actually produced and reproduced by discourse. It is within the spectrum of these definitions that most of the work conducted from a CDA/CDS perspective takes place, to which we now turn.

5.3.2 Critical discourse analysis and critical discourse studies

There are at least three distinct—but interrelated—approaches to analysis from a CDA/CDS perspective, which engage in productive intellectual and empirical cross-pollination. Fairclough's approach uses textual analysis and is largely based on Halliday's Systemic Functional Linguistics (1978), also drawing on Bakhtin's (1981, 1986) notions of interdiscursivity and dialogism. The critical and sociological aspects of his work draw on Gramsci (1971), Bourdieu (1977), and Foucault (1972, 1980), among others. Drawing on the above, Fairclough's work uncovers how discourses come to be formed as a result of a combination of pre-existing discourses, genres, and texts, with particular social and political goals (Jaworski and Coupland 1999). Fairclough's scholarship includes examinations of advertising, media, and political discourse. For instance, in his most cited book, *Language and Power* (2001), Fairclough uses the concept of *synthetic personalization* to refer to how language is crafted in mass-oriented discourse in order to create a sense of direct contact with and concern for the consumer of the discourse.

Wodak and colleagues have developed the *discourse-historical approach*, which uses textual analysis in combination with other elements that are understood historically—that is, considering their development over time. Departing from Fairclough's examination of discourse produced for massive consumption, the scholarship from this perspective investigates, often through ethnographic methods, the mechanisms of social inequality achieved through naturally occurring discourse. Thus, their work in the Austrian context has analyzed the construction of national identity, as well as how discourses can contribute to maintaining the status quo, by, for instance, justifying and obscuring discriminatory practices in society (Wodak et al. 1999).

Teun A. van Dijk's sociocognitive approach addresses, among other issues, the reproduction of racism and prejudice toward different stigmatized groups in Europe, more recently in Spain, and also in Latin America. Van Dijk makes many of his books freely available on his personal website for download, which at the time of writing contained over a dozen volumes. For instance, in the downloadable *Elite Discourse and Racism* (1993), he argues that public elites, such as politicians, scholars, and journalists, work in complicity with the mass media, which he describes as "white institutions and business corporations" that work for the "cause" of the dominant groups in society by shaping the attitudes and ideologies toward the powerful majorities. Thus, van Dijk's work along these lines has analyzed media to demonstrate how knowledge, beliefs, and ideas are internalized in people's minds, leading, on one hand, to the construction of the elite in particular ways (e.g., as benevolent), and on the other, justifying different forms of discrimination against other groups in society.

5.3.3 The dialectics of discourse

Foucault has famously stated that discourses are systems that talk about and also form the same objects to which the discourses refer. Echoing Foucault, Fairclough claims that language and society exist in a dialectical relationship, thus forming each other. In this view, analyses of language as a system independent of society, its culture, and its power structures suffer from a peculiar paucity—like studying X by only looking at Y. Therefore, analyses using critical discourse approaches see discursive events as two-way processes: they are products of social structures, institutions, and situations, but also producers of them (Fairclough and Wodak 2004). Although there are many differences in how scholars using these approaches may define and analyze discourse, what they share is an interest in challenging and critiquing particular discourses and in investigating how these constitute and are constituted by other social and cultural phenomena. Therefore, a key goal these scholars share is to expose the purposes served by the discourses under study. Given that a key commonality CDA/CDS approaches share, as explained in detail by Wodak and Meyer (2009), is the inclusion of four elements: discourse, critique, power, and ideology, all of the work of these scholars deals with how discourses are used to exert power, oppress, or otherwise *other* individuals and groups for political reasons. Because of the nature of these goals, it is not surprising that the work of the leading scholars in CDA/CDS—and that of others working across disciplines in the rest of the world—often focuses on negatively deployed discourses.

5.3.4 Discourse, critique and power across disciplines

In his work, Foucault sought to make explicit the ways in which power is found in discourses. When viewed through a Foucauldian lens, discourses always encompass forms of power. Scholarly work that has as one of its central goals the examination and uncovering of discourses of domination cannot be separated from power and ideology. For instance, Steuter and Wills (2009) analyze the discourses of dehumanization through an examination of how the wars in Iraq and Afghanistan are covered in Canadian newspaper headlines. They show how the "enemy" (Arab and Muslim leaders, as well as citizens) is constructed as sub-human through the use of animal metaphors, which lead to a positioning of these as expendable. They argue that beyond rhetorical representations, these practices lead to racist abuses and even genocide. In a similar vein, Bhatia used a corpus of official United States government documents and public political discourse produced between 2001 and 2004 in order to analyze the Bush administration's portrayal of the war on terrorism. She found that, unsurprisingly, the rhetoric was full of dichotomizing discourses making *us* vs. *them* divisions. More interesting, however, was the construction of discourses that automatically positioned people disagreeing with such ideologies as condoning the actions of terrorists.

Critical feminist scholars within cultural studies and in other disciplines often employ analytic approaches from a critical discourse perspective. Iyer (2009), for instance, examined the discourses of patriarchy based on popular media news articles in India, which covered stories of women entrepreneurs in stereotypical ways. Smythe (2006) conducted a Foucauldian analysis of literacy advice given to mothers in the nineteenth and twentieth centuries. Drawing on over three hundred literacy advice publications from Britain and North America, she shows how this type of advice is grounded in conceptualizations of the "good mother," with implications for the reproduction of gender inequalities in society, among other consequences.

Pennycook (1998) wrote a highly cited book length treatment of the colonial discourses still attached to English, from a Teaching English to Speakers of Other Languages (TESOL) perspective. He argues that the central ideologies within TESOL are rooted in the cultural constructions of colonialism. He posits, for instance, that theories, practices, and contexts of English language teaching should be understood in the historical context of colonialism. He adds that colonialism produced the prevalent ways of thinking and behaving in the West. Some of these ways of thinking are present in the discourses that construct dichotomies between self and other. Furthermore, Pennycook claims, these dichotomizing discourses construct the West as masculine and mature and the Orient, for instance, as feminine and childish.[1] These negatively deployed discourses about the East and West also contain sub-discourses that depict children and women in pejorative ways.

A key departure between the study of discourse from a CDA/CDS perspective and the one taken in this book is that my intention is not to uncover such types of discourses—that is, negatively oriented ones—but rather, to make explicit the ways in which linguistic minorities discursively construct the continuation of their languages in the new generations. Hackett and Moore (2011) provide an accessible definition of discourse that fits the focus of this volume. To them, discourses are "those shared, structured ways of speaking, thinking, interpreting, and representing things in the world" (4). Following this conceptualization, I take discourses to mean a collection of ideas and opinions—ideologies—about a particular topic, or more concisely, the shared ways of thinking and speaking

---

[1] Pennycook draws to some extent on Said's (1978, 1993) analyses of some of these issues.

about things in the world. In other words, the book deals with how families that participated in an ethnographic research project talked about HL development. Thus, in this book discourse is operationalized as shared ways of thinking and speaking about HL development.

Many of the analysts working in these traditions have attempted to expose, challenge, and substitute discourses of exclusion with discourses of inclusion. As a result of the work of these scholars and many others working within critical studies, cultural studies, feminism, queer theory, ethnic studies, race studies, to name a few, a new community has emerged: the political correctness discourse community. Therefore, even within the work of discourse studies, the dialectics of discourse becomes evident. In other words, talking about exclusionary and oppressive language has the effect of creating a counter-discourse that challenges and changes the way people, objects, and topics are talked about. Subsequent iterations of this dialectic, then, have the potential to change ideology, transform society, and establish a more just social order.

5.4 Discourse and ideology

Attempts to define discourse would be incomplete without at the very least a mention of the nature of language. Indeed, ways of understanding discourse are inherently connected to theories of language. A definition of discourse from a critical perspective sees language beyond referentiality. In other words, language is not only reflective of the world, but constitutive of the world. Thus, rather than just seeing language as neutral, transparent, and transmissive, critical discourse analysts view language as political, interested, and directly implicated in power relations and in the reproduction of inequality. Therefore, echoing Gee and other scholars discussed in this chapter, language is seen and treated as highly ideological.

A critical probe into discourses is bound to uncover ideologies, and ideologies of language have particular bearing on the present analysis. As we saw in the previous chapter, *language ideologies* refer to people's and communities' implicit and explicit beliefs, attitudes, and values regarding the worth of their languages. These ideologies also include how those languages ought to be used in their daily lives (Baquedano-Lopez and Kattan 2008). Pêcheux saw discourse as "the place where language and ideology meet" (Fairclough and Wodak 2004: 262). Indeed, ideologies—including ideologies of language—are most commonly expressed discursively; therefore, I maintain that the concepts of discourse and ideology are intimately and necessarily intertwined.

5.5 Chapter summary

Based on a review of conceptualizations of, and approaches to viewing, the notion of *discourse*, in this chapter I have developed a tentative definition of this term in relation to heritage languages. Thus, HL discourses can be understood as shared ways of thinking and speaking about HL development and maintenance. Given that this is a rather broad and encompassing definition, it obscures the remarkable variation found across disciplines and areas of research that utilize this notion in one way or another.

There are good reasons why discourse has been labeled elusive and indefinable. Common operationalizations range from purely linguistic to holistically social. On the linguistic extreme, the focus of analysis is on the structures of text beyond the sentence, whereas social perspectives view discourse as social practice. The latter, often exemplified by critical approaches such as critical discourse analysis and critical discourse studies, see discourse as not neutral, but highly ideological. Therefore, definitions of discourse from these perspectives are always implicated in discussions of ideology, critique, and power. However, an argument can be made that regardless of whether a discursive approach privileges linguistic structure or broader social practices, this does not automatically preclude the utilization of critical analytical lenses or the incorporation of critique. As I demonstrate in Chapters 11 and 12, it is possible to conduct microlinguistic analyses of parent-child interactions from a critical perspective. In these chapters, I attempt to include examinations of power relations as expressed through discourse as well as the way power is established, enacted, maintained, and embodied in discourse.

This book does not align entirely with critical discourse analysis and critical discourse studies given that these approaches often look at the ills of society and their relationship to discourse. Instead, this book's conceptualization of discourse seeks to describe how minorities discursively construct the continuation of their languages. Yet, the perspective taken in this book does attempt to follow Foucault's view that the existence of discourse is determined by social context, particularly institutions, and at the same time, discourse makes possible the production and continuation of the social context. In this view, institutions are not only discursively produced, but actually produced and reproduced by discourse. It is within the spectrum of these definitions that much of the work presented in the book takes place.

Part II: **The discursive construction of heritage language development**

6 Discourses of heritage language development I: A preliminary typology

6.1 Introduction

In the previous chapter we studied some of the ways in which the notion of *discourse* has been conceptualized and used across disciplines. Such discussion enabled us to arrive at an operationalization of discourse for the purposes of the present chapter and in subsequent discussions throughout the book. In this chapter, I propose a preliminary typology containing some of the various discourses surrounding linguistic minority families' conceptions of the development and maintenance of heritage languages. Specifically, the chapter presents 10 discourses as follows: utility, cohesiveness, identity, affect, aesthetics, validation, correctness, opposition, access, and cosmopolitanism. Ethnographic data are used in order to illustrate each of the discourses.

Although there appear to be countless themes, factors, ideologies, advantages, consequences, and other issues associated with HL development and bilingualism/multilingualism, these have not been discussed in terms of discourses. Therefore, the next section introduces a data-based typology of discourses, reviews some of the ways in which these have been defined and used, and proposes discourses as a way of categorizing HL development perspectives present in families and scholarship. Given that ideologies of language are present in all aspects of human life, these ideologies are often made visible through language users' discursive interactions. The discourses of HL development and loss, therefore, can be found in both public as well as private settings, and in both settings, language ideologies are discoverable in their ways of talking about HL development. This section, then, attempts to make public the private discourses of HL development found in a selection of Hispanic Canadian homes. This is accomplished through a thematic analysis of the participants' discursive constructions of Spanish language development and maintenance. The data for this categorization of discourses were generated through the ethnography in Metro Vancouver that was described in Chapter 1. The following section describes the procedures employed in this analysis.

6.2 Thematic analysis of data

A total of 65 audio-recorded interviews were conducted in Spanish with members of 34 Hispanic families. The data were transcribed in Spanish and analyzed keeping in focus the overriding theoretical proposition (Yin 1994), language socialization, which had also guided the data collection and selection. Formal coding began in June 2005 using the qualitative data analysis software package N6, at that time the latest version of NUD*IST (Non-Numerical Unstructured Data Indexing Searching and Theorizing), which allowed researchers to manage, code, analyze, and report on text data. This computer program was used to help in the coding and identification of emerging themes across the interviews. In April 2006, I converted and transferred the NUD*IST project into NVivo 7, in that year the newest version of N6 and NVivo 2 combined, and coded the remaining data using this program.

The coding of each interview was performed using several steps that included the following:

1. Listening to audio-recording: I listened to each recording in order to recapture the original atmosphere and character of the interview and to note important contextual features.
2. Reading fieldnotes: I read the fieldnotes focusing on initial ideas and looking for additional details.
3. Listening to audio-recorded memos: I listened to the memos that were recorded immediately after each interview where I captured my first impressions of the information.
4. Reading fieldwork journal: I reviewed the notes contained in my research diary looking for any analytic thoughts I had recorded.
5. Manual coding: I read a printout of the interview transcript,[1] taking notes in the margins and assigning descriptive codes.
6. Using NVivo: I imported the interview transcripts to NVivo and entered the codes as free nodes.[2]
7. Organizing free nodes in NVivo: Once all the interview coding had been entered in NVivo, I created *tree nodes* and organized the *free nodes* into *child nodes* within the *tree nodes*.
8. Verifying coding: I went over the *child nodes* to verify that *free nodes* had been classified correctly. I also merged *child nodes* as necessary, creating larger categories, until a small number of broad themes emerged.

As Palys (1997) explains, qualitative study is iterative in nature. "An iterative process is one that is cyclical, but not merely repetitive. Instead, the term also connotes increasing sophistication or change" (298). This brings images of a

---

[1] The interviews were transcribed verbatim in the languages in which they occurred.
[2] A node is a collection of references about a specific theme, place, person or other area relevant to the analysis.

spiral making its way increasingly deeper into the data. An emergent and iterative approach was therefore used in the data collection and analysis stages, in an attempt to go ever deeper into participants' experiences during interviews.

It should be noted that the theory of interview used in this study was what Talmy (2010) has termed *interview as research instrument*. Although this book section discusses discourses of HL development, the analysis of the interviews on which this chapter is mainly based did not take a discursive perspective. That is to say, the interviews were not explicitly conceptualized as speech events nor openly analyzed as socially situated and co-constructed practices (Talmy and Richards 2010). While acknowledging this as a limitation of the current analysis, it is also important to note that the entire project was conceptualized, implemented, and completed over a period of several years, making it impossible to consider this emerging perspective *a posteriori*. Additionally, the *interview as research instrument* perspective continues to be the dominant approach in applied linguistics, so it is hoped that interested scholars find this work just as valuable as analyses that theorize interviews differently.

Finally, the analysis presented in this chapter should be seen as a summary for discussion and illustration purposes and not intended to function as a full research report, and as such, the data generation context is incomplete. Further data collection and analytical context for the data excerpts included herein can be found elsewhere (e.g., Guardado 2008a, 2009, 2013a). Therefore, it is hoped that the reader is fully aware that these texts have been removed from their interactional setting and *recontextualized* (Bauman and Briggs 1990) for the purposes of the current discussion.

6.3 The discourses of Spanish as a heritage language

6.3.1 Utility

A commonly cited motivation for HL development and maintenance was often expressed in the form of utilitarian discourses. Echoing the majority of studies published as L1 maintenance or HL development projects, this study's participants talked about HL development in terms of future economic benefits for their children through enhanced business and employment opportunities. The participants saw HL development as key to their children's future successful careers, hence leading to their eventual social mobility. The examples below serve to illustrate the discourses the families used in reference to utility.

When Mr. Pedroza spoke of HL development in economic terms, he saw it as becoming his daughter's savings box: "Necesita el español, porque ese será el **plus** de ella. Su caja de ahorros para el futuro. Su alcancía para el futuro" [She will need Spanish because that will be her *plus*. Her savings box for the future. Her piggybank for her future] (Interview: 05/31/05). Mrs. Aguirre asserted: "Si tienen tres o cuatro [idiomas] es mejor" [if they have three or four [languages] it will be better] (Interview: 05/14/05). In these particular statements the two participants were beginning to construct a discourse that built on the extrinsic aspect of their motivation (Petri 1991) to promote the first language, because of the tangible rewards that this promised, namely, future economic benefits. As Mrs. Aguirre spoke: "Además que puede ser muy bien aprovechada ya después cuando ellas crezcan ya en su campo de trabajo. Te permite moverte mucho más fácil" [it can be used to their advantage in the future when they grow up; in their line of work. It allows you to be more mobile] (Interview: 05/14/05). Therefore, mobility and flexibility in employment were goals they expected to achieve as part of their "investment" (Norton 2000) in the linguistic marketplace.

Moreover, some of the children in the study were aware of this goal and the potential positive effects of bilingualism in their career aspirations. They had internalized these ideologies and were also able to produce discourses that were similar to those of their parents. A 13-year old female participant, Olivia, asserted: "Yo quiero ser criminologista o profesora. Si soy profesora puedo enseñar español, inglés o francés. En criminología si necesitan traducción o algo en español, yo lo puedo hacer" [I'd like to be a criminologist or a teacher. If I become a teacher I can teach Spanish, English or French. In criminology, if there is a need for translation or something related to Spanish, I can do it] (Interview: 09/28/06).

Therefore, their construction of Spanish and its role in their families encompassed views that connected it to the production and re-production of linguistic, cultural, symbolic, and economic capital (Bourdieu 1986). The families believed that their children's future success and well-being largely hinged on the maintenance of Spanish and its potential for facilitating better opportunities in life. In sum, these families constructed Spanish maintenance through utilitarian discourses that referred to it as a tool for attaining a better socioeconomic status. If He's (2012) *benefits hypothesis* is correct, then it is possible to argue that the fact that families attach this type of instrumental value to the HL may be a factor leading to successful HL development.

6.3.2 Cohesiveness

Discourses surrounding the creation and maintenance of cohesion was a recurrent theme in the data. These discourses were constructed both in relation to family and at times also broadened to the local Hispanic community, which clearly reflects He's (2012) *rootedness hypothesis*. Although the latter were found in the data, their use was not as abundantly or fervently expressed. By contrast, as expected, intergenerational communication and family unity were pervasive elements in all of the families' discourses of HL development. In fact, when asked about their main motivation for pursuing Spanish maintenance, many of the parents pointed out family communication as the most important. When I asked Mrs. Pérez why she was so committed to Spanish maintenance, her answer was unequivocal: "Por mis padres. Toda la familia está en España. Si mis padres no se pueden comunicar con los nietos, me matan" [My parents. The whole family is in Spain. If my parents cannot communicate with their grandchildren, they will kill me] (Interview: 05/12/06). Although other families did not make such extreme case formulations, this rhetorical device enabled Mrs. Pérez to construct a cohesion discourse that accentuated its importance in her own family.

In constructing the discourses of family cohesion the families often drew on other elements, such as the quality of their relationships with different family members. More interesting—and relevant to the discussion—however, was the explicit deployment of language ideologies in their discourses. Mrs. Pérez's husband was from Afghanistan, but the only heritage language that the parents were committed to transmitting to their children was Spanish, thereby excluding Persian. According to Mrs. Pérez, her husband deemed Spanish a more "useful" language internationally, compared to Persian. Therefore, ideologies were in competition and in the case of this family, utilitarian motives were privileged over cohesiveness.

Mr. Pedroza explained that his nuclear family members had a strong family relationship, which was made possible by their language, stating: "Estamos sostenidos por un mundo de palabras, todas dichas en español" [We are really sustained by a world of words, all of them spoken in Spanish] (Interview: 05/31/05). The family accepted the fact that their public life in Canada was conducted in English, but their private home life and their connection to their family in Colombia could only be mediated by their mother tongue. As other scholars have argued, when families shift to a second language often they feel they are losing their children (Skutnabb-Kangas 1999) because they are no longer able to connect with them in the language in which they are most comfortable communicating. Because of this, it is not surprising to find emotionally charged statements of cohesiveness in the families' discourses of HL development.

6.3.3 Identity

The families' opinions of HL development were full of explicit identity discourses. One of the most pervasive features of these was the construing of Spanish language as "part of who we are;" "part of our roots." The families stated that their ability to successfully maintain the home language in a dominant language environment gave them a stronger identity and sense of self. They claimed that the L1 was a necessary resource for maintaining cultural tradition and fostering ethnic identity in the new generations. Furthermore, it was crucial for them to maintain Spanish as the basis for cultivating a Hispanic cultural identity and for building up their children's self-esteem culturally in order to save them from future identity contradictions (Rodríguez 1982). In other words, to help them become proud of who they were in order to value their origins and to have a strong ethnic point of reference. They saw Spanish as part of their culture and identity, in the same sense that Anzaldúa (1987) talked about the need to be proud of her language in order to be proud of herself.

This analysis also points to the relationship between language and culture as well as to a strong interdependence between the two. Mrs. Corral stated about her children: "El español es necesario para su identidad cultural" [Spanish is important for their cultural identity] (Interview: 04/29/05). Mrs. Amado felt that if her children did not maintain Spanish: "Van a perder su propia identidad. Es importante para ellos mantener sus raíces" [They'll lose their very identity. It's very important for them to maintain their roots] (Interview: 05/17/05). Mrs. Steinberg asserted: "Identidad cultural e idioma es lo mismo. Se puede llegar a la cultura a través de otro idioma, pero se pierde mucho en el camino" [Language and cultural identity are the same. One can learn the culture through another language, but one loses a lot along the way] (Interview: 06/24/05). Thus, a significant aspect of the construction of Spanish maintenance discourses for the families was its key role in promoting a strong attachment of their children to their original cultures. They regarded Spanish as essential in the healthy development and continuous shaping of their children's sense of self.

Additionally, many parents had a sense of the dynamic ways that identity and language are interrelated. Mr. Maradiaga, for instance, argued for the importance of Spanish in the development of an ethnocultural identity. At the same time, he maintained that it was cultural identity that was necessary for maintaining Spanish, indicating that a strong cultural identity would allow their children to want to maintain Spanish, highlighting the dynamic interrelationship that exists between cultural identity and HL development and revealing an iterative relationship between the two. Fishman (1999) wrote extensively on this relationship, and a similar connection could also be made between some of his previous work and the next discourse (1996a).

6.3.4 Affect

The families' comments contained many examples of discourses addressing emotions. Furthermore, the discourses themselves were often expressed emotionally. This was not only true for the discourses of affect themselves, but also for most of the other categories. Thus, the affective discourses could be analyzed at many different levels. One aspect of these discourses was related to the role of the Spanish language in their emotional well-being and that of their children. Hence, they addressed aspects of their affective domain as a crucial part of their language socialization goals. The parents assigned a vital role to home language development and maintenance in the transmission of values by stressing the emotional and moral benefits. In constructing these discourses, the families drew on popular and academic notions related to the psychological consequences of not transmitting the language. In this way, they connected the successful continuation of their children's Hispanic roots and Spanish language with their affective domain as well as their social, mental, and moral development. Thus, the HL development discourses positioned Spanish as playing a central role in supporting the family members' emotional well-being and as an intimate element of their identity.

Mrs. Asturia, a member of a Spanish language Scout group, stated that the family participated in the group because of the opportunity it provided to use the language and "Les ayuda a crear un poco de independencia y de autoestima" [to boost their [children's] independence and self-esteem] (Interview: 01/13/06). The parents felt that the children would benefit from socialization that allowed them to value all cultures, but at the same time, to feel proud of their own roots, holistically raising children some of them described as more emotionally stable human beings. As Mrs. Aguirre asserted: "Todo esto le refuerza esa parte emocional, y yo digo que puede a la larga pues dar seres humanos, espero, más seguros y más fuertes, más orgullosos de sí mismos" [HL development/group participation] reinforces the emotional aspect and I think that in the long run it can, I hope, foster human beings that are more secure, stronger, and prouder of themselves] (Interview: 05/04/06).

These discourses constituted Spanish development and maintenance as key to the construction of some children as experts at certain times, which contributed to the enhancement of their self-esteem. For instance, of all the benefits Mrs. Aguirre saw in La Casa Amistad for her daughters, she ranked the emotional advantages as the most important. She believed that her daughters benefited from their involvement in the language development of other children—novices—which assigned them an identity as "experts," further strengthening their own self-esteem. Likewise, Mrs. Ruedas' oldest daughter, Olivia, often found herself playing the role of an expert in El Centro de Cultura where she assisted the teachers with the rest of the students. This, according to Mrs. Ruedas, was important for Olivia's self-esteem when her language ability was recognized and valued and she was portrayed as an opportune resource in the class activities. In this way, the families produced discourses that asserted the children's Spanish skills played a role in their emotional security and affective well-being.

The most poignant versions of the affective discourses were produced when parents talked about their ability to communicate with their children and others close to them. A common manifestation of this discourse was often a version of "Los sentimientos no se pueden transmitir en inglés" [feelings cannot be transmitted in English] (Mrs. Corral, Interview: 05/29/05). Mrs. Corral added that when her son said to her in English "I love you" it did not mean much. She added: "Si él me dice 'I love you' yo no le entiendo. Y si me dice "ay te amo mamá" allí me toca el alma" [If he says to me "I love you" (in English) I don't understand it. But if he says to me "oh, I love you mom" (in Spanish), he touches my soul]. Mrs. Nuñez said: "Necesito desahogarme, necesito escuchar mi lengua" [I need to unwind; I need to hear my tongue/I need to listen to my language] (Interview: 05/31/05). Arguably, He's (2012) *positive-stance hypothesis* deals with aspects of the *affect* discourse, a relationship that seems to suggest that engaging in the production of this type of discourse in families may be related to successful HL socialization practices. These discourses also echo comments in Fishman's (1996a) work related to the ways speakers display emotional attachment to their languages which they view as particularly special and beautiful, a notion that points to a link between affect and the next category of discourse.

6.3.5 Aesthetics

Many participants referred to their language as "such a beautiful language" as if Spanish were vested with inherent splendor and magnificence. These discourses were produced spontaneously during interviews, family interactions, and impromptu lectures parents gave to children during group gatherings. For example, Mrs. Ruedas regularly attempted to encourage her children to become more aware of their own cultural origins and to appreciate the beauty of their language. She once admonished her 13-year old daughter for being ashamed of speaking Spanish in public, telling her: "Que te de vergüenza mentir, pero no hablar un idioma que es tan bonito" [You should be ashamed of being dishonest, but not of speaking such a beautiful language] (Interview: 05/25/05).

Mr. Hernández, one of the parents who participated with his children in the Spanish language Scout troop, once talked to the group about the beauty of Spanish and the value of maintaining it alive in the group (Mr. H=Mr. Hernández):

> Yo quiero decirles que estoy contento que hablen la lengua española, castellano. Este en sí es un idioma muy bonito, y una de las cuestiones muy importantes de este grupo es (xx) y conservar eso. A los nuevos y a todos, yo les pediría que insistieran en hablar en español, que traten de hablarse en español. Es un idioma muy lindo ¿okay? Y este este también me da de veras mucho gusto ver a todos que hablan muy bien español y me permití invitar a unas otras personas amigos ... a mí me gustaría que conserváramos eso de que les hablen <u>hablan perfectamente</u> inglés como ustedes pero a mí me gustaría que más bien les hablaran que hablaran siempre en español que es parte de lo que nos distingue de los demás. (Observation: 06/24/06)

[I'd like to tell you (pl.) that I'm happy to see that all of you speak the Spanish language, Castilian. This is a very beautiful language, and one of the most important features of this group is (xx) and to maintain that. To the newcomers, I would like to ask you to persevere in speaking in Spanish to try to speak Spanish with one another. It's such a pretty language, okay? And u::m um I'm also very glad to see that everyone speaks Spanish so well and I took the liberty of inviting some people who are friends of mine ... I would like all of us to maintain that practice of talking to them they speak English perfectly like all of you but I would like you to always speak to them to always speak Spanish because it's part of what distinguishes us from others]

As the extract shows, he constructed a discourse with positive assessments of the Spanish language, ("This is a very beautiful language"), and stated that maintaining it was one of the Scout group's objectives and appealed to the children to continue using it. Subsequently, he began a second round of positive assessments with the statement "It's such a pretty language," expressing satisfaction with the children's Spanish development and appealing to them to persevere in their efforts. He added that the endeavoring to maintain the Spanish language was not only an important feature of the group, but the language was also a key cultural element that united Hispanics and distinguished them from other cultures, thus, perhaps unwittingly making an 'us-them' contrast category (Hester 1998). Although his words seemed aimed at fostering cultural pride in the children, thus contributing to strengthening their cultural identities, the discourse used could also unintentionally transmit "othering" views to the children, as it contained positive appraisals of the Spanish language and possibly implying negative assessments of other languages. Regardless, the fundamental point of presenting this excerpt is to illustrate a prevalent discourse in the families which constructs the beauty of their HL.

6.3.6 Validation

Having lived their entire lives as a cultural and linguistic majority in their countries of origin, many families used a variety of strategies to come to terms with their new reality. Hence, this discourse focuses its attention on families that saw themselves relegated to the status of subordinated linguistic minorities. They used discourses designed to construct themselves in a legitimate light. This became particularly important in relation to their children, as some of their fears were apparent in their discourses of cultural and linguistic validation.

In a context where Spanish does not enjoy a high status, families that have enough social, linguistic, and cultural capital (Bourdieu 1977) can exert their agency in order to offset the potential linguistic devaluing effect of the wider society. It has been argued that linguistic-minority families' cultural practices may contrast greatly with those of the larger society (Pease-Alvarez 2002). In the so-called mainstream society often their home language is not valued, has no use, or both, and their cultural values clash with those of the dominant populace.

The devaluation of the social, cultural, and linguistic competencies of immigrant parents and their children has been addressed by numerous scholars, such as Li (1999), Rodríguez (1982), Schecter and Bayley (2002) and Valdés (1996). It has been posited that families' efforts to transmit their home languages to their children is a necessary step in order to empower themselves and to validate themselves (Zhou and Trueba 1998), and to give them voice to affirm their own culture (Pennycook 2001). The parents' discourses about the role of the grassroots groups as socializing agents and as spaces for reiterating the value of Spanish to their children highlights the role that this valorization may play as a critical prerequisite in minority-language transmission (Li 1999). The validation discourse made frequent references to the safe houses the families had created (i.e., grassroots groups) and the activities they conducted there, which fulfilled the function of providing an authentic context for Spanish practice and for validating the families' language and cultures. Because the language used in their activities was Spanish, the validation discourse that portrayed these as important socializing spaces for the children was reflected in their daily and weekly reality. These groups provided opportunities for the children to experience linguistic and cultural immersion and to further validate the usefulness of their language. These opportunities were particularly unique in the Vancouver context where Spanish does not enjoy strong ethnolinguistic vitality, turning these groups into sites of production and reproduction of discourses of validation. In this way, the various language and cultural activities conducted helped turn these spaces into "agents of linguistic legitimation" (Jaffe 2005: 26).

Mr. Herrera, for instance, felt that beyond La Casa Amistad, his children's opportunities to practice and become meaningfully involved in a Spanish-rich context were low. His family did not have an extended family circle to provide an authentic context for language practice, and the only opportunity to access such linguistic resources was La Casa Amistad. In the same vein, Mrs. Pérez felt that El Centro de Cultura gave her the opportunity to provide her children with an authentic context for Spanish practice and validation. She stated: "Veo que es muy bueno que mis niños vean que hay otras personas que hablan español aparte de mí" [I am aware that it's good for my children to see that there are other people, besides me, who speak Spanish] (Interview: 05/12/06). Many parents produced similar discourses that asserted that it was essential for them to show their children that Spanish was a useful language and that there was a whole world out there where Spanish was the medium of communication. Others, like Mrs. Aguirre and Mr. Ramírez, who provided rich Spanish socialization to their children at home, wanted to go further and immerse them in a context where they could have a consistent Spanish socialization experience that went beyond what they experienced within the family context or during their annual trips to their home country.

Thus, an analysis of the discourses of validation used by the families shows that the grassroots groups were places where the existence of their language and culture became validated, indicating to their children that their culture had a legitimate place in the world and their language was a legitimate means of communication. In the Canadian context, this also meant the children should feel proud of their home language and could expect their "right to difference" (Mr. Pedroza, Interview: 05/31/05) be respected and their voices heard and understood.

6.3.7 Correctness

An ideology of correctness was prevalent both in the parents' meta-discursive conceptualizations of HL development—such as those generated during our interviews—as well as in their day-to-day interactions with their children—such as the ones analyzed in Part III of this book. A less common—and yet explicit and clearly intentional—form of displaying an ideology of correctness can be seen in the lecture by Mr. Hernández, which was presented under the aesthetics discourse. This was particularly evident in his insinuation that Spanish was vested with certain cultural, moral, and social values. The implication of these assumptions was that communication in Spanish in the group was the only "proper speech," or the only culturally, morally, and socially appropriate way of speaking, albeit in that particular context. It follows that socializing the children through discourses of correctness was seen as a necessary prerequisite for influencing their linguistic ideologies, with the intended goal of affecting their practices. Likewise, speaking Spanish in the home context was equated with "linguistic correctness," construing English as a threat (Woolard and Schieffelin 1994) to the development of strong Spanish language ideologies.

In daily linguistic interactions between adult caregivers and children, ideologies of correctness were abundant and frequent. These manifested themselves quite explicitly in discourse and sometimes relatively implicitly. For example, parents used a range of linguistic tools in their efforts to foster sustained home language use. This included using direct imperative forms such as *speak Spanish*. These often carried a particular intonational contour in order to further—and unequivocally—constitute them as orders. Other times, caregivers used less directive forms, in which the message was expressed tacitly (Clyne 1996). One such form included commands phrased as clarification requests, as in uttering

I don't understand when a child speaks in English, in order to correct the linguistic anomaly, namely, the child's failure to use Spanish in that context. This type of utterance, however, often had a meaning that was quite different from what was actually said. In my analyses I found that these types of utterances could be paraphrased as "I heard your answer, but I'm not going to accept it and I will pretend not to understand it until you say it in Spanish, the 'proper' language in the family." One of the corrective forms of feedback used by parents with their children (analyzed in detail in Chapter 11) are what I call cross-code recasts (CCRs). As an implicit form of corrective practice, CCRs are meant to prompt a code switch from English to Spanish. The very fact that parents saw the need to make a "correction" when children used English was clear indication that an ideology of correctness was evident in their discourses. In other words, the above linguistic tools formed part of the discourse of ordering, a common feature of the correctness discourse. Based on the above, correctness can be conceived in various related ways. At one ideological level, it may refer to using the correct code for the situation and context. At another, it may be understood to mean using any language form that deviates from the parents' (and others in power) evaluation of what the standard or prestigious variety of Spanish is, which of course includes dialectal differences and regionalisms.

A final feature of the correctness discourse is its silencing function. When care-givers use imperatives such as *speak Spanish* or clarification requests, as in *I don't understand,* the correctness discourse performs a further task, that of silencing. Given that many parents disapprove of any type of code-switching, or code-mixing, the correctness discourse often also contains ideologies of purity. Linguistic purity, in this case, refers to attempts at avoiding *low prestige* varieties, such as *Spanglish* (for a detailed discussion of the linguistic systematicity and social functions of Spanglish, see Zentella 1997). Given that individuals living in multilingual societies readily incorporate elements of the languages used in their environment into their own linguistic toolkit, discourses that chastise children for drawing on all of their linguistic resources at the same time is tantamount to denying their hybridity and their identity as multilingual individuals.

6.3.8 Opposition

Perhaps the most common ideological and discursive thread found at macro- and micro levels of analysis of the ethnographic dataset is one of resistance. Oppositional discourses were pervasive both implicitly and explicitly in daily life for all participating families. While some parents used rhetorically gentle discourses to index their *oppressed* condition as subordinated linguistic minorities, others spoke more directly and almost militantly about the need to work *in defense of Spanish* or used war metaphors to refer to the *battles* they were fighting against assimilation. These discourses talked about Spanish as a language relegated to second and third class. The more radical discourses found in the data portrayed Spanish as a socially weak, underdog language, which needed protection and whose speakers faced systematic oppression.

Arguably, at the broadest level, engaging in any discussion regarding the families' commitment to the promotion of the HL can in itself be seen as a discourse that challenges the prevalent assimilative forces. As well, by merely engaging in conversations with like-minded families about participating in grassroots HL development organizations, such as the ones in this study, these families can be seen as producing discourses that contest the official language structures. Adapting an idea from hooks (1989), minority families' asserting their identities through discussions of HL development, is in itself a discursive act of resistance.

On the moderate end of the oppositional discourse continuum, parents talked about their dreams, aspirations, goals, and strategies for pursuing what they referred to as an uphill journey in socializing their children into Spanish use, and covertly challenging the dominant linguistic practices. For instance, Mr. Morales, a medical doctor from Colombia, spoke of the Spanish language Scout group in which his family participated as enabling them to further resist assimilation into the dominant culture:

> De una u otra manera ... los niños en ese momento están aprendiendo ya sea a través de la comida o de la música o de cualquier otra palabra que surge en los momentos que se reúnen y van a vivenciar y en ese momento los niños están aprendiendo algo propio de nosotros. Es una manera de inculcarles algo diferente, pero diferente con relación a nuestra cultura, no a la cultura de acá canadiense, sino a la cultura latina. (Interview: 01/13/06)
>
> [One way or another ... the children are learning, either through food, music, or words that emerge in their sessions, and they have lived experiences and are learning something unique to us. It's a way of inculcating into them something different, but different because it's related to our culture, not to the Canadian culture, but to the Latin American culture]

Mr. Maradiaga, one of the leaders of the Scout group, frequently spoke of the challenges they faced with regards to the home language socialization of his daughters using oppositional discourses in the form of war metaphors that alluded to a type of war against assimilation. Their daughters had reportedly been ambivalent about their cultural identities and about Spanish. However, the parents reported that through hard work and perseverance they were experiencing some successes in their efforts of fighting the assimilative forces and reversing their daughters' rejection of their cultural identity. They saw this as an important victory in the struggle to raise awareness of who they were culturally and in consolidating their language abilities. Mr. Maradiaga stated that although it had been a major struggle to socialize the girls into the use of Spanish, finally "Las batallas más grandes ya se han ganado" [The biggest battles have been won] (Interview: 05/09/05) and in the last few years, things had changed for the better.

Again using the war metaphor, Mr. Maradiaga added: "La guerra no está ganada, pero hemos ganado una batalla" [We have not won the war, but we have won a battle] (Interview: 05/02/05), echoing comments made also by a father in a study on multilingualism and identity (Rothman and Niño-Murcia 2008), in which the parents expressed similar attitudes about the challenges they faced in relation to the societal assimilative forces. Mr. Pedroza, a lawyer from Colombia, created the most explicitly oppositional discourses of HL development. His discourses echoed critical cultural scholarship that argued for minorities' "derecho a la diferencia" [right to difference/right to be different] and the need to work "en defensa de nuestro idioma español" [in defense of our Spanish language] (Interview: 05/31/05). Additionally, he produced discourses that depicted the struggle for Spanish as a "huge problem" but also as a "huge possibility," clearly attempting to utilize rhetorical devices that juxtapose a negative state of affairs with its potential, thus avoiding speaking from a deficit-view-of-the-world perspective.

All the discourses produced could be categorized as oppositional, including the ones on the politics of identity and ethnolinguistic validation. Despite most of the families' ability to function in an English–speaking context, many chose to develop—or join—a Spanish-language group in which they could affirm and attempt to maintain their sense of identity and transmit it to children in the community. Yet, some of the discourses produced by the families reflected an overt attempt to resist assimilative forces prevalent in the schools (Pacini-Ketchabaw, Bernhard and Freire 2001) and in the wider community (Schecter and Bayley 1997), and were constructed as "oppositional discourses" (Pratt 1991) emerging from Canadian multiculturalism contact zones.

6.3.9 Access

The study participants' constructed discourses of Spanish maintenance as a key that opened doors—the door-opening metaphor was pervasive in their discourses. Mrs. Ovando stated: "we are aware that being bilingual opens many doors" (Interview: 05/24/05). Mrs. Vanegas equated being bilingual with being "educated" and saw future employment opportunities as becoming available by knowing more than one language: "El mundo se mueve en rededor de la gente preparada, de la gente bilingüe. Tienen mejores oportunidades, están mejor preparados, y lógicamente es el futuro de ellos ... y se abren puertas por todos lados inimaginables. Las puertas se abren en cuanto a trabajo" [The world revolves around educated people, people who are bilingual. They have better opportunities, are better prepared, and obviously that is their future ... doors open in the most unimaginable places. Doors open regarding employment] (Interview: 04/23/05). Mrs. Vanegas further stated: "Hablar dos idiomas, tres, cuatro, cinco idiomas es una gran ventaja" [To speak two languages, three, four, five languages, is a great advantage]. Therefore, the families' access discourse revealed that they did not only count on Spanish to provide these opportunities, but also saw it as a starting point for learning other languages, and thus, increasing their professional potential. This was also evident in the parents' own interest in learning other languages. Some of the parents, like Mrs. Delgado, already spoke three languages. She was already fluent in Spanish, English, and French, and was studying Italian at the time of the interview.

In Mrs. Pérez' discourse, the doors that were opened through Spanish were not necessarily the doors of economic opportunity or other languages, but the doors of cultural knowing and awareness. Such notions were particularly applicable in this case because the Spanish language is associated with cultural, racial, religious, dialectal, and regional diversity. To Mrs. Pérez, the Scout group and El Centro de Cultura, along with the family's other Spanish language socialization efforts, were key to helping open those doors: "Y claro, una vez ya lo tienen [idioma español], pues te abre muchas más puertas y puedes apreciar toda una cultura, no una, muchas, como España, Méjico, Guatemala, Argentina. Es que es maravilloso, claro imagínate. Aparte te abre las puertas para aprender otras lenguas latinas" [And of course, once they have it [Spanish language], it opens many more doors for you and you can appreciate a whole culture, not one, but many, like Spain, Mexico, Guatemala, Argentina. Because it's so wonderful, for sure, imagine. Besides, it opens doors for learning other Latin (Romance) languages] (Interview: 05/12/06).

Like Mrs. Pérez, other families went beyond the economic benefits they expected Spanish to afford their children. Mrs. Aguirre's discourse addressed the transferability of skills from one language to another (Cummins 1981, Crawford 1992b, Krashen 1996, Cummins 2000), as evidenced in this quote: "Yo creo que abriéndote el canal de un idioma más, estás abriendo las opciones para otros idiomas" [I think that by creating an avenue for another language, one is broadening the options for other languages] (Interview: 05/14/05). The family's efforts in HL development were directed at creating access opportunities for their daughters to build on that knowledge and learn other languages; forming the linguistic foundations the children could draw from in their future language learning endeavors.

Thus, the above analysis shows the families appeared to say that not passing on the language and culture to their children would be equivalent to stealing from them, robbing them of access to their history, their heritage, their future economic opportunities, and the opportunities for them to learn other languages more easily. The parents' discourses about Spanish show they recognized the value of linguistic resources in society and identified their potential for accessing other forms of capital. They were interested in adding to their linguistic wealth, and were aware of its potential for being converted into symbolic, cultural, and economic capital (Bourdieu 1986).

6.3.10 Cosmopolitanism

Not all participating families used cosmopolitan discourses in our interviews. In fact, these discourses were only found in interview data with families with a post-secondary education. Those families who did speak this way, produced discourses of cosmopolitanism that unequivocally articulated with contemporary conceptualizations of the topic in the literature. There was no doubt that when they spoke about Spanish maintenance, they spoke of it as an important catalyst for socializing their children into a progressive worldview. Of all the participating families, the Fernández-Maradiaga and Aguirre-Ramírez families emphasized this notion most strongly in their discourses. These parents seemed to subscribe to a syncretic notion of cultural identity that strongly embraced their own culture. At the same time, they were aware that their children's sense of identity was different from their own. Mrs. Fernández stated in this regard: "La identidad cultural de las niñas es un híbrido. No podemos hacer un pequeño mundo dentro de estas cuatro paredes. Ellas tienen que conocer su cultura, pero tampoco encerrarlas en eso. No se puede. No estaríamos logrando nuestros objetivos, de que ellas tengan una visión amplia" [The cultural identity of the girls is a hybrid. We can't create a mini-world inside these four walls. They have to know their culture, but we can't enclose them in it. It can't be done. We wouldn't be achieving our goals for them to have a broad outlook] (Interview: 05/09/05). The family was aware of the outside influences on their daughters' evolving identity and understood that they could not enclose them in a cultural bubble. Additionally, as asserted by Mrs. Fernández, one of their aims was to socialize them into a "broad world outlook." This "outlook" discourse can be seen as consistent with pursuing an understanding and appreciation of other cultures, drawing from them in the course of their identity formation.

The Aguirre-Ramírez family used a similar discourse. They placed a central value on bilingualism and multilingualism as part of a belief system that included valuing all languages and cultures equally. Mr. Ramírez stated the family was interested in transmitting a sense of value for languages other than Spanish. They explained they wanted to raise children who were "interesados en otros" [interested in others], echoing scholars studying cosmopolitanism (e.g., Delanty 2006). They added that they wanted their daughters to "... absorber todo lo que están viviendo a su alrededor, pero sin perder las raíces y las tradiciones que traían o que tenemos en México" [... absorb everything they [were] experiencing in their surroundings, but without losing their roots and the traditions they brought or that we have in Mexico] (Interview: 04/15/06), thus socializing them into hybrid identities as Canadians, which to them meant embracing an affiliation to a broader identity beyond that of Latin American or Mexican. They produced a HL development discourse that described Spanish in the context of the Canadian multicultural milieu as key to socializing their children "ciudadanos del mundo" [to be citizens of the world] and incorporating aspects of the Canadian cultural fabric into their identification.

These types of discourses were produced by the Fernández-Maradiaga family both in relation to their home as well as to the Scout group of which they were leaders. Their socialization discourse cast Spanish maintenance as an essential factor in providing their daughters with "una visión más amplia del mundo" [a broader vision of the world] (Mr. Maradiaga, Interview: 05/09/05), thus enabling them to function through many cultural systems. Their views on HL development revealed a cosmopolitan discourse that related their daughters' socialization experiences with local, national (i.e., Canada and Guatemala), and global perspectives (Starkey 2007) and promoted identity development that benefited from multiple cultural sources (Kastoryano 2000).

When the conversation focused on the Scout group, the discourse also shifted toward a promotion of good citizenship and contributing toward social change. The parents, as Scout leaders, promoted active citizenship through informal education activities in an attempt to mold the Scout members' value systems and identities, raising awareness of their roles and responsibilities to their families, their communities, society, and the environment. Through this, they intended to foster the children's social consciousness as their contribution to the community and to effecting social change. Mr. Maradiaga stated their aim was "... formar la conciencia en los niños acerca de tener una razón por la cual existir, con una conciencia social en todos los aspectos de la vida" [... to form the conscience of the children about their reason to exist, with a social conscience in all aspects of life] (Interview: 11/05/05). Their discourse of HL development presumed a commitment to the community, to the environment, to social change, and to cultural diversity, in line with some of the current conceptualizations of cosmopolitanism (e.g., Smith 2007). Thus, the families' discourse of HL development revealed that to them—and contrary to popular opinion—HL development went beyond preserving an elusive past and was meant to raise cosmopolitan people who can relate at local and global levels.

6.4 Chapter summary

In this chapter, I have presented a first attempt at analyzing HL development from the perspective of *discourse*. Taking discourses of HL development to mean shared ways of thinking and speaking about HL development and maintenance, I have proposed 10 categories under which these can be classified. In this preliminary attempt, it has already become clear that language ideologies cannot be separated from all aspects of social life. Indeed, all of the discourses of HL development discussed in this chapter contain linguistic ideological traces and in some cases are inherently ideological. One of the main purposes of organizing language minority families' ideas about HL development in this way is to begin to look at how families construct HL development discursively. This helps lay the foundation for engaging in discussions of how discourses may influence the outcomes of HL development efforts in families and communities. The discourses introduced in the foregoing chapter had varying frequency in the data and alluded to different aspects of the families' aspirations and ideas associated with HL development.

Utility, for instance, was identified as the most frequently manifest in comments regarding economic or professional opportunities and the notion of "successful careers" and socioeconomic mobility. Cohesiveness was mainly discussed in terms of family unity, and, of secondary importance, connection to the local Hispanic community. Intergenerational and international family unity appears to be a strong component and motivator of a discourse of cohesiveness. Implicit reference was made to the parallel between intimate family relations necessitating an equally intimate family linguistic code for communication. The identity discourse in the data often made explicit connections to the heritage language as an intimate part of the family members' being and history. As such, parents talked about HL development and maintenance as critical to positively influencing their children's psychology and self-esteem. In a more extreme case, HL loss was equated with the child's loss of identity altogether. Many parents conceived of HL and cultural identity as having a symbiotic relationship.

The discourse of affect was discussed as a twofold construct. Not only did families talk about the importance of their HL for expressing their emotions, but they often spoke affectively about all aspects of their HL. Heritage language maintenance was talked about in terms of its role in their children's social, mental, and moral development, and subsequently, of the parents' ability to be more influential in their children's overall socialization. In addition to these key factors, proficiency in the HL led to the "promotion" of some children to the role of "experts" in the grassroots classroom, which undoubtedly had a positive influence on the children's feelings of self-worth in association with the HL but also in general.

A discourse of aesthetics was also identified in the data. Even though this notion may be seen as somewhat problematic, it is not a surprising finding. This type of folk linguistic analysis has been discussed in the literature before. Still, while many of the parents in this study emphasized the beauty of Spanish, one might ask if this was done at the expense of the beauty of other languages; in other words, by focusing on the "aesthetic splendor" of Spanish, is the beauty of other languages inadvertently suppressed? Given the emotional way in which these parents—and speakers of other languages generally—often discuss their own languages, it is impossible to ignore the close connection of this discourse to the discourse of affect.

Other discourses addressed the relative lack of a Spanish ethnolinguistic vitality in Vancouver and seemed to be constructed as ways of providing legitimate, public, and concrete spaces where Spanish could be spoken and cultural values shared (validation); the Spanish language was talked about explicitly and implicitly regarding what parents saw as culturally, morally, and socially appropriate forms (correctness); and more politically in how Spanish was often spoken of as needing protection from subordination by the dominant language and culture (opposition). Indeed, the use of war metaphors underscores the seriousness with which many parents took their task of HL development. Therefore, opposition was enacted in many different ways, from asserting a non-dominant identity, to participating in grassroots groups such as the ones described herein.

Two discourses constructed HL development and maintenance in progressive terms that would provide more idealistic opportunities to the new generation. For instance, HL development was often referred to for its ability to "open doors" to employment opportunities, success in learning other languages, and cultural awareness. Likewise, parents that used the door-opening metaphor felt that failing to pass on the HL to their children was equivalent to robbing them of a range of opportunities that their "linguistic wealth" could bring them. Likewise, while not the most frequently referred to in relation to HL development, cosmopolitan views—when they did arise—were strong and clearly explained. The parents whose comments are interpreted herein as cosmopolitan in nature had attained higher levels of formal education and seemed to possess analytic tools to reflect on their families' experiences and the linguistic resources to express them. These parents embraced their children's hybrid identities as a feature of their upbringing in a society other than that of their immediate heritage. They felt that supporting such an identity would encourage their children to acknowledge and have respect for other cultures and their languages, and would ultimately help them to become "citizens of the world." These beliefs reflected a value system that centered on social harmony and community participation, made possible in part by heritage language and culture preservation.

7 Discourses II: Mapping the literature

7.1 Introduction

In Chapter 6, I introduced a preliminary typology of dominant HL development discourses that emerged from an ethnographic study with Hispanic families in Canada. In this chapter, I scrutinize a segment of the HL development research literature with this evolving discourse typology lens in an attempt to ascertain whether this may be a scholarly direction worth pursuing. After briefly describing the inclusion criteria and introducing the studies reviewed, I discuss several features of the most common discourses found in the research literature. Finally, I review the publications that were found to contain the most discourses, followed by a discussion of the least common discourses according to the typology presented.

7.2 Testing the typology

In the preceding chapter I took a broad look at the discourses of HL development used by a group of Hispanic families. These discourses, both individually and collectively, tell the story of heritage language development and maintenance among the participants, some of whom knew each other through common social networks, including micro grassroots HL development organizations. In this sense, I may go out on a limb and refer to these as dominant—albeit contextually situated—discourses of heritage language development. The analysis demonstrates that these discourses are in fact used in families and communities and that this typology may be a starting point for taking a discourse-based approach to the study of HL development. This tentative—and evolving—taxonomy has been applied to the literature that is most relevant to HL development with the outcome that the proposed discourses also exist in this body of knowledge and across a wide range of linguistic groups and contextual characteristics. Therefore, in this chapter I provide a summary of how this discourse typology articulates with the extant scholarship within a specified period of time.

7.3 Selection of studies

The data for this analysis come from a multi-phase literature review based on the basic inclusion criteria described below. Articles were initially selected if they had a HL development focus, and reported the results of an empirical study. When multiple publications were based on the same study (e.g., Schecter and Bayley 1997, 2002), the most comprehensive one was chosen. Studies in various national contexts focusing on the development and maintenance of diverse immigrant languages were included.[1] Criteria for exclusion: articles with a purely quantitative focus; articles reporting HL development strategies but not exploring participants' reasons for HL development; articles examining minority parental attitudes towards bilingual education in general, as opposed to attitudes towards their desire to enroll their children in a HL program. The selection of articles underwent an iterative process of verification and refinement of the application of the criteria. Thus, although the literature review initially included 47 articles, on closer examination through three rounds of analysis guided by the selection criteria, this number was reduced to 24 sources that were deemed relevant and appropriate for the final analysis. All of the articles that were part of the final analysis (with the exception of Lily Wong Fillmore's seminal 1991 article) were published after 1999, with a majority (21) published in 2005 or later.

7.4 Identifying discourses within studies

The initial discourses were identified as dominant HL development discourses among the 34 families that participated in my 1.5-year, multi-site ethnography in Metro Vancouver. The table below was developed after the completion of the ethnography over a period of about two years (2011–2013). Taking the dominant discourses identified in that study as a point of departure, this literature review project sought to gather evidence in order to quasi empirically establish whether these discourses are in fact widely used, and subsequently to propose this typology as a starting point for taking a discourse-based approach to the study of heritage language development.

In order for the discourses proposed in the previous chapter to form a useful framework to other scholars, these need to be clearly defined, which is the aim of Table 7.1. This said, however, there remains a high degree of overlap inherent in the majority of these HL development discourses, which I discuss in the following chapter. Let me just say for now that this overlap is not always consistent (i.e., *Identity* sometimes but does not always include *Affect*), so it is worthwhile to try to keep them separate. The criteria in Table 7.1 are examples of orientations to HL development that might be found in each discourse. This table was consulted in order to ascertain whether the discourses proposed in the previous chapter were

---

[1] One study that examined Indigenous language socialization was included as it was sufficiently similar to the rest of the studies in approach and content.

Table 7.1 Discourse identification criteria.

Discourse	Criteria
Utility (Instrumental)	The HL as a means to different pragmatic ends, such as: – economic (e.g., business and employment possibilities) – socio-economic (useful for ascending the social class ladder) – fostering overall academic achievement (it is frequently HL bilingualism, and not simply HL development, that is presented as instrumental in accomplishing a range of concrete goals)
Cohesion	HL development as key in fostering a sense of unity, continuity, and understanding in: – the family (nuclear and extended) – the ethnic community (in the host and home countries; with peers and intergenerationally)
Identity	HL development as part of identity formation for: – showing ethnic pride – showing ethnic and/or linguistic solidarity – cultural maintenance and continuity – linking to ethnic roots – enhanced self-image
Affect	The HL as: – a code that enhances emotional connection (especially to family members) – a means to express emotion – a code in which affective matters are thought about and discussed – a code that provokes an affective reaction in others (i.e., to please someone by speaking the desired language) – a tool for building (or severing) affective ties to the past
Aesthetic	The HL as: – something inherently beautiful or expressive—either on its own, or in comparison with other languages – something to be proud of because of its beauty and expressivity
Correctness	HL ideologies surrounding 'correctness' in relation to: – age-appropriate proficiency – literacy – mixing languages – accuracy (in grammar, vocabulary, etc.) (discourses may be present in reported practices or attitudes towards any of the above by parents, children, teachers, or community members)
Access	Door-opening metaphor depicts the HL as: – key to learning other languages – crucial to communicating with a wider range of people (including those in the heritage country) – important for facilitating adaptation to dominant culture through HL school participation

(continued)

Tab. 7.1 (continued)

Discourse	Criteria
Opposition	Defensive ideologies and practices that construct the HL (and culture) as: – needing protection and shelter – participating in power struggles with other languages at the institutional level – participating in power struggles with speakers of other languages – experiencing oppression by society or societal forces
Validation	The HL seen as being validated by particular spaces; HL development efforts in these spaces validate HL speakers **Spaces that validate the HL include:** – the home – travel to places where the language is spoken by the majority or a large minority – ethnic group events – community language schools – community groups where the HL is spoken – the regular education system (i.e., bilingual programs) **People that are validated by the HL include:** – *children* (e.g., hearing and speaking the HL spoken outside of their domestic circle; being publicly recognized as 'experts' or having an advantage because of their HL knowledge; interacting with peers with a similar cultural upbringing in the same context of immigration) – *parents* (e.g., helping their children with their homework when it is in the HL; using their HL to communicate with other adults in public spaces; socializing their children according to their values in public, and feeling the support of other parents trying to accomplish the same goal) – *parents, children, communities:* social and emotional support; validation of cultural values, practices, and beliefs
Cosmopolitanism	HL as key to fostering: – a progressive worldview – simultaneous local and global affiliations (multiple belonging) – hybrid/globally oriented identities – intercultural understanding – multicultural and multilingual awareness and appreciation – a desire to make a positive contribution to society and the world

present in the selected publications. Naturally, the table provides a preliminary guideline that will benefit greatly in the future from the insights of those who use and modify it.

Table 7.2 Selected sources.

Selected sources	
Cho (2008)	*Nicholas (2009)
Chumak-Horbatsch (1999)	Oriyama (2010)
Comanaru and Noels (2009)	Pacini-Ketchabaw et al. (2001)
Dagenais and Day (1999)	Park and Sarkar (2007)
Decapua and Wintergerst (2009)	Pease-Alvarez (2002)
Gibbons and Ramirez (2004)	Schecter and Bayley (2002)
Iqbal (2005)	Slavik (2001)
Li, G. (2006)	Sodhi (2007)
Li, X. (1999)	Tannenbaum (2005)
MacPherson and Ghoso (2008)	Thomas and Cao (1999)
Maguire (2005)	Wong Fillmore (1991)
Nesteruk (2010)	Xiao (1998)

Table 7.2 contains an alphabetic list of the studies that were included in the final analysis through the lens of the above criteria. Care was taken to ensure that a range of languages and contexts were included. As has been made clear throughout this book, I take the stance that HL development processes are intimately tied to a variety of individual and broader factors (familial, social, ideological, historical, cultural, political, educational, economic, among others). These factors, I contend, are not static but constantly in flux and in dialectical relation with one another. Given that the goal of this book is to provide an up to date picture of the research domain—from micro- and macro perspectives—and to suggest ways forward, I find it necessary to constrain the analysis to a relatively short period of time, one which, hopefully, will still be reasonably similar and relevant when the insights drawn finally reach interested readers. Therefore, two decades was deemed an appropriate cut-off point for inclusion, a time period that yielded sufficient linguistic diversity and a wide enough range of studies.

7.5 Discourses in the research literature

A meticulous examination of 24 publications using a detailed set of criteria revealed that the typology proposed in this book is compatible with contemporary popular and scholarly discourses of HL development. Figure 7.1 provides a visual representation of how the discourses were distributed in the sample of studies. As this graphic indicates, discourse representation ranged between three and 21 out of the 24 publications. That is, the discourses were found in the literature at least 12.5% of the time and as much as 87.5% of the time. The most

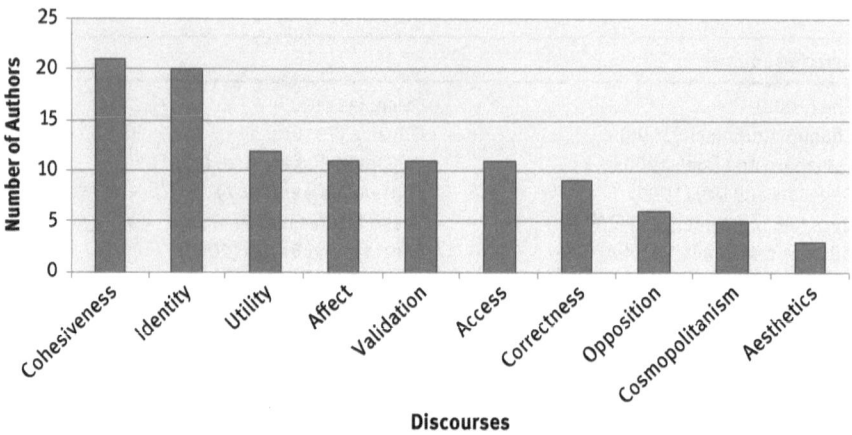

Figure 7.1 Frequency of discourses in the literature consulted.

common discourse running through the selected sources was *cohesiveness*, with 21 out of 24 publications containing some version of this discourse. Please refer to Table 7.3 for a breakdown of how each of the discourses was distributed across the selected sources. The first discourses I discuss in this section are the ones found to be more representative across the sources examined. Thus, my discussion progresses from most to least frequent.

7.5.1 Discourses of cohesiveness

The classic study on the issue of family cohesiveness could well be Wong Fillmore's, which speaks about the consequences of language loss for family unity and communication, especially in how it can negatively affect early childhood socialization. A frequently quoted excerpt from Wong Fillmore's (1991) article is the following, also quoted in Chapter 2:

> When parents are unable to talk to their children, they cannot easily convey to them their values, beliefs, understandings, or wisdom about how to cope with their experiences. They cannot teach them about the meaning of work, or about personal responsibility, or what it means to be a moral or ethical person in a world with too many choices and too few guideposts to follow. [...] When parents lose the means for socializing and influencing their children, rifts develop and families lose the intimacy that comes from shared beliefs and understandings (343).

Wong Fillmore's seminal article paints a bleak picture for minority family cohesion when children lose their first language. More recently, Thomas and

Table 7.3 Distribution of discourses in the literature consulted.

Sources	Cohesiveness	Identity	Utility	Affect	Validation	Access	Correctness	Opposition	Cosmopolitan	Aesthetics
Cho (2008)	✓	✓	✓	✓	✓	✓	✓	✓	✓	
Chumak-Horbatsch (1998)		✓		✓	✓		✓			
Comanaru and Noels (2009)	✓	✓	✓							
Dagenais and Day (1999)	✓	✓		✓		✓			✓	
Decapua and Wintergerst (2009)	✓	✓	✓	✓	✓	✓				
Gibbons and Ramirez (2004)		✓	✓	✓				✓		✓
Iqbal (2005)		✓		✓						
Li, G. (2006)	✓	✓				✓	✓	✓	✓	
Li, X. (1999)	✓	✓	✓	✓			✓	✓		
MacPherson and Ghoso (2008)	✓	✓	✓			✓	✓			
Maguire (2005)	✓					✓				
Nesteruk (2010)	✓	✓	✓	✓		✓			✓	
*Nicholas (2009)	✓	✓				✓				
Oriyama (2010)	✓	✓	✓			✓	✓	✓	✓	✓
Pacini-Ketchabaw et al. (2001)	✓	✓	✓	✓				✓		
Park and Sarkar (2007)	✓	✓	✓			✓	✓	✓	✓	
Pease-Alvarez (2002)	✓	✓					✓			
Schecter and Bayley (2002)	✓	✓	✓	✓	✓	✓	✓	✓		✓
Slavik (2001)	✓	✓	✓			✓				
Sodhi (2007)	✓	✓				✓				
Tannenbaum and Berkovich (2005)	✓			✓						
Thomas and Cao (1999)	✓									
Wong Fillmore (1991)	✓			✓					✓	
Xiao (1998)	✓	✓								

Cao (1999) wrote about a Vietnamese family where cohesiveness had become a serious concern due to the loss of the home language in the new generation. The authors lament the fact that language failed the family members when the topic of conversation deviated from "routinized interactive exchanges" (109), rendering parents and children virtually unable to talk about anything other than such habitual daily interactions. Some publications, such as that of Dagenais and Day (1999), contain discourses of cohesiveness also in relation to the broader heritage ethnolinguistic community. They write that a mother in their study wanted "... her child to maintain oral competence in Vietnamese so that she [could] develop close ties with the Vietnamese community in Vancouver and with family in Vietnam" (113). Therefore, the analysis showed that both forms of cohesion found in the data-set are also available in the research literature.

7.5.2 Discourses of identity

Not surprisingly, the second most common discourse that appears in the research literature is identity. Out of the 24 studies reviewed, 20 addressed the role of identity in HL development. This distribution is entirely consistent with the data on which the taxonomy was developed and with data collected for other studies in the past (e.g., Guardado 2002). Therefore, together with the discourse of cohesiveness, it is not unreasonable to propose these as dominant discourses of HL development. In fact, several of the publications examined contained the term *identity* in their title. Interestingly, the ubiquitousness of the discourse of identity in the literature should not be taken to imply a monolithic construct or an uncontroversial use of the term. On the contrary, there was considerable diversity in the conceptual stance taken among many of the sources. For instance, the dominant identity discourse in the literature asserted that linguistic minorities' ability to successfully maintain the home language gives them a stronger identity and sense of self. Pacini-Ketchabaw et al. (2001) reported that participating Latin American families saw L1 maintenance as a way to foster Latino identity. This discourse was also found in Schecter and Bayley (2002) who found that the heritage language was seen by their participating families as "a necessary social resource for maintaining cultural tradition and ethnic identity" (79). This stance was of high frequency in my own ethnographic data set which was used in the generation of the taxonomy under examination. Conversely, Pease-Alvarez reported that many parents saw the relationship between language and cultural identity in synonymous terms. Thus, the parents' discourse on language loss included identity loss. Again, this finding is consistent with segments of the data set. However, based on some of her participants' experiences, Pease-Alvarez surmised that HL development might not be necessary for cultural identity maintenance—presumably, at least not equally for all individuals.

Yet another dimension of the identity discourse found in the literature was participants' sense of obligation to learn or maintain the HL because of their family background (Comanaru and Noels 2009, Oriyama 2010). Oriyama talks about her Japanese descent participants in Australia feeling the need to raise their children fully proficient in Japanese. Some of her participants went so far as to claim that being Japanese in Australia, without the language—or without 'proper' Japanese—made them non-Japanese. Comanaru and Noels reported that some of their participants in Alberta, Canada expressed guilt at disappointing others for their lack of heritage language proficiency. As Canadians of Chinese descent, they felt a sense of *obligation* to maintain Chinese because of their heritage. An identity discourse with a similar sense was also found in Nesteruk's (2010) study, whose participants felt guilt and shame for not doing enough to see that the family heritage was continued in the next generation. There were other dimensions to the discourse of identity in the literature, such as the feeling of belonging and loyalty toward other multilinguals (Dagenais and Day 1999), a stance that points to the possible development of unique cross-group cultures among new generations in diaspora.

7.5.3 Less frequently found discourses

The five discourses in the middle of frequency were distributed in this way: utility, 12 studies; affect, 11 studies; validation, 11 studies; access, 11 studies; correctness, nine studies. The utility discourse category yielded interesting results. The analysis reveals that in some of the studies, the utilitarian discourse referred to economic benefits in a straight-forward manner. One of Sakamoto's informants explicitly noted the status Japanese language enjoyed and wished that eventually their children's linguistic capital (Bourdieu 1977) would lead them to successful careers. This feeling held particularly true for participants who had lost their first language when very young (Kouritzin 1999). Other times, this discourse appeared more multidimensional. For Richard, a man of Cree descent in Kouritzin's study, the usefulness of the Cree language traversed several dimensions, as illustrated by his words: "Cree could accommodate the Cree wants and needs more than English could. English became lacking; it was not as colorful; it was not as useful—it was dry. Cree became a more colorful world, became a more precise world. You could describe things in Cree you couldn't describe in English" (71).

An aspect of the utility discourse in Dagenais and Day's study as analyzed through the criteria set was an assertion of the 'usefulness' of the English language in the world. The discourse was extended to include the heritage language, but not because of its utilitarian nature, per se, in the sense that English was.

It connected at various levels within the family and was understood as an integral component of the children's trilingualism, which in itself was seen as useful, more than the heritage language by itself.

The discourses of affect were not found as frequently—or explicitly—as such in the literature as I had anticipated. Only slightly under half of the studies contained discourses identified as affective. Their pervasiveness, however, should not be ignored given that some intriguing instances of the affective discourse were coded. For instance, Tannenbaum's (2005) findings seem to problematize the role of affect in HL development. Affective relationships with the L1 can be avoided by using the L2, or the L1 can be used as a significant tool for affective meaning making in the family. Language can be seen as a tool for cutting ties with the past or for providing the past with continuity in the new country—in spite of past negative experiences. What is striking about the discourse of affect is that the very act of talking about HLs can be emotional in itself. The affect discourse seems to be ever-present in discussions of HLs, either explicitly or implicitly. This was the case in the data set and also in the research literature.

The discourse of validation, also with 11 instances in the literature, was found to mirror the data set at least at two levels: personal validation and societal validation. At the personal level, Decapua and Wintergerst (2009) described a German family's trip to Germany. When the oldest child in the family took daily excursions on her own to different cities, she was able to fully appreciate the German-language descriptions of exhibits in various museums. She was also able to communicate effectively with the German-speaking people around. These experiences seemed to have a validating effect on her in how they made her feel that her language was valid and had a place in society. At the societal level, some studies also resonated with the data set. Sodhi (2007: 294) reported that the Sikh women in her study created a "third space" in their hearts and minds, which allowed them to embrace their new hybrid identities and thus "the best of both worlds." "Safe houses" such as these—not only mental, but also physical—were found in the data set to have a powerful validating effect on members.

The discourse of access also had 11 occurrences in the literature examined. The review revealed that it mirrored the proposed taxonomy, particularly in the allusion in the discourse to a door-opening function. Park and Sarkar's (2007) study used a HL development discourse of access to language learning and to academic achievement. Decapua and Wintergerst (2009) contained a discourse of accessing other cultures. Li, X. (1999) and Li, G. (2006) revealed the presence of discourses of access to participants' roots and family connections and to their host cultures. The discourse in Nicholas's (2009) study with Hopi Native Americans referred to accessing other ways of thinking through language, and Maguire's (2005) study in Quebec, Canada, referred to language maintenance as a doorway into the world. Therefore, the HL development discourses found in the literature were almost perfectly in line with the analysis conducted in Chapter 6.

The final discourse in this grouping, the discourse of correctness, also was not without multiple dimensions, reflecting the data set reported in Chapter 6. In Schecter and Bayley's study (2002), the discourse of correctness often referred to dialectal differences and regionalisms, which were unacceptable by some of the highly educated Mexican parents living in California. This was echoed in Cho's (2008) study where parents monitored their children's use of MSN (an online chat tool) in efforts to ensure they used correct forms of Korean. Another type of this discourse was also present in this study as the parents insisted on the correct honorific forms in Korean. Chumak-Horbatsch (1998) contained discourses referring to how the quality of the Ukrainian the children spoke was very important to parents. In Oriyama's study (2010), the correctness discourse equated speaking poor Japanese to childishness and therefore immaturity, a discourse that is often found also among adults studying an additional language. A further dimension of the correctness discourse, as analyzed in the previous chapter, was the preference for language purity. Sakamoto, for instance, reported that parents attempted to create a home environment that kept the development of different languages rather separate, thus discouraging language mixing. Although Pease-Alvarez's (2002) article only contained two other discourses (identity and cohesiveness), the discourse of correctness arose strongly in relation to code-switching. According to Pease-Alvarez, some of the participants used discourses against mixing languages and other participants spoke in favour of this practice. Parents, in particular, seemed to hold negative opinions of code-switching, seeing it as an index of linguistic incompetence. Children, however, were much more inclined to view language-mixing and switching behaviour in positive terms.

7.5.4 Least representative discourses

The least common discourses found in the literature were opposition, cosmopolitanism, and aesthetics. Depicting the discourse of opposition as having low representation in the literature may be deceptive. Arguably, as also posited in Chapter 6, all efforts to transmit heritage languages to the new generations, or even engaging in conversations about such goals, can be interpreted as acts of resistance. These activities produce discourses laden with ideologies that implicitly contest the dominant and even official language structures. Therefore, oppositional discourses may be seen across all the studies. Additionally, oppositional discourses of the rhetorically gentle type as well as the more forceful ones were unequivocally present in the literature. In Pacini-Ketchabaw et al.'s (2001) study, there was a somewhat gentle, but clear, discourse of resistance toward assimilating forces. One of the parents, in an attempt to ensure her two sons did not assimilate too rapidly to the dominant culture, challenged the resistance she encountered at school, mainly in reaction to the teacher's insistence that the family use English at home. The mother used an explicit discourse of opposition when she stated that, even if she knew enough English to communicate with her children, she would choose Spanish as it was the school's role to teach them English and the family's role to teach them Spanish. A less gentle discourse of opposition can be found in Li's (2006) article. One of the participants, Mr. Ma, spoke explicitly about discrimination being "very much alive in society" and a prevalent attitude "against the Chinese community" that he hoped would be diminished by the learning of English by the next generation.

The fact that cosmopolitanism discourses were largely absent from the literature could be seen as a predictable outcome. A commitment to heritage languages and cultures may be viewed as narrow thinking based on nostalgia and on attempts to cling to a romantic past, whereas a cosmopolitan outlook is more readily interpreted as progressively looking to the future. Only five out of the 24 studies contained some type of discourse that could be described as cosmopolitan (Dagenais and Day 1999, Park and Sarkar 2007, Cho 2008, Nesteruk 2010, Oriyama 2010), but in some cases this discourse was only alluded to in passing as part of larger themes. There were only budding traces of the discourse, but by and large, the scholarship on HL development has not, as of yet, taken up this relationship in and of itself. Thus, while focused discussions on the relationship between HL development and cosmopolitanism are still largely absent from the discourses, this is not to say that cosmopolitan discourse surrounding HL development exists only in exceptional cases or not at all. Further scholarly work looking at this relationship is needed to arrive at a fuller picture of this discourse in discussions of HL development. Chapters 13 and 14 are attempts to engage in this conversation.

Finally, the least discussed discourse in the literature was aesthetics, with only three studies containing any references to this category (Schecter and Bayley 2002, Gibbons and Ramirez 2004, Oriyama 2010). Oriyama, for instance, writes that one of his participants "likes Japanese as a language and believes that Japanese often has better expressions [than English]" (86). Whereas the lack of cosmopolitan discourses in the HL development literature may be seen as a shortcoming by some readers, the relative absence of aesthetics discourses could be welcome news by some who may interpret this almost non-existence as a possible sign that certain views that assign certain languages inherent characteristics, such as magnificence and beauty, and other languages primitivity and repulsiveness, may be on the decline. Finally, of the 24 studies reviewed, it is interesting to note that three publications (Schecter and Bayley 2002, Gibbons and Ramirez 2004,

Oriyama 2010) contained nine out of the 10 discourses, with only cosmopolitanism being absent, and Oriyama contained eight, with only affect and opposition discourses not present.

The results of the examination presented in this chapter show that it is possible to take a discourse approach to discussions of HL development and to engage with the research literature in such deliberations. All 10 discourses proposed in Chapter 6 based on an ethnographic data set were found to exist in a selection of 24 studies from across languages and contexts when examined through a prepared set of criteria. This indicates that the proposed discourse typology does in fact help tell the HL development story. However, as was made evident throughout the last two chapters, implicitly, but also at times explicitly, discourses are anything but discrete and clearly defined entities. Discourses are always enmeshed in broader—and deeper—ideological stances and systems of meaning making. In the next chapter, I atempt to engage with such intricacy.

7.6 Chapter summary

In this chapter, I have presented the results of applying a discourse typology to a selection of publications that address HL development issues. I showed that the discourse typology developed as a result of ethnographic research is compatible with the academic discourses on this topic. To ascertain if this typology of HL discourses could extend to a broader circle of languages and cultural settings, I initially reviewed 47 relevant articles written on HL development and related topics in the past 20 years. Upon a close reading of the selected articles, I narrowed the list of empirical sources to 24, where evidence of the discourses could be found.

I grouped the discourses that appeared in these 24 studies according to frequency, and then discussed them for their unique findings and contributions to the literature. I then examined some of the factors that might have led to certain discourses being more frequent than others. Examples from the literature helped to demonstrate nuance and contribute to our conceptualization of the different discourses of HL development and bilingualism generally. In terms of a broad-sweeping conclusion, none of the higher discourse frequencies were remarkable. Cohesiveness and identity, for example, are well-established motivators of HL development. Some of the lower frequency discourses may have been such because of (1) recency to the field and thus lack of scholarly publications discussing these constructs (i.e., cosmopolitanism); (2) less emphasis currently being put on certain aspects of HL development or language in general (i.e., aesthetics); and (3) the fact that some discourses seem to underlie other, more prominent ones, and thus when singled out, appear to receive less attention (i.e., opposition as possibly present in all of the discourses in some way or another). Although I had begun to engage with some of the overlapping characteristics of the 10 discourses identified and discussed in Chapter 6, the border-crossing qualities of the discourses of HL development—which reflect the fuzzy nature of discourse categories more generally—became exceptionally clear when applying this typology to the body of HL scholarship.

8 Discourses III: Problematizing the discourse typology

8.1 Introduction

In Chapter 7, I applied the discourse typology to a set of HL development studies in order to test its applicability to the body of knowledge in this research area. Through this analysis, I showed that the typology is at least consistent with the academic discourses on the topic, albeit loosely applied. In the present chapter, however, I intend to complicate the typology by deconstructing its artificial boundaries and looking at the deeper structures of the categories. I first provide a rationalization for taking a discourse-based approach to HL development. I then describe some of the ways in which the discourse boundaries are blurred and look at their various interrelationships, subdivisions, and characteristics. I end the chapter with some possible implications of taking a discourse-based approach to HL development.

8.2 Rationalizing a discursive approach to heritage language studies

An understanding of a variety of issues and factors, such as the individual, familial, and societal benefits of HL development is well established in the sociolinguistics research literature (e.g., Kouritzin 1999, Schecter and Bayley 2002). More explicit analyses from the perspective of discourses, however, have not been attempted. It is by and large recognized in several interrelated traditions of discourse analysis (Foucault 1980, Fairclough 1992, Gee 1999, Wodak et al. 1999, van Dijk 2008) that discourses are a social practice. Furthermore, in line with comprehensive macro and microanalyses of discourses on a range of topics, as shown in Chapter 5, I take the position that discourses are produced by particular ideologies, situations, and contextual realities, and at the same time are constitutive of them. Following these theoretical and research traditions, this chapter takes the stance that discussions of factors affecting HL development, and of the consequences of maintenance and loss, can be profitably enriched by drawing on the ample interdisciplinary scholarship on discourses. Therefore, the chapter revisits the diversity of meanings present in the families' discursive constructions of language development and maintenance. I argue that, as is the case with all discourses, talk about HL development contains elements that indicate their origin. At the same time, this talk has the potential of effecting, or at least contributing to enacting, HL development in the new generations.

8.3 Overlapping discourses of heritage language development

The existence of a persistent overlap across discourse categories and their recursive interrelationships was revealed in the course of conducting the research on which the chapters in Part II are based. This was evident both in the data from which the discourse typology was developed, as well as in the meta-examination of the research literature. As Gee (2005) posits, there are no discrete discourse boundaries. These are constantly changing and new ones being created, contested, or reconfigured all the time. He argues that it does not matter so much how we count the discourse categories as what the discourses do. They, he continues, are "defined in relationships of complicity and contestation with other Discourses, and so they change when other Discourses in a society emerge or die" (31). Clearly, the discourses analyzed in this book also do not exist as discretely defined entities; rather, they are fluid and in flux as a result of social life factors and processes of ideology formation and socialization, among many others. Likewise, each of the discourses can be further divided into additional discourses that have complex relationships among themselves and with other categories, and the categories themselves can be grouped in different constellations of discourses.

8.3.1 Interconnected constellations of discourses and their attributes

A conceptual mapping of the discourses points to the existence of three discourse clusters. These groupings also display characteristics found in the discourses and are subject to the same types of interlinkages. In terms of interrelationships among all the discourses of HL development, *affect* emerges as the most central. An example of this is provided by Fishman who argued that there is a strong relationship between language and identity (1999). More specifically, as in his work *In Praise of the Beloved Language: A Comparative View of Positive Ethnolinguistic Consciousness* (1996a), he wrote about the positive opinions—discourses—espoused by speakers of languages from around the world about their own languages and how their languages are connected to ethnicity, religion, land, among other relationships. Fishman collected praising comments about different languages from all over the world and would sometimes read one of these comments to speakers of other languages and asked them to guess what language the comments were about. Almost invariably, he asserted, they guessed the comment was about their own "beloved language." This, *inter alia*, points to the role that affect plays in the construction of people's perspectives on their own mother tongues, which arguably, also indexes a link to identity. I return to the significance of *affect* as an umbrella term shortly.

Cluster 1 comprises identity, validation, cohesion, and aesthetics, with affect occupying the node position connecting all others. Cluster 2 is made up of three discourses: utility, access, and cosmopolitanism, and Cluster 3 only contains opposition and correctness. The discourse of *identity* in Cluster 1, for instance, can be easily sub-grouped with *cohesiveness, affect,* and *validation.* Likewise, thematic trends in the *identity* discourse include issues of ethnic/cultural pride, cultural continuation, and validation, the L1 as a link to family heritage, and multilingual identities as a common ground for the formation of friendships (e.g., Maguire 2005). The distribution of discourses into clusters, with affect in the node position, implies a dominant conceptualization of HL development as including at least the following: loyalty, nostalgia, history, self-esteem, emotions, passion, interconnectedness, continuity, belonging, acceptance, self-worth, family, and a feeling of prestige, among many other connotations. The central unifying umbrella term for Cluster 1, which according to this view, can be seen as largely dominant in the typology, is the notion of *pride.*

Pride, then, may be understood as a meta-discourse of HL development, one that encompasses a variety of branches, some of which are present in Cluster 1. A sense of pride is possessed by families subscribing to a HL development project and developed by those individuals who succeed as the subjects of this project. Conversely, the lack of a sense of pride in the heritage language may lead to an unwillingness of families to transmit the heritage language to their children. This unwillingness may be the result of negative experiences in their home countries, and these experiences themselves possibly leading to negative language ideologies for families uninterested in pursuing HL development. More often, however, these language ideologies are the result of persistent hegemonic forces in their home cultures and in their host cultures. As was discussed in Chapter 4, there is a paradox of cultural reproduction in the way families often endeavour to contest the official language and social structures on one hand, and reproduce these ideologies in their practices, on the other. The lack of a sense of heritage language pride may also be the result of the inability—for whichever reason—of individuals to develop and maintain their heritage language. As we discussed in the previous chapter in relation to the discourse of identity, lack of proficiency in the heritage language sometimes leads to guilt on both parents and children. This sense of guilt is often related to feelings of shame. This shame arises from the belief that individuals and families were responsible for passing on the family heritage to the new generations and having failed. Hence, meta-discourses of pride lie at the opposite end of the language ideological spectrum, in relation to negative ideologies that may include a sense of shame. The *pride* discourse umbrella, then, can be contrasted with linguistic and cultural assimilation, emotional detachment from the heritage language and sometimes even heritage language devaluation as a result of hegemonic language ideologies.

Cluster 2, made up of three discourses, utility, access, and cosmopolitanism, implies a notion of HL development as a *key* that opens doors. *Access*, a discourse of HL development, may also be seen as the central concept in this cluster, and thus, also an umbrella term. Although the *access* meta-discourse is not as dominant as *pride*, it seems to play a significant role in the discourses of HL development in general. It is applicable to intimate connections to family, community, and culture, as well as to materially instrumental or broader goals such as socioeconomic mobility, intellectual growth, and a global sense of place. Furthermore, each of the discourses in this and in the other two clusters can be discussed in terms of their local associations. *Access*, on one hand, overlaps with *utility*. The HL is *useful* when *accessing* people's own ethnic community. The frequent use of the 'door opening metaphor' in participants' discourses is further evidence of this overlap as the language is seen as a key that opens different types of doors, including those leading to economic opportunities. On the other hand, *access* overlaps directly with *cosmopolitanism*. *Access* is part of a cosmopolitan outlook when seen as a passageway to other cultures and communities. Cohesiveness is also part of cosmopolitanism when seen as the glue that unites the global village. Identity is also part of the cosmopolitanism umbrella when seen as a way of being in the world, and hybrid identities are the substance of cosmopolitanism when individuals draw on more than one cultural system as a source of identification.

Opposition and *correctness* make up Cluster 3. Together, they add the critical edge to the discourses of HL development. The fundamental component of this cluster is its *political* substance. The *political* meta-discourse suggests that when seen in these terms, the number of discourses of HL development may not be a suitable measure of their significance. Despite being the smallest grouping, *politics* is a deeply rooted meta-discourse in HL development. Language is laden with ideology. Heritage language development and maintenance perhaps even more so given that sites of language maintenance are sites of ideological struggle. Heritage languages, as the underdogs in this interaction, strive to subsist in the midst of perpetual threat. Seen in this light, HL development seems to lie between politics and emotions.

The upshot of this discussion is the impossibility of speaking of discourses of HL development without acknowledging their inherent interrelationships. All the discourses are implicated with one another. No matter which way we look at them, their interconnectedness is clear. Thus, discourses can be understood in terms of *interconnected constellations of discourses* that can work in a multitude of configurations and sub-divisions.

8.4 Implications of typologizing discourses

Drawing on ethnographic research data, the preceding chapters have proposed a discourse based approach to the study of HL development. Despite the arguments made above in regards to the complex interrelationships among discourses, I posit that dominant discourses of HL development may be found in ethnolinguistic groups. In my analysis I have taken a rather broad look at the discourses of HL development. These discourses, although not discreet, provide a first attempt at using this lens as a way of engaging in discussions on the topic. I do not intend, however, for this meta-view of HL development discourses to be seen as exhaustive; rather, this is to be understood as a preliminary effort of this nature. Many other discourses were identified and considered as part of this project, but it was beyond the scope of a preliminary model to attempt to provide a more comprehensive examination. It is expected that many other discourses of HL development may be proposed, and alternate relationships attempted, in future work.

8.4.1 Theoretical implications

An objective of the chapters in Part II was to illustrate the diversity of discourses related to HL development that circulated among the participating families, many of which have also been discussed amply in the literature, albeit sometimes implicitly. At the same time, through this discussion I intended to further stress and describe the conceptual and practical complexity of the HL development issue. The postmodernist contention that "truth" and "knowledge" are plural, contextual, and historically produced through discourses has been found to be very much the case with the many dimensions of the HL development phenomenon. From this perspective, the analysis has attempted to challenge the essentialist myth related to HL development, specifically around linguistic minorities' interest in preserving and transmitting their cultural and linguistic heritage. Therefore, the chapters in Part II serve to support the view that the discourses of HL development are as complicated as any other social phenomenon and these are interrelated and changing through time, space, socio-economic, and other contexts. Moreover, this analysis may enable scholars to look at HL development from a different perspective by providing discursive resources to "talk about" it in different ways. Thus, these collective of discourses can be seen as a typology that may help further theorize HL development. This preliminary operationalization offers a potentially useful heuristic to probe factors affecting HL development in families.

8.4.2 Empirical implications

Likewise, the outcomes of this analysis may be a starting point for researchers to relate this heuristic usefully to the substance of their own data and contribute to building a framework for future HL development study. One possible application of this emerging framework could be found in cross-linguistic comparisons of HL development. In this regard, the creation of a research instrument drawing on the present typology is already underway. Once finalized, this instrument may be initially tested with a segment of the Hispanic population in Edmonton, Canada, and subsequently, with a cross-linguistic sample in order to draw preliminary similarities, differences, and idiosyncrasies in these populations and to begin to refine the model. Further research and theoretical scrutiny will no doubt expand and fine-tune this line of inquiry or otherwise dismiss it as unproductive.

8.4.3 Dialectical implications

Given that discourses are constitutive of and constituted by social reality (Wodak et al. 1999), the contexts and situations in which discourses emerge shape and affect them. Similarly, discourses of HL development may have an impact on families and communities' sociolinguistic realities. It is possible that families may be putting too much faith in HL development—by expecting so much from it—leading one to wonder whether they may be setting up themselves for future disappointment. Can HL development deliver on the promises implied in the (especially positive) discourses? It is my contention that regardless of whether these expectations are too ambitious or not, the fact that these desires are being thought and expressed discursively, in itself, may have an effect on what families do practically. Following Foucault (1972), who saw discourses as "practices that systematically form the objects of which they speak" (54), I would like to end this book section with the claim that making these discourses explicit and public may contribute to the spread of a HL development ideology and thus, ultimately contribute to the promotion of heritage languages.

8.5 Chapter summary

In this chapter, I have attempted to problematize the boundaries of the discourses in the typology that I have been building from Chapter 6 in order to begin a discussion of the fluidity of discourses of HL development, and examine the possible implications of this lack of stability. It is helpful to conceptualize of the overlap and interconnectivity present in the discourse categories in terms of constellations, or clusters, that are interrelated in different ways. By looking at the discourses in this manner, larger macro—or umbrella—discourses seem to emerge which unify elements from different clusters. *Pride* and *affect* are examples of these. Therefore, in this chapter I set out to show that identifying a number of discourses and the similarities and dissimilarities among them can help larger, meta-discourses to emerge and possibly unify the numerous areas of intersection and division.

As shown, sometimes the discourses relate to one another in more linear ways, such as the HL being thought of as useful for accessing the home or other cultures. Other times, they seem to take on more abstract relationships; for example, the way that HLs can be talked about for their ability to express emotion better than the L2, or how, no matter what is being said about the HL, the comment itself is being expressed *affectively*. It was my goal in this section of the book to show that insofar as discourses can be seen to "form the objects of which they speak," the possible interrelatedness of the discourses of HL development and the promotion of HLs have potential to form an interesting and productive avenue of research in HL studies, from data collection to organization and interpretation to analysis.

An issue that could not be overlooked in these last two chapters, however, is the one posed by attempts to identify discourses across the literature where examining discourses was not the aim. As every study seeks to answer a particular question or set of questions, these inform what data are useful, and thus, make their way into the published research findings. Clearly, the processing of data shapes the kind of picture that emerges in a particular study, which directly influences the discourses of HL present in the literature. A central limitation of the present analysis, then, is related to the fact that no research questions, methods, or complete sets of data of the studies were accessed, examined, or contrasted with one another. Therefore, it is impossible to know for certain whether the studies in which all 10 discourses were represented and those which only displayed a few are being accurately portrayed in this meta-analysis.

Part III: **Socializing strategies and metapragmatic practices**

9 The role of community

9.1 Introduction

This chapter begins Part III of the book by addressing one aspect of the heritage language development strategies found in families, namely their recognition of, and capitalizing on, the socializing power of the community. I first engage with some of the issues that have been researched in relation to communities more broadly as a way of highlighting their potential for families and individuals. Then I draw attention to the relationship of HL development specifically to communities. The core of the chapter is grounded in three grassroots community groups that explicitly pursued language and culture maintenance and this discussion is enriched by the description of additional organizations with similar and also different goals. Based on ethnographic data, I outline the informants' motivations for starting and joining the groups and underscore some of the key perceived benefits that are drawn from participation in the groups. I end the chapter with an interpretation and discussion of the role of the grassroots groups for the participants.

9.2 Why are communities relevant?

When it comes to HL development, the unit of analysis should be the family. This does not mean that HL development occurs equally across family groups. What this suggests is that the family is the central collective that facilitates socialization and maintenance processes. It is assumed that the family alone, especially the nuclear family, is not always—or frequently—able to facilitate this process without help. It takes a village to maintain a minority language, but it is the family that mediates between the individual and the village. Since the village— the community—is embedded in the broader society, or, the "national culture," it can play a buffer role between the minority family and the larger society. This relationship and embracement gives the family and its members a sense of community that validates their place in society and provides sources of support and belonging. In the previous chapters I described and provided examples of issues and concepts emerging from families' experiences in their own homes, communities, and in society in general. However, we have not analyzed in detail the key role that community groups play in HL development. In the section that follows, I briefly discuss research from particular traditions, which, in addition to being of relevance to the issues that are the focus of this chapter, may also provide further useful background to the entire discussion of the book. The role of communities as sources of practical and emotional support, coping mechanisms, and many other factors are discussed. This research helps to describe and analyze how, in the absence of extended families, the village can be recreated in diaspora as a key means of helping families socialize their children into favourable linguistic ideologies and as a source of essential types of support to adults.

9.2.1 Introducing the role of community through sense of community

The concept of sense of community (SOC) has been developed and empirically tested in dozens of studies following Sarason's (1974) foundational work. McMillan and Chavis (1986) define SOC as "a feeling that members have of belonging, a feeling that members matter to one another and to the group, and a shared faith that members' needs will be met through their commitment to be together" (9). In this work, McMillan and Chavis have described the fundamental elements of sense of community: membership, influence, integration, and fulfillment of needs as well as shared emotional connection. As part of this work, they have also delineated the process of developing positive relationships, connections, and support networks as central to the survival and improved well-being of communities.

One specific line of inquiry has focused on resiliency. Sonn and Fisher (1996, 1998) have explored the resilient ways in which communities respond to adverse or stressful conditions, such as oppression and change. In their research with Colored South Africans,[1] Sonn and Fisher (1996) found that because of their mixed ethnic ancestry, members of this group found themselves in-between cultures in the context of Apartheid. The researchers found that these individuals relied on mediating structures and alternative activity settings (e.g., extended family, schools, churches, sporting groups) from which they could derive community benefits such as a sense of psychological relatedness, belonging, and security. Thus, through their participation in these activities they were able to resiliently reconstruct and maintain social and cultural identities that had been devalued, and as a consequence, denied to them. Sonn and Fisher likened the functions of these alternative settings to those fulfilled by Black churches in the United States.

---

[1] A mixed ethnic group living in South Africa with a predominantly European ancestry combined with several South African tribes and other ethnic groups (e.g., Indian).

9.2.2 The therapeutic role of churches in Black communities

McMillan and Chavis (1986) briefly address the sense of community prevalent among Blacks, especially in relation to group membership, shared values, and shared emotional connection, but without specifically focusing on the role of Black churches in the lives of these groups. In related lines of scholarship, however, the study of the key role that churches play in Black communities in the United States has been increasing since the 1980s. Gilkes' (1980) seminal work first identified the therapeutic function these groups play for the church membership (e.g., validation of experience). For example, informed by systems theory and group relations theory as their conceptual frameworks, McRae, Carey and Anderson-Scott (1998) have studied the ways in which different Black churches adjust how they operate depending on the needs of their membership. Although to my knowledge sense of community was not named explicitly in their work, the role Black churches play in the lives of their members can be understood as a function of the sense of community that is fostered through participation in that group. One of the key roles of the churches, McRae, Carey and Anderson-Scott (1998) found, was as supportive networks. Their research, based on focus group discussions with members of four Black churches in the United States, showed that Black churches offer a system-centered approach to dealing with the community mental health needs of African American populations. One of the traditional missions of the Black church has been to provide their community with material and psychological support. Black churches have served as mutual aid groups, providing for African Americans a sense of belonging, role models, interpersonal learning, and safe environments in which to share and express ideas and feelings. These churches, according to McRae et al. (1998), function as bridges that connect members to others who share similar values and religious beliefs. Because they foster feelings of acceptance and provide support to members, they often see the church membership as a family. In fact, they found that members who were from out of state relied on the church to fill the void left by the absence of family.

Grassroots groups, such as churches, are key players in the identity, social, and cultural development of communities. This is strongly the case for Black communities in the United States. This process, Mays (1986) asserts, ought to be analyzed as situated in particular socio-historical contexts. For African Americans, such socio-historical reality is embodied in the slave trade. Mays argues that in order to understand the development of identity for Black slaves, it is necessary to see it as departing from that of the White master. These communities, and the shared social life of their members, shaped their identities and for this reason affiliation to the church became necessary as it provided comfort and practical support.

A sense of culture, family, pride, and self-respect was not available to Black slaves outside of the church context, which became a sort of protective sanctuary for them. The severe racial segregation that prevailed during slavery brought about the ghettos. In order to survive, these marginalized communities had to rely on the only resources they had at their disposal: each other. Therefore, the entire community had to take on the task of caring for its members. They became sources of material and emotional support and raised their children as big extended families. This is not surprising, given that the extended family has been identified as a strong feature of Black communities (McAdoo 1995). The extended family unit has also been identified as a central feature of many other groups, such as Asian groups, and has been connected to an ideology of community centrality (Arthur 2000). The extended family is also a key cultural orientation for Hispanic populations and has been examined using the term of *familism*.

9.2.3 Hispanic familism

Familism refers to core values that emphasize loyalty to the nuclear and extended family as a unit and relying mainly on this family for support. It can be described as a collection of strong feelings of identification and attachment of individuals with both their nuclear and extended families (Sabogal et al. 1987). With this attachment come strong feelings of loyalty, reciprocity, and solidarity within the family. Familism is a construct that has been examined in the context of Koreans (Kim 1990), Chinese (Lau 1981), and other groups. Familism has been shown to exist in all ethnic groups and in all individuals, to varying degrees, and it has been found to be one of the most important cultural values of Hispanics. The existence of familism in Hispanic cultures has been documented in a wide body of research, especially in psychology. It has also been found that Hispanics exhibit a significantly higher level of familism compared with other groups. For instance, it is suggested that familism is a more common feature of Latino families in the United States diaspora as they often display more cohesion, intergenerational exchange, and family support than do Anglos. Building on the above line of scholarship in combination with fieldwork with Hispanic community groups, a situated type of familism is proposed later in this chapter.

9.2.4 The role of grassroots community groups in HL development: British Columbia

The role of grassroots community groups has received little attention in its own right within the literature on HL development. Studies often provide a cursory commentary on the existence of community groups or complementary language schools within a certain minority language context, but a review of the relevant literature suggests that the role that these groups play in the multifaceted process of child language and culture socialization remains largely unknown. The following sections draw on data from an ethnographic study conducted between 2005 and 2007 in the Hispanic community of Metro Vancouver. These sections highlight the various roles that grassroots groups have played in the children's heritage language socialization, and in the lives of the participating families, among other functions. In this part of the chapter I tell the stories of how the groups emerged out of desires and needs of community members in relation to their children's Spanish language socialization. In general, I found that families formed or became involved in these support groups in order to transmit language and culture to their children. Moreover, the study revealed that the families further exerted their agency by strategically turning these spaces into "safe houses" to resist assimilation and into venues for the Spanish socialization of their children, which enabled them to also transmit cultural values, such as familism. In the following section, I provide a brief introduction to the organization of each group, its purpose, and activities.

9.2.4.1 El Grupo Scout Vistas

Organization
El Grupo Scout Vistas was a Spanish-language boys and girls Scout troop. Its members met every Friday evening from 5:00 to 8:00 p.m. in a community school. The family of each child contributed about $50 a year to cover insurance costs. They also covered additional expenses like uniforms, fieldtrips, and other activities. By the time I learned about the group, it had gone through several incarnations since its initial formation in December 2000. Mr. Maradiaga, co-founder, had been a Boy Scout in Guatemala from the time he was 11 years old and Mrs. Fernández, his wife and co-founder, had been a Girl Guide in the same country as well.

Purpose
According to the founders, philosophical differences between their conceptualization of scouting and that of Scouts Canada were a primary motivator in the couple's decision to officially join the independent Scouting Movement through Baden-Powell Scouting Association (BPSA) British Columbia in March, 2004. The leaders stressed that the objectives of their group were not limited to playing games and having fun. There was a much deeper impetus that attempted to educate and socialize children and youth into values related to physical fitness and nature. This scouting group differed from traditional scouting groups in

its emphasis on fostering a social consciousness in the children, which would help them to become responsible and contributing citizens of the larger society. But perhaps the way in which the group departed the most from other scouting groups was in its facilitation of the transmission of Spanish language and literacy as well as Hispanic culture.

Activities

Most of the activities conducted in the Scout group took place on the community school grounds. These activities could be classified into language and literacy related, Scouts proper, arts and crafts, games, and sports. Therefore, the Scouts engaged in weekly activities designed to promote Spanish language and literacy learning in the children. In order to support this goal, a mini-library project was proposed by Mrs. Fernández, and implemented with the support of all the parents. Every week, between 30 to 40 books in Spanish were brought from members' homes and spread on a table where a parent volunteer would loan them to the children. This proved to be an exciting time for the children.

Scouts proper activities were varied and numerous. With one hundred years of history from which to draw, the Scout Movement had already accumulated a plethora of traditional games and skills that had become classics in Scout groups around the world. In addition to a variety of games, these included knot tying, book binding, insignia sewing, wood carving, and other Scout-related arts and crafts. Besides Scout-based arts and crafts, they also engaged in more culturally related types of arts and crafts. This became particularly common during the Christmas holiday season. For example, one Christmas project involved the creation of a *nacimiento* (nativity scene) in a showcase at the local public library. Although the Scout Movement has no religious affiliation, these activities were planned in a meeting with the consensus of all the parents. In response to a question I posed to the group leaders sometime later about this thematic choice, they explained that the intention was purely cultural and that such initiatives were fully directed by parents.

Outdoor activities varied widely and, like indoor events, were based on the regular Scout curriculum as well as other activities that were unique to this group. Outdoor activities involved recreational, community service, survival, and other purposes. In general, I observed that all the children had a positive attitude toward outdoor events and they seemed to enjoy them a great deal. Activities in the outdoors included camping trips at least twice a year, hikes during the day and also hiking expeditions during the night, which focused specifically on orienteering and learning about nocturnal animals. The Scouting troop also participated in removing invasive weeds from parks, tree planting, park clean ups, competitions in cross-country marathons, visits to bird sanctuaries, tours of the coast guard, taking part in Chinese New Year and Santa Claus parades, fundraising for hurricane victims in Central America, among others. During camping trips, Scouts learned about survival skills, fire building, cookery, archery, and a range of other Scout staple abilities. Some parents usually accompanied the group on fieldtrips, who assisted with transportation and supervision.

9.2.4.2 El Centro de Cultura

Organization

El Centro de Cultura was founded and registered as a non-profit organization in 1999. The group rented indoor space in a community centre owned by City Hall in a municipality about 30 km from downtown Vancouver, and each family paid $50 a year to cover the cost of rent. There was ample space available and furniture arranged for group work, but no playground-type equipment. Overall, the facilities at the centre lent themselves to more structured, school-like work as opposed to free play and open activities. The families came together once a week for one hour, three times a month, but between set up for classes and clean up afterward, the group members only had 45–50 minutes of actual class-time available. There was considerable national origin diversity in this group's composition, and hence, cultural and dialect diversity, which according to the parents greatly enhanced the participants' experiences as they were exposed to a variety of cultural practices and linguistic richness.

Purpose

The original goal of the founding parents was to create something like an *escuelita* (little school) and also have a sharing of skills among Latin families, such as guitar and cooking lessons. Reportedly, the comprehensive plan was not fully successful due to the lack of volunteers; however, the *escuelita* did work as intended and continued to operate in a similar manner—run by a small group of volunteer parents—in 2012 when I last made contact with some of the members.

Activities

The group classes were organized in three levels by age (3–5, 6–9, and 10–15 year olds). Mrs. Martínez, who had been a parent-participant since 2000, explained that she became a teacher in the group "by accident" and had already been teaching for several years by the time of our interview. She initially resisted taking this role because she had not been trained as a teacher, but when they were unable to find anyone else to fill this role, she reluctantly accepted. Overwhelmingly, the teachers of the two older groups almost exclusively conducted form-focused and literacy-based activities without a noticeably significant emphasis on communicative competence or performance. Many of the lessons observed had a dictation, grammar, and/or translation focus, and were also textbook-based. Following instructions and other practices traditionally associated with formal classroom learning seemed pervasive in all of the classes observed. For example, the objective of Mrs. Perez's class was to teach the children grammar, regardless of what language was used to teach it. Besides socialization into traditional school-like lessons conducted in English, the children were socialized to linguistic attitudes that emphasized Spanish through English translation and the privileging of grammar.

The focus of Mrs. Nieve's class (teacher of the youngest age group) was on various types of arts and crafts, puzzles with Spanish syllables, and bingo games with cards containing pictures of an assortment of objects that included fruit, vegetables, and everyday items. These activities were supplemented with various children's songs, action games, and stories. In general, the content was based on colours, numbers, and letters. The materials used came from books brought from Mexico, photocopies from different early childhood education (ECE) books, and from other sources. Because Mrs. Nieve had been trained as an ECE teacher in Mexico, the work in her class was varied and usually based on activities she used in her teaching prior to immigrating to Canada. The most significant feature in terms of language use was Mrs. Nieve's efforts to maintain the focus of the children on speaking Spanish. There was considerable variety in the types of strategies she used to achieve this goal, including explicit requests, translating the children's utterances, and sometimes recasting their utterances with the appropriate Spanish words substituted. In Chapters 11 and 12, I specifically describe and analyze some of these strategies in their interactional context.

9.2.4.3 La Casa Amistad

Organization

La Casa Amistad was formed by a mother in September 2004. Six families from various Spanish-speaking backgrounds met for about two hours after school once a week at the time I did fieldwork in the group between 2005 and 2006. The meeting space was rented for $25.00 per session and each of the families contributed $30.00 a month. This contribution covered supplies, the cost of hiring a teacher (at $30 per hour) for one hour every two weeks and the rental of a place for families. The place was called Family Centre (a pseudonym), which was an actual house located in a residential area.

Purpose

The non-profit organization that rented the space to the group described the place as "A resource centre for families with young children to meet, make new friends, gain a sense of community, and receive ongoing support and assistance in an effort to raise healthy, happy children." Although the Amistad families met and conducted their activities independently from Family Centre, the space seemed fitting to the goals of La Casa Amistad. The setting and equipment available to them made it a welcoming place for families, especially those with small children.

The Group's mission statement, written in English in September 2004, read: "Mission Statement—purpose is to meet regularly to pass Spanish speaking language and culture to our children." Elaborating on her mission statement, Mrs. Bedward, founder, explained that her idea was to get other people involved, who could help her by teaching her and her children, and other families' children, Spanish through a variety of activities. According to her, because she left Mexico when she was seven years old, she did not know the type of activities that would be suitable for the group. In her words: "I was trying to get together a group to create the cultural contacts and the cultural environment, and the child-centred play environment that would bring that knowledge back into my life and back into theirs." In order to accomplish these goals, Mrs. Bedward proposed a number of activities to the original six families that met for the first time, including arts and crafts, a book club, games, songs, birthday celebrations, and themed activities such as *Día de Muertos*, *Navidad*, and *Día de Reyes*, among others. She also proposed a simple division of labour, assigning jobs to different parents. The jobs included such customary roles as treasurer, accountant, and membership manager.

Activities
This group struggled with self-definition, and as a result, questions regarding the type of activities on which to base the group aroused ongoing tension. At the time of fieldwork, it had already become clear to all parents that a decision needed to be made regarding how the group's activities would be conceptualized: semi-structured, arts, crafts, and games-driven activities vs. structured, school-like literacy-oriented activities. Two not entirely separate issues were also causing tensions: 1) the multilevel nature of the Spanish language abilities of the children—and some of the parents—in the group and 2) the balance in parental involvement in conducting the group activities. The latter issue, which had lingered for some time, had already been partially addressed by the decision to hire a teacher—for two hours a month—a few months after the group was formed. The common denominator in all the parents' agendas for participating in the group seemed to be HL development. They were committed to the promotion of the Spanish language in their children and sought out opportunities to pursue this goal. Deep down, however, their goals seemed to transcend language; they sought out opportunities for cultural awareness and transmission, identity formation, and family value creation.

9.2.5 The role of grassroots community groups in HL development: Alberta

This chapter's discussion of the fundamental supporting roles that community groups play in relation to a broad range of issues among immigrant communities is enriched and expanded by recent work conducted with additional groups in neighbouring Alberta, Canada. Findings emerging from research with grassroots groups that did not explicitly pursue language and culture maintenance were found to offer comparable benefits to participants. Some of the functions identified in these were similar and others were different to those of the core community groups discussed earlier in this chapter. Nevertheless, all were equally relevant to the overall arguments posited here.

9.2.5.1 The Co-Op

As reported in Guardado and Becker (2013), research conducted in 2008 examined the experiences of two Chilean families in relation to the factors contributing to HL development among their children. The families lived for two decades in a housing co-operative (The Co-Op) that had been built as a result of efforts by Chilean exiles in the city of Edmonton. According to the study participants, The Co-Op became a mini-version of Chile in the middle of the city and as such, offered them a sense of place and belonging in diaspora. What they derived from the group, however, went much further and had special meaning for residents of all generations. For adults, it provided continuous opportunities for the open use of their language and for socializing their children into the cultural orientations and other elements that were important to them. The Co-Op was important for the children as it helped them feel part of a close-knit community that embraced them and cared for them as their own when their parents were unavailable due to work or other commitments. Given these community cultural practices, it is not surprising that the ties the children developed with their neighbours were stronger than the ones they had with their kin in Chile. The surrogate family relationships they formed were explicitly named by the participants who stated in interviews that these community members became their aunts and uncles (Guardado and Becker 2013). Thus, while growing up, the children reportedly experienced different types of ethnocultural discovery that gradually shaped their sense of ethnic self as adults. During their life in The Co-Op, the two families reported having the opportunity to naturally and collectively engage in a sort of language socialization that for immigrant minorities in general is only possible within the home domain.

9.2.5.2 REPARA

In a recent study on heritage language development, Becker (2013) examined the experiences of several Chilean community members in Edmonton, two of whom belonged to a grassroots organization, *Recordar para Actuar* (REPARA). This group was formed by second- and third-generation activist youth whose families came from Chile as exiles in the early 1970s. The main goal for founding the group was to document the progressive political culture and activities of the first generation, which included the study participants' own parents and grandparents. It has been documented in a number of studies that Chilean exiles in the 1980s and 1990s engaged in significant work for the Chilean solidarity movement internationally (Paredes 2003, Simalchik 2006) as well as in Canada (Baeza 2004, del Pozo 2006, Ginieniewicz and Schugurensky 2006, Landolt, Goldring and Bernhard 2009, Shayne 2009, Palacios 2011). With this body of scholarly work as a backdrop, Becker's research zoomed in on the ways two second and third generation descendants of exiles described Chilean culture, their positioning in relation to this conceptualization, and the role their community involvement played in their HL attitudes and practices.

The culture with which these participants identified was more similar to the one their parents knew when still in Chile in the early 1970s—aspects of which they brought with them to exile—as opposed to the contemporary culture they found when visiting Chile at different points in their own lives. More concretely, however, participants related to the "refugee culture" narratives in the midst of which they were socialized and which eventually "became the pulse of their diaspora identities" (Guardado and Becker 2013: 65). This locally constructed way of identifying was reportedly part of the motivation for founding the group, and at the same time, their diasporic identities were enhanced and fostered by their engagement in REPARA. Therefore, their openly political work in this grassroots group served a deeper purpose beyond documenting the solidarity movement activities of their senior relatives and raising awareness of their significance. Their identity seemed rooted in the local community, which included the Chilean refugee culture that evolved in Edmonton. Their group participation served as a means to accessing members of that refugee culture with whom they interacted in a variety of Spanish that in some ways was frozen in time in their diasporic community. As with the other groups analyzed in this chapter, REPARA served an important function in the validation, re-creation, and shaping of the participants' identities.

9.2.6 Motivations for starting the groups

The main motivation for the founders of El Centro de Cultura and La Casa Amistad in creating these groups arose largely out of the fear that members of the new generation would grow up without speaking the language of one of their parents. Indeed, both of the families that headed up these groups consisted of intercultural/interlingual marriages, dramatically diminishing the opportunities for heritage language transmission in the home. The need to seek out opportunities for language practice, especially in a naturalistic context, was therefore cited by these leaders (and most of the families) as an important reason for their participation in the group. El Grupo Scout Vistas was the only one of the three British Columbia groups whose founding motives were not first and foremost language transmission—at least in my interpretation of the participants' perspectives. As mentioned above, the initial motivation for breaking away from Scouts Canada was due to philosophical differences, but it was also due to cultural differences as one of the founders, Mr. Maradiaga, explained: "... la solución es simple, la creación de un grupo scout de estructura latina: nosotros ... nosotros tenemos diferencias culturales abismales con ellos. Entonces y tenemos la concepción del escultismo desde otro punto de vista" [... the solution is simple, [which is] the creation of a Scout group with a Latin American structure: we ... we have fundamental cultural differences with them. And we have a Scouting conception from a different perspective] (Interview: 11/05/05). Regarding their second motivation, social change, they felt that "El aporte del grupo es la formación de niños para que después como adolescentes, jóvenes adultos y como adultos puedan ser útiles a la sociedad" [The group's contribution is forming children, who later as adolescents, young adults, and adults, can be useful to society] (Mr. Maradiaga, Interview: 11/05/05).

The group's third motivation revolves around the transmission of language and culture. What is interesting about this group, however, is that this transmission took place under the larger scouting umbrella; by definition, the role of the Scout group was to pursue goals related to community service, environmental awareness, and global citizenry. However, the leaders had aims that went beyond the mandate of Scouting. In this sense, the third major reason for starting the group was to contribute to the local Hispanic community, and in order to do so, knowledge of its language and culture(s) was necessary. Mr. Maradiaga and Mrs. Fernández explained how they intended to reach the community and contribute to the recognition and strengthening of the Hispanic culture as well as to the conservation and continuation of the culture and Spanish language in the new generations of Hispanics in the Metro Vancouver area. Thus, within the broader ethical framework of this group, language and culture transmission served a part of the more far-reaching objective of community service and social connectivity—locally and globally.

9.2.7 Motivations for group participation

The main reasons for joining given by the families generally echoed those given by the grassroots group founders for forming the groups. While all of them, regardless of the group in which they participated, had heritage language promotion in common, the parents also identified many other reasons for being part of the groups. For example, they referred to the grassroots groups as spaces where they felt a sense of belonging, where they could "ser como son" [be who they really were], and as places where they could promote social relations, build a social network, and promote family values. Other reasons included fostering in the children a sense of attachment to Spanish and an awareness of the Spanish-speaking world from a young age, so as to ensure that Spanish language and the parents' associated cultures felt natural to the children as they grew up. It was hoped that the achievement of this goal would have positive implications for intergenerational communication with parents and grandparents, and would increase their children's sense of self-esteem and cultural pride. The groups, being extra-domestic, were also desirable because they served as sites of validation where the children could see the heritage language and culture in a familiar context, but one not limited to the home and to single-parent input. Also, as informal to semi-formal, family-oriented community environments, many parents relished in the chance to be a part of their children's learning outside of the home. To a significant extent, the adults interviewed by Becker (Guardado and Becker 2013) in Edmonton also talked about their lives in The Co-Op as children in very similar terms. In the next section, I outline some of the perceived benefits of participation in the groups. As it becomes clear below, the benefits of participation tended to expand upon the original reasons for joining.

9.2.8 Interpreting the role of the grassroots groups

9.2.8.1 Creating language and cultural spaces

The notion of *safe house* is related to Pratt's (1991) concept of *contact zones*. She describes these zones as "social spaces where cultures meet, clash, and grapple with each other, often in contexts of highly asymmetrical power" (23). Therefore, when dominant and marginal cultures meet, they face tensions that arise from their unequal relations of power as well as their potentially disparate cultural value orientations and languages. In the face of these latent conflicts emerging from asymmetrical relations and clashing interactions, or contact zones, Pratt argues that "people need places for healing and mutual recognition, safe houses in which to construct shared understandings, knowledges, claims on the world that they then bring into the contact zone" (36). Some immigrants in multicultural societies, regardless of their integration status or level of fluency in their additional languages, may feel unable to completely feel a sense of belonging in their new environments.

Many of the families profiled in this book expressed feelings that evoked the safe house notion when talking about their participation in their respective grassroots groups, where they found a kind of refuge. When describing their experiences in Canada, they alluded to the pain of displacement, the reality of contact zones full of the complexities of living in a new culture, speaking a new language, living without extended family, and attempting to socialize their children to particular cultural values and linguistic behaviours. For instance, mothers referred to the groups as spaces in which they could socialize in Spanish and have the opportunity "para soltarse" [to loosen up] in their own language. Thus, the groups were like safe houses for the parents—particularly for the mothers—where they could express themselves freely, in atmospheres they described as "emotional." For Mrs. Martínez, El Centro de Cultura was a space where its members could be themselves and could express themselves in their mother-tongue. They saw these environments as spaces where their language and cultures were validated and where they could display these cultural elements to their children and socialize them according to their cultural values. Mrs. Aguirre spoke of La Casa Amistad as a place that evoked a feeling of safety, comfort, and nostalgia that her family associated with "la casa de la abuelita" [granny's house] (Interview: 05/14/05), arguably one of the strongest connections to home language in diaspora. Thus, the groups enabled families to successfully foster social relations, form a sense of community, and promote values such as familism, which made it possible for them to provide a more authentic language socialization experience to their children.

There was also a strong sense that these safe houses provided a feeling of connectedness that served a therapeutic function. Mrs. Martinez, quoted above, more closely exemplified this interpretation:

> Las mamás se quieren sentar a platicar, es un *break* y a platicar en su idioma, y como dije la mayoría tienen esposos que hablan otro idioma, entonces tú no te ... cuando tú hablas otro idioma no estás tan relajado como cuando hablas tu idioma porque a mí me dicen "cuando hablas español tu cambias, y cuando hablas inglés eres diferente," así que eso ... eso es otro cosa que te hace ir a estos lugares, aquello de que es para tí, cuando hablas otro idioma, tú te sientes que no casi así ... y cuando hablas tu idioma ... es tan relajado y te sueltas, ademanes y expresiones y lo que sea no, entonces eso para ellos también ... es un-es un momento de- de ser como son, de ser latino y eso es- es otra de las cosas que por lo que la gente va ahí también, y es una lástima que no-que no continúen yendo. (Interview: 04/06/06)

[The mothers want to sit and talk, it's a *break*, and to have a conversation in their language, and as I told you, most of their husbands speak another language, so you don't ... when you speak another language you aren't as relaxed as when you speak your language because people tell me "when you speak Spanish you change, and when you speak English you're different," so that ... that's another thing that makes you go to these places, that which is for you, when you speak another language you feel like no, almost like that ... and when you speak your language ... it's so relaxed and you loosen up, gestures and expressions and what have you, right? So it's the same for them, it's a-it's a moment to-to be the way you are, to be Latin American and that is-is also another reason people go there, and it's a shame that they don't continue going]

As suggested by Mrs. Martínez, Spanish was for them a comfort language, a language that penetrated multifaceted levels of their selves. For Mrs. Martínez, the group benefits had a deeper value, which was the emotional connection that came from the connection to the mother tongue (Hispanic parents participating in Dagenais and Day 1999s study made similar comments). Spanish enabled them to connect to their most intimate part of their identity and allowed them to be who they truly were. It gave them the opportunity to socialize in Spanish, which provided a direct link to their innermost self. As Mrs. Martínez spoke: "... y cuando llegas a esos lugares, te abres, te relajas, te-te quitas lo canadiense y te quedas latino, te quitas como—como sin el pellejo de que te pones todo el tiempo de canadiense ..." [... and when you arrive at those places you open up, you relax, you—you remove the Canadianness and are simply Latin American, you remove as if-as if you don't have the Canadian skin you put on all the time ...] (Interview: 04/06/06). To Mrs. Martínez, being in the group was like stripping herself of the Canadian identity she had carved out of English over the decades, leaving the bare mother-tongue self.

Thus, the participating families constructed social spaces and networks that enabled them "to form bonds, support each other, develop a critical consciousness, and construct subversive cultures" (Canagarajah 2004: 134) through which they resisted assimilation and further facilitated their efforts to socialize their children into their values and practices. However, assuming that just by bringing together people from the same cultural and linguistic background will automatically translate into a safe house would be simplistic. This would ignore the complexities of culture, particularly in the Latin American world where linguistic/dialectal and cultural diversity exist in combination with racial, religious, regional, and other types of diversity. Nonetheless, the participants' voices clearly revealed feelings of being heard, understood, and respected in the safe houses they had created in the grassroots groups. These feelings seemed to be absent in the experiences of other families in my ethnography who spoke of dislocation, but did not take part in any of the grassroots groups.

9.2.8.2 Linguistic and cultural validation

The discourse of validation was rich in the families' conceptualizations of these settings. The safe houses the families had created and the activities they conducted also fulfilled the function of providing an authentic context for Spanish practice and for validating the families' language and cultures. Because the language used in their activities was Spanish, these were important socializing spaces for the children. These grassroots groups provided opportunities for the children to experience linguistic and cultural immersion and to further validate the usefulness of their language. These opportunities were unique in the Vancouver context where Spanish does not enjoy strong ethnolinguistic vitality, but perhaps even more critical for the families in the Edmonton studies where the Hispanic population was drastically smaller—particularly in the 1970s and 1980s. Therefore, the various language and cultural activities conducted by participants or the ones in which they engaged naturally in the course of their informal interactions helped turn these spaces into "agents of linguistic legitimation" (Jaffe 2005: 26).

An example of this legitimation was provided by Mr. Herrera who felt that beyond La Casa Amistad, his children's opportunities to practice and become meaningfully involved in a Spanish-rich context were low. His family did not have an extended family circle to provide an authentic context for language practice, and the only opportunity to access such linguistic resources was La Casa Amistad. In the same vein, Mrs. Pérez felt that El Centro de Cultura gave her the opportunity to provide her children with an authentic context for Spanish practice and validation. She stated: "Veo que es muy bueno que mis niños vean que hay otras personas que hablan español aparte de mí" [I am aware that it's good for my children to see that there are other people, besides me, who speak Spanish] (Interview: 05/12/06). Many parents constructed a similar discourse and asserted that it was essential for them to show their children that Spanish was a useful language and that there was a whole world out there where Spanish was the medium of communication. Others, like Mrs. Aguirre and Mr. Ramírez, who provided rich Spanish socialization at home to their children, wanted to go further by also immersing their children in a context where they could have a consistent Spanish socialization experience that went beyond what they experienced at home or during their annual trips to Mexico.

My analyses of these grassroots groups indicate that in contexts where Spanish does not enjoy a high status, families that have enough social, linguistic, and cultural capital (Bourdieu 1977) at their disposal can exert their agency in order to offset the potential linguistic devaluing effect of the wider society. It has been argued that linguistic-minority families' cultural practices may contrast greatly with those of the larger context (Pease-Alvarez 2002). In the so-called mainstream society often the language of minorities is not valued, has no use, or both, and their cultural values clash with those of the dominant populace. The parents' views about the role of the grassroots groups as socializing agents and as spaces for reiterating the value of Spanish to their children highlight the role that this valorization may play as a critical prerequisite in minority-language transmission (Li 1999). The families' perspectives reflect an attempt to resist assimilative forces prevalent in the schools as well as in the broader community and were constructed as strongly oppositional.

9.2.8.3 Social relations

Familism also displayed strong connections to language and culture development and maintenance. Given that most of the study participants were immigrants who had no blood relatives in Canada, cultivating social relations was an important goal in their lives. Most group members interviewed stated they had established close relationships with other members. As Mrs. Aguirre spoke about La Casa Amistad: "La parte más fuerte del grupo es la parte social" [The most powerful aspect of the group is the social aspect] (Interview: 05/04/06). Like other parents, she also referred to her group as a special space where the way of relating with each other was "muy latina" [very Latin] and that the expression of feelings came more naturally. Despite their seemingly successful integration into the broader society, many families still felt more comfortable interacting with people that shared much of their cultural background and experiences, and their groups seemed to provide such a space. Additionally, group attendance was seen as a "leisure activity" by many parents. They often commented that part of the reason the grassroots groups fulfilled such a function was the symbolic and physical space that was created and the propensity of that space to cultivate friendships among the participants. It is clear that the families valued social relations highly as a strong socializing factor in the linguistic and moral development of their children and in the well-being of the whole family unit.

As indicated earlier, many Vancouver families who did not join any grassroots groups—even long-term Vancouver residents—expressed feeling disconnected from the wider society and stated that forming close relationships with other Canadians was not easily accomplished. They also shared that cultivating these relationships with other Canadians of Hispanic descent was not as easy as they had expected. They spoke of being on the margins of both cultures while feeling members of neither (Suárez-Orozco 1993). This was in part due to the diffuse nature of this population in Vancouver, and in Canada in general. Numerous participants spoke of feelings of frustration and isolation and in some cases, a strong feeling of physically living in Canada, but keeping more in touch with the social reality in their countries of origin. However, families that were able to create or join existing social networks, and therefore cultivate close friendships, particularly with other Spanish-speaking families, felt that these social systems played a crucial role in their lives, especially given their lack of extended family. They also felt these affiliations provided various types of support and became important language socialization agencies for their families in their efforts to transmit their language and cultures.

Since Hispanic immigrants in Canada may see other fellow Hispanics in their communities as their extended family (Suárez-Orozco 1993), based on my analysis, I argue that families that participated in grassroots groups created spaces where they promoted values such as familism and saw aspects of family attachment, including family solidarity and family involvement, as key in the development and maintenance of their home language. Inspired by Sabogal et al.'s (1987) definition of familism and based on extensive iterative cross-case analyses, I propose the term *diasporic familism* to explain unique attitudinal, affective, and behavioural features displayed by participants in immigrant grassroots groups. My notion of diasporic familism refers to the set of close family-like ties that evolve among non-kin individuals and families living in diaspora. In the absence of blood relatives, core groups are formed by individuals and families in which members rely on each other for the types of solidarity, mutual support, and other forms of reciprocity that are traditionally found in nuclear families. This definition shares characteristics with the sense of community construct, particularly in relation to the feelings that families experience in these alternative activity settings. Furthermore, most study participants defined themselves in relation to membership in large families. They longed for the support they were used to receiving from family members, saw their families as resources for heritage language exposure and as sources of support for language and cultural maintenance, and as one of the main motivations for striving to achieve these goals (as language development and maintenance in the children fostered intergenerational communication and relationships). Not having such benefit was stressful and a source of sadness for some of the parents and their children, many of whom actively sought out proxy family relationships.

Additionally, family values, communication as well as language development and maintenance were clearly interrelated for all the families. The majority of the families, especially those without relatives living near them, spoke of a deep family emptiness that became excruciating during key periods of their adaptation in Canada and under certain circumstances thereafter (e.g., personal and family crises). Mrs. Aguirre, for instance, reported experiencing pain when the family immigrated to Canada because of the lack of the family support that she was used to in Mexico. However, because their nuclear family had become members and active participants in La Casa Amistad, the whole family seemed to consider the group as a *surrogate extended family*.

9.3 Parallels across communities

There are many commonalities between the roles of Black churches and other community-based groups when compared to the grassroots organizations described in this chapter, both in Alberta and in British Columbia. Just as Black churches have been described as a bridge connecting individuals with a larger group (McRae, Carey and Anderson-Scott 1998), the Hispanic grassroots groups are social organizations that are based on the desire for language and culture socialization. These grassroots groups are a bridge that connects families to a larger group who share a similar culture as well as language beliefs, values, and practices. The existence of supportive social networks has been an essential resource and a source of resilience for African Americans, largely through churches, but also in relation to other groups. Both the HL development grassroots groups and the Black churches have provided their members with material, emotional, and psychological forms of support. These groups have provided safe environments—safe houses—where members feel a sense of belonging. In this manner such supportive and non-threatening environments have functioned like extended families for both types of groups. In them, they have found a refuge from physical subjugation as well as otherwise perceived oppressive or highly assimilative forces, where they have enjoyed feelings of safety, comfort, self-respect, and nostalgia. Both for Black church members and for Hispanic HL development group participants, these extended families have helped them validate themselves as individuals and as valued members of their communities.

In contrast to the founding motivations of the Black Churches, most of the grassroots groups described in this book had as their primary objective the transmission of Spanish language and Hispanic culture(s) to their children. Upon close examination, however, many of the benefits of participation in these groups mirrored or approximated those experienced by members of Black Churches. For example, the community service activities conducted by the members of El Grupo Scout Vistas echoed the "giving back" to the community attitudes of Black Church members reported by McRae et al. (1998). Other commonalities between both types of settings include the transmission of cultural awareness, values, and pride, a sense of cultural relatability, safe houses, and the creation of extended families among members. Insofar as grassroots community groups can facilitate the creation of extended family-like situations, parallels can be drawn between Hispanic immigrants in Canada (e.g., in Vancouver and Edmonton) and Black Church members whose original family support networks often were reportedly in other parts of the United States. Also, just as "Black churches provide a sense of achievement and worth by involving [African Americans] in roles that are valued and respected and that may not be available in the dominant society" (McRae, Carey and Anderson-Scott 1998: 786), the psychological benefits (e.g., increased self-esteem, cultural validation) that Hispanic families, and especially youth, derived from participation in the Canadian grassroots groups arguably provided fertile soil for language development and maintenance.

9.4 Grassroots groups as primary communities

Building on the growing body of scholarship in the area of sense of community (e.g. Sarason 1974, Heller 1989, Smith 1991, Mankowski and Rappaport 1995) as well as on their own research, Sonn and Fisher (1998) explain that even though individuals typically belong to various groups, which provide some of the material for their sense of community, they are also grounded in a primary community, which "is the one that provides the values, norms, stories, myths, and a sense of historical continuity" (461). They posit that because ethnic groups are sources of cultural knowledge, which we may understand as values, beliefs, behaviours, and ways of meaning-making, these groups play the role of primary communities. It is conceptualized, then, that the grassroots community groups that are the focus of this chapter, also constitute primary communities for the Hispanic families and their children that participated in the group activities.

The individual and familial benefits that members of these primary communities derived from their participation were multiple and broad-reaching. In addition to the core objectives of the groups in relation to language, culture as well as identity development and maintenance, some of the benefits that resulted from the resourcefulness of the groups worked at a superficial, albeit important, level in terms of material support in the fulfillment of everyday needs. Members also benefited from the different dimensions of the diasporic familism that was fostered, particularly in the feelings of solidarity, loyalty, and reciprocity they developed. One of the strongest forms of support appeared to be the sense of empowerment they felt in the groups. I posit that a validated or empowered person is more likely to promote speaking their stigmatized and possibly unsupported minority language and encourage its continued use with their children.

Echoing the theory postulated by McMillan and Chavis (1986), these grassroots groups clearly displayed several of the elements that are central to a sense of community. Membership in the grassroots groups was an important aspect of the family members' feelings of interconnectedness. The group members also appeared to influence the group activities and the roles of other members through their active participation and at the same time, participants were influenced by the dynamics of the groups in a variety of ways. McMillan and Chavis argue that these forms of influence are important to the development of a sense of community in groups. Both in material and affective senses, the groups also provided their members with support in the fulfillment of needs. Similarity of experiences among members has been described as central to the integrative role in community, and this is something that both brought members together and kept them together. Finally, McMillan and Chavis posit that a shared emotional connection is the definitive factor in a true sense of community and this is perhaps one of the strongest threads found in the grassroots groups examined in this chapter.

9.5 Chapter summary

In this chapter, I have highlighted some of the many functions of community in HL development by looking at examples from my ethnographic study of Hispanics in Vancouver as well as summarizing two studies conducted in Edmonton. When researching HL development, it is important to see the family as part of community and to understand both social levels as being engaged in a dynamic and reciprocal process. In this sense, while often overlooked, the community and its functions can be just as fruitful a social unit of analysis in HL development situations as the family.

Because the role of grassroots community groups has only recently been recognized and not examined in much depth in HL development studies, it is useful to draw comparisons with the benefits of community groups to other minority communities, such as members of the Black Church in the United States. Looking to these more established groups which have received some scholarly attention also sheds light on useful factors to consider when beginning to look at the effects of grassroots groups on HL development; for instance, Mays' reminder that socio-historical contexts need to be taken into consideration in examinations of this type is an important point. The social, emotional, psychological, material, and other benefits of participation in groups which older studies have identified help to orient examinations of the role of grassroots community groups in HL development.

Looking at the fundamental functions of Hispanic participation in grassroots groups is reinforced and supported by their common cultural value of familism. The grassroots groups examined in this book provided near-ideal sites where the expression of familism was welcome and natural. In turn, this value stood a better chance or at least added another avenue of HL socialization for the children. Based on my analyses of several exemplar grassroots community groups, in this chapter I have proposed the term of diasporic familism to refer to the set of close family-like ties that evolve among immigrants. In the absence of blood relatives, core groups are formed by these individuals and families in which members rely on each other for the types of solidarity, mutual support, and other forms of reciprocity that are traditionally found in nuclear families. Benefits specific to the Vancouver grassroots groups included contextualizing and validating the HL outside of the home or biological family circles; time set aside for HL literacy activities; exposing their children to the cultural and dialectal/linguistic diversity in the Hispanic community in Vancouver among many others shared by participants.

Importantly, these spaces were found to be prominent in all the discourses of HL as introduced in Chapter 6. What grassroots group participation meant for the parents and their children was evidently present in the discourses they produced. Notably, these discourses were full of ideological statements about the languages in the lives of their children and how this linguistic interaction impacted their socialization processes. The way families that participated in grassroots groups constructed HL development discursively suggested that their heritage language and culture aspirations were closely tied to their experiences with other group members. This I believe is a substantial indication that community, however it is defined, is a central aspect of HL development for families and as such should also be an important dimension of analysis in these investigations.

10 Family language and literacy practices

10.1 Introduction

Community and family have long been seen as inextricably interdependent in HL development pursuits. The bonds of community and family together are so influential that Fishman wrote they are the "real secret weapon" (Fishman 1991: 458). Whereas community plays a centrally supportive role in the well-being of families and individuals, and consequently in their ability to realize their HL development goals, the family domain is the locus for heritage language continuity *par excellence*. Therefore, this is the first of a three-chapter series in which I introduce, describe, analyze, interpret, and discuss key policies, concepts, and practices that impact on language development and maintenance. In this chapter, I first address some general matters of concern to family activities. Then, I describe significant practices through revealing cases drawn from two different studies. These cases range from relatively unsuccessful home language practices leading to language loss in one family, to several highly successful cases utilizing a variety of strategies to pursue the development of ethnic identity, oral language proficiency, literacy, critical thinking, as well as the transmission and continuation of family and cultural values.

10.2 The home context and heritage language development

As has been emphasized in previous chapters, the language and culture ideologies that families espouse can be expected to have a strong impact on the home language policies that are implemented and the language practices that emerge. In other words, the language use choices that parents and children make have immense consequences for their future ability to communicate well, especially at more complex levels. For the immigrant family, being surrounded by the hegemonic forces and assimilative discourses of the dominant society often requires that the family make a tremendous effort to resist these forces in order to preserve their minority language and culture—at least in the home domain. In Canada, where there are virtually no large concentrations of certain ethnolinguistic groups, such as Hispanics, or regular waves of HL newcomers that would facilitate a more natural or unstructured development and maintenance of the language, families must pay special attention to creating frequent and engaging activities that necessitate the use the HL for participation.

Many studies have highlighted the roles of language socialization activities on HL development (Field 2001, Ochs 2002, Nonaka 2004, Garrett 2005, Friedman

2006, Howard 2008, Ochs and Schieffelin 2008) and have examined ways in which ethnolinguistic minority families and their communities use innovative techniques to encourage their children to use the HL. One of the common threads throughout successful language socialization strategies appears to be the children's level of enjoyment of the activity; fun makes children unaware of their learning process and therefore is an integral part of what could be called a "natural" (subconscious) socialization process. Moreover, most games, musical activities, and other types of activities that are commonly found in HL community groups have a moderate to strong social component. As was alluded to in Chapter 9, peer-group membership plays a central role in child and adolescent inclination toward HL development. However, when peer-groups are united and validated through gratifying language socialization activities, it would seem that the benefits of the activities are multiplied. The understanding of "enjoyment" may depend on individual factors such as age and interests. Younger children, for instance, might be more engaged by playful activities such as painting or arts and crafts, whereas older children might prefer more challenging or even "school-like work" such as that found in some of the grassroots groups. What seems to be important is the provision of engaging opportunities for enjoying explicit language socialization activities and generating interest in children to participate. Obviously, the activities in and of themselves are secondary, as there is no *panacea* activity that will ensure successful HL development.

In the remainder of this chapter, I summarize five case study families emerging from two different qualitative projects conducted several years apart. Through these cases, I attempt to draw attention to family circumstances, policies, and practices that impact language development and maintenance in different ways. The first case serves to briefly exemplify outcomes on the less successful end of the HL development spectrum. The other four cases highlight factors, characteristics, and strategies on the other end of this continuum.

10.2.1 A mother's lonely struggle

The central participant of this case is Lisa, a 33-year old divorced mother of three children who had supported herself from the time she was a teenager in her home country. Lisa's family had lived in Vancouver since 1991 after arriving from El Salvador. Lisa took part in a multiple case study I conducted in 2001 (see Guardado 2002, 2006) during which I made several visits to her home. During my visits, I noticed that the children tended to rely heavily on television and video games for entertainment. Apparently, watching television was one of the few activities in which they engaged together as a family. I also observed that the children spoke English all the time, to Lisa and to one another. In our conversations I heard a very frustrated parent. Lisa was outspoken and showed irritation with her children's language situation, particularly their lack of proficiency in Spanish and the strong forces of assimilation outside the home. The children only spoke in English in and outside the home. She talked at length about how her children, Dolores aged 7, Tony aged 9, and Francisco aged 13, had great difficulty understanding and speaking Spanish. She described in much detail how the children had significant weaknesses in Spanish in terms of syntax, lexis, and pronunciation: "Pues el vocabulario en español es muy limitado. La pronunciación también es mitad inglés y mitad español. La pronunciación definitivamente que les causa muchos problemas y la verdad que ninguno de ellos puede leer o escribir en español" [Their Spanish vocabulary is very limited. Much of their pronunciation is also half Spanish and half English. Pronunciation definitely gives them many problems and none of them knows how to read or write in Spanish] (Lisa, Interview: 06/15/01).

She explained that their understanding of spoken Spanish was poor and their literacy was nonexistent, and because of this lack of proficiency, they refused to speak it and were therefore losing the HL. It is unclear, however, whether there was a cause-effect relationship or simply a correlation as their refusal to speak Spanish might have been due to other factors. Regardless, the language situation at that time was stressful and disappointing for Lisa, who according to her own account, was trying hard to raise her children bilingually. This quote addresses the language use patterns at home: "Ahorita hablan en inglés todo el tiempo ... yo les hablo en español y ellos me contestan en inglés. Entienden, pero no lo quieren hablar. El inglés es definitivamente mejor que el español" [Right now they speak English all the time ... I speak Spanish to them and they respond in English. They understand it, but are reluctant to speak it. Their English is definitely much better than their Spanish] (Lisa, Interview: 06/15/01). Lisa's words echoed those of other participants whose children had also embraced English as their dominant language. Such parents had described their children's efforts to use the HL, but these efforts had only allowed them to produce what they often referred to as "a deteriorated Spanish." Lisa stated that her children, on the other hand, not only refused or were unable to produce any significant amount of Spanish, but had difficulty understanding her words. This reality was exacerbated by several factors, including having only one parent to model the HL, being born and raised in Vancouver without ever visiting their mother's country of origin, and also their circle of so-called Spanish-speaking friends with whom they only interacted in English. Additionally, Lisa was quite proficient in English, a situation the children seemed to take full advantage of in all home interactions.

Frustratingly for Lisa, Hispanic friends did not seem to provide any advantages to her children in terms of heritage language practice because they spoke

English with them: "Tienen amigos latinos. El problema es que solo se hablan en inglés. Yo lo que creo es que estan perdiendo el español porque casi solo pasan afuera de la casa y allá siempre estan hablando inglés" [They have some Latin friends. The problem is that they speak English among themselves, too. I believe that the reason they're losing Spanish is because they're outside the house most of the time and all their friends speak English] (Lisa, Interview: 06/15/01). Lisa often stated that she felt alone in the struggle to transmit the language, as everyone outside the home spoke English, making it so much more difficult. She expressed frustration at making efforts to foster Spanish at home, only to see the entire broader community speaking English, effectively hampering her efforts.

10.2.2 The role of family intimacy

The same year, I also conducted a case study with Carmen, a single mother from Colombia. She was happy to talk about her Vancouver-born, 17-year-old daughter Fay's heritage language development and maintenance. In sharp contrast with Lisa's feelings, Carmen was enthusiastic about her daughter's language abilities and talked at length about their linguistic lives, from the time Fay was born. It soon became clear that the special moments that mother and daughter had shared together, bonding through a variety of activities focused on children's literature, music, song, dance, poetry, arts, and story telling had been highly significant in fostering the heritage language. Carmen described these activities as the most treasured in her heart and the most influential in her daughter's HL development. She stated: "... leíamos cuentos infantiles en español. Tenía yo música infantil en español de diferentes países de Latinoamérica, la cual escuchábamos con frecuencia" [... we would read children's stories in Spanish. I also had children's songs in Spanish from different Latin American countries, which we listened to very frequently] (Carmen, Interview: 05/31/01).

Therefore, for Carmen, her socialization project consisted of much more than a strong desire for her daughter to maintain the heritage language. It also went beyond attempts to persuade her daughter to use Spanish at home. One of the strongest discourses produced in her characterization of her ideologies and experiences with language with her daughter was that of affect. Moreover, the *pride* meta-discourse cluster seemed to dominate (see Chapter 8 for a discussion of this meta-discourse). Therefore, affect, identity, and cohesiveness were spoken of frequently. Additionally, an unexpected outcome of focusing strongly on arts, pop culture, and literature was the fact that Fay developed L1 literacy on her own. Carmen stated: "Un día ella me dijo, 'mami déjame te lea esto.' Yo casi me caigo para atrás. '¿Pero quien te enseñó?' le pregunté. Ella aprendió sola. Ella se autoenseñó a leer en español. Tanto era su interés en el idioma" [One day she said to me, 'mommy, let me read this to you.' I just about fainted. 'Who taught you?' I asked. She had taught herself. Such was her interest in the language]. Additionally, Fay had clearly been strongly attached to her culture, and Carmen believed that it had been one of the most important factors in her daughter's maintenance of the language: "Yo creo que yo no puedo apartar la parte afectiva del idioma, que definitivamente creo que es lo que más ha influenciado para que esta niña no haya perdido el idioma" [I don't think I can separate the affective aspect from the language, and I definitely think that's what has had the most influence on her language maintenance] (Interview: 05/31/01).

To Carmen, as decried by Lisa earlier in the chapter, the lack of a larger ethnolinguistic community was a significant hurdle in transmitting the home language and culture: "En los últimos 12 años, yo he sido su contacto principal con el español" [In the last 12 years, I have been her main contact with Spanish]. She realized that the opportunities for heritage language practice provided by the home were limited, given that she was the only parent, but also emphasized the need to take advantage of the few opportunities that the home provided for language use and transmission: "Tiene que utilizarse ciento por ciento en una forma en que se utiliza diariamente, como se utilizaría si viviéramos en nuestro país de origen" [It has to be used widely in all aspects of daily life, as if we lived in our own country]. She remarked, like Lisa, that having Latin American friends did not provide any advantages in terms of heritage language practice because all the children spoke English among themselves. Despite the absence of a large L1 community in Vancouver, Fay had developed a high level of proficiency in Spanish. Carmen attributed Fay's accomplishments to several factors. In part, she attributed her success to her attachment to the culture through her frequent visits to places associated with the Latin American culture (i.e., Montreal, where Carmen's brother lived with his family; Miami, where they had other relatives). As she stated: "El contacto con mi familia materna fue muy importante para mantener el español. También el hecho de que nosotros viajamos todos los años ya sea a Miami o a alguna región donde hay algún familiar que habla español o conexión latina. También yo creo que eso influyó en su idioma. Para ella fue muy natural continuar con el español" [The contact with my maternal family has been very important in maintaining the language. Also the fact that we travel to Miami or other places where there's some kind of connection with Latin America, like a relative that speaks Spanish, had an impact on her language. It was very natural for her to maintain Spanish] (Interview: 05/31/01).

Thus, the extended family played a key role in HL development for them. Extended family members had helped expose Fay to language and culture in an important way, and in some instances, she had been able to almost completely immerse herself in a Latin American-like setting, even in places like Miami or Montreal, just because of her close kinship relationships in those cities. As was the case with the families discussed in the previous chapter in relation to diasporic familism, Carmen saw her family as a resource for home language exposure and sources of support for language and cultural maintenance, and as one of the main motivations for striving to achieve those goals. Perhaps Fay also felt attached to her family members, even though all of them lived thousands of miles away, and embraced the home language as a family connection and as a way of having access to them and to what they represented in her life. Carmen stated that at least every other year, Fay had the opportunity to visit family in Colombia, Montreal or Miami, in addition to family members visiting Vancouver.

According to Carmen, more than anything, the construction of a unique space for mother-daughter interaction, mediated by Spanish language and culture, appeared to have played a crucial role in the development of the language use patterns and identity of her daughter. Additionally, the exposure to positive Latin American role models with whom Fay could identify undoubtedly played an important role. Importantly, the ability of her mother to provide her with opportunities to be in touch with part of her roots, albeit in geographically distant places, was a privilege to which many families do not have access.

10.2.3 "Language injections"

Mrs. Aguirre and Mr. Ramírez were middle-aged professionals from Mexico. They took part in my extended ethnography—many years after the first two cases described above—along with their three daughters: Perla, Florencia and Penelope (ages 2, 5, and 6 at the beginning of the study). They were a somewhat privileged, transnational family living in an affluent neighbourhood in Metro Vancouver, Canada. Having studied in a private bilingual school from kindergarten to grade 12, Mr. Ramírez was already fluent in English when he arrived. When the girls moved to Canada at the ages of two and a half and four (the youngest was born in Canada), they already spoke Spanish well. The family attributed the relative ease with which they learned English to the fact that they already had a solid foundation in their L1. Mrs. Aguirre remembered that shortly after their arrival, people in Vancouver started to question their decision to still speak Spanish to the girls, but apparently, the parents were immovable in their stance: "Pueden decir misa, pero nosotros vamos a seguir detrás de que ellas sigan hablando el español" [People can lecture us, but we are going to

10.2 The home context and heritage language development

continue emphasizing they keep speaking Spanish] (Interview: 05/14/05). The family made a deliberate and firm decision to create and maintain a rich Spanish language socialization milieu in which the girls could develop their Spanish language and literacy abilities.

In general, the family maintained a Spanish-only policy at home, but this was not enforced at all times. As is the case in many immigrant families, a combination of both languages was often used. Mrs. Aguirre and Mr. Ramírez spoke Spanish to the girls all the time. The girls spoke Spanish back to them most of the time. Among themselves, Florencia and Perla tended to use English—especially during play—although they were often reminded to use Spanish. With Penelope, however, the girls tended to use Spanish because otherwise—they explained—she did not understand them. These language patterns were affected by variables such as the time of year, the interactants, and the context. For instance, it was not unusual for them to start speaking in English to Mrs. Aguirre right after school, because according to her, they still had not "... cambiado el casete en sus cerebros" [... changed the tape in their brains]. This was especially so when there had been a significant incident that the girls were excited about and wanted to relate it to their parents quickly.

The family had created a strong Spanish-language environment and often engaged in explicit activities to promote the language at home. However, their most significant shared activity seemed to be an annual visit to Mexico. They saw this as an exceptional situation for the family to spend time with their large extended family there; it was an opportunity that many other families with similar HL development goals did not enjoy. For them, it was a regular routine that for the past five years—almost as long as the girls' lives—they had taken them at the same time, to the same place, to do the same thing: spend time with the family. It was an event that the girls anticipated with excitement and it was also by far the most important mechanism for the girls' HL development. In an interview with the girls about their language behaviour, the topic of Mexico came up unexpectedly (Martín=interviewer):

```
[Excerpt 10.1]
Florencia:   ¿y te digo porque me gusta más México?=
Martín:      ¿porqué?
Florencia:   ¿que aquí?
Martín:      si
Florencia:   porque
Perla:       allí
Florencia:   allí tengo a todos mis primos
```

```
Translation
Florencia: Can I tell you why I like Mexico better?
Martin:    why?
Florencia: than here?
Martin:    yes
Florencia: because
Perla:     there
Florencia: I have all my cousins there
```

What led to their comments about Mexico was a question about why they thought Spanish would be useful in the future. Florencia offered to reveal why she liked Mexico better, explaining that her cousins lived there. This suggests that the girls had a strong connection and affiliation to their family in Mexico, which undoubtedly had a strong influence on their socialization to speak Spanish and display a Latin American cultural identity. Therefore, the trips back to the ancestral country represented an essential language development and maintenance strategy and clearly all the family members valued the socialization experiences that these visits provided. These trips, the mother explained, were the centre of their annual language socialization cycle. For them one cycle ended in Mexico and a new one began in Vancouver in September upon their return. The girls' Spanish proficiency was at its highest when they returned and over the following months it slowly decreased, until they received, in Mrs. Aguirre's words, their next "Spanish injection" the following summer. Mrs. Aguirre described the incentives and interest of the girls during their stays in Mexico and the effects of these stays on the girls' Spanish, especially at the end of the cycle when it became a struggle to keep them from switching to English:

> Es como que cada año tienen un curso intensivo nada más de español, porque allá nadie les habla en inglés, nadie. Durante todo el año que estamos aquí, o durante los diez meses que estamos aquí, tú puedes ver el proceso de cómo el español se va quedando atrás. Ahorita ya es pleito. Ahorita ya es reto. Aquí me hablas en español. Yo especialmente les he marcado, en español ... y no te entiendo. Y como ellas saben que yo no hablo bien, entonces para ellas es algo real. Pero como me ven que afuera a veces hablo, me dicen, si entiendes. Entonces les digo, sí, si entiendo, pero si tú no hablas el español yo pido un boleto para México, no pido cuatro. Porque en México nadie te va a entender en inglés. Ese eso es como un incentivo, o a lo mejor amenaza ... para que lo hablen ¿me entiendes? Les encanta, lo están esperando. La pasan muy bien. Quieren hacerlo. (Interview: 05/21/05)

> [It is as though every year they take an intensive course solely in Spanish because there nobody speaks to them in English. Nobody. During the whole year when we are here, or during the ten months we are here, you can see the process through which Spanish gets left behind. Now it is problematic. It is a challenge.

"Here, you speak to me in Spanish." I have especially emphasized it to them, in Spanish ... "and I do not understand." And since they know I do not speak [English] well, for them it is real. But, since they see I sometimes speak when we are out they say, "you do understand." So, I say, "yes, yes, I understand, but if you do not speak in Spanish I will only get one ticket to Mexico, not four [Mr. Ramírez often stayed behind working or joined them at a later time]. Because in Mexico nobody will understand you in English." It is like an incentive, or perhaps a threat ... so that they speak it, do you know what I mean? They love it; they are looking forward to it. They have a great time. They want to do it]

Mrs. Aguirre recalled an incident soon after their arrival in Mexico that year when Florencia and Perla had gotten into an argument, in English. She witnessed the whole exchange, but did not understand what had happened. She asked the girls and, still in the excitement of the moment, they tried to relate in Spanish what each had said to the other and it proved quite confusing. Perla reacted by turning to Florencia and saying: "Mejor peleemos en español de nuevo" [We had better fight again in Spanish] (Interview: 10/16/05), ending the conflict with her comment. Upon their return in September, they were still having their arguments in Spanish. There was no doubt that the girls had a high level of Spanish proficiency and seemed comfortable switching between Spanish and English.

Having spent a significant period of time with the family as an ethnographer,[1] I can attest to the language proficiency of the girls, which was observed to be high. This was further corroborated through elicited and collected spoken and written language samples in both languages. Their Spanish literacy did not seem to be age-appropriate, but sufficiently comprehensible. Both Mrs. Aguirre and Mr. Ramírez stated that their goal was for the girls to develop a reasonable level of literacy:

> Es una habilidad fácil de perder. Aunque no lo hables, siempre lo vas a entender. El segundo nivel es que además lo puedas hablar. Pero el hecho que lo puedas hablar no necesariamente implica que lo vas a poder escribir. Entonces, esa es la tercera habilidad y que queremos buscar que no se pierda. (Mr. Ramírez, Interview: 05/14/05)

> [It is an ability that is easily lost. Even if you do not speak it, you will always understand it. The second level is that you can also speak it. But the fact that you can speak it does not necessarily imply that you will be able to write it. Therefore, that is the third ability and we would like for it not to be lost]

They made it clear that they wanted their children to understand it, speak it, and write it, and that it was with writing that they had the most trouble. They felt that it was easy to lose writing ability and for that reason they wanted to emphasize this area. The family seemed quite confident about the girls' maintenance of the language, but appeared to view literacy as the "final frontier" to conquer.

---

[1] Officially 18 months, but informally, about 24 months.

10.2.4 Family literacy and the role of transnationalism

The Ruedas-Blanco parents, Mrs. Natalia Ruedas and Mr. Dimas Blanco, were professionals from Peru who moved to Canada in 2001. They were also part of the ethnographic study, along with the previous family and the one that follows. Their children were Graciela, Rogelio, and Olivia (ages 4, 11 and 13 at the beginning of the study). The family had a fairly flexible Spanish-only policy at home. The parents spoke Spanish only, and generally, the children were also encouraged and expected to adhere to this rule. However, in practice it did not always hold. The two older children tended to speak some English to each other, but rarely in a sustained manner. The parents considered them English-dominant and were aware that English was what came naturally to them. They often tended to reply in English, but they were reminded to try to switch to Spanish. Mrs. Ruedas stated that when such instances occurred, the parents "… insistimos en que sea en español aunque se demore más" [insist[ed] that they switch to Spanish even if it takes them longer] (Interview, 03/29/06).

According to their family arrangement, Mrs. Ruedas stayed home and took care of the children's extracurricular activities. Mrs. Ruedas in particular, was the one responsible for supporting the children's Spanish literacy development, and to a lesser degree, also responsible for exposing the children to the language at all times. However, Mr. Blanco always reminded them to focus on Spanish and called from work to check on their language usage. Whenever he called he asked Mrs. Ruedas: "¿Y los niños han escrito algo en español este día?" [Have the children done any writing in Spanish today?] (Mrs. Ruedas, Interview: 05/25/05). Mrs. Ruedas stated that although she was the one involving them in Spanish literacy and oracy activities, it truly was a family endeavour and both parents supported and reminded each other. They felt that if they left it up to the children, they would just switch to English and the Spanish language would be left behind. Therefore, the family pursued their goals even if these entailed a huge mental, emotional, and time commitment.

Olivia and Rogelio regularly exchanged formulaic expressions in English mixed in with Spanish as in "**Hurry up!** Hace rato que te estoy esperando" [Hurry up! I've been waiting for you for so long] (Home observation: 03/29/06). There were times, however, when they engaged in English-only speaking episodes, especially when arguing, but as soon as an adult entered their physical interactional space, they switched to Spanish. This was also true when Graciela, the youngest of the three, happened to be playing in English. The older siblings only spoke in Spanish to Graciela because they claimed that she understood Spanish better—a claim also made by the case family discussed above—but Graciela responded in English to them. To her parents, Graciela only spoke in Spanish and even demanded it from them. Sometimes when they watched movies on DVD, Graciela would tell Mrs. Ruedas: "Ponme como hablo yo" [Put it on the way I speak] (Home observation: 09/28/06), meaning that she wanted to watch the version dubbed in Spanish. The language use patterns in the home exhibited language socialization at different levels. The older children were being socialized by the parents regarding the Spanish-only rule, but this socialization was playing out on another level for Graciela, their younger child, who spoke Spanish to her parents, but answered in English to her older siblings, a likely indication that she was aware that her siblings were English dominant, or a result of her own socialization into the linguistic behaviour of her brother and sister as well as the broader community.

This family made use of several language and literacy development strategies. These strategies often combined oracy and literacy-oriented activities and other times they focused on one particular area. For instance, cooking was an activity that Olivia enjoyed and in which she enthusiastically participated. Mrs. Ruedas explained in the following quote how Olivia took the initiative in this activity:

> Mi hija mayor ya llega por allí y me dice "mami me gustaría aprender a hacer cosas de la cocina", entonces le explico en español y lo entiende y a veces me dice, "pero ¿qué es esto?" y le explico en español y no se lo digo ... a menos que sea un ingrediente que ella nunca ha escuchado en español y le digo "es lo que acá se llama tal cosa" y al final ella lo recoge en su cabeza como español. (Interview: 05/25/05)

> My oldest daughter comes to the kitchen and tells me: "Mommy, I'd like to learn how to make things in the kitchen," so I explain to her in Spanish and she understands and sometimes asks me: "but, what is this?" and I explain it to her in Spanish and I don't tell her in English ... unless it's an ingredient that she's never heard in Spanish and I tell her: "it's what here is called such and such a name" and in the end she picks it up in her head in Spanish]

Mrs. Ruedas saw this as an opportunity to teach her daughter vocabulary related to cooking and to explicitly socialize her into using Spanish in another domain of language use.

Other home language activities involved the whole family. About nine months after my initial home visit the family subscribed to a satellite television service. Mrs. Ruedas explained that part of the purpose for this acquisition was to expose the children to television programming in Spanish. Their provider was *Telelatino* (TLNTV), which offered Italian and Spanish language programming. Mrs. Ruedas and Olivia enjoyed watching Spanish *telenovelas* (short soap operas) together and the whole family watched a variety of shows ranging from newscasts to talk and game shows. The children seemed to enjoy the programs. When I asked Mrs. Ruedas whether the children ever made negative comments about the Latin

American programming, contrasting it with the North American one, she stated that both parents actively promoted the children's interest in the shows. She felt that as with everything related to the Latin American culture, parents needed to be "... creativos para que los niños tengan ese interés, sino nunca vas a poder [hacer] que acepten y que les guste" [... creative so children become interested, otherwise you'll never get them to accept it and to like it] (Interview: 05/25/05).

Mrs. Ruedas looked for ways of exposing the children to Spanish on an ongoing basis, so she often took advantage of special occasions and events such as Easter. Although in Peru it was not customary to celebrate *Easter* with *Easter Egg* hunts, she liked to incorporate it into their activities, but with a pedagogical purpose. In the quote below she explained how she designed the activity:

> Yo les hago pistas, como buscar un tesoro y a cada uno le hago diferentes pistas y les escribo todo en español. "¿Que es lo que más te gusta comer?" por ejemplo. Si hay uno que le gusta la pasta, entonces donde guardo la pasta, allí escondo el huevito. Es una manera de que lean el español y ... siempre trato de que de alguna manera estén expuestos ¿no? (Interview: 05/25/05)

> [I give them clues to find a treasure and prepare special clues for each one and I write them in Spanish, for example: "What do you like to eat the most?" If one of them likes pasta, for instance, then I hide the egg in the area of the cupboards where I store the pasta. It's a way for them to read Spanish ... I always try to expose them to Spanish somehow]

They also used to have some type of literacy activity at home at least once a week, but Mrs. Ruedas lamented that unfortunately it was not always possible. Their family in Peru regularly sent them materials in Spanish such as books and comics, which they used for literacy-related activities. One activity they often conducted was having the children copy texts from Spanish books in order to practice writing and to increase their vocabulary. Other times the children read a book in English and talked about it in Spanish. All in all, Mrs. Ruedas was always looking for family activities that provided the children with practice in Spanish language and literacy. She explained that "en la casa tienes que ser creativo con el español: danzas, canciones, juegos, etc. Puede ser divertido para los chicos y a la vez ellos pueden internalizar un poco" [At home you need to be creative with Spanish: dances, songs, games, etc. It can be entertaining for the children and at the same time they can internalize some of it] (Interview: 05/25/05).

It is evident that Mr. and Mrs. Ruedas did everything they could to promote a strong L1 identity in their children. The children's own internalization of the relevance of this identity through personal connection to their family members in Peru was perhaps a positive and unforeseeable consequence of their parents' efforts. This connection to family members in Peru seemed key to their maintenance of Spanish and of their ethnic identity. Regular communication with extended family members by phone was undoubtedly a major factor in HL development, as the whole Ruedas-Blanco family emphasized the strong ties they maintained with family in Peru. Perhaps more importantly though, according to Mrs. Ruedas, both adults and children had a strong nostalgia for Peru. She stated that "Los niños viven pegados a la familia" [they live[d] glued to the family] (Interview: 05/25/05) that they had left there. She added that the children had strong emotional ties to their cousins, uncles, aunts, grandparents, and even their pets. Almost every summer, or during Christmas, the family spent time in Peru. These trips were always a source of great excitement for the children, who prepared well in anticipation of each trip making plans for how they would like to spend their time with family there and making a list of the special dishes and treats they did not want to forget to eat during their stay. They seemed to view Peru as an extension of their life in Canada, one that was in some ways richer and closer to their individual beings as well as collectively as a family. Because of the significance of Peru to the children, they were also somewhat ambivalent about the geographical spaces in which they moved and lived. Olivia, the eldest of the three children, once said that she wanted to move back to Peru and stay there to be with her whole family. Rogelio was undecided and said that he wanted to live both there and also in Canada. One day I asked Olivia, then aged 14, about her national identity and her attachment to Canada or Peru. She said that she felt more Peruvian than Canadian, but felt undecided about her geographical preference. There were many things she liked about Canada (e.g., nature) and about Peru (e.g., family).

In an interview with Olivia, she indicated a clear desire to return to Peru. She enjoyed her life in Canada, but missed her family in Peru so much that she was willing to move back there just to be closer to them. Olivia's strong connection to her family in Peru is arguably a significant factor in her own maintenance of Spanish as one of the main causes of L1 loss appears to be the failure of Hispanic parents to promote a strong L1 identity in their children. Olivia's HL proficiency was high and her connection to family life in Peru, as was the case for the Aguirre-Ramírez girls, likely played a strong role in her successful HL socialization experiences.

10.2.5 Engaging in critical family literacy

Idalia Fernández and José Maradiaga, leaders of the Scout group described in the previous chapter, are the parents in the final case family profiled in the present chapter. They were a professional couple from Guatemala who immigrated to Canada in 1995 with their two-year old daughter, Idalia (Idalita). Diana, their younger daughter, was born in Canada in 1997. At the time I started my ethnographic fieldwork in 2005, the girls were 8 (Diana) and 13 (Idalita). In addition to their work with the Scout troop, the family reportedly worked tirelessly toward HL development in the home context as well. Although their repertoire of strategies was ample, in this chapter I would like to hold up one of their initiatives as an exemplary literacy practice. Family literacy refers to parents, children, and other family members' participation in literacy activities in home and community settings, either initiated purposefully or occurring spontaneously in their daily lives (DeBruin-Parecki and Paris 1997).

It is currently claimed that language and literacy develops more successfully when children engage in reading activities with family members (Anderson et al. 1985, Teale and Sulzby 1986, Saracho 2002), a belief that seemed prevalent in the Fernández-Maradiaga family. Along with culture and spoken language, written language was emphasized and promoted by them. Upon entering their home, visitors might readily notice their collection of Spanish literature for children as well as school textbooks in Spanish (e.g., math). During our interviews, the parents also proudly pulled stacks of books from their shelves to show me, which contained many collections in various genres including literature, textbooks, comics, and reference books. They had materials for teaching Spanish literacy and other subjects, which they had obtained from Guatemala and from other Latin American countries. They explained that they had content area textbooks, as well as literacy textbooks, that were appropriate for their children's age at that time and books saved for future years.

The parents used various strategies to support the girls' language and literacy development. Mrs. Fernández explained that the girls' vocabulary in English was more varied than in Spanish and sometimes they tended to get confused with words. Whenever the girls used the wrong word or used an English word in their speech, their mother asked them to write the Spanish word five times on a piece of paper. The girls were present when this strategy was described and their reaction was just to nod and shrug their shoulders as if to indicate that it was a commonplace and uneventful routine. Besides addressing issues that arose from interactions in daily life, the parents also engaged the children in more structured and focused family literacy activities.

An example of the family's regular literacy activities was one undertaken by Mr. Maradiaga. This activity involved regular sessions of reading, discussion, and explanation using a small whiteboard. It was based on two books. The parents selected a first book, *El Hombre que Calculaba* (The Man Who Counted, Tahan 1972), whose story was set in the Middle East. It was a book that related the adventures of a man who used his mathematical abilities to solve problems he encountered in his travels, to amaze and entertain people, to resolve disputes, and to do justice. This book was somewhat advanced and was used mainly to support Idalita's language development and to promote her mathematical understanding.

Diana also participated in this book activity, but at a more elemental level as the book was recommended for children over 14 years old whose Spanish competence was age-appropriate. A second book, *El Libro de la Selva*[2] (The Jungle Book, Kipling 1987), was used for Diana's sake.

The learning activity based on these two books was conducted two or three times a week for 30–60 minutes, usually before bedtime. There was no fixed schedule for this activity and they simply looked for the right time when the girls were willing, were not too tired, and did not have much homework. The following is a description of the routine: Mr. Maradiaga read to them and when the girls did not understand a word, they interrupted and he explained. In the case of *El Hombre que Calculaba*, Mrs. Fernández stated that "Al final cada capítulo es entendido en su totalidad incluyendo el problema matemático (en el caso de Idalita)" [in the end each chapter is understood in its entirety including the math problem (in Idalita's case)] (Mrs. Fernández, E-mail communication: 02/08/06). She added that this activity helped Diana increase her vocabulary, but the mathematical problems were beyond her level. When working with *El Libro de la Selva*, however, Mrs. Fernández asserted that Diana also understood it in its entirety. The girls' attitude, according to Mrs. Fernández, was good. She wrote: "La respuesta es bastante positiva, y es mejor de la esperada, comentan de lo que se les ha explicado y en el caso de Idalita ha entendido muy bien la parte filosófica de la matemática. A Diana, le gusta escuchar las narraciones de la historia y las ironías que se presentan" [The response is quite positive and better than expected. They comment on what's been explained, and in the case of Idalita, she has understood the philosophical aspect of mathematics very well. Diana likes to hear the stories and the ironies that come up] (Mrs. Fernández, E-mail communication: 02/24/06).

In terms of the rationale for their book choice, they explained that initially they considered other books such as the bible, popular novels, and children's stories. However, they felt these books were not appropriate. She said: "Solamente se cumplían parte de los objetivos pero no todos, algunos libros son alienantes" [They fulfilled only part of our objectives and some of them are alienating] (Mrs. Fernández, E-mail communication: 02/21/06), in the sense that the content provided a view of the world that was narrower than what they intended to promote. Because part of their broader language and literacy socialization objectives included countering "... la hegemonía de una cultura" [... the hegemony of the culture] (Mrs. Fernández, Interview: 05/02/05), they wanted to use books that allowed them to pursue the goal

---

[2] The parents were leaders in a Spanish-language Scout group and this book was the basis for the philosophy of the Scout section in which Diana was a member. See Guardado (2008, 2009 and Chapter 9 in this book) for a detailed description and analysis of the group.

of interrogating the dominance of Anglo-Canadian culture. They felt *El Hombre que Calculaba* was ideal for several reasons. She explained that they wanted to foster vocabulary development, philosophical understanding, and to improve their skills in mathematics. She also wrote: "El que tengan una base sólida intelectual con conocimientos en muchos aspectos, en la ciencia exacta y las ciencias sociales" [So they have a solid intellectual basis with knowledge in various areas, in the exact sciences and in the social sciences] (E-mail communication: 02/21/06). Additionally, she wrote that another important reason was to give the girls an opportunity to "Que aprendan que la cuna de las ciencias no es exactamente Occidente, la historia se desarrolla en Medio Oriente, Bagdad" [... learn that the cradle of the sciences was not exactly in the West, the story is set in the Middle East, Baghdad] (Mrs. Fernández, E-mail communication: 02/21/06).

Mrs. Fernández also explained that part of the reason *El Libro de la Selva* was selected was because this book enabled them to help improve Diana's comprehension through detailed explanations of the vocabulary and also explanation of the moral of the reading. According to the parents, the relevant moral of the book highlighted attributes of adaptability and survival in various circumstances, as well as responsibility, courage, friendship, and mutual support and solidarity, traits highly valued and dynamically promoted in other activities in which the family participated, such as the Scout group. *El Libro de la Selva* was the basis for the philosophy of the Scout section in which Diana was a member. This initiative provides a concrete and vibrant example of the range of possible family literacy practices that go beyond a focus on basic decoding-based or text-bounded practices. This example illustrates possible family literacy initiatives that can potentially connect language, culture, and identity in novel ways.

10.3 How do the above practices fare?

The home practices described in this chapter suggest that the case families' goals of socialization were multidimensional and included not only language, literacy, and academic content, but also goals to socialize their children to particular values and identities. They attempted to foster holistic learning in their children in order to cultivate their moral development, and in some cases, a non-alienating stance as well as a broad worldview. In such cases, they assumed postcolonial attitudes and positioned their activities as oppositional discourses (Pratt 1991) in relation to the dominant society. Likewise, at least some of the families sometimes produced what may be interpreted as cosmopolitan discourses. Thus, through their language and literacy activities they endeavoured to foster a flexible and progressive—rather than a traditional—way of thinking, one that emphasized the possession of adaptable dispositions and values, and aspired to the promotion of social justice and a rejection of what they appeared to construct as prevailing grand narratives (Lyotard 1984) (e.g., the supremacy of the Western world).

It has often been argued in the education literature that promoting family literacy should be a key educational goal. Given that in such a scholarship it has been proposed that family literacy activities should be promoted as a valuable practice in families by encouraging parents to realize that children's schooling begins at home with parents as children's first teachers (Bhola 1996), the language and literacy socialization practices in which some of these families engaged were in line with such propositions and could be characterized as exemplary and worthy of emulation. The practices in some of the homes boldly transcended decoding-oriented literacy practices, recasting family literacy as a critical family literacy that not only focused on meaning-making and citizenship learning, but one that also interrogated the dominance of Western-origin meta-narratives, revealing ubiquitous societal assimilative forces, and at the same time fruitfully connecting language, culture, and identity. Many of these home practices were imbued with a variety of critical discourses, including discourses of opposition and of correctness.

It has been found that a family literacy program that incorporates components that go beyond just a focus on reading and writing seems to offer more possibilities for success (DeBruin-Parecki and Paris 1997). This suggests that some of the family initiatives described in this chapter can have a positive effect on the education of their children. Since the promotion of family literacy activities and parental involvement with school has been suggested to have a strong potential to break down existing educational inequalities (e.g., those based on class and ethnicity) (Brain and Reid 2003), cases like the ones described can fruitfully inform educational policy and practice.

In this chapter I described some of the life circumstances and practices prevalent in five different families. Arguably, all of the parents could be heard speaking of a strong desire for and commitment to heritage language development and maintenance in their children. Therefore, even though the outcomes in Lisa's lonely struggle departed greatly from those of the other families, it may be impossible at this point to pinpoint exactly what went wrong for them. The foregoing analyses, however, hopefully provided the reader with some insights into what some of the dominant factors at play might be in relation to such disparate outcomes. The common denominator among all families, except Lisa's, was the open implementation of home language use strategies, such as some kind of family language policy. In other words, they made a conscious effort to encourage their children to speak Spanish and had an explicit or implicit plan that they followed. Additionally, several factors seemed to have contributed to the children's maintenance of the heritage language and culture in these families. For instance, Carmen reported that many features of their family life were responsible for Fay's success, including the special time they spent together and the relationship that developed between the two through Spanish as well as her arguably rare ability to provide Fay with travel opportunities to keep in touch with her roots locally and abroad. Whether the family practices reported by Carmen and observed during my frequent visits were the ones—or the only ones—to which Fay's successful heritage language socialization process can be attributed remains an open question. What I know for certain is that the last time I checked in with the family, as Fay approached her thirties, is that her commitment to the Hispanic culture and use of the Spanish language had solidified in a way that seemed natural and part of who she was as an adult.

Finally, one facilitating factor in children's L1 culture and identity development seems to be the frequent connection to the L1 culture, particularly, their attachment and regular contact with family locally and abroad. Frequent visits to the home country formed an important strategy used by many of the families described in this chapter (see Ahmed 2016 for similar findings). However, it is important to note that availability of resources and other conditions to make frequent trips abroad are inconsistently distributed across families in my studies and possibly even more so in the larger population. In other words, not everyone gets to be transnational or to prescribe an annual language injection to their children. Lisa faced many barriers to heritage language transmission and possibly had the least resources available to her. For Lisa, visits to El Salvador with her children were not in the realm of her life circumstances, a reality that might or might not have been a determining—or even an important—factor in the heritage language fate of her children. In the case of the Fernández-Maradiaga family, even though they had access to a variety of resources that they used creatively and frequently, they did not enjoy such a luxury either.

10.4 Chapter summary

The family cases I have described in this chapter serve to illustrate just how central the family is as a mini-community in HL development processes. These provide insights into some of the HL aspirations, frustrations, and successes of families as well as the family-specific activities and dynamics that emerge in them. As the family is the primary language socialization group of the child, an analysis of language practices and dynamics in the family domain can be very revealing—if not somewhat predictive—of language development and maintenance outcomes.

I have shown that HL development is challenging for Hispanic immigrants in Vancouver, a city with a relatively small and diffuse Hispanic population. Assimilative forces are strong, and opportunities where Spanish can be used are virtually non-existent for families. As a result, factors such as peers, literacy activities, as well as fun and excitement (e.g., for travel) have been shown to have a positive effect on child and youth HL socialization. Based on the analyses with the families showcased in this chapter, it is possible to draw some conclusions regarding circumstances that can be considered more conducive to HL development success. For instance, HL development is more likely to take place in families where parents are aware of their children's HL situation and as a result use explicit measures to support its development (i.e., through explicit policies and strategies). Additionally, affective factors such as intimacy, excitement, identification with the home country and culture, and the child's personal interest in the HL and HL-related activities, bode well for heritage language development. Overall, engaging in rich family time such as travel, HL activities conducted by the family together (including literacy and games), and participation in grassroots groups like the ones described in Chapter 9 make up part of a healthier HL picture.

At the most general ideological level, a desire for HL development is essential for it to take place—without this desire, it is unlikely to occur in minority language environments where the HL is not necessary for communication. This is not to say that there are not powerful forces internal and external to the home that have a major influence on the families' ideologies, practices, and circumstances related to the HL. Nevertheless, this desire is only the first step of a thousand-mile journey that cannot be walked alone. Family—however broadly defined—is key to advancing in this journey.

11 Family language policy and language regulation

11.1 Introduction

The goal of this chapter is manifold. First it provides an overview of the research literature in regards to heritage language policy, planning, and management. In particular, this section of the chapter acknowledges the emergence of the family language policy area of research and establishes the rationale for examining how multilingual families regulate language use. This aspect of the goal involves briefly reviewing the research literature that reports on metadiscursive comments made by parents as a way of providing an understanding of some of the lines of analysis more commonly undertaken in regards to HL policy and regulation within families. The area of the literature that is emphasized is that which engages in microlinguistic analyses of interactional data, within which the analyses presented in this part of the book are situated. A key goal of the chapter is to describe the analytical methodology, conversation analysis, as well as to engage in a discussion around transcription theory and conventions. In this chapter, I also define and exemplify essential terms used in applied linguistics, linguistic anthropology, and in other traditions, and show how these can be used to examine strategies found in multilingual caregiver-child interactions. Indeed, the key analytic constructs that form the backbone of the following chapter are introduced in this chapter. In short, it is the goal of this chapter to establish the foundational background for the technical analyses to be conducted in the chapter that follows.

11.2 Family language planning and management

Many studies have emphasized the practical difficulties families face in maintaining a HL in the home (Chumak-Horbatsch 1999, Iqbal 2005, Guardado 2006, Li 2006, Torres 2006, Muñiz 2009, Xie 2010), whose findings have drawn our attention to the seriousness of these struggles for families. To my knowledge, not many studies have demonstrated empirically what such difficulties look like in practice through analyses of interactions. Scholarship on HL development with a specific focus on metaregimentation of language use in families, then, is still in its infancy (see similar comments by Lanza 2007). Work by Spolsky (2009) and Kopeliovich (2010) are examples of the few that highlight the need to focus on home language policies and management, which would help expand aspects of this research line. Lanza's (2001) pioneering work in Norway with a focus on English as a heritage language has strongly advanced this line of inquiry. She posits that when investigating any aspect of the linguistic development of children, research needs to "focus on the micro-level of interaction ... through a discourse perspective on language contact in parent–child (caregiver–child) interaction" (201) whether the topic of examination is interaction itself or a different issue. Following this line of inquiry, the central concern in the next two chapters is to delve into the finer details of caregiver-child interactional data with a particular focus on what have variously been referred to as directives (Matychuk 2005), prompting (Ochs 1996), insisting strategies (Döpke 1992), parental discourse strategies (Lanza 1997/2004), and metapragmatic devices (Guardado 2013a), among other terms in use.

A closely related area that is currently evolving out of the language planning literature is family language policy—a combination of child language acquisition and language policy scholarship (King, Fogle and Logan-Terry 2008). Fishman's work reviewed in Chapter 1, particularly that which deals with intergenerational communication, language planning, and more broadly with the sociology of education, can be seen as precursors to this evolving field. Family language policy includes aspects of language ideologies (Spolsky 2004) and is currently defined as overt planning related to the use of language among family members (King, Fogle and Logan-Terry 2008, Fogle and King 2013). This work, although not specifically addressing heritage language socialization, is relevant to the arguments presented in this book given that family language policies tend to emerge from particular language ideologies and are therefore central to heritage language regulation and use in the home. For that reason, this and the following chapter can also be seen as a response to King, Fogle and Logan-Terry (2008) who argue that there is a lack of language policy work with a focus on "the intimate context of the home" (908).

11.3 Metadiscursive reports of language regulation

Our understanding of linguistic-minority families' opinions and beliefs about heritage language development and maintenance is already established in the sociolinguistics literature (e.g., Kouritzin 1999, Schecter and Bayley 2002). Yet, the linguistic practices resulting from the families' beliefs and policies are less frequently discussed explicitly (for exceptions see Zentella 1997, Lanza 2001, Schecter and Bayley 2002, Lanza 2007, Fogle and King 2013). Furthermore, the research that has provided actual interactional data collected from naturalistic family communicative events is considerably less abundant (Lanza 2007). Thus, I contend that there is a dearth of empirical evidence demonstrating how families attempt to persuade, encourage, or otherwise coerce their children to speak the heritage language while immersed in a dominant-language environment.

With that in mind, I review some exemplars from the relevant research literature that address parents' opinions about HL development. This overview facilitates the preliminary framing of the present chapter as I specifically draw attention to some of the studies that have analyzed linguistic exchanges between family members, particularly between adults and children. Thus, such studies provide the immediate backdrop for this and the next chapter. The data excerpts are drawn mainly from my ethnographic study with Hispanic families in Metro Vancouver in order to begin to investigate what linguistic tools the families employed in their daily interactions with the intention of managing their children's linguistic practices.

Many of the preceding chapters have frequently alluded to the rapidly growing scholarship examining several interconnected issues related to HL development such as rationales, attitudes and beliefs, causes and consequences as well as the role of ethnic identity in the various HL socialization processes. The parents' self-reports on home language policies and enforcement constitute a frequent theme in the literature. This recurring result, often part of larger issues, has frequently described the adult caretakers' attempts to ensure their children use the HL in day-to-day home communications and have often also reported on their frustrations in their efforts to achieve this goal. Studies of this nature include Piller (2001b), Park and Sarkar (2007), Li (2006), Zhang (2005), Eunjin Park (2006), Søndergaard and Norrby (2006), Kopeliovich (2010), and Guardado (2002). I should preface this discussion by noting that many of these studies did not intend to provide specific descriptions or analyses of how the participating parents enforced such strategies interactionally and therefore these were not included in their reports.

Piller's (2001b) study on home language planning is an analysis of publicly available data posted on online forums that promote bilingualism, as well as recordings of interviews with middle-class interlingual couples who also agreed to record their own private conversations. Among other issues, Piller discusses the parents' self-reports of their language planning and strategy use, particularly stressing the families' efforts to emphasize the heritage language to their children. Therefore, the prevalence of strategy choice and consistency in the parents' reports are proposed as key factors in their language development and maintenance success.

In Park and Sarkar's (2007) research, the authors did not intend to explain how Korean language regulation was accomplished, so they only noted that parents in their study attempted to promote the language in their children by speaking it at home, presumably as an implicit strategy. Li (2006) studied biliteracy and trilingual development in Chinese immigrant families living in Canada. As part of a variety of issues, she reported on the families' Chinese-only policies and implementation efforts in the home, the children's resistance to using the heritage language, and the concomitant parents' frustrations. Li's findings further highlight the lack of certainty in the uncomplicated transmission of the parents' attitudes to their children, without specifically shedding light on the regulation of Chinese language. Zhang (2005) provides a rather detailed account of how the participants attempted to enforce heritage language use at home. For instance, one of the fathers reportedly refused to respond to his daughter's written messages to him unless they were written in Chinese. The parents also reported that they often "reminded" their children to use Chinese, which was the extent to which the topic was pursued. In a New York study, E. Park (2006) reported on the language socialization of politeness in Korean-American families. The families appeared to view the heritage language as the carrier of culture, and as part of this goal they frequently attempted to convince their children to use the heritage language with statements like "say it in Korean." Likewise, based on a study on Danish language maintenance in Australia, Søndergaard and Norrby (2006) described language management in general terms by explaining that participating parents insisted their children spoke Danish at home.

Despite the prevalence of self-reports on language regulation in the literature, the degree of insightfulness in this particular regard varies widely. In her study profiling a Russian-speaking immigrant family in Israel, Kopeliovich (2010) provides a poignant account of the families' language attitudes and practices, focusing on the families' enormous struggles in their HL development efforts. Particularly, the mother's use of "battleground" analogies to describe her attempts to promote Russian language development and maintenance in the family underscore the scope of the struggles they contended with in daily life. At times, the mother's ardent statements sounded almost militant. She attempted to manage language use through direct requests to switch to Russian and would often say to her children "I won't speak to you unless you talk to me in Russian" (168). Interestingly, as I have also written elsewhere (Guardado 2002), the children were more inclined to speak Russian with their father, who did not attempt to force them to speak Russian.

The interview-based study I conducted with Hispanic families in Vancouver over a decade ago (Guardado 2002) has provided some of the insights already addressed in this book. The goal of the project was to investigate the parents' perspectives on their children's language loss or maintenance, and based on what they told me I posited at that time that the type and tone of the discourse used to persuade their children to speak the heritage language might have had a facilitating or detrimental effect on their children's HL development.

This argument was based on their accounts of how they pursued the goal of HL development and also on the factors to which they attributed their children's success in HL development, in the case of fully bilingual children. Additionally, this interpretation resulted from the fact that the parents who had been less successful in their HL development efforts reportedly used a particular approach: demanding that their children speak Spanish (e.g., we tell them that they must speak Spanish; we force them to speak Spanish). Interestingly, the parents whose children had been the most successful in HL development never used this aggressive kind of discourse. Quite the opposite, they claimed to use a softer and encouraging tone and to frequently engage their children in conversations about their feelings toward heritage language use. Therefore, although no parent-child interactional data were systematically analyzed in that study, it began to point out the ways in which parents regulate language at home as part of their language socialization goals.

11.4 The linguistic interactional picture

Although most—mainly interview-based—studies have discussed a variety of issues around identity, attitudes and beliefs, rationales, causes and consequences related to HL development, fewer investigations have presented actual interactional data or have analyzed caretaker-child linguistic interactions in daily life. Of these, some notable studies have provided detailed and insightful analyses of language practices in HL classes, such as the work of Agnes He (2001, 2004, 2006), and in less academic settings such as doctrina classes (Baquedano-Lopez 2000), Scout troop activities (Guardado 2009), careful examinations of code-switching across several generations (Zentella 1997), as well as thick descriptions of language and cultural practices across geographical settings and family life situations (Schecter and Bayley 2002).

Lanza (1992, 1997/2004, 2001, 2007) has conducted some of the work available in relation to the analysis of linguistic interactional data in heritage language contexts. Her language socialization research on English as a HL in Norway has provided an enhanced understanding of a variety of aspects related to the linguistic interactions of multilingual families. Some of these include practical aspects of the one person-one language strategy of interaction (Ronjat 1913), the contextually sensitive code-switching practices of very young children (Lanza 1992, 1997/2004), the key role of the mother tongue in the continuation of (national, ethnic, cultural) identities across generations (Lanza and Svendsen 2007), and parental use of discourse strategies (Lanza 2001, 2007 see also Döpke 1992). In relation to code-switching, her research challenges prevailing, although somewhat implicit, views that this practice in infants might be due to lack of linguistic awareness and a sign of linguistic confusion. She provides evidence that there is no difference between the code-switching patterns of two-year olds compared to older bilinguals. Lanza also posits that code-switching in multilingual interactions is used as a communicative resource and suggests the speaker is sensitive to not only formal but also social functions of language. Also of crucial relevance to Chapters 11 and 12 is Lanza's work on parental discourse strategies. Taking a discourse perspective, although using slightly different terminology than the one I use in this book, Lanza (1997/2004) categorizes and analyzes some of the common linguistic strategies used by parents and care-givers in their efforts to promote some language practices (e.g., use of heritage language) and to discourage others (e.g., mixing). Based on fieldwork with a Norwegian girl, Siri, and her parents (mother: English L1; father: Norwegian L1), Lanza identified the following strategies:

1. Adult requests for clarification: these are instances of other-initiated repair in which an adult interlocutor informs the child that there is a gap in understanding, whether real or artificial. Adult requests for clarification roughly correspond to Ochs' (1988, 1991) Minimal Grasp and Expressed Guess strategies.
2. Adult repetition of the content of the child's utterance, using the other language. This is a simple translation.
3. A move-on strategy: the conversation simply continues.
4. Adult code-switches.

I return to some of these points in the next chapter when I analyze excerpts of interactional data.

In a similar line as Lanza's work, a few studies have reported on actual interactional data from families where Spanish is used in the context of English as the dominant societal language. Studies in this category, like Lanza's, have gone beyond merely providing an account of parents' self-reports and have presented a linguistic picture of home language use. Delgado (2009) investigated the language socialization of a Mexican-descent family in Tucson, Arizona, focusing on whether their linguistic practices reinforced or hindered the maintenance of Spanish. Her research design included a combination of conversation analysis and language socialization in an attempt to describe how talk was organized in the family. Delgado's findings provide insights into the daily life of the family and the mother's desires and efforts to promote the HL for herself and the children, the family members code-switching practices, and the challenges faced by all. Delgado found that both the children and the mother engaged in this language practice for the same reason: the mother code-switched in order to accommodate the children's weak language skills and the children code-switched in order to compensate for their lack of Spanish proficiency. Delgado describes her study as a "fine grained" analysis of the family's sequential organization of talk, particularly code-switching. If the reader expects to find a turn-by-turn analysis of the interactional data as is the norm in CA-informed studies, however, it is not to be found in the written report.

Zentella's (1997) already classic, two decade, three-generation ethnographic study of working-class Puerto Rican families in New York's *El Barrio* marks a move forward in our understanding of language use—particularly the grammatical structure and social significance of code-switching—in bilingual and multilingual communities. Among a multitude of insights, Zentella aptly demonstrates through thick description and analyses of family linguistic interactions how code-switching served a variety of functions in the families, such as social control, language teaching, comprehension, and management. Lanza's (1992, 1997/2004) research in Norway, reviewed above, has also provided compelling arguments regarding the nature of language mixing/switching in very young children.

Schecter and Bayley's (1997, 2002, 2004) work covers a variety of issues, including attitudes and factors affecting HL development as well as strategies the families used in their attempts to enact language maintenance. Drawing on interview, observation, and recorded linguistic interactional data, they discussed the ways in which parents encouraged their children to use Spanish and how the children were admonished when caught departing from it. They pointed out that parents would often remark "¡Habla español!" (speak Spanish!) when children interacted in English with each other (Bayley and Schecter 2004). They reported, nevertheless, that even though statements such as this were found, the strategy that was used by parents the most was indirect requests, which was meant to get the children to switch to Spanish. What sets Schecter and Bayley's work apart from other studies addressing parents' metadiscursive comments of language regulation is that in addition to presenting parental self-reports, they also analyze the observed interactional implementation of such strategies in a highly contextualized manner.

Building on the extant HL development scholarship, such as the studies briefly reviewed above, research is now orienting towards emerging fruitful avenues of investigation. I recently examined the ideologies, practices, and socialization processes (Guardado 2009) found in some of the families and voluntary groups described earlier in this book. This work linked microlinguistic interactions to macro societal forces in the analysis of informal home and community heritage language communication among adult caretakers and children. The analysis presented critical snapshots of heritage language socialization, promotion of favorable language ideologies, as well as the resistance to, and reproduction of, hegemonic linguistic forces among participants.

11.5 Heritage language socialization and conversation analysis

Understanding the microlinguistic processes that form the heritage language socialization practices of multilingual families requires more than just parental self-reports of language use; this endeavour calls for the close examination of face-to-face interactional transcripts (Lanza 2001, 2007). Although there is intrinsic value in analyzing interview-based parental reports of children's linguistic behaviour, it is necessary to collect recorded speech of children's actual utterances in order to understand the home interactional picture in all of its contextual dimensions (Lanza 2001). Expanding on Lanza's call for a "conversationally oriented approach" (202) to the study of heritage languages within a language socialization framework, I explore the applicability of conversation-analytic principles in uncovering and understanding the discourse strategies present in family interactions.

Applying conversation analysis to heritage language socialization research is an important feature of this book, but not an entirely unique contribution within language socialization. It has been used successfully in several other studies taking this theoretical perspective (He 2006, Talmy 2008, Delgado 2009, Talmy 2009, He 2013, Talmy 2015, He 2016). Agnes He has skillfully employed CA tools in the analysis of naturally occurring interactions among Chinese as a heritage language (CHL) speakers of various ages. For instance, she has analyzed the co-construction of forms of participation and the interactionally negotiated nature of HL identities (2006). In other research, He (2013) has utilized CA in the analysis of the meaning and various functions of code-switching for speakers of CHL. She found that code-switching serves to sequentially create context among CHL interactants, make requests, engage in self and other repair, etc. Research of this type demonstrates that even though CA has traditionally de-emphasized context, when combined with a contextualized theoretical and methodological perspective, such as language socialization, it can facilitate the fine-grained analysis of heritage language interactions. Indeed, a contextually specific, CA-informed approach has the potential to strengthen language socialization research on parental discourse strategies. Thus, I argue that an applied CA perspective (ten Have 2001, 2007) offers powerful tools for analyzing and understanding interconnected issues of metapragmatic regimentation of language use and therefore, promises to help open productive lines of inquiry, potentially making innovative contributions to this area of research.

11.6 Conversation analysis

The field of conversation analysis was founded by Harvey Sacks in the 1960s and 1970s in collaboration with Emanuel Schefloff and Gail Jefferson (1974). CA refers to the systematic study of how people use language in everyday conversation, or *talk-in-interaction*. Its development was stimulated by Harold Garfinkel's ethnomethodology (members' methods) (1967), which focused on the "social structure of everyday lived experience" (Liddicoat 2007: 2). Goffman (1967) further emphasized the study of everyday interaction as a way of uncovering important social information, directly influencing his graduate students, Sacks and Schegloff (Heritage and Clayman 2010). However, although Garfinkel also had a direct influence on their work, Sacks and Schegloff developed their own distinctive approach to sociological research (Sidnell 2010).

Conversation analysis can be understood as the "grammar" of conversation and as such, assumes there is overwhelming order in how people speak—that is, interlocutors construct conversation in orderly ways. From a CA perspective, there is a commitment on the part of the analyst to work with what conversation participants see and hear and on what actions are produced, or "done," by conversation elements (e.g., pauses, prosodic features) and what interlocutors "orient to" (Schegloff 2007). In other words, CA privileges participants' perspectives by grounding its arguments in their observed behaviour (Grancea 2007).

CA understands talk-in-interaction as sequences of actions and emphasizes the sequential organization of these actions (Schegloff 2007). Some of the key conversational constructs that apply to the analyses presented in this book include *turn-taking* organization (how speakers change), interactional *adjacency pairs* (conversation turns tend to occur in pairs), *preference* organization (preference for certain actions/responses), and *repair* (dealing with problems in conversation). Turn-taking, one of the core concepts in CA (ten Have 2007), refers to the orderly ways in which interactants take turns in conversation with minimal gap and overlap. Turn-taking describes the rules and components for the organized construction and allocation of turns at talk (Grancea 2007). In their seminal article on CA, Sacks, Schegloff and Jefferson (1974) describe the nature of turn-taking in conversation as follows:

> It has become obvious that, overwhelmingly, one party talks at a time, though speakers change, and though the size of turns and ordering of turns vary; that transitions are finely coordinated; that techniques are used for allocating turns, whose characterization would be part of any model for describing some turn-taking materials; and that there are techniques for the construction of utterances relevant to their turn status, which bear on the coordination of transfer and on the allocation of speakership (699).

The simplest rules of turn-taking described by Sacks et al. state that in conversation, the next speaker can be selected by the current speaker, a speaker can self-select, or the speaker can continue speaking. The implementation of these rules is locally and interactionally achieved turn by turn. Turn-taking in conversation tends to occur in pairs. An adjacency pair (AP) is a sequence of two adjacent utterances by two different speakers in conversation and ordered as a first and a second. For instance, a question is usually followed by an answer. The first utterance (the question) is referred to as the *first pair part* (FPP), and it initiates the action; the answer is the *second pair part* (SPP) and it completes or flows from the initiation (Liddicoat 2007). Example of AP:

A: What's your name? (FPP)
B: Daniel (SPP)

Some SPPs are easier to perform than others (Liddicoat 2007). This can be explained in terms of *preference organization*. Preference organization refers to how in a particular conversation, "certain actions may be avoided, or delayed in their production, while other actions are normally performed directly and with little delay" (Liddicoat 2007: 909). It is widely accepted in CA that there is a preference for agreement and expected responses in talk-in-interaction (Sacks 1973/1987, Pomerantz 1984, Liddicoat 2007, Schegloff 2007). Interactants in conversation clearly design and deliver SPPs containing agreements to assessments and acceptances to invitations in a short and direct manner and without delay. These are *preferred* actions and their direct and immediate production is generally treated as routine and unexceptional. Pomerantz (1984) has called these overtly stated responses *preferred turn shapes*. On the other hand, disagreements, declinings, objections, refusals, and other forms of misalignment are *dispreferred* (Pomerantz 1984, Schegloff 2007) and their direct and immediate production is usually considered rude and unacceptable. These types of actions are uncommon in casual conversation. What is customary and expected is for dispreferred responses to be marked by hesitations, hedges, pauses, delays, clarification requests, excuses, false starts, and so on. Therefore, an index of preference is contiguity—preferred SPPs (e.g., agreements) tend to happen contiguously with their FPP, while dispreferred SPPs (e.g., rejections) may be delayed and contain hedges and hesitations, and as a result occur farther away from their FPPs (Liddicoat 2007). In lay language, when we agree with someone or accept their invitations, there is generally no noticeable hesitation or pause before our responses and this is because these are not difficult or potentially embarrassing responses. When we are preparing to deliver bad news—a negative response such as a disagreement, a rejection, or a declining—we are more likely to attempt to soften the response and this process causes us to stumble, pause, or produce false starts, which delays the response.

Finally, repair refers to the means speakers use to handle language problems that emerge in conversation (Liddicoat 2007). It is the ways in which conversation participants address and potentially resolve problems of mishearing and misunderstanding (ten Have 2007) and is sometimes set off by a complaint or clarification request such as "I don't understand" or "what did you say?." In such instances, it is referred to as *other-initiated repair*. Other-initiated repair tends to occur later in the turn sequence and may be preceded by a delay, thus providing an opportunity for self-repair. Although other-initiated repair may be common in certain specific conversational contexts (in classroom settings or between adults and children), research shows there is overwhelming preference for self-repair in conversation (Schegloff, Jefferson and Sacks 1977). It is argued that through monitoring, speakers *notice* erroneous or inappropriate output, triggering a self-initiated and self-completed correction.

11.6.1 A few words on transcription

Readers might have noticed that I presented transcriptions of naturalistic interactions in previous chapters without providing an explanation of transcription conventions. One of the reasons for this was that the analyses conducted there were not as detailed as the ones presented in the next chapter. Additionally, given that Chapters 11 and 12 are based entirely on microlinguistic analyses of naturally occurring family interactions, I deemed it essential to provide this type of explanation in this chapter instead. Doing so in Chapter 4 where some interactional data were analyzed, for instance, would have positioned this key information too far from where it is the most relevant.

Ochs (1979) contends that "transcription is a selective process reflecting theoretical goals and definitions" (44). Thus, this is an appropriate point to also lay out some of my own biases about how the data are presented in the book. The analyses conducted in these two chapters, more than in any other chapter, epitomize the micro perspective promised in the sub-title of the book. When it comes to transcribing interactional data, many choices present themselves to the transcriber and analyst. These may vary along a wide range of styles and degrees of specificity. Analysts working solely from a thematic analysis perspective often limit their transcription to summarizing what was said in the conversation. Since their focus is on the content of the data—often generated through interviews—detailed transcription of the interaction is not needed and in fact, they argue, such detail can undermine the smooth flow of ideas in the data.[1] Other analysts working from the same thematic analysis perspective sometimes transcribe the speakers' utterances verbatim, but without making any effort to capture the features of the interaction. The focus then is on capturing meaning. Often this type of transcription involves loosely transcribing complete "repaired" utterances; that is, utterances without false starts, pauses, and other features of casual unscripted speech.

Throughout the book I take a multi-level approach to transcription. Thus, multiple transcription versions are presented in different sections as appropriate for the goal at hand. That is, in chapters where the focus is mainly on the gist of the content, my transcripts are more "standardized" and "repaired" (as in the case of Chapters 6, 9, and 10). At times my transcripts are more "ethnographic" and include speakers and turns at talk, but without providing a fine-grained representation of their interaction. Excerpt 1 in Chapter 10 is a case in point. Given that the analyses presented in Chapters 11 and 12 are directly informed by conversation analysis, the conventions used in the transcripts are based on the Jeffersonian notation system, a widely accepted method for transcribing talk developed by Gail Jefferson (1984). Following Jefferson (1983), who points out that although it seems inappropriate to only highlight the features that are analytically relevant, excessive detail can limit access to some readers. Notwithstanding the above, the talk notations in the excerpts contained in these two chapters may not always be relevant to the analysis or if they are, may not necessarily form part of the analysis conducted at the particular place where these excerpts appear. I have attempted to provide a relatively detailed transcription in an effort to keep it consistent throughout the two chapters.

The type of transcription work contained in these two chapters is painstaking. It involves the meticulous timing of pauses in tenths of seconds. A pause of two tenths of a second is generally considered significant when considering the interactional organization of turn-taking. In fact, from a CA perspective whenever there is a pause equal to or greater than two tenths of a second (notated as 0.2), it is assumed that *something is up*. For this reason, it is critical to note such pauses in the transcript when approaching data from a micro-analytic perspective. When we consider that everyday speech is filled with a complexity of features such as silent pauses, filled pauses, false starts, hesitations, repetitions, overlaps, ellipsis, and so on, we begin to realize how meticulous and time-consuming the transcription work has to be. It is not surprising, then, that the fine-grained transcription of one minute of naturally occurring conversation can take one hour or longer.

---

[1] However, see Talmy (2010) and Talmy and Richards (2010), for a counter-argument.

To further complicate matters, one concern with this type of detailed transcription is striking a balance between depicting the features of the interaction as accurately as possible within the constraints of text and producing a transcript that is readable. Another complication emerges with the transcription of translated speech. Decisions about how to approach the transcription of interactions containing code-mixing and code-shifting need to be made carefully, especially when the intended readership may only be proficient in one of the languages in the mix. According to Jefferson (1983), certain methods of transcribing talk (such as *eye dialect*[2]) may make the speakers look "stupid" rather than capture important features of the interaction. This type of transcription presents speakers as a caricature. Clearly, given that stigmatized linguistic behaviour such as code-mixing and code-shifting is generally pervasive in data generated in multilingual settings, it is critical that the balancing act between readability and accurate interactional representation be harmonized with interactant self-respect. Paraphrasing Duff (as cited in Roberts 1997), naturalistic talk ought to be transcribed in a way that allows the analyst to examine the medium without presenting the messenger in a stigmatized way. In other words, the human side of transcription has to be preserved so as to represent interactants in a dignified manner.

Another balancing act related to data representation is posed by the need to reconcile the language ideologies of the analyst with the readability of the text in which the data are embedded. In an article on the politics of transcription, Roberts argues that some journals and other publishers are adamant about only including English translations of data transcripts, a practice that has the effect of denying "the whole social person" (Roberts 1997: 170). She posits that such practice serves to stress the "power of English to represent everyone and everything." Such strong ideological statements are particularly detrimental when the subject matter of a publication is precisely the validation and promotion of minority languages and the challenging of the dominant language structures in society and the world. Since most of the interview data on which this book is based were produced in Spanish, I had to translate the majority of excerpts into English. The interview excerpts that were originally produced in English are indicated with a note [original in English]. Otherwise, it should be assumed that excerpts are translations. In the spirit of the language ideologies advocated in this book; that is, the ideology to acknowledge and validate different languages (L1, L2, L3, etc.), I made a deliberate decision to provide the original quotes followed by translations. Interaction excerpts include both Spanish and English given that code-mixing

---

[2] Nonstandard respellings (e.g., *wuz*) that tend to denigrate speakers by portraying them as uneducated or rustic (Preston 1985).

and code-shifting are integral to the analyses I conduct in these two chapters. It is also an attempt to facilitate the verification of the analysis by readers.

In this book I take the position that one of the most illuminating sources of information regarding HL development is not how families say they talk—it is how they actually talk. I believe that it is their spontaneous conversation produced *in-situ* that provides the most insights. For this reason, the transcriptions in these chapters are meant to provide as much information as possible, while being mindful of the caveats discussed above. These transcriptions do not only contain the words spoken by the participants, but also attempt to capture how these words were spoken (e.g., rising intonation), in what conditions (e.g., speech overlaps), and some of the contextual features of the utterance (e.g., background noise). Obviously, not even the best transcription in the world can represent linguistic behaviour accurately in text. Written text is only a partial depiction of what was spoken—only a sketch at best. Therefore, we need to keep in mind that when analyzing transcribed talk we are only looking at part of the picture; part of the story. I hope, however, that the notation system I use in this chapter provides a clear enough representation of some of the salient features in the talk analyzed. These transcription conventions, presented in Table 11.1, are based on the ones developed by Gail Jefferson (1984) and adapted from the modified system used by Wooffitt (2001).

Table 11.1 Transcription conventions.

Symbol	Name	Description
(0.5)	Timed pause	The number in brackets indicates a time gap in tenths of a second
-	Hyphen	A dash indicates the sharp cut-off of the prior word or sound
(.)	Micro-pause	A dot enclosed in a bracket indicates a pause in the talk of less than two tenths of a second
.hh		A dot before an 'h' indicates speaker in-breath; the more 'h's, the longer the in-breath
hh		An 'h' indicates an out-breath; the more 'h's, the longer the out-breath
(( ))	Double parenthesis	A description enclosed in a double bracket provides additional information. It may indicate a non-verbal activity, for example ((looking at Angela)). It may provide grammatical information in a translation, for example ((pl.)) indicates the original word in Spanish was marked for plural. It can also enclose comments or background information, for example, ((the answer 'si' could be in response to a non-verbal question))
:	Colon	Colons indicate that the speaker has stretched the preceding sound or letter. The more colons the greater the extent of the stretching

(continued)

Table 11.1 (continued)

Symbol	Name	Description
(×)		An 'x' enclosed in single parentheses indicates the presence of an unclear word in the recording. The number of 'x's enclosed indicates the number of unclear words
(guess)	Parenthesis	The words within a single bracket indicate the transcriber's best guess at an unclear fragment in the recording
.	Dot	A full stop indicates a stopping fall in tone. It does not necessarily indicate the end of a sentence
Under	Underlined speech	Underlined fragments indicate speaker emphasis
↑↓	Up/down arrow	Pointed arrows indicate a marked falling or rising intonational shift. They are placed immediately before the onset of the shift
CAPITALS	Capitals	With the exception of proper nouns, capital letters indicate a section of speech noticeably louder than that surrounding it
° °	Degree symbols	Degree signs are used to indicate that the talk they encompass is spoken noticeably quieter than the surrounding talk
> <	Greater than/ Less than symbols	'More than' and 'less than' signs indicate that the talk they encompass was produced noticeably quicker than the surrounding talk
=	Equal sign	The equal sign indicates contiguous utterances
[	Bracket	A left-hand bracket indicates the beginning of overlapping speech, shown for both speakers. It also indicates that speakers start a turn simultaneously
Bold		**Bold** typeface indicates the text was originally spoken in English

In the following section I introduce a series of concepts associated with corrective feedback, which I have found useful for thinking about and analyzing heritage language regulation in families. The above notation conventions are used in the data presented below.

11.7 Concepts associated with language regulation

11.7.1 Self-repair

Self-repair has been studied from various research perspectives, including CA in L1 settings (Schegloff, Jefferson and Sacks 1977) and classroom discourse in L2 settings (Kasper 1985). Self-repair often falls within the scope of communicative and psycholinguistic perspectives on second language acquisition. From a psycholinguistic perspective the notion of self-repair is based on complex theories of monitoring behaviour, such as *The Perceptual Loop Theory of Monitoring* (Kormos 1999), which constitutes the foundation of self-repair. Some of the interactions observed in my ethnography contained a type of corrective behaviour that could be characterized as self-repair. Although it was less common than the adult-initiated correction styles that are introduced later, there were some unambiguous manifestations of self-corrective behaviour by the children. These incidents usually involved code-mixing, as shown in the example below, rather than full-fledged code-switching. For example, in the following excerpt Graciela produced the Spanish equivalent of the word *French* almost immediately after finishing an utterance that included the word in English: (Teacher=Mrs. Nieve):

```
Teacher:   ¿fuiste a la escuela hoy Graci?
           |did you go to school today Graci?|
Graciela:  a::h si a French |yes to French class|
Teacher:   ¿si? |yes?|
Graciela:  al (.) francés |to French|
```

Mrs. Nieve, a parent-teacher in El Centro de Cultura, had a strictly enforced Spanish-only policy in her class and she usually modeled the expected behaviour by never speaking any English during class herself. In this interaction, although Graciela produced a word in English (French), Mrs. Nieve did not orient to it. However, Graciela corrected herself, pointing to her awareness of the language policy in the class, and suggesting she noticed that she had engaged in what was seen as an inappropriate practice for that setting.

11.7.2 Corrective feedback

Corrective feedback (CF) has a long history in first and second language acquisition research (e.g., Pemberton and Watkins 1987, Lyster and Ranta 1997, Matychuk 2005). In first language learning, scholars have used the term *motherese* (also *baby-talk, parentese, child-directed speech, caretaker speech*) to describe parents' and other caregivers' communication style with infants and toddlers (Philips 1973, Newport, Gleitman and Gleitman 1977, Ochs 1982, Schieffelin 1990). The term is frequently used to describe how adults alter the language they use with young children through shorter sentences and simplified grammatical structures (Matychuk 2005).

When studied as part of motherese, corrective feedback is provided in the form of explicit and implicit directives, which are tools used by parents to foster, expand, and regulate the linguistic practices of their children. Explicit directives are somewhat akin to prompting (e.g., "say thank you"), which refers to "caregivers providing explicit instruction in what to say and how to speak in a range of recurrent activities and events" (Ochs 1986: 5). Prompting behaviour has been observed in families in a variety of settings that include White working class families in the United States, Sesotho-speaking families in Africa, and Senegalese Wolof communities (Miller 1982, e.g., Demuth 1986, Eisenberg 1986, Schieffelin 1986, 1990, Rabain-Jamin 1998). These explicit directives are used to elicit from children the required language form. In order to accomplish this goal, they typically use an imperative form with a specific prosodic feature for emphasis (e.g., word or syllable stress), which is sometimes followed by some type of reprimand with the aim of further constituting their utterances as orders (Ochs 1996). In monolingual societies, prompting is commonly used to lead children to use a particular speech form, to "correct or expand children's utterances to be socially appropriate and grammatical" and to "repeat and paraphrase their own speech" (Paugh 2005: 57).

Implicit directives are used by adults as non-literal means of regulating children's linguistic behaviour. These are phrased in the form of hints or suggestions meant to produce the desired linguistic behaviour without explicitly naming it, but often relying on prosody. Ochs (1986) suggests that prosodic features have a strong prompting effect, even when they are not accompanied by explicit directives. When functioning as corrective feedback, motherese can also refer to how adults provide subtle corrections to children regarding their language errors (see, e.g., Sommerer 2006). These subtle corrections in the form of reformulations without the error are often referred to as *recasts*.

Analyses of parental reports as well as observed naturalistic interactional ethnographic data show that one of the most pervasive language socialization strategies the adults in the study employed with children to instruct them to switch to the heritage language and to cultivate favorable linguistic ideologies was the use of speech acts such as explicit and implicit directive forms. My observations indicate that explicit directives—commands—were by far the more common type of the two strategies as they seemed to come automatically to the parents. This is evidenced in the following example, which took place in La Casa Amistad, described in Chapter 9 (Mrs. C=Mrs. Clavel):

```
Child 1: ((Speaking in English)) (xxxxxxxxx)
Child 2: the program (xxx)
Perla:   (xx) but (xxx) over there=
Mrs. C:  =in SPANish hey hey hey. What's the matter my friends?
```

The context of this interaction was an arts and crafts project led by Mrs. Clavel. The children were caught having switched to English entirely, prompting an admonition from Mrs. Clavel. As with explicit prompting, her directive was initiated by an imperative form that carried a particular intonational contour (Ochs 1986), which she followed with a rhetorical question. A much more extensive analysis of a similar, but longer, extract is conducted in the next chapter.

11.7.3 Recasts

In second language acquisition, recasts are a common form of corrective feedback given to language learners (Schmidt 1990, Lyster and Ranta 1997, Lyster 1998, 2001, Sheen 2004, Carpenter et al. 2006, Ellis and Sheen 2006, Nassaji 2007). A functional definition is provided by Nicholas, Lightbown and Spada (2001), who describe recasts as reformulations of a speaker's incorrect utterances made by listeners. Part of the appeal of recasts is that they acknowledge the content of a speaker's utterance, helping maintain the flow of communication and providing an alternative model (Nicholas, Lightbown and Spada 2001). However, some scholars call for a cautious construal of their usefulness as they consider recasts too ambiguous due to the repetition of the speaker's statements. Recipients of recasts, it is argued, may interpret them as focusing on meaning, thus causing them to overlook the error made (Lyster 1998). Additionally, *noticing,* or paying attention to speech, has been suggested to activate language acquisition (Schmidt 1990). Yet, because of the implicit nature of recasts, without directly calling the speaker's attention to the error, the speaker may not notice a correction was made. To illustrate, the following is an example of a recast that may take place in an English as an additional language classroom:

```
Student:  She go yesterday
Teacher:  She went yesterday
```

11.7.4 Cross-code recasts

While there is already a relatively long tradition of research on recast usage in monolingual as well as in second language learning contexts, its use in HL development contexts has not been examined. Whereas the type of recasts regularly discussed in the second language acquisition literature refers to within-code corrections, in this chapter I introduce what I term *cross-code recasts* (CCRs), which are meant to prompt a code switch. The analysis in my ethnographic data set showed that caregivers used two main types of recasts. They used recasts to provide negative evidence to children regarding incorrectly formed utterances (e.g., verb forms, lexis, syntax), which were similar to the recasts investigated in the established domains of recast research cited above. The other type of recasts adult care-givers used were intended to offer a subtle code correction, that is, to keep the children focused on speaking Spanish. The following segment illustrates how the recasts used by adults were clearly meant to provide to the children a reformulation of an utterance spoken in the wrong code (i.e., English), thus surreptitiously regimenting their language use:

```
Graciela:   this is black
Teacher:    ese es negro |this is black|
```

In this example, Graciela started the interaction with a phrase spoken in English and Mrs. Nieve used a CCR in response (ese es negro; this is black) by simply translating Graciela's utterance. Thus, Mrs. Nieve contributed to the flow of the interaction, while providing a clue to Graciela that something was "up" in her utterance, without actually saying it. In other words, she corrected her implicitly while still acknowledging the content of Graciela's words. This brief and de-contextualized excerpt may seem like an ordinary and inconsequential translation, in some respects similar to the translations reported by Lyster and Ranta (1997) based on research in a French immersion context in Montreal, Canada and to Lanza's (1997/2004) *adult repetitions* in Norway. However, as it is shown in the next chapter, the deployment of this strategy did much more work than just translate or repeat Graciela's English utterance. Several researchers have argued that because of their implicit, and therefore ambiguous nature, the modifications made in recasts may not be noticeable to learners. For instance, Lyster and Ranta (1997) suggest that other forms of correction, such as metalinguistic feedback, clarification requests, and teacher repetition of the error may be more effective than recasts.

11.7.5 Clarification requests

Clarification requests attempt to address problems of incomprehensibility, unlike recasts or commands, which seek to make a correction. Pragmatically, however, the clarification requests found in my interactional data were also meant to prompt a code-shift. Adult care-givers often used directives that exhibited non-explicit features, such as requests for clarification or statements of lack of understanding, or even of puzzlement (e.g., "I don't understand," "I don't know what you're saying"). These implicit clarification requests were frequently formulated as questions or as other types of statements that were meant to function as directives given the context in which they occurred (e.g., children speaking in

English). These are similar to the clarification requests that Ochs (1988, 1991) has termed *minimal grasp* and *expressed guess* strategies. Lanza (1997/2004) has also found these types of strategies in her research on English as a HL in Norway. The following is a typical example of the type of indirect discourse parents often used to convey the message to children that they were using the wrong code for the social situation. (bold=English in original):

```
Olivia:   I want an iPod
Mother:   no te entiendo
Olivia:   yo quiero un iPod
```

In this particular interaction, the context made it sufficiently clear what it was that Olivia wanted and that her mother understood her request ("I want an iPod"). However, the mother formulated a directive explicitly by framing it as a request for clarification of her utterance, to which Olivia oriented, as evidenced in her next turn where she produced the utterance her mother was expecting. Much more was going on in this interaction, but we get to some of those details in the next chapter when we look at the entire episode.

11.7.6 Lectures

An uncommon, but nevertheless significant, characteristic of the children's language socialization processes was the parents' use of explicit pleas urging the children to persist in their efforts to use Spanish within and outside their homes or grassroots groups. One case in point was a talk given by one of the parents at the end of a Scout group nature hike that was organized as part of a larger event that included an outing with parents and other children. This lecture was, in all probability, motivated by the pervasiveness of English in the children's speech during the leisure activities of the day when the children ran and played in the large park and ocean front open area where the event took place. The parent's talk was an invitation to the children to become more aware of the value of the Spanish language and to encourage them to continue speaking it. This lecture is analyzed in the next chapter where it serves to illustrate the role of lectures in the families.

11.8 Chapter summary

In this chapter, I have reviewed the relevant family language policy, planning, and management literature and introduced some of the key concepts I see as relevant to the process of heritage language regulation. I also provided basic examples of how these concepts are embodied in the linguistic strategies that parents and other adult caregivers utilize in order to manage their linguistic interactions, motivated by their language ideologies. As well, I have presented the linguistic tools the participating families employed in their daily interactions with their children in their efforts to promote the continued use of the HL in family communication. In an attempt to build on and productively expand the existing heritage language development scholarship, it is also my goal in this chapter to set the stage for investigating the discursive practices in which ethnolinguistic minorities engage in their efforts to foster the development and maintenance of the HL. For this purpose, I introduced conversation analysis as a promising methodology in this area when combined with language socialization as well as introduced a sense of what a CA-informed analysis of these strategies might look like. However, a turn-by-turn analysis of extended interactions was not attempted at this time, given that the purpose of the chapter was to only lay the foundation for the analytical work that is performed in Chapter 12.

The body of research relevant to HL development has traditionally relied on thematic analyses of interview-based data. Many of these studies have reported on parents' perspectives on heritage HL development in their children and have reported on their recollections of how they engage in the regulation of their children's language practices through directives of different types. However, with some notable exceptions, how these practices play out in their linguistic interactions has not been extensively explored or demonstrated in the research literature. Expanding on King, Fogle and Logan-Terry's (2008) words, work on home language policy and regulation has the potential to address key gaps in HL development by closely examining "what families actually do with language in day-to-day interactions; their beliefs and ideologies about language and language use; and their goals and efforts to shape language use and learning outcomes" (909). Although this is an avenue of inquiry which is still just evolving, it can arguably benefit from various analytic perspectives; in this book I propose conversation analysis as a discourse analytic method for studying caregiver-child discourse in HL socialization contexts. Thus, the next chapter provides analyses of heritage language interactions through the use of CA-informed tools that enable a deeper look into the data.

12 Heritage language regulation

12.1 Introduction

Having introduced in the previous chapter the terminology, analytical tools, transcription conventions, and examples of linguistic devices employed by families to foster sustained heritage language use, this chapter examines these metapragmatic devices in detail and as they are used in daily interactions. Drawing on conversation analysis, introduced in Chapter 11, the chapter locates language-regulating practices in the context of HL development on a continuum from complete explicitness to relative implicitness; however, it suggests that successful strategies may not necessarily be related to degree of explicitness, but to interactional turn shape. I argue in this chapter that some processes of metapragmatic regimentation of language use and the resulting responses to their deployment may have the effect of unwittingly oppressing children by silencing them. Given that much heritage language research has relied on self-reports of linguistic practice in families, I demonstrate the potential of CA tools for conducting detailed analyses of their actual practices in relation to linguistic regulation. The current analysis, then, shows that CA offers a practical set of tools for uncovering the interactional shape of caregiver-child interactions in HL development. Therefore, I cover some of the more common heritage language regulation strategies that parents and grassroots group members use to encourage their children to speak the heritage language and look at the potential implications of these strategies for validating or denying budding hybrid cultural and linguistic identities.

As was the case when first introducing the thematic analysis in Chapter 6, in this chapter I would like to describe the procedures that were followed in the analysis of naturalistic interactions. These data were carefully examined through the language socialization lens in chronological order and through several iterations. This analysis was conducted in the following steps:

1. Scanning data: I examined all naturalistic interactions several times (audio and video) in order to note important contextual features and to obtain a preliminary sense of language socialization patterns
2. Pre-coding: I used the software application *Transcriber* to listen to recordings. During this stage I made general transcriptions, took notes, and labeled salient segments
3. Pre-selecting interactions: I reviewed rough transcriptions and labeled segments that seemed clear enough for detailed transcription
4. Detailed transcription: I transcribed clear segments in detail, noting overlapping talk, pauses, prosodic features, etc. (see transcription conventions in Table 11.1)

5. Coding: I reviewed detailed transcripts, particularly noting exchanges in which speakers oriented to language (implicitly or explicitly), to activities, or which seemed to contain features especially relevant to language socialization. These segments were labeled and categorized
6. Re-contextualizing interactions: I examined fieldnotes and journal entries in order to recall and identify details of the circumstances surrounding the recorded activity/interaction
7. Extract selection: in the process of writing, I carefully examined detailed transcripts and selected exemplars for inclusion in the book. These were generally representative of language socialization patterns observed or evocative of a critical incident
8. Detailed analysis: the analyses contained in the book were first conducted in the actual process of writing the initial report (Guardado 2008a) and expanded with the assistance of notes and codes previously generated as a basis

12.2 Lectures as a defensive language socialization practice

The first excerpt is meant to provide an example of how lectures were at times used as a mechanism of defense against the prevailing assimilative forces in society. Defensive socialization has been described as a strategy used by immigrant parents in the face of dominant societal values that differ from their own (Knafo and Galansky 2008). The immigrant experience inevitably reveals a clash of values that can generate tension and stress in the lives of families and individuals. In response to this potential collision, many immigrant parents—and local minority parents for that matter—often engage in practices designed to "pre-arm" their children with counter-arguments and rationales that are more in line with their own values (Goodnow 1997). In view of such observation, I have analyzed this linguistic practice—lectures—as a form of defensive socialization. The first language excerpt, introduced in Chapter 6 as an example of a discourse of aesthetics, took place in the Grupo Scout Vistas. The fathers of some of the children had been Scouts as children. One such parent sometimes became involved in the activities and joined the troop for the opening and closing ceremonies of the day. At times, he had words of encouragement for the children. One Saturday morning the troop went on a long hike, which concluded with a barbecue in a park, in which all parents participated. At the end of the event, the Scout troop was called to stand in a horseshoe formation for the closing ceremonies. Mr. Hernández, one of the parents, addressed the group about Spanish and the value of keeping it alive in the group (Mr. H=Mr. Hernández) (Observation: 06/24/06):

[Excerpt 12.1] "a very beautiful language"
```
1  Mr. H:  yo quiero decirles que estoy contento que hablen
2          la lengua española, castellano. Este en si es un
3          idioma muy bonito, y una de las cuestiones muy
4          importantes de este grupo es (xx) y conservar
5          eso. A los nuevos y a todos, yo les pediría que
6          insistieran en hablar en español que traten de
7          hablarse en español. Es un idioma muy lindo
8          ¿**okay?** Y este:: este también me da de veras mucho
9          gusto ver a todos que hablan muy bien español y
10         me permití invitar a unas otras personas amigos
11         míos e:h van a seguir como más bien nutrias pero
12         igual hay algunos lobatos que a mí me gustaría
13         que conserváramos eso de que les hablen <u>hablan
14         perfectamente</u> inglés como ustedes pero a mí me
15         gustaría que más bien les hablaran que hablaran
16         siempre en español que es parte de lo que nos
17         distingue de los demás. ¿Estamos? ¿(Les parece)
18         alguien tiene alguna pregunta o alguna otra
19         (xxxxxx)? ((a child asks a question about who the
20         new children were))
```

Translation
```
1  Mr. H:  I'd like to tell you (pl.) that I'm happy to
2          see that all of you speak the Spanish language,
3          Castilian. This is a very beautiful language,
4          and one of the most important features of this
5          group is (xx) and to maintain that. To the new-
6          comers, I would like to ask you to persevere
7          in speaking in Spanish to try to speak Spanish
8          with one another. It's such a pretty language,
9          okay? And u::m um I'm also very glad to see that
10         everyone speaks Spanish so well and I took the
11         liberty of inviting some people who are friends
12         of mine e:h they are going to start mostly as
13         Otters, but there are some Timberwolves also and
14         I would like all of us to maintain that practice
15         of talking to them <u>they speak English perfectly</u>
16         like all of you but I would like you to always
17         speak to them to always speak Spanish because
18         it's part of what distinguishes us from others.
```

```
19            All right? (do you agree?) Does anybody have any
20            questions o::r some other (xxxxxx)? ((at this
21            point a child asked a question about who the new
22            members were))
```

Mr. Hernández's initial utterance was designed to recognize the efforts and gains of the children by congratulating them for their Spanish skills (lines 1–2). He then used a discourse of aesthetics, which contained a positive appraisal of the Spanish language: "This is a very beautiful language" (line 3). This discourse stated that maintaining Spanish was one of the Scout group's objectives (lines 4–5) and appealed to the children to continue using it (lines 6–7). Subsequently, he constructed a discourse that was similar to the previous one with a second round of positive assessments: "It's such a pretty language" (lines 7–8), expressing satisfaction with the children's Spanish development (lines 8–9) and appealing to them to persevere in their efforts (lines 12–13). Finally, he acknowledged the children's language circumstances of living in an English dominant context (line 14), showing empathy for them, and made a final plea based on his own hopes for the children and the group. To close this sequence, he made a statement about the uniqueness of the group members based on the Spanish language and culture (lines 16–17).

Mr. Hernández's discourse contains several appeals to the children to use Spanish, which were interspersed with positive assessments of the language and statements of exaltation regarding the children's language abilities. This combination of moves was designed to highlight the children's success in learning and maintaining Spanish as well as to further sensitize them to the importance of continuing to do so, in a move that could be heard as a preemptive socialization strategy. In contrast to the use of more forceful commands (e.g., speak Spanish!), these explicit directives contained positive discourse, such as "I'd like to ask you," instead of "you must." As I argued in Chapter 11 and elsewhere (Guardado 2002), the type of encouragement that parents give to their children to speak the heritage language may have a facilitating or a detrimental effect. The communication style used by Mr. Hernández had the potential of promoting a positive attitude in the children as it couched an implicit directive within a positive appraisal of the children and the heritage language.

Mr. Hernández announced there were new members in the group and attempted to emphasize the expected standard linguistic behaviour in order to prevent the newcomers from altering the established language dynamics. He recognized the children's linguistic choices and suggested that their preferred language might not be Spanish, which seemed to motivate his appeal to them to continue speaking Spanish. As part of that plea, he also indicated that Spanish use was valued and expected in the group. In order to have a stronger rhetorical impact, thus regulating heritage language use, he proclaimed Spanish as a key cultural element that united everyone ethnically, distinguishing them from other groups in Canadian society.

Although his call to the children did much more work than just emphasize the heritage language management efforts of the parents (see Guardado 2009, for further analysis), much of the *illocutionary* force of his speech—the speaker's intention—attempted to strongly socialize the *newcomers* and *oldtimers* to the linguistic practices of the group, thus attempting to inoculate them from code-switching or full language shift. He strongly attempted to "defend" Spanish by depicting and rendering it the only "proper speech" in the group and equated Spanish with "linguistic correctness," implicitly portraying English as a threat (Woolard and Schieffelin 1994).[1]

12.3 Cross-code recasts and conversational expansions

The next interaction comes from El Centro de Cultura, one of the grassroots groups that were discussed in Chapter 9. It was recorded in Mrs. Nieve's class, the smallest of the three classes in the group, with only three pre-school children in it. The interaction took place in the context of an arts and crafts activity with a focus on body parts, clothing items, colours, and other related lexical items, which could be characterized as somewhat typical of pre-school settings. The lesson started with Mrs. Nieve giving the children photocopies with pictures of clothing items and a non-gender specific doll. Mrs. Nieve's warm up activity consisted of asking the children to name the items on the papers, which was done in less than two minutes, as the children had no difficulty naming them. The children were told that first they would colour the pictures and then they would cut them out. After cutting them out they would dress the doll as a girl or a boy.

Recasts, as defined in the previous chapter, are reformulations made by listeners of a speaker's incorrect language use. Recasts acknowledge the content of a speaker's utterance and focus on communication while providing an alternative model (Nicholas, Lightbown and Spada 2001). Cross-code recasts (CCRs), on the other hand, are meant to prompt a code switch through a subtle code correction in the form of a repetition in the "correct" language. CCRs are similar to the *adult repetitions using the other language* reported by Lanza (1997/2004, see

---

[1] Although it may seem as if Mr. Hernández's use of the term "castellano" (Castilian) created a dialectal hierarchy where the variety spoken in Spain was assigned a higher status than Latin American varieties (as is often the case), this was not so. Many Spanish speakers in Latin America use this term (castellano) even when referring to their local variety. It is a way of distinguishing it from the other languages of Spain and Mr. Hernández appeared to use it in this sense.

also Juan-Garau and Pérez-Vidal 2001). As the next example demonstrates, the recasts used by adults in the grassroots groups (and in their homes) were clearly meant to provide the children with a reformulation of an utterance spoken in the wrong code (i.e., English), thus regimenting their language use (Mrs. N=Mrs. Nieve) (Observation: 01/25/06):

```
[Excerpt 12.2] "this is black"
1   Graciela:   this is black
2   Mrs. N:     ese es negro |this is black|
3   Graciela:   negro |black|
4               (4.1)
5   Graciela:   black se dice negro |black is said black|
6   Mrs. N:     exactamente |exactly|
7   Graciela:   black se dice NEGRO |black is said BLACK|
8   Mrs. N:     SI |YES|
```

In this context, Graciela started the interaction with what appeared to be a *think-aloud*[2] episode, using a phrase spoken in English. Mrs. Nieve recasted Graciela's utterance in line 2 (ese es negro). Then in line 3 Graciela produced a preferred response by repeating the content word "negro"—the translation provided by Mrs. Nieve. The 4.1-second pause in line 4 appears to be the end of the sequence and the topic. However, given Graciela's self-selection for another turn, it is clear the pause provided Graciela with "thinking" time. The significantly long silence before producing "black se dice negro" in line 5 is an indication that Graciela was still engaged with the content of Mrs. Nieve's cross-code recast produced in line 2. In line 6 Mrs. Nieve confirmed Graciela's realization. Graciela's turn in line 7 is significant as she not only repeated her previous utterance, but also pronounced "negro" with heavy word stress and loudness of voice, to which Mrs. Nieve, possibly influenced by Graciela's enthusiasm, also responded with a loud and high-pitched "SI."

This extract shows that Graciela produced an utterance in English, which departed from the official language policy in the group (i.e., to use Spanish only), prompting Mrs. Nieve to use a CCR in response. Graciela appeared to learn a new semantic relationship through Mrs. Nieve's modeling of the item "negro." Although she likely knew the word "negro" prior to this episode, the corrective feedback Mrs. Nieve provided seemed to get her attention, triggering her realization that "black se dice negro." The 4.1 second pause in line 4 suggests Mrs. Nieve's CCR might have led to Graciela's noticing the problematic code use,

---

[2] Verbalized mental activity used while conducting a task (Davey 1983).

prompting her to verbalize her recognition, as the emphasis in "NEGRO" indicates. Her repetition of the utterance and the emphatic production of "NEGRO" clearly index enthusiasm, an arguably positive and desirable attitude in any language acquisition situation.

This analysis shows that Mrs. Nieve's recast acknowledged the content of Graciela's utterance and, although no extensive communication followed, Mrs. Nieve's stance generated topic expansion and the generation of several additional turns, leading to the closing of the interaction in a way that invited communication. By focusing on the meaning of Graciela's utterance and providing an alternative model to follow, rather than simply issuing a command to switch languages, Mrs. Nieve created a positive environment in which she continued to positively reinforce and support Graciela's noticing and repetition of the correct utterance and commentary. Although this is a brief extract, it effectively illustrates the potentially facilitating force of CCRs in adult-child interactions in the processes of heritage language regulation.

12.4 Requests and negotiation

As opposed to issuing direct imperatives to the children, as I analyze later in the chapter, at times parents used firm, but somewhat less stern strategies. The following excerpt illustrates the use of polite requests. It also took place in El Centro de Cultura while Mrs. Nieve's group of pre-school aged children worked on arts and crafts projects. The child participants in the interaction were two girls from one of the other classes that had joined Mrs. Nieve's group for the activities of the evening (Mrs. N=Mrs. Nieve) (Observation: 01/25/06):

```
[Excerpt 12.3] "very hard words"
 1  Mrs. N:  ¿Luisa y Cheryl podrían tratar de hablar tantito
 2           español?
 3           |Luisa and Cheryl could you try to speak a little
 4           Spanish?|
 5           (0.4)
 6  Luisa:   okay
 7  Cheryl:  si |yes|
 8           (1.9)
 9  Luisa:   claro |sure|
10  Cheryl:  the words (.) we're saying are very hard words
11  Mrs. N:  ¿como cual? |like which one?|
12           (1.0)
```

```
13  Cheryl:   I don't know=
14  Luisa:    =I don't know
15  Mrs. N:   ¿entonces como sabes que son muy difíciles?
16            |then how do you know they are so difficult?|
17  Cheryl:   ('cause) I forgot them
```

In this example, Luisa and Cheryl were engaged in conversation in English prior to the interaction shown; therefore, in line 1, Mrs. Nieve directed them to use Spanish. After a noticeable pause (0.4 seconds), Luisa agreed, but with a markedly unenthusiastic "okay" in line 6. In line 7, Cheryl also agreed with a similarly produced "si" (yes). After a significant pause of 1.9 seconds, Luisa—line 9—reiterated her agreement with a "claro" (sure), again using clearly flat intonation. However, in line 10, Cheryl attempted to justify their use of English, namely, that the words they were speaking in English were too hard to be said in Spanish, to which Mrs. Nieve responded with an information question: "¿como cual?" (like which one?). Following a 1.0 second pause, in line 13 Cheryl informed her that she did not have such information, which was immediately reiterated by Luisa in line 14, as evidenced by the contiguity of her utterance (=). Mrs. Nieve asked how they knew these were difficult words in line 15, indicating that she was not satisfied with their previous replies, to which Cheryl countered that the evidence attesting to the difficulty of those words was provided by the fact that they had forgotten them.

Despite the significantly soft *locutionary* force (Austin 1962) of Mrs. Nieve's directive—the literal meaning of her utterance—, its *perlocutionary* force—the action performed as a result—can still be heard as dispreferred. However, given its moderate design, the participating children were still encouraged to orient to a stance of negotiation (see also Brooksbank 2017). The pauses in lines 5, 8, and 12 clearly indicate the children were in disagreement with the directive. Their utterances in lines 6, 7, and 9, contextualized with flat intonational contours, confirm this assertion. This excerpt illustrates how in response to a command that was framed as a request, the children oriented to a challenge to a power figure—an adult and teacher. Even though some tension was evident in the exchange, the conversation still continued as Cheryl and Luisa co-constructed a challenge to Mrs. Nieve, the teacher, and politely but confidently, opposed the rules and made a case for speaking in English.

The metalinguistic discussion in this interaction illustrates the nature of conversational negotiation generated by Mrs. Nieve's request and indicates resistance on the part of the children in response to her request. In the process of resisting the rule they co-constructed an explanation for why the words were hard, namely, that if those had not been difficult words, they would not have forgotten them. This is also evident in the use of English in the last three turns by Cheryl and Luisa, suggesting their negotiation was at least partly successful, thus further confirming the dispreferred nature of their responses to the request and the instantiation of their resistance.

12.5 Clarification requests and conversational closings

The next excerpt occurred in the home of the Aguirre-Ramírez, the middle-aged professionals from Mexico that were discussed in Chapter 10. A Spanish-only rule prevailed in this home. It became clear in multiple interviews with the parents and the children that the parents employed an assertive heritage language regulation style. They repeatedly commented on the three children's persistent habit of speaking English among themselves, and both parents'—but particularly Mrs. Aguirre's—constant reminders to use Spanish. The following excerpt took place in that particularly hard line language context as three-year old Penélope made herself busy at home while her sisters were in school. Penélope was holding a piece of paper in her hand when her mother inquired about it (Mrs. A=Mrs. Aguirre) (Observation: 01/12/06):

```
[Excerpt 12.4] "un paper"
1    Mrs. A:      ¿que es eso Flo-Penélope?
2    Penélope:    es un (0.2) paper=
3    Mrs. A:      =¿es un QUE?=
4    Penélope:    =un °paper° (xx[x)
5    Mrs. A:                  [no entiendo
6    Penélope:    (xxxx)
```

Translation
```
1    Mrs. A:      what is that Flo-Penélope?
2    Penélope:    it's a (0.2) paper=
3    Mrs. A:      =it's a WHAT?=
4    Penélope:    =a °paper° (xx[x)
5    Mrs. A:                  [I don't understand
6    Penélope:    (xxxx)
```

Mrs. Aguirre started the interaction by asking Penélope what it was she had in her hand. In line 2, Penélope seemed to struggle momentarily (0.2 second pause) just before producing "paper," an indication that she might have been unsuccessfully looking for the word *papel* in Spanish. In line 3 Mrs. Aguirre spoke immediately after Penélope used the English word "paper," which Mrs. Aguirre did not accept. The contiguity of line 3 with line 2 suggests there was a sense of urgency in Mrs. Aguirre's queries. She attempted to encourage Penélope to use the right Spanish word, raising her voice in the word "¿QUE?" (WHAT?), clearly indicating emphasis. In her reply, Penélope again used the word "paper" and was still talking, possibly explaining what it was she had in her hand. However, as soon as Penélope pronounced "paper," failing to repair, Mrs. Aguirre appeared to decide that she had heard enough. She only seemed interested in Penélope's code choice, evidenced in her overlap in line 5. There was no uptake of the message on her part once she had made her point through an implicit directive ("I don't understand") phrased as a clarification request. Rather than simply using a direct command (e.g., "speak Spanish"), Mrs. Aguirre drew on other linguistic resources to call Penélope's attention to the appropriate linguistic behaviour. Ochs (1988, 1991) has termed these types of clarification requests as minimal grasp strategies. She explains that terms such as "I don't understand" or puzzled facial expressions are commonly used to initiate the clarification of a presumably unintelligible utterance.

In implicit directives, which are often phrased as clarification requests, the message is expressed indirectly (Clyne 1996). However, given that this was a common occurrence in her family, it can be argued that the clarification requests in lines 4 and 6 together contained an explicit command through their prosodic features (i.e., loudness of voice). In addition, these types of directives tend to rely on conversational *implicature* (Levinson 1983) in order to produce contextually situated meanings. Implicature is used to explain utterances that mean more than what is said. In the interaction above, Mrs. Aguirre's utterance ("I don't understand") had a meaning that was quite different from what she actually said. Her utterance could be paraphrased as "I heard your answer, but I'm not going to accept it and I will pretend not to understand it until you say it in Spanish, the 'proper' language in the family." Penelope was expected to draw this inference from Mrs. Aguirre's utterance "I don't understand" and produce the Spanish word *papel*. The implicature of Mrs. Aguirre's utterance was an explicit directive to display a particular language behaviour. Through her linguistic actions, Mrs. Aguirre was making an obvious attempt to reinforce the Spanish-only rule at home, making it clear that at least in this interaction she was not interested in the content of three-year old Penélope's words, but in the code she used. This extract illustrates how the heritage language regulation processes found in the family created tensions that could interrupt the natural flow of communication, in this case, between a mother and her three-year old daughter. Mrs. Aguirre's attempts to strictly regulate her young daughter's language practices prompted an abrupt closing of the conversation, possibly also negating Penélope's budding ethnolinguistic identity.

12.6 Commands, resistance and sequence closings

In grassroots group gatherings, some parents were dubbed the "language police." They frequently reminded the children to use Spanish through various forms of directives. Commands were by far the most common type of heritage language regulation strategy observed during grassroots group activities as well as in everyday home interactions. These seemed to come spontaneously to the caregivers, as shown in the following example. It took place in El Grupo Scout Vistas as Mr. Maradiaga was leading an activity designed to help the children learn the Scout *promise*, which is part of the fundamental philosophy of the Scout Movement (see Chapter 9, and particularly Guardado 2009, for a more detailed description and analysis of the Scout activities). The Scout leaders had prepared slips of paper with the words of the Scout promise. These were distributed to groups of two or three children, who were instructed to put them in order. While working on the activity, Mrs. Fernández, one of the Scout leaders, discovered the children in one of the small groups departing from the official normative standard (Spanish-only), prompting a stern scolding (text in bold was originally spoken in English) (Mrs. F=Mrs. Fernández; Mr. M=Mr. Maradiaga) (Observation: 02/24/06):

```
[Excerpt 12.5] "why black?"
1              ((children speaking English in background))
2    Child:    (xxx)
3    Child:    what?
4    Child:    WHY BLACK?
5    Mrs. F:   ↑español
6    Child:    ↓oh
7              (8.0) ((background noise and talking))
8    Mr. M:    en caso de (xx) de que no usen la coma
9              déjenla los dos puntos la coma esos déjenlos
10             o- obvienlas no se preocupen de eso lo que me
11             interesa más es el (xxxxxx) déjenlos la coma
12   Mrs. F:   en ↑españo:l (.) Tatiana
13             ((extended pause before Mr. M moved to the next
               phase of the activity))

Translation
1              ((children speaking English in background))
2    Child:    (xxx)
3    Child:    what?
```

```
4   Child:   WHY BLACK?
5   Mrs. F:  ↑Spanish
6   Child:   ↓oh
7            (8.0) ((background noise and talking))
8   Mr. M:   in case (xx) you don't use the comma leave
9            it the colons the comma those leave them o⁻
10           obviate them don't worry about that what I'm
11           interested in mostly is the (xxxxxx) leave the
             comma
12  Mrs. F:  in ↑Spani:sh (.) Tatiana
13           ((extended pause before Mr. M moved to the next
             phase of the activity))
```

After noticing that some of the children had switched to English or were code-mixing (lines 1–4), Mrs. Fernández reminded them to speak Spanish, using rising intonation, to which a child (line 6) responded with an *oh* particle using falling intonation. A few seconds later, Mr. Maradiaga continued with additional instructions for the children (line 8), after which, Mrs. Fernández restated her admonition in line 12, again using rising intonation with an elongated vowel in the last syllable, as Tatiana had not complied with her request.

It was discussed in the previous chapter that in many societies, prompting is commonly used to lead children to use a particular speech form or to speak in a way that is grammatically and socially appropriate (Paugh 2005), and in the case of bilingual children, to teach them 'proper' uses of both languages (Howard 2008), among other goals. In line with these functions of prompting, the grassroots parents used directives to elicit from the children the required code—Spanish. In order to accomplish this goal, they typically used imperative forms accompanied by relevant prosodic features for emphasis, which were frequently followed by reprimands to further establish the imperative functions of their speech (Ochs 1996). As previously discussed in the book, the prompting effect and sense of urgency of imperatives, even without explicit directives, is significantly augmented by the use of prosodic features.

The above excerpt is therefore a clear-cut case of directives phrased as commands. The fact that Mrs. Fernández's directive (line 5) used an imperative form that carried a particular intonational contour suggests that it was designed for "doing ordering" and to send the unequivocal message to children to switch to Spanish. What this turn does to children, however, is frustrate them. A child's dispreferred second pair part (SPP) in line 6 uses the particle *oh*, which Heritage (1984) has analyzed as a *change-of-state token*. Heritage has demonstrated that this particle has several functions in conversation and usually means *news receipt* and a change of state in the recipient of a previous turn. It refers to an assessment of the first pair part that often signals disagreement with its propositional content. He argues that intonational delivery is important in interpreting a change-of-state-token, which in some cases leads to a sequence closing. Therefore, the falling intonation used in "oh" in line 6, combined with the long pause in line 7 (8.0 seconds) are easily interpretable as an index that the child was disappointed at the command issued and that it had the effect of closing the sequence. Furthermore, Mrs. Fernández's even more stern command in line 12, evidenced by the rising intonational contour and stretched vowel sound, further constituted the severity of the admonition, effectively ending the children's participation in the conversation.

12.7 Implications of the analyses

In this chapter, I presented a CA-informed analysis of the HL socializing strategies used by adult caregivers in their attempts to encourage and regulate young Hispanic Canadian children's heritage language use. A cursory review of the types of interactions included may suggest that the analyses conducted located language regulation strategies in the participating families on a continuum from complete explicitness to relative implicitness. Table 12.1 may soon make it clear, however, that the level of implicitness of the directives used was relatively unrelated to their effects on the interactions. Commands and requests, which were classified as explicit in the table, both produced dispreferred turn shapes and stances of misalignment. However, a turn-by-turn analysis revealed that whereas commands ended conversations, requests tended to foster negotiation. Therefore, even though both have been described as sharing some features (explicitness, resulting turn shape), they are also seen in contrast to each other in terms of their actual effects on conversation.

Table 12.1 Summary of metapragmatic strategies and characteristics.

	Lectures*	Commands	Requests	Cl. Requests	CCRs
Stance	N/A	Misalignment	Misalignment	Misalignment	Alignment
Turn shape	*	Dispreferred responses	Dispreferred responses	Dispreferred responses	Preferred responses
Action performed	*	Conversational closings	Metalinguistic negotiation	Conversational closings	Conversational expansions
Type	Explicit	Explicit	Explicit	Implicit	Implicit

Even more strikingly, clarification requests and cross-code recasts were both classified as implicit in Table 12.1. Nevertheless, while clarification requests generated dispreferred turn shapes that motivated misalignment between the interactants, CCRs fostered alignment through preferred turn shapes. Therefore, CCRs were found to engender conversational expansions while clarification requests produced abrupt conversational closings. I posit that explicitness and implicitness are generally unrelated to what these strategies do in conversation given that how they are perceived and oriented to is based on their illocutionary force, which is ultimately consequential to communication.

In a 2002 article I argued that the type and tone of discourse parents used to encourage their children to speak the HL could have a facilitating or detrimental effect on their children's language development and maintenance. While that argument was based on interview data that elicited parents' accounts of how they pursued the goal of HL development, in this chapter I showed, based on microanalyses of parent-child talk in interactions, that the approach parents use to encourage children to speak the HL can indeed have a facilitating or a detrimental effect on communication with their children. The present analysis revealed that it is not the implicitness or explicitness of the linguistic strategies that can have a detrimental or facilitating effect, but the rhetorical force of the linguistic intervention. Although illocutionarily—the speaker's intention—the utterances summarized in Table 12.1 are arguably similar, the locutionary—literal meaning—and perlocutionary—or result—forces are considerably different.

The analyses presented in this chapter closely resemble aspects of Lanza's (1997/2004) findings in Norway. Building on concepts and terminology proposed by Ochs (1988, 1991), Lanza categorized the parental discourse strategies along a continuum based on their potential for fostering "a monolingual or bilingual interactional context" (207). Seeing the present interactional analyses through Lanza's analytical lens, it is clear that all of these metapragmatic strategies attempt to create a monolingual interactional context. Indeed, although commands make the strongest bid for a monolingual context, all other strategies carry a similar illocutionary force. Minimal grasp and expressed guess strategies (Ochs 1988) are both contained in clarification requests. Adult repetitions (Lanza 1992, 2001, 2007) are somewhat equivalent to CCRs. Therefore, as Figure 12.1 shows, the present categorization is best represented on a continuum that highlights the effect that the deployment of these monolingually oriented metapragmatic strategies have on the interaction.

Conversational Closing			Conversational Expansion
Commands	Clarification Requests	Requests	CCRs

Figure 12.1 Continuum of parental metapragmatic strategies.

12.7 Implications of the analyses — 201

A methodological implication of this chapter in relation to the 2002 study stems from the potential of using CA tools in investigations of heritage language socialization. By using these tools, the chapter provides interactional evidence for my earlier hypothesizing that the nature of discourse employed by parents to encourage their children to speak the heritage language can be potentially conducive to maintenance or to loss. Thus, through triangulation of different types of data and analytic techniques, it is possible to strengthen the research findings of thematic analyses.

A key thread found in the emerging themes was resistance of various types. All the strategies used by parents had either motivations or effects associated with forms of resistance. Commands, for instance, produced strong resistance and annoyance in the children and had a sequence closing effect. Requests to speak Spanish, although facilitating negotiation, also had a strong resistance component. Although the children affirmed their identities through resistance, this identity affirmation in itself also constituted an act of resistance (hooks 1989). The lectures occasionally given to the children as a defensive socialization technique, were also a resistance performance on the part of the parents in a preemptive attempt to confront the hegemony of English and *inoculate* the children against code-switching or full language shift. Clarification requests created tensions that interrupted the natural flow of communication between caregivers and children, which generated strong resistance and the closing of conversations. A recent study using Child Language Data Exchange System (CHILDES) data also highlights this issue (Brooksbank 2017).

Although parental planning of language use tends to be treated as a side issue in HL development scholarship (Piller 2001b), the goal of the present chapter—and one of the goals of this book—is to attempt to bring home language planning, policy, regulation, and use to the forefront of research. It is my belief that these factors and processes are at the heart of this research area as the linguistic interactions taking place between parents and children are some of the key sites of struggle upon which family language ideologies are contested. These analyses constitute an attempt to begin to "lift the hood" on the linguistic mechanisms operating in multilingual families. Thus, I examined the characteristics of the turns engendering dispreference and disagreement between adults and children in daily interactions. Additionally, emphasis was paid to the design of the dissenting responses and the actions performed by these sequences. The metalinguistic practices analyzed reveal parents' attempts to revalorize Spanish in the English-dominant Canadian context in order to construe it as a "power code" (Hill 1985).

Since speech is often a coercive force (Philips 1998), some of the very explicit processes of metapragmatic regimentation of heritage language use found in the data show that when parents coerce children to speak in a particular way, this practice often has the effect of unwittingly oppressing children by silencing them.

Thus, through the resistance manifested in some of the above interactions, the children affirmed their identity and their right to use the language with which they were most comfortable. In effect, they countered what they seemed to perceive as a rejection of the linguistic affordances that characterized their evolving and potentially hybrid ethnolinguistic affiliations and practices.

12.8 Chapter summary

In this chapter, I have addressed the metalinguistic management of language use within families and grassroots community groups, a key aspect of HL development, which is often ignored in this area of research. I proposed using language socialization in combination with tools borrowed from conversation analysis in order to examine how heritage language regimentation takes place. For instance, lectures provided clear examples of how HL development discourses are utilized to strengthen the lecturer's call. This form of defensive socialization is a strategy used by immigrant parents in response to clashing cultural values in order to "pre-arm" their children with counter-arguments and rationales that are in line with their own culture. Indeed, the lecture given at the beginning of the chapter served not only to reinforce or validate parents' heritage language attitudes and home practices, but also necessarily, to inform the children of the language values and expectations of the Scouting group.

While cross-code recasts as well as metalinguistic negotiations have different effects on conversation, both seem to show respect for the ultimate agency of the child. In the case of CCRs, this effect, in turn, led to conversational expansions, which arguably, would be conducive to HL development given the expanded interactional opportunities. Clarification requests, on the other hand, tend to focus on form rather than function or meaning, which may have detrimental effects on conversation continuity. In the analysis presented, the deployment of a clarification request seemed to abruptly end the interaction. Unsurprisingly, commands were the most common form of heritage language regulation observed; paradoxically, my microlinguistic analyses found them to be the least desirable, although a growing body of research suggests that these are the most common within families.

The analyses presented in this chapter showed that the level of implicitness and explicitness of the directives used was unrelated to the effects that they produced. One of the arguably undesired consequences of certain metapragmatic strategies, such as commands and clarification requests, is that they—presumably unintentionally—deny the children's right to hybridity in relation to their identities and linguistic practices. It is argued that these negative consequences of their deployment make a case for the introduction of a variety of rhetorically softer strategies in families in order to diminish this unfavorable effect.

Part IV: **Family, community and education in global perspective**

13 A cosmopolitan turn in heritage language studies?

13.1 Introduction

This chapter takes up the cosmopolitanism discourse proposed in Chapter 6. It draws on a much larger collection of ethnographic participants' comments in order to relate this notion to HL development. I first define relevant concepts, such as Generation 1.5, Third Culture Kids, cosmopolitanism, and transnationalism. Then I outline a multilayered view of identity within a HL development discussion, and examine what a cosmopolitan turn in HL development may mean for theory, heritage language socialization, and research. The chapter concludes by positing the intersection between HL development and cosmopolitan identities as a potentially fruitful dimension to be considered in discussions about the emergence of new hybrid identities. The discussions contained in this chapter serve as a catalyst for the ruminations I mull over in the next chapter.

13.2 Generation 1.5 and Third Culture Kids

Identity is a key concept that helps set off the discussion in this chapter. The study of identity development has a long tradition that has built on the work of Freud (1923/1961) and Erikson (1950). In applied linguistics, the relationship between identity and language learning has generated significant scholarship in the last decade. Postructuralists define social identity as the way individuals understand and view their relationship to the world and how that relationship is constructed in their lifetimes (Norton 2000). Language is the chief tool that members of social groups use in order to transmit their values and beliefs to individuals, which helps form individuals' emerging identities. The language itself codifies many cultural elements, such as ideas about language and aspects of the speakers' worldview.

Two terms intricately connected to identity and HL development that are of critical relevance to the arguments made in this chapter are Generation 1.5 and Third Culture Kids (TCK). Generation 1.5 (Rumbaut and Ima 1988) refers to those individuals who immigrate as children or teens to a new country. They are believed to grow up with characteristics of the first and the second generation of immigrants without fully fitting in either category (Ryu 1991). Although scholars have taken up various parameters to circumscribe membership in Generation 1.5

(e.g., age at immigration, linguistic ability, stage of education at time of immigration), of interest to this chapter are their putative bicultural and multicultural identification and characteristics (Park 1999). The general consensus is that these are immigrant youth who have different complex experiences and identifications from those of the first or the second generation. Thus, there is currently an increased interest in investigating the unique position in which Generation 1.5 individuals may find themselves, the features and challenges of their lived experiences, and as a consequence, the distinctive ways in which these youth negotiate and construct their identities (e.g., Roberge 2002, Harklau 2003, Talmy 2005, Kim 2008). Work of this nature also needs to address the unique ways they may learn to view, make sense of and interact with the world as a result of their experiences.

The factors to which I would like to draw attention in this chapter relate to these individuals' highly complex identities, especially their potentially multicultural dimension, fluidity and dynamic nature, and hybridity. These individuals are able to move across generational, cultural, and linguistic boundaries in their social lives. Their ability to function and feel comfortable in different physical and symbolic spaces is related to their greater adaptability, transnational experiences, and as Hurh (1993) has posited, their cosmopolitanism as evidenced by their creativity and ability to simultaneously identify with both their ethnic past and their adopted society.

The term TCK (Fail, Thompson and Walker 2004) is used to describe individuals who spend a significant period of time in two or more ethnic and language cultural groups, and as a consequence, embrace elements of those groups into a third culture (Useem, Useem and Donoghue 1963). In a sense, their identities become greater than the sum of their parts. Generation 1.5, TCK, and HL learners share a variety of characteristics as they grow up in a culture (or cultures) that is not their parents' original cultures and tend to develop identities that incorporate components from all of them. These experiences allow them to function as complex multicultural individuals with adaptable features who engage in transnational activities and embrace highly cosmopolitan characteristics.

13.3 Cosmopolitanism

The notion of *cosmopolitanism* promises to be useful in discussing issues of identity affecting the above individuals. Along with *transnationalism,* a related term, cosmopolitanism has become a popular concept in recent scholarship in fields such as sociology and cultural geography. Faist (1998) defines transnationalism as emergent communities comprised of individuals who are settled in different national societies and who share common religious, territorial, linguistic as well as other interests and relationships across national boundaries. It can apply to the experiences of individuals and families who maintain strong cultural and familial ties to actual or imagined communities (Anderson 1983) in their countries of origin while living in the diaspora.

The notion of cosmopolitanism is not new. Etymologically, it comes from the Greek term *kosmopolitês*, which translates as *a citizen of the world* (Roudometof 2005). Cosmopolitanism connotes mobility of people, ideas, cultures, images, or objects (Germann Molz 2005) across spaces and a relationship between the local, the national, and the global (Starkey 2007). Thus, it refers to a "global sense of place" (Massey 1994: 12) that indicates a shift in collective and personal cultural identities that cultivates the recognition of others (Delanty 2006). A cosmopolitan disposition allows individuals to draw on the country of origin as a source of identity (Kastoryano 2000, Appiah 2006). At the same time, it promotes in them a "stance of openness towards divergent cultural experiences" (Hannerz 1990: 239) and a feeling of being at home in the world (Brennan 1997). In other words, it assumes the possession of adaptable dispositions and "a commitment to global solidarity and global cultural diversity" (Smith 2007: 39) that nurtures multiple belonging. It can be understood as a synergy of many cultures, with at least two dominant ones. The relationship between transnationalism and cosmopolitanism, then, is that while cosmopolitanism refers to the attitudes and identities (the ideology), transnationalism describes the individual experiences. I continue to engage with—and expand on—these ideas in the next chapter.

Although cosmopolitanism has not been discussed in direct relation to HL development in the applied linguistics literature, associated terms have at times been indirectly referred to by scholars (e.g., He 2006). It is argued in this chapter that cosmopolitanism offers sufficient explanatory power to be extended fruitfully to discussions of identity in the HL development and maintenance scholarship.

The foregoing discussion in this chapter has dealt with various interrelated concepts that have relevance to discussions of identity for individuals living in multicultural and multilingual societies. In particular, these concepts encapsulate many of the characteristics that immigrant youth and the children of immigrants may experience. Although these children and youth may or may not fit definitions of Generation 1.5 or TCK specifically, I believe that considering such concepts in relation to cosmopolitanism can help elucidate key features of identity surrounding HL learners. Therefore, the foregoing descriptions are intended as an introduction to the possible cultural identifications of linguistic-minority children.

13.4 Growing up ethnic or pan-ethnic?

The participants in my ethnography used a variety of terms to refer to cultural identity. These terms sometimes referred to specific ethnic identities (e.g., Mayan), nation-state identities (e.g., Guatemalan, Canadian), or pan-ethnic identities (e.g., Hispanic or Latin American). The Aguirre-Ramírez parents often referred to identity in terms of national origin, equating nation-state identity with ethnic identity, and other times used more encompassing identities. For instance, they felt that the maintenance of their own cultural roots meant the maintenance of a Mexican identity, as quoted previously when Mr. Ramírez talked about their daughters' possible adoption of various cultural elements based on their experiences in Canada: "Para absorber todo lo que están viviendo a su alrededor, pero sin perder las raíces y las tradiciones que traían o que tenemos en México" [To absorb everything they [were] experiencing in their surroundings, but without losing their roots and the traditions they brought or that we have in Mexico] (Interview: 04/15/06). Likewise, Mr. Maradiaga often used the term "Guatemalan." At times the term seemed to encompass the whole nation-state and at other times, a more particular one, a Mayan Guatemala that emphasized his ethnicity. Thus, he seemed to refer to a generic cultural identity, a nation-state identity, but also an ethnic identity, Mayan, which illustrated the complex ways in which identity was experienced and portrayed by the families.

The socialization of pan-ethnic identities was evident in the comments the families made about their home activities, as well as the activities in which they participated in their grassroots groups. Since the groups had members from 10 different Spanish-speaking countries, this national origin diversity translated into cultural and dialect diversity. The following is an example of how issues of pan-ethnicity came up in one of the grassroots groups, La Casa Amistad, during an activity led by Mrs. Aguirre. The activity required the children to become involved in all aspects related to running a restaurant, including finding a name, creating the menu, and finally preparing the items in the menu. After introducing the activity, Mrs. Aguirre helped the children name the restaurant. This is an excerpt from the interaction that took place (Mrs. A=Mrs. Aguirre):

[Excerpt 13.1]
1 Mrs. A: ¿Cómo le ponemos al resrorán?
2 Child 1:   España
3 Child 2:   México
4 Perla: Español
5 Mrs. A: ¿que tal 'Latino'?
6 Mrs. A: algo que unifique más

```
Translation
1  Mrs. A: what should we name the restaurant?
2  Child 1:   Spain
3  Child 2:   Mexico
4  Perla: Español
5  Mrs. A: how about 'Latino'?
6  Mrs. A: something more unifying
```

Mrs. Aguirre instructed the children to name the restaurant and several options were offered by everyone. She clearly avoided the use of a name that was specific to a particular country, so she attempted to elicit other ideas from the children (lines 5 and 6). She explained she was looking for a name that was more unifying in the Spanish-speaking world or at least in Latin America. Mrs. Aguirre offered "Que tal *latino*?" [How about *Latino*?] and then repeated "algo que unifique más" [something more unifying], and further elaborated on this idea before deciding to have a vote (excerpt not shown), in which España (Spain) obtained the most votes, although Restorán Latino was used in the end. Throughout this interaction, Mrs. Aguirre's efforts to elicit a particular type of name for the restaurant showed clear efforts to socialize the children into pan-ethnic identities.

13.5 Growing up around other languages and cultures

Another aspect of the families' socialization efforts that pointed to a hybrid and highly complex identity orientation in their children was their stance toward other languages and cultures. All the families placed great importance on having multilingual abilities and pursued these goals through Spanish-only policies at home, participation in HL development grassroots groups, enrolling their children in French immersion programs, among other initiatives. Therefore, the families did not only count on Spanish to provide special opportunities, but also saw it as a starting point for learning other languages, and thus, increasing their professional and meaning-making potential. This was also evident in the parents' own interest in learning other languages. Indeed, many of the parents were multilingual themselves and actively engaged in activities that promoted multilingualism in their children and other members of the community. This attitude toward other languages and their speakers was also evident in the efforts made by the families in El Centro de Cultura, one of the grassroots groups, by accommodating three Chinese-speaking students in the group who were interested in learning Spanish.

Although many previous studies have highlighted the potential economic benefits families assign to multilingualism, in Mrs. Pérez' case, she was more interested in promoting cultural and linguistic awareness in her children. Such notions were particularly applicable in this case because the Spanish language is associated with cultural, racial, religious, dialectal, and regional diversity. To Mrs. Pérez, a key to helping open those doors was provided by the Scout group and El Centro de Cultura, two groups in which she participated along with the family's other Spanish language socialization efforts. She stated in this regard: "Y claro, una vez ya lo tienen [idioma español], pues te abre muchas más puertas y puedes apreciar toda una cultura, no una, muchas, como España, Méjico, Guatemala, Argentina. Es que es maravilloso, claro imagínate. Aparte te abre las puertas para aprender otras lenguas latinas" [And of course, once they have it [Spanish language], it opens many more doors for you and you can appreciate a whole culture, not one, but many, like Spain, Mexico, Guatemala, Argentina. Because it's so wonderful, for sure, imagine. Besides, it opens doors for learning other Latin (Romance) languages] (Interview: 05/12/06).

Like Mrs. Pérez, other families did not only use utility discourses but also went beyond the economic benefits they expected Spanish to afford their children. For instance, Mrs. Aguirre seemed to address, at least in part, the transferability of skills from one language to another (Cummins 1981, Crawford 1992b, Krashen 1996, Cummins 2000), as evidenced in this quote: "Yo creo que abriéndote el canal de un idioma más, estás abriendo las opciones para otros idiomas" [I think that by creating an avenue for another language, one is broadening the options for other languages] (Interview: 05/14/05). The family's efforts in HL development and maintenance were directed at creating opportunities for their daughters to build on that knowledge and learn other languages; forming the linguistic foundations the children could draw from in their future language learning endeavors.

The families' views about other cultures were exemplified by the Aguirre-Ramírez parents. Mr. Ramírez stated that the family was interested in transmitting and reinforcing the notion that there is more to language than just Spanish. They wanted the girls to really understand "... que no solo es el español. Que hay otros idiomas" [... that it is not only Spanish. There are other languages] (Mrs. Aguirre, Interview: 05/14/05). It appears that the main thrust in the family was to raise children who were aware of their roots and proud of who they were. At the same time, they wanted them to value the place where they lived, the languages that were spoken, and the cultures that were practiced in that milieu. Mrs. Aguirre believed that the girls' experiences were enriched

> ... de toda la oportunidad que tienen de convivir con diferentes personas, de diferentes países, y creo que de alguna manera siempre las lleva a pensar en la propia, en las suyas,

en lo que nosotros acostumbramos a hacer, en todo lo que pretendemos llegar a hacer ¿no? creo que el reto que dice Orlando [Mr. Ramírez], que mantengan la [cultura] de nosotros y asimilen las partes positivas de las demás y que aprendan a respetar las diferentes [culturas] ... ese yo creo que es la base, o sea, la teoría aquí en Canadá es una de que tu respetes al otro individuo como es, en sus creencias, en sus formas de actuar, mientras NO interfieras en tu ... no en tu espacio, sino que no provoque un daño al otro, lo que es la libertad, ser libre, y hacer lo que tú ... a donde tú quieras llegar, pero sin dañar a otros, entonces yo creo que esa parte es muy rica para ellas. (Interview: 04/15/06)

... by all the opportunities they have to coexist with different people from different countries and I think that in some form it always leads them to think about their own [culture], in what we customarily do, in everything we intend to do, no? I think the challenge Orlando [Mr. Ramírez] is referring to, that they maintain ours [our culture] and assimilate the positive aspects of other cultures and learn to respect different [cultures] ... that is what I think is the base, that is, the theory here in Canada is one that holds that you respect other individuals as they are, their beliefs, their behaviours, as long as you DO NOT interfere in your ... not in your space, rather that does not harm others, what liberty is, to be free and to do what you ... where you want to go, but without harming others, so I think that aspect is very, very enriching for them]

Mrs. Aguirre and Mr. Ramírez's cultural beliefs reflected their understanding of Canadian multiculturalism, one in which all the different cultures ideally cohabit in the same geographical and socio-politico-cultural space, without interfering with one another's cultural practices. Living in such an environment—a cultural market of sorts—the family members could choose to take what appealed to them and incorporate it into their own lives. The parents felt that the children would benefit from a socialization that allowed them to value all cultures, but at the same time, to feel proud of their own roots, holistically raising children that they appeared to describe as more emotionally stable human beings: "Todo esto le refuerza esa parte emocional, y yo digo que puede a la larga pues dar seres humanos, espero, más seguros y más fuertes, más orgullosos de sí mismo, pero además, interesados en los otros" [All this reinforces that emotional aspect and I think that in the long run it can, I hope, foster human beings that are more secure, stronger and prouder of themselves, but in addition, who are interested in others] (Mrs. Aguirre, Interview: 05/04/06).

In other words, they felt that the promotion and maintenance of their own cultural roots and an appreciation of other cultures was the ideal balance with which to grow up:

A lo mejor es el reto ¿no? Porque sí sería triste que perdieran esas tradiciones por absorber otras y no porque unas sean necesariamente mejores que otras, no, sino porque esas tradiciones vienen de tus raíces ¿no? entonces, ese es el reto, tal vez lograr que las niñas, este, mantengan ese espíritu abierto ¿no? para absorber todo lo que están viviendo a su alrededor, pero sin perder las raíces y las tradiciones que traían o que tenemos en México ¿no? (Mr. Ramírez, Interview: 04/15/06)

[Maybe that is the challenge, no? Because it would indeed be sad if they lost these traditions as a result of absorbing others and not because some are necessarily better than others, no, rather because these traditions stem from their roots, no? So, that is the challenge, perhaps that the girls, uh, maintain that open spirit, no? to absorb everything they are experiencing in their surroundings, but without losing their roots and the traditions they brought or that we have in Mexico, no?]

13.6 Growing up with a broader vision of the world

As part of the process of awareness raising, culturally and linguistically, in Canada's multicultural context, the children in this ethnographic study, and to some extent the adults, might have been developing syncretic identities that were, in many ways, unlike those of their counterparts either in their countries of origin or in Canada. Moreover, the identities they attempted to socialize the children into also considered the other languages and cultures of the community as having a significant role in their identity development. These issues were highly reminiscent of descriptions of Generation 1.5 individuals and TCK, whose characteristics resemble those of heritage language learners in my data set.

Indeed, Mrs. Fernández and Mr. Maradiaga claimed to subscribe to a syncretic notion of cultural identity that embraced much more than their own culture. Mrs. Fernández asserted: "La identidad cultural de las niñas es un híbrido. No podemos hacer un pequeño mundo dentro de estas cuatro paredes. Ellas tienen que conocer su cultura, pero tampoco encerrarlas en eso. No se puede. No estaríamos logrando nuestros objetivos, de que ellas tengan una visión amplia" [The cultural identity of the girls is a hybrid. We can't create a mini-world inside these four walls. They have to know their culture, but we can't enclose them in it. It can't be done. We wouldn't be achieving our goals for them to have a broad outlook] (Interview: 05/09/05).

Additionally, they seemed to suggest that an additional language, in this case Spanish, was also key to present and future learning and to accessing otherwise inaccessible physical, symbolic, and cultural spaces. When asked why he felt it was important for his children to maintain their Spanish, Mr. Maradiaga told me:

Un niño cuando habla más de un idioma intelectualmente crece. Ha habido estudios creo, que los niños son más inteligentes ¿no? Tienen otra visión del mundo que es lo que la otra parte que queremos darles a ellas. Otro punto de vista, varios puntos de vista y que ellas después escojan ¿no? La identidad cultural es necesaria para lograr mantener el español. No se puede saber de su cultura si no se sabe su idioma. Yo no puedo conocer más a fondo de los chinos, de los japoneses, porque no hablo la lengua de ellos. Ellos me podrán pasar una información platicándolo, pero no es lo mismo. A las niñas les da una visión más amplia del mundo, no de un lugar más pequeño, pero del mundo (Interview: 05/09/05)

[A child that speaks more than one language grows intellectually. I believe there have been studies; children are more intelligent, no? They have another vision of the world, which is the other aspect we want to give them. Another point of view, many points of view and later they can choose, right? Cultural identity is necessary in order to maintain Spanish. We can't know about the culture if we don't know the language. I can't have a deeper knowledge of the Chinese and the Japanese, because I don't speak their language. They could give me some information through conversation, but it's not the same. The [Spanish] language gives the girls a broader vision of the world, not of something that is smaller, but of the world]

In this quote Mr. Maradiaga asserted that there were two main reasons he felt HL development was important. First, it was important to their children's sense of cultural identity, and second, it would provide the girls with a "broader vision of the world." This quote referred to the benefit of being able to function, think, and conduct analyses through two or more cultural systems (Schecter and Bayley 2002), enriching people's worldview as well as increasing their meaning-making capabilities.

Echoing the Fernández-Maradiaga parents, Mrs. Aguirre and Mr. Ramírez often stated that the maintenance of their own cultural roots and an appreciation of other cultures was an ideal balance they pursued. The values that the family espoused reflected a view that being Canadian meant embracing an affiliation to a broader identity beyond that of Mexican or Latin American. Mr. Ramírez concluded with a question that he also answered: "¿Qué significa ser canadiense? Ser ciudadano del mundo" [What does it mean to be Canadian? To be a citizen of the world] (Interview: 05/14/05). This suggests that the family attempted to socialize the children into identities as global citizens.

13.7 Growing up cosmopolitan

The families included in this chapter held the view that Spanish maintenance was an important catalyst in socializing their children into a progressive worldview. First of all, the parents implied to subscribe to a syncretic notion of cultural identity that strongly embraced their own culture. At the same time, they were aware that their children's sense of identity was different from their own. The Fernández-Maradiaga family was aware of the outside influences on their daughters' evolving identities and understood that they could not enclose them in a cultural bubble. Additionally, as asserted by Mrs. Fernández, one of their aims was to socialize them into a "broad world outlook." This outlook can be seen as consistent with pursuing an understanding and appreciation of other cultures, drawing from them in the course of their identity formation.

The Aguirre-Ramírez family had similar views. They placed a central value on bilingualism and multilingualism as part of a belief system that included valuing all languages and cultures equally. Mr. Ramírez stated the family was interested in transmitting a sense of value for languages other than Spanish. They explained they wanted to raise children who were "interested in others," echoing scholars studying cosmopolitanism (e.g., Delanty 2006). They explained they wanted their daughters to absorb the cultural contents of their experiences in their surroundings, while at the same time holding on to their heritage, thus socializing them into hybrid identities as Canadians, which to them meant embracing an affiliation to a broader identity beyond that of Latin American or Mexican. To them, Spanish maintenance in the context of the Canadian multicultural milieu meant socializing their children to be citizens of the world and incorporating aspects of the Canadian cultural fabric into their identification. These goals were associated with their cosmopolitan stance and their efforts to ensure their daughters have access to increased mobility, a characteristic of global citizenship (Lin 2003), in their future lives.

The Fernández-Maradiaga family also pursued these notions in various ways. Their socialization aims included a construction of Spanish development and maintenance as an essential factor in providing their daughters with a broader vision of the world. These goals entailed enabling them to mediate their thought processes and behaviours through more than one cultural system (Schecter and Bayley 2002), enhancing their world outlook as well as diversifying their abilities for meaning-making across different physical, cultural, and symbolic spaces. All of this was part of their attempt to relate their children's socialization experiences with local, national (i.e., Canada and Guatemala), and global perspectives (Starkey 2007) as well as to promote identity development that drew from multiple cultural sources (Kastoryano 2000). Their idealistic HL socialization goals also entailed maintaining an open attitude toward other cultures (Hannerz 1990), and preparing them for creative thinking and intercultural flexibility (Ting-Toomey and Chung 2007).

In addition to the above points, the broader study (Guardado 2008a) documented how the family's language socialization aims included promoting good citizenship. The maintenance of Spanish language and culture were central to this goal. Based on interviews and observed interactions, Mr. Maradiaga and Mrs. Fernández' understandings of good citizenship assumed the maintenance of Spanish language and culture. Likewise, they felt that for the children a cosmopolitan outlook presupposed developing a strong sense of belonging related to their original cultures and languages as well as an appreciation for other cultures and languages. It presumed a commitment to the community, to the environment, to social change, and to cultural diversity, in line with some of the current conceptualizations of cosmopolitanism (Appiah 2006, Smith 2007). For them, language and cultural maintenance, good citizenship, and cosmopolitanism were intertwined in various ways.

Thus, the families' construction of Spanish maintenance went beyond more usual constructions related to future economic benefits as expressed in utility discourses. It was aimed at maintaining strong cultural identities that were influenced by their transnational activities. Nonetheless, it also encompassed important elements of cosmopolitanism. Contrary to popular opinion, HL development was not just about preserving a mythic past; it was about raising their children as cosmopolitan people with the ability to establish social relations and to bridge gaps between local and global ways of thinking. Heritage language development was constructed in a progressive rather than a nostalgic and conservative sense, and as a way of creating a synergy of many cultures in the language socialization experiences in which they sought to immerse their children. In this way, the families influenced the development of their identities in particular ways that fostered a global sense of place (Massey 1994).

The above discussion indicates that the families' constructions of Spanish development and maintenance in their children were directly associated with identity. However, as Figure 13.1 shows, their stances toward cultural identification were found to be highly complex and multilayered. The families appeared to be interested in socializing their children into locally defined ethnic and nation-state identities; however, this did not mean rejecting more encompassing affiliations such as pan-ethnicity. On the contrary, it was part of their view of Spanish as key to maintaining different, and often situated, levels of identity,

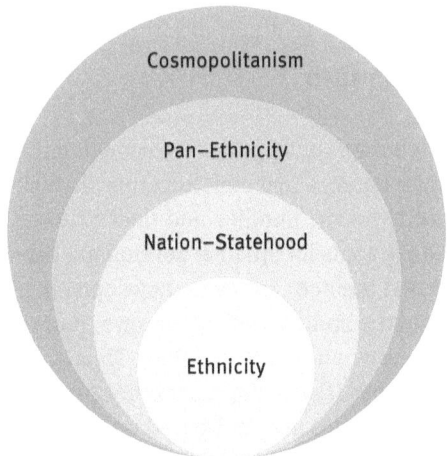

Figure 13.1 A multilayered view of identity.

being legitimate members of, and identifying with, a pluralistic society, as well as adopting a cosmopolitan outlook that emphasized global citizenry, and thus, a broader vision of the world. As individuals born elsewhere but growing up in a highly diverse society, the children in these families share many features with Generation 1.5 and TCK and are likely to become the adults their parents aspired for them to be.

I argued above that the participating families' constructions of HL development echoed those found in current academic discourses of cosmopolitanism. One of the traditional criticisms directed at cosmopolitanism has been its elitism. It is important to note that some of the families in the study were somewhat more privileged than the general Hispanic immigrant population in Canada. Such characteristic can be seen as consonant with a cosmopolitan orientation. However, many contemporary scholars of cosmopolitanism (e.g., Robbins 1998, Ribeiro 2003) argue that it is time the term be extended to unprivileged individuals with a variety of experiences given the increasing movement and interdependence of humans across geographical and virtual spaces.

A direct link between cosmopolitanism and HL development in this regard stems from particular ideologies about HLs prevalent in recent decades. Multilingualism among members of the upper classes in North America has been equated with what we might call cosmopolitan worldviews. Multilingualism among minorities has been seen as a problem and the chief cause for linguistic minority children's failure in school and in society. Scholarship in the last three decades has done much to change this deficit view and to highlight the positive effects of multilingualism in individuals and society. It is this key moment that makes it possible to propose a cosmopolitan turn in relation to HL development for elite and non-elite populations alike.

13.8 Implications of a cosmopolitan turn

This chapter has shown, by drawing on ethnographic data, that many families use discourses of HL development and maintenance that construct this phenomenon as a crucial source of cultural identity for the families and their children. However, beyond this frequently reported rationale for Spanish development and maintenance, these parents also constructed their children's HL development as a passport to a worldview that went beyond the limits posed by narrower notions of identity, such as ethnic, nation-state, or even pan-ethnic identities. Thus, these findings imply that for the participating families HL development is not a narrow goal, motivated by "backward" and nostalgic thinking, and based on the families' desires and efforts to cling to their past through their HL. Rather, HL development should be seen as the result of an open-minded stance with wide-ranging and far-reaching goals that can positively affect the broader society and at the same time promote enhanced intercultural relations, adaptable thinking, mutual understanding and learning as well as synergistic problem-solving.

Although the relationship between identity, L2 learning, and HL development has been abundantly documented elsewhere, the findings demonstrate that for the families, the relationship between HL development and identity was much more complex than previously shown. In line with other research, the chapter analyzed some of the ways in which parents constructed HL development and maintenance as part of their goals to instill in their children an ideology of pride and self-worth rooted in their culture. However, the families' desire to meaningfully connect to their nation-states of origin and their cultures does not imply or preclude the lack of desire to establish meaningful connections and affiliations with diverse groups spread across time and space. In addition to socializing their children into Spanish ideologies and Hispanic/Latin American cultural identities, these parents also attempted to inculcate a sense of value for other cultures and languages in the community, including English—a language ideology of inclusion. In this way they worked to add a hybridized, cosmopolitan layer to their children's identities. Thus, Spanish maintenance was constructed as a tool that would enable children to develop syncretic identities that included a broader worldview. Through the development and maintenance of the language and the cultures of the parents, families endeavoured to socialize their children into values aimed at promoting good global citizenship. Thus, their conceptualization of identity did not only refer to often-cited notions that index generic and static identities. Theirs was one that pointed to multilayered and dynamic identities that encompassed a broad range of their experiences and those of their children and the effects of these experiences on their children's evolving identities.

For certain individuals, such as the families profiled in this chapter, adopting a cosmopolitan stance may be seen as a key move to developing and maintaining minority languages and cultures because individuals do not define themselves in nation-state, geographical terms only, but see themselves as citizens of a much larger conglomerate. Although linguistic minorities may maintain a strong affiliation with a particular nation-state or cultural group, as in the case of transnational families, their cultural associations may be much more fluid and dynamic—more flexible—as cosmopolitan individuals. These individuals, like TCK, may tend to adopt and adapt aspects of the cultures they interact with and embrace more syncretic identities.

The future in this research area promises to be a remarkable one as educators, scholars, and other social actors witness and examine how bilingual and bicultural identities are negotiated and perhaps transformed into multilingual and multicultural identities as local, transnational, and cosmopolitan identities are re/constructed in the emerging global context. This chapter has only started to point out the ways in which the participating families constructed Spanish maintenance as a passport to a cosmopolitan worldview, suggesting the need to further expand our conceptualization of HL development and identity. I propose this understanding as a starting point for future scholarly discussion surrounding HL development and identity and as an avenue for research in this emerging area within applied linguistics. I conclude by positing the interrelationship between HL development and cosmopolitan identities as a potentially fruitful dimension to be considered in discussions about the future of emerging Canadian, and perhaps global, identities. These notions are further explored and extended in the next chapter.

13.9 Chapter summary

In this chapter, I have engaged with the notion of cosmopolitanism, which for the purposes of this book I am recasting as a discourse of HL development. As part of this discussion, I introduced the concepts of Third Culture Kids and Generation 1.5. Both of these have been described as people who take elements from their parents' or their own childhood cultures and the host culture, a process that results in the forging of a cultural identity that is not entirely that of their parents' upbringing, nor that of their host-country-born peers. Just as a bilingual person is not two monolinguals inhabiting in a bilingual's body, so are Third Culture Kids and Generation 1.5 not two separate and essential identities housed in one person—they are unique individuals whose identities are the product of two (or more) cultural and linguistic experiences. The argument that I have advanced is that the nature of their unique identities disposes these individuals to having a cosmopolitan outlook, a latent possibility that is expressed discursively by parents.

I also distinguished between the notions of transnationalism and cosmopolitanism. While transnationalism has more to do with the individual's experience across borders (such as the development of ethno-national communities in the diaspora), cosmopolitanism may depart from nationalist origins, but ultimately expands out to the individual's sense of belonging in the broader global community. In feeling such borderless belonging, the cosmopolitan individual is primed to become a conscientious world citizen. Because identity and HL development are intertwined, it is worthwhile to investigate this cosmopolitan avenue of identity, especially because most if not all children of immigrants experience linguistic and cultural hybridity to some extent.

Although the study on which this chapter is based did not set out to investigate cosmopolitanism, it became clear that the parents from whom data were collected were observed to explicitly socialize their children into a sense of global ethnic inclusivity (and even hybridity). In fact, parents seemed to see the fact of their children's developing multilinguality and multiculturality as not only being a key to accessing other languages and cultures, but also as tied into an entire value system of good citizenship, which included multilingualism and multiculturalism. Data from the grassroots groups show that this consciousness was alive in those groups as well, as some activities sought to socialize the children into cosmopolitan identities within the community sphere. Parents also felt that encouraging their children to value other cultures and languages would have a boomerang effect on how they viewed their own roots. Ultimately, then, valuing their own roots through valuing those of others would have a strongly positive influence on their self-esteem and sense of self-worth in Canadian society.

14 From multiculturalism to cosmopolitanism

14.1 Introduction

Drawing on recent work on cosmopolitanism, global citizenship, and critical applied linguistics, this chapter builds on the previous chapter in order to continue to extend the concept of cosmopolitanism as a viable goal within education, particularly in Canada where the studies were conducted, but with possible implications for broader contexts. Special attention is paid to the inclusion of global citizenship goals in K-12 language programs in general, and in heritage language curricula in particular. I make a case for the consideration of the concept of cosmopolitanism as a key guiding principle at different levels of education in formal, non-formal, and informal settings. I argue that in the Canadian context, multilingual education could play a more prominent role in educational agendas as it has the potential to promote cosmopolitan ideals. I conclude that in the framework of official bilingualism and multiculturalism, cosmopolitanism can fruitfully add to discussions about the role of education in the emergence of a Canadian identity.

14.2 The global race to "be" global

There is a growing trend in higher education worldwide toward internationalization and the promotion of global citizenship. As well, many public and private school systems in disparate geographical settings are beginning to incorporate related objectives in their curricula. This tendency has also gained momentum in Canada as university presidents, school board and ministry of education officials as well as other individuals in positions of influence, endeavour to offer a world-class education. In this frantically racing and evolving context, critics argue that these efforts are often motivated by economic goals as a result of prevailing ideologies surrounding globalization. Indeed, market economics seem to control processes of globalization (Wodak et al. 1999). It comes as little surprise, then, that a growing debate in critical education within academic circles today stems from an increasing trend toward the commodification of education at all levels (Giroux and Myrsiades 2001, Naidoo and Jamieson 2005, 2008). Objectives related to human interconnectedness and the recognition and cultivation of global cultural diversity are less frequently emphasized. Moreover, although it is indisputable that language plays a key role in such processes, its significance is not always recognized.

14.3 Transnationalism, cosmopolitanism and global citizenship

Although closely related to each other—and sometimes used interchangeably—the constructs of transnationalism, cosmopolitanism, and global citizenship are not synonymous concepts. I explained in Chapter 13 that transnationalism refers to communities comprised of individuals settled in different national societies. Some of the characteristics of these groups and individuals are that they may embrace common religious, territorial, linguistic, and other interests across national boundaries (Faist 1998). The concept of cosmopolitanism has been employed for over two millennia, having been first used by the ancient Greek. It is said that Diogenes, a fourth century B.C. philosopher, famously declared, "I'm a citizen of the world." Cosmopolitanism as a concept, then, was first developed by the Greek school of philosophers known as the *Cynics*—co-founded by Diogenes—to refer to universal love for mankind regardless of origin or political affiliation. The concept was later redefined and expanded by Greek *Stoic* philosophers in the third century B.C., who emphasized ethics and added the principle of living in harmony with the universe. Almost 2,000 years later, Immanuel Kant proposed a federation of nations and perpetual peace, ideas that expounded cosmopolitan ideals and harmony among diverse peoples.

Today, there is a myriad of definitions of cosmopolitanism—or cosmopolitanisms—such as economic, moral, cultural, and other forms. To revisit the definitions provided in the previous chapter, a review of contemporary characterizations of cosmopolitanism reveals that it is understood as mobility of people, objects, images, cultures, and ideas (Germann Molz 2005) across diverse spaces. It also suggests a relationship between the local, the national, and the global (Starkey 2007). Thus, it connotes a "global sense of place" (Massey 1994: 12) that emphasizes a repositioning of personal and collective cultural identities that fosters the recognition of others (Delanty 2006). A cosmopolitan outlook assumes a "stance of openness towards divergent cultural experiences" (Hannerz 1990: 239) and a feeling of hominess in the world (Brennan 1997). Despite some perspectives that argue for the contrary, cosmopolitanism also allows individuals to draw on the country of origin as a source of identity (Kastoryano 2000, Appiah 2006). Thus, a cosmopolitan disposition does not preclude narrower identifications based on local or national loyalties. In other words, it nurtures multiple belonging through the possession of adaptable dispositions and "a commitment to global solidarity and global cultural diversity" (Smith 2007: 39).

Thus, cosmopolitanism is to be understood as a symbiotic blend of cultures where two or more are dominant. To sum up, the distinction between transnationalism and cosmopolitanism is that the former describes the experiences of individuals across borders and the latter refers to the attitudes and identities that these and other individuals may possess and subscribe to. It focuses on the moral responsibilities we have toward all human beings regardless of nationality, religion, political affiliation, color, language, geographical location, and social status, as an ethical obligation and an act of human rights promotion and preservation. Therefore, despite an abundance of cosmopolitanisms, one element they share is that all humans should see themselves as members of one community—one group—and that this community should be nurtured and protected.

In July 2008, then Senator Obama stated: "The burdens of global citizenship continue to bind us together. Partnership among nations is not a choice; it is the one way, the only way, to protect our common security and advance our common humanity" ("A World That Stands as One," Tiergarten, Berlin, Germany). Even though Obama was speaking from a particular perspective—a political agenda—that draws on the discourses of terrorism and "homeland security," the essence of his arguments still holds. It does provide an example of the diversity of the locations where the discourses of global citizenship can be found today, discourses that call for a federation of nations à la Kant. The idea of global citizenship has been around since ancient times, since the first recorded use of the term *kosmopolitês*, and has gained considerable currency in recent decades as a result of unrelenting globalization processes.

The terms of global citizenship, globalization, internationalization, and cosmopolitanism can often be sources of much conceptual confusion. Although they are potentially highly complex constructs that are understood differently in diverse disciplines and contexts, here I attempt to provide a simplified distinction between them. Essentially, internationalization is a form of reaching out to the world intentionally and purposively. Globalization, on the other hand, refers to global forces affecting our lives just like gravity, whether we like it or not. Cosmopolitanism is an embracement of the human, cultural, and moral features of globalization and internationalization. I see an important distinction between global citizenship and cosmopolitanism. However, given that the concept of cosmopolitanism is less understood and does not have the buzzword status that global citizenship has today, I loosely refer to global citizenship as a close equivalent to cosmopolitanism—an ideological steppingstone, if you will. Additionally, since processes of globalization tend to create favourable conditions for hybrid identities to evolve (Hall and Du Gay 1996), it is possible to draw on the concept of global citizenship as a mid-point between parochial and cosmopolitan identities.

Although Kant's ambitious proposition of permanent peace among nations and peoples continues to elude humankind—as it perpetually has—the time may be ripe for educational scholarship and policy in Canada to harvest elements of over two millennia of cosmopolitanism propositions. The sections that follow are a modest attempt to address this argument.

14.4 Cosmopolitanism and education

14.4.1 Higher education

Many universities across Canada are pursuing goals of internationalization (mainly through an increase of the international student population) and promoting global citizenship among all university members. The University of Toronto, The University of British Columbia, and the University of Alberta are promoting global citizenship goals through rhetoric in their vision and academic plans, as well as concrete initiatives "on the ground." For instance, the University of Alberta's previous vision, part of former President Indira Samarasekera's *Dare to Deliver* (2011)[1] University Plan, stated that the university attempted to benefit an Alberta whose citizens and communities "are increasingly global as well as national and local" (7). The Global Education Network at this university is housed in the Department of Educational Policy Studies in the Faculty of Education. Inspired by the 2004 conference "Educating for Human Rights and Global Citizenship," one of its main goals is to engage in local-global efforts that address social justice. The key players in this initiative at the time of writing were professors Ali Abdi and Lynette Shultz, who at that time were also spearheading the Global Citizenship Curriculum Development (GCCD) project, which attempted to establish this university as an institution that was "recognized internationally as a leader in the field of global citizenship education." As part of this initiative, the team worked to incorporate global citizenship content into existing curricula, develop an undergraduate course on global citizenship, and develop a Global Citizenship Certificate Program.

The University of British Columbia states in its institutional vision that it fosters "global citizenship, advances a civil and sustainable society, and supports outstanding research to serve the people of British Columbia, Canada and the world." It further ascertains its commitment to these goals in its latest strategic plan, "*Place and Promise: The UBC Plan*" (2009) where commitments, goals, and actions around global citizenship, social sustainability, aboriginal education, community engagement and other promises are carefully articulated.

Interestingly, global citizenship goals are absent from the University of Toronto's discussion paper entitled "*Towards 2030: Planning for a Third Century of Excellence at the University of Toronto.*" It is only mentioned once in passing in the Synthesis Report of the above document: "the University benefits greatly from the multicultural

---

[1] The University of Alberta's new institutional strategic plan, *For the Public Good*, was launched in September 2016, after this project was completed.

milieu of the Toronto region, and the ethno-cultural diversity of our student body. These facets of the University help our students to become global citizens, but are not a substitute for travel and study abroad" (2008: 43). And yet, the University of Toronto has one of the most innovative and practically oriented initiatives around global citizenship focusing on K-12 education. With funding from the Canadian International Development Agency's (CIDA) Global Classroom Initiative, the Comparative, International and Development Education Centre (CIDEC) at the University of Toronto is working on a number of projects with a global gaze. One of their projects is *Educating for Global Citizenship in a Changing World*, a freely downloadable book for practicing teachers and teacher educators in school settings in the Toronto area.

14.4.2 Language education

As for discussions of cosmopolitanism in relation to language, there are at least two important contributions. Guilherme (2007) critically examines the possibilities English as a global language offers for acting as cosmopolitan citizens without the loss of local cultural identifications and ideologies. To this end, she calls for a critical pedagogy that makes learners aware of their rights and obligations as members of various local and global communities. She argues that in this way, intercultural freedom leading to cosmopolitan citizenship can be pursued.

Popp (2006) links bilingualism to cosmopolitanism through an analysis of *Dora the Explorer*, Nickelodeon's foray into the pre-school television viewership. The programming is designed with the assistance of a team of education, Spanish, and Latino culture experts and draws on Gardner's (1993) multiple intelligence theory. Each episode features seven intelligences, including bilingualism. Each episode also tells stories drawn from Hispanic cultural experiences and has *Dora* use both English and Spanish in her interactions. *Dora* has been a tremendous economic success for the network and has popularized *Dora* as the "bilingual heroine." Popp argues that parents, particularly non-Hispanic parents, see *Dora*'s bilingual practices as helping their children accumulate cultural capital and giving them certain distinction. He posits that this capital can be readily converted into notions of cosmopolitanism. Thus, parents see the series as helping their children become cosmopolitan themselves.

14.4.3 Canadian K-12 curricula

With the goal of understanding this issue from the public school system perspective in Canada, I conducted an examination of Canadian educational policy and curricular documents. This work consisted of a preliminary analysis of the K-12 curriculum documents for social studies and language programs in ten provinces and three territories with the goal of identifying if, and to what extent, these programs promote objectives of internationalization, global citizenship, and cosmopolitanism.

Early findings from provinces in the Prairies and Western Canada show that explicit objectives and content related to global citizenship and cosmopolitanism are absent from the British Columbia and Yukon documents. Implicit content related to these concepts is also mostly absent. The Prairie Provinces of Saskatchewan, Manitoba, and Alberta, on the other hand, paint a very different picture. Not only are these concepts an integral part of the social studies and language programs in K-12, but global citizenship is a central tenet of the language programs specifically for the three provinces. The language program curricula are based on the *Common Curriculum Framework for International Languages, Kindergarten to Grade 12*, which is a joint project of the Western Canadian Protocol for Collaboration in Basic Education. The Common Curriculum follows an integrative framework of language learning which progresses spirally through all grades, starting from kindergarten (see Figure 14.1). The four pillars that support the curriculum are: applications, language competence, global citizenship, and strategies. Thus, global citizenship is introduced in grade three in social studies, but it becomes central in language programs from kindergarten.

The above summary suggests that current trends in the Canadian public school system are moving toward the promotion of broader worldviews, at least in some provinces. Additionally, a growing research literature suggests that there seems to be a trend among middle class Anglo Canadians toward bilingualism, mainly through French immersion. In the United States, Mandarin Chinese seems to be appealing to non-Chinese background populations (Weise 2007). There is increasing anecdotal evidence that this is the case in Canada as well. Research

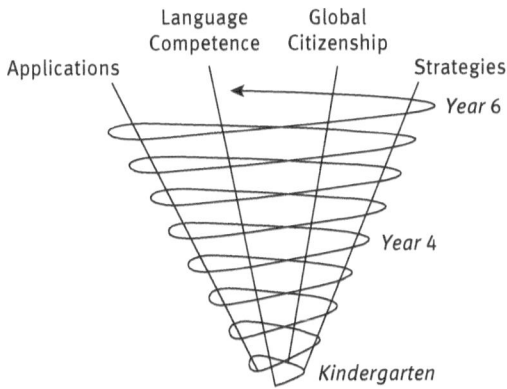

Figure 14.1 Spiral progression model.

has shown that middle class immigrant families are also being drawn by the popularity of French immersion (e.g., Dagenais and Berron 2001, Guardado 2008a). These tendencies point to a growing recognition of the value and desirability of multilingualism in Canada, a goal that has been recently stressed by several Canadian scholars (e.g., Duff 2007a). Given that immigrant Canadians, such as the Hispanic families discussed throughout this book, make direct connections between heritage languages and a broader vision of the world, and considering that language education programs in some provinces also make similar connections and have built such goals in their curricula, it may be time to emphasize these goals in educational policy and practice. It is suggested in this book that societal multilingualism may lead to cosmopolitanism in Canada, and that this move will benefit all society. This calls for a renewed, more ethical version of cosmopolitanism. A frequent critique of cosmopolitanism is its elitism. Today's cosmopolitanism, however, has a new cast of characters (Robbins 1998). These emerge from the increasing movement and interdependence of individuals across geographical and virtual borders, which include nannies, guest workers, and members of various diasporas. I argue that it is time to think beyond a restricted and elitist cosmopolitanism and to move toward a *popular cosmopolitanism*, a notion that accounts for the desires, experiences, and forms of capital of privileged and less privileged populations alike.

14.5 From multiculturalism to cosmopolitanism

An important aspect emerging from the foregoing analysis relates to multicultural and educational policy. Canada embraced an official multiculturalism policy within a "bilingual framework" in the early 1970s. However, the Canadian "bilingualism framework" seems to be fully supported across Canada only if it is French-English bilingualism. This was a good start in the 1960s when both languages (and associated cultures) were made official languages of the country, but four decades later, it is time to take the next steps. The implication that official multiculturalism should also be understood as multilingualism, at the moment does not seem to be of enough concern to those in positions of influence (e.g., policy makers, school teachers). There is need for a better understanding of how these official policies facilitate school boards' efforts in fostering heritage languages, and how provincial ministries of education, school boards, and school districts across the country interpret Canada's official multiculturalism policies as well as how they implement—or fail to implement—support programs. Integrating HL programs more assertively in schools and creating more opportunities for minority and majority students to work together on language issues would be an important step to take. It would be a key move away from a stance that privileges the Anglicization and cultural assimilation of Canada's linguistic minorities and toward adopting a position that champions the diversification of thinking and multilingualization of Canada's Anglo majority as well as a way of promoting a cosmopolitan orientation in all of Canada's populations alike. If this is not a reasonable move for educational policy, then, we have to ask ourselves: Is Canada's ideology of multiculturalism a deeply rooted value reflected in educational policy or is it only a "celebratory multiculturalism"?

14.6 Cosmopolitanism in educational practice

Within education and applied linguistics, cosmopolitanism has been discussed in relation to a number of perspectives. There appears to be a link, albeit loose, between this notion and the current emphasis in the academy on developing "global citizens," particularly in college and university presidents' discourses. More specifically, however, Allan Luke (2004) has called for a major rethinking of the teaching profession as cosmopolitan work. He argues that this reconceptualization requires the "cultural, linguistic, epistemological diversification and, potentially, hybridisation of the very educational institutions where we work" (1439). He adds that this would entail the reenvisioning of a new transcultural and cosmopolitan teacher "with critical capacities for dealing with the transnational and the global." This would also require the ability to converse with educators, researchers, curriculum developers, and educational bureaucrats physically as well as virtually across regional and global boundaries, especially in relation to the various forms of diversity that now are commonplace. Part of this ideal would require envisioning a world where everyone can speak as equals and "expanding the purview, scope, and gaze of the school curriculum" (Luke, Luke and Graham 2007: 12). To date, Luke's theorizing of critical pedagogy from a cosmopolitanism perspective, particularly his propositions regarding teacher education, offer the most theoretically comprehensive and practical applications of this notion in education.

14.7 Cosmopolitanism and Canadian identity

Based on the above discussion, it is crucial to conceptualize the promotion and maintenance of minority languages in more progressive and encompassing terms that highlight the positive effects of this process and its role as a bridge to the promotion of multilingualism in society. Since classrooms are the locus for change

(MacDonald and Monkman 2005), teachers need to more decisively promote supportive classroom communities (Brown 2007). Thus, these classrooms need to become sites where languages and cultures, both minority and majority, are valorized and where both, linguistic-minority and majority students are given opportunities to foster positive multicultural attitudes and to cultivate their potential for multilingualism (Duff 2007a) as part of the school's official ethos and agenda. This way, all students might have opportunities to develop strong cosmopolitan identities and grow up to be citizens who are not only tolerant of difference, but who embrace and value difference as a key social and human resource. Thus, these cosmopolitan citizens will develop dispositions and stances of openness towards diverse cultural experiences (Hannerz 1990), construct identities that combine local and broad senses of belonging (Luke, Luke and Graham 2007), and assume more adaptable dispositions as well as a stronger commitment to local and global cohesion and ethnolinguistic diversity (Smith 2007). Arguably, these are highly desirable assets in the current climate of unprecedented cultural exchange and globalization. Thus, a cosmopolitan turn promises to contribute to the educational needs of a rapidly changing global context.

Teachers in North America continue to be mostly monocultural and monolingual (Nieto 2001, Rodriguez 2007). Given that teaching around and with difference is the most challenging question in education today (Luke 2004, Luke and Goldstein 2006), the above goals are not attainable unless their pursuit is extended to teachers so they develop interest and skills in additional languages and become more aware of multicultural issues (Nieto 1999), potentially leading to their own development of a broader vision of the world. Only then, I believe, the goal of advancing an effective culturally responsive pedagogy in multicultural and multilingual settings will be within reach.

14.8 Chapter summary

In this chapter, I have further engaged with the discourse of cosmopolitanism and global citizenship in relation to heritage languages and language education, but also in relation to education at all levels within the Canadian context. I pointed out that although cosmopolitanism has traditionally been seen as a feature of the world's elite, in recent times its ideals have become popularized through political discourse, educational discourse, such as the vision statements and mandates of post-secondary institutions, as well as popular media. The millennia-long history of these concepts seems to offer hope that these will not fall into disuse, but rather take on new meanings and with them, reach and enrich all walks of life.

A key argument that I have advanced in this chapter is the possibility of a cosmopolitan curricular focus at different levels of education within the Canadian context. I suggest that this has possible implications for the development and enrichment of a Canadian identity, particularly if multilingual education features prominently in promoting such a focus. Part of the rationale for this proposal is that if Canada is to call itself a country that embraces all cultures and their languages, then there should be more purposeful and explicit educational policies and practices that support this ideal. I posit that cosmopolitanism-inspired curricula are a promising avenue worthy of consideration to begin achieving this goal. Whether or not all schools have an explicit mandate to promote diversity through visions and activities that are inspired by cosmopolitanism, the ever-globalizing world brings an inevitable diversity to all manner of learning contexts, and thus has the potential to be an exceptional opportunity for building intercultural and international mindfulness. I believe that cosmopolitanism-inspired multilingual and multicultural education has the potential to support heritage speakers, but also to foment a sense of unity, equality, and understanding between these heritage speakers and monolingual speakers of the official languages, thus nurturing an educational context that draws on the strengths and uniqueness of all Canadians alike.

15 Final reflections and ways forward

15.1 Introduction

In the preceding chapters, I engaged with several concepts and theories that I regard as closely tied to and inseparable from heritage language studies, namely discourse, ideology, and language socialization. After writing this book, I realize that I could have written a separate book on heritage languages in relation to each of these lenses, as the sources of data and other available information would have provided plentiful material for discussion. However, my goal from the start was to provide as holistic a view as possible based on my empirical work and thinking on the topic over the last two decades. To reach such a goal, I needed to look at the heritage language area from diverse theoretical and methodological vantage points provided by various traditions of linguistics and anthropology, enhanced by conceptual insights from philosophy, sociology, psychology, and education— in short, a distinctly interdisciplinary enterprise. Indeed, my interest in writing this book the way I did was fed by a desire and perceived need to investigate and better understand heritage languages with the aid of concepts and tools from other disciplines. As such, it was a disciplinary border-crossing project at several levels. Because the perspective of language ideology provides a bridge between social theory and linguistics (Woolard 1998), throughout the book I attempted to uphold an analytical stance that considered power relations, which was informed by ideas from various critical schools. As well, I believe that a focus on intimate family communication provided an opportunity to link the study of heritage languages to the important issues of family daily life. It is my hope that the several bridges that I attempted to construct between heritage language studies and other scholarly as well as folk dimensions will serve as foundational points for the further development of this critical area of study. In this closing chapter, I intend to briefly recapitulate some of the ideas that I have discussed and possibly offer some final thoughts for facilitating the flow of these ideas into future conversations.

15.2 Signposting to new conversations

In the five chapters that comprised Part I, my objective was to introduce aspects of the foundational research literature and the key concepts and theories that worked in concert to form the lens through which I intended to consider heritage languages. Chapter 1 introduced the research literature and described the methods of research that were used in the gathering of the different datasets on which I based my arguments. I also presented some basic concepts related to heritage languages and considered issues of terminology. Chapter 2 provided the historical trajectory of heritage language studies beginning with the perspective of Joshua A. Fishman's work, followed by an overview of selected aspects of the HL research literature. Although limited in scope and number, the themes and issues taken up in this overview began to set the stage for heritage languages from different vantage points throughout the book.

The three chapters that followed, Chapters 3, 4, and 5, did the heavy theoretical lifting by engaging with the central theories that provided the analytic bite to a multiplicity of aspects of heritage languages, supporting and leading to the many arguments made. Chapter 3, Heritage Language Socialization, afforded the central theoretical and methodological paradigm guiding the arguments advanced in the book. Because of its roots in anthropology, language socialization has been intimately related to my ethnographic stance in one way or another from the beginning of fieldwork almost two decades ago. As a result, language socialization has performed multiple functions both in the preparatory work for this book, as well as during its writing, operating as the guiding epistemology, overarching theory, and focal topic. Crucially, a fundamental consideration in this chapter was the recent recognition of heritage language socialization as an area of research in and of itself. Thus, I initially traced the evolution of language socialization from work that focused mainly on monolingual communities to second language and multilingual contexts. I followed up with a discussion of the roles that foundational investigations in the latter contexts played in the subsequent naming of work that deals specifically with heritage languages as *heritage language socialization*.

Chapter 4 introduced language ideology, one of the key concepts that acted as a continuous thread—sometimes invisibly, but other times prominently—in all the chapters of the book. As a young notion discussed in various fields, mainly anthropology, linguistics, and education, language ideology does not yet have a unified body of research—and perhaps never will. As a result, there is a diversity of definitions, some functional and others critical, some highlighting linguistic aspects and others casting a broader social net. As an even newer addition to heritage language studies, this notion is only beginning to be discussed explicitly and as such, lacks an operationalized definition. As I hope has been made clear in this book, for the purposes of engaging with this scholarly area, I view heritage language ideologies as the tentative systems of beliefs, understandings, justifications, and judgments held by minorities about their heritage languages, including when, where, how, and to what ends they should be used. Ideologies of heritage languages also include desires and expectations regarding the relevance of these languages and language varieties in the lives of the new generations. These multiple systems are generally implicit, but ever present in the back of people's minds as they go about their daily lives and grapple with the challenges of interacting in the broader society in a language which they are sometimes not proficient. They also deal with these issues on a day-to-day basis with their children, both in and out of the home, so even if metadiscursivity is not always part of their daily talk, the tensions are nevertheless latently ever-present in their interactions. Thus, even though definitions of ideology are so complex, so multiple, and so contested, what this book has attempted to do with ideology is to use these—albeit convoluted—understandings as a way to confront concepts that are difficult to grasp and relate them practically to family interactions.

Together, the five chapters in Part I of the book provided the disciplinary, theoretical, conceptual, and epistemological backdrop against which the discussions were set. Fittingly, Chapter 5 closed Part I by engaging with yet another contested concept: discourse. This chapter concluded Part I and provided the *segue* into Part II, which in its 3 chapters, proposed *discourse* as a way of discussing and researching heritage languages. The way I understand language ideology and discourse, as the terms are used in this book, they are inseparable. If language ideology stands between language and society, discourse may be seen as mediating between language and ideology itself. Part of the purpose of introducing discourse into studies of heritage languages responded to my growing awareness of a pervasive practice among linguistic minority speakers, dominant language speakers, and members of the academy: talking about heritage languages in a complexity of ways. In my research and reflections, I observed the diversity of ideologies about dominant and minority languages that were present in these ways of talking about languages and saw a certain theoretical parallel with ways of talking about terrorism, patriarchy, the poor, and so on. Just as those ways of talking—discourses—were laden with ideas, beliefs, and evaluations about terrorism, patriarchy, and the poor, the ways of talking about heritage languages were also not neutral or value-free. As a result, unwittingly, I started thinking about heritage languages in terms of discourses loaded with judgments, commonsensical characterizations, and popular empiricist depictions of their place in society and in the intimate lives of individuals linked to them. Another aspect of the impetus that drove me to this type of discussion was that both of these concepts—discourse and language ideology—are also interested notions that deal with critique and power and as such, are contested and the source of much debate and contradiction. Discourses of heritage languages are indeed inconsistent, heterogeneous, and highly situated collections of ideas, opinions, and ways of thinking and speaking about heritage languages.

Chapters 6, 7, and 8, respectively, introduced a typology of discourses, reported on an analysis of how this typology articulated with the HL research literature, and attempted to begin a discussion of the affordances and shortcomings of using a discourse-ideological approach to heritage language studies. Whether this is a sensible take on the study of heritage languages remains to be seen, but a recurring question when I think of discourses of heritage languages—which remains unanswered—is whether and to what extent discourses impact families and society. There is evidence that public discourses can affect families and individuals' beliefs and practices in various ways, sometimes negatively, such as in the case of discourses of what constitutes good or bad parenting (Okita 2002). Thus, following Foucault (1972), who saw discourses as "practices that systematically form the objects of which they speak" (54), I posited that making the discourses of heritage languages explicit and public—assuming these discourses are supportive—may contribute to the spread of a HL development ideology and thus, ultimately contribute to the promotion of heritage language development.

The focus of Part III of the book was on the multifaceted strategies deployed by parents with the goal of fostering the socialization of the heritage language. These multifaceted socializing agents resided in different sites, including the home, community, and even in various transnational spaces. The chapters in this section (9, 10, 11, and 12) dealt overtly with the practical enactment of much of what I had discussed in the book. Indeed, the ideologies of language espoused by the participants and other actors described in the various studies reviewed and analyzed are acted upon at the individual, family, and community level. As I sufficiently alluded to in Chapter 9, the relevance of community ought to come to the fore in HL development discussions, and even if *community* itself is conceptualized in multiple ways, these varied views are arguably all relevant to heritage language studies. All ethnolinguistic groups conceive and establish grassroots organizations of some type, given the role of communities as sources of practical and emotional support and coping mechanisms, among others. Different populations, and particularly immigrant minorities, form groups in order to satisfy needs they identify in their new culture. These needs may be related to religion, housing, education, ethnolinguistic and cultural connection as well as other special interests, but regardless of their central mandate, the language of choice in these groups tends to be the heritage language, and as such, almost all of these groups are *de facto* heritage language socialization settings.

As Joshua A. Fishman advised us time and time again, there is just no substitute for family when it comes to HL development. But even what constitutes family *per se* may differ across cultures and possibly across groups within cultures. Many groups, for instance, define family mainly as parents and their children (i.e., nuclear family), while other groups place much more emphasis on the extended family. Indeed, in many cultures today it is common for extended family members to live together within the same household. Hispanics, in particular, tend to exhibit high levels of familism. In some ways reminiscent of members of Black churches who derived a sense of family and belonging from them, many Hispanics tend to seek out surrogate extended families in the context of immigration for a variety of reasons. These groupings can be informal and unstructured or highly organized and systematically designed with clearly laid out agendas, at times with the mission to foster cultural values and heritage languages. If, as Fishman has declared, home is the real secret weapon of HL development, when the "village" is recreated in diaspora through collections of surrogate extended families, opportunities emerge for ethnolinguistic communities to pursue some of the most central HL development aims, namely the recognition of, and capitalization on, the socializing power of communities.

I have no doubt that the above conditions present many opportunities for so-called "town-gown" relationships. As post-secondary institutions across the globe are increasingly advancing goals of community engagement and even writing these objectives into their visions and missions, HL scholars are called upon to take note of this opportune historical moment. Grassroots community groups like the five investigated in British Columbia and Alberta, as described in Chapter 9, are ideal places for these academic investigators to practice a scholarship that transcends one-way relationships based on academic agendas alone. These groups can be seen as ideal starting points for understanding the needs and desires of communities in relation to their HLs and cultures, and engaging in work that can directly benefit the communities.

Chapters 11 and 12 made it clearer than any other chapter that one of the central goals of this book was also to attempt to bring parental language planning, regulation, and use to the forefront of research, although as of yet, this sub-topic has frequently been treated as a secondary issue in HL development scholarship (Piller 2001b). It is my belief that these issues are at the heart of this research area as the linguistic interactions taking place in families are some of the key sites of HL development struggle. These analyses constitute an attempt to begin to uncover the linguistic mechanisms operating in multilingual families, such as the characteristics of the turns engendering dispreference and disagreement between adults and children in daily interactions. Additionally, emphasis was put on the design of the dissenting responses and the actions performed by these sequences. The metalinguistic practices analyzed in Chapter 12, in particular, reveal parents' attempts to revalorize Spanish in the English-dominant Canadian context in order to recast it as a valuable language (Hill 1985). Since discourse often functions coercively (Philips 1998), some of the explicit processes of metapragmatic regimentation of language use analyzed suggest that parental discourse that attempts to manage and dictate children's language practices may have negative effects on family communication, a result that can arguably also be detrimental to their HL socialization goals. In light of the analysis presented in this chapter, which highlights the complexities found in the day-in-day-out struggles of families committed to HL socialization, it is possible to understand why many parents feel that the pursuit of multilingualism practices against a backdrop of monolingualism ideologies sometimes becomes a battle that seems almost impossible to win.

In Part V of the *Handbook of Language Socialization*, whose chapters specifically address many of the issues discussed in the present book, Duranti, Ochs and Schieffelin (2012) introduced the set of chapters by explicitly referring to the "complex networks of informal and formal social institutions that regiment, or attempt to regiment, cultural and symbolic values associated with different linguistic varieties and discursive expressions" (485). In several chapters of the present book, I have addressed a variety of ways in which informal institutions, such as the family and grassroots community groups, directly or tacitly attempted to regiment the value of the languages in the children's lives. The linguistic practices found in these and other settings were frequently designed to socialize the children into language ideologies that in the view of the adult caregivers supported the development and maintenance of the heritage language. The words of Duranti, Ochs and Schieffelin echo the language practices found in the families and grassroots groups that I have analyzed in this book, which once again emphasize the complexity of heritage language socialization and add to its further theorization.

The two chapters in Part IV of the present book, Family, Community and Education in Global Perspective, constitute my attempt at proposing a possible cosmopolitan turn for heritage language studies. I argue that the emergence of cosmopolitan identities, particularly rooted ones, may be more realistic today than has ever been in the last two thousand years. Fishman (1999) declared that English monolingualism, for instance, negatively affects global business practices, clearly rejecting the idea that globalization makes local languages irrelevant. On the contrary, he argued that just as Latin, an international language in its time, became irrelevant because of the emergence of local languages, so can English. I believe that we are slowly beginning to realize the effect of globalizing forces on families and their languages, the relevance of transnational practices, and the largely untapped but growing potential of heritage languages in an increasingly interconnected world. In a rooted cosmopolitan world, where individuals derive sources of identity from the local community, but act and nurture global loyalties, heritage and other world languages may not replace English, but will hopefully co-exist and foster ethical cooperation across ideological, cultural, and geographical borders.

15.3 Research directions

Looking to the future, I have no doubt that all of the issues and specific lines of inquiry discussed in these chapters will continue to attract scholarly attention. Through this work, our understanding of the interaction of discourses, ideologies, and heritage language socialization will be given increasing granularity. To illustrate, I return to one thread from Chapter 3, namely, heritage language socialization in linguistically mixed families. It was stated that this demographic faces multiple complexities in the language socialization of their children. Considering the recent calls for increased research around interlingual family language policy, socialization, and related issues, I am positive that researchers will find that this demographic offers fertile ground for examining the central issues of discourse, ideology, and heritage language socialization. If, as Ochs and Schieffelin have stated, learning language "goes hand-in-hand with acquiring sociocultural knowledge" (1995: 74), HL development within the highly complex interactional dynamics of interlingual families must involve intricate processes of negotiation and socialization into highly varied and hybrid cultural values and practices. Ethnographic data using a language socialization perspective and other lenses have much to uncover and explain regarding the linguistic lives of families made up of various ethnolinguistic combinations. Ochs and Schieffelin (2008) posit "that the coexistence of two or more codes within a particular community, whatever the sociohistorical and political circumstances that have given rise to them or brought them into contact, is rarely neutral in relation to children's developing linguistic and sociocultural competence" (10). Viewing the family as a community of sorts, it is argued that the social, linguistic, and political circumstances of interlingual families pose significant challenges given the various interacting power relations.

For interlingual parents, the complexities associated with HL socialization, along with the concomitant emotional, physical, and financial burden they often shoulder, can lead to feelings of confusion, guilt, anxiety, and frustration. As Tsushima and Guardado found, this state of affairs is compounded by interlingual parents' relative lack of access to knowledge regarding multilingual parenting and family language planning. Therefore, in addition to deepening research into the complexities, possibilities, and limits of HL development in interlingual families, it is of critical urgency that scholars ensure that knowledge created with families also returns to families in order to clarify ambiguities and inform their daily practice of heritage language. This presents an ideal opportunity where the community engagement proposed earlier can take place. Indeed, this scholarly knowledge should also reach other stakeholders, such as community leaders, school personnel, health professionals, and other stakeholders who at times are in a position to provide linguistic advice to families.

Another area that warrants closer research attention is related to issues of class. Most of the families that participated in the studies that helped inform this book were of middle-class background. All of the families that were profiled and analyzed in detail were in several ways privileged, at least enough to have obtained higher education qualifications. Their privileged status gave them access to material and symbolic resources that enabled them to engage in the heritage language socialization activities analyzed herein, including the formation of grassroots groups. Less advantaged families arguably face greater challenges in regards to HL socialization goals. They may also lack the disposable time and income as well as the social networks to participate in these groups. Unfortunately, given the socioeconomic composition of the various grassroots groups that were examined, no data were collected which would allow rigorous analyses of the ways in which language and class might have interacted in these groups. This is considered a limitation of the present work. If possible, it would be valuable to identify research sites in the future where families of different socioeconomic backgrounds participate and interact. This might allow analyses of pertinent questions of how ideologies of class related to language use manifest themselves in grassroots organizations such as the ones examined in this book.

15.4 In closing

As I write the final paragraphs of this book, I cannot avoid the unconscious awareness that even though my reflective work on heritage languages has been extensive, by no means have I expressed everything emerging from my ruminations. I have written enough, perhaps, for this work to serve as a starting point for future conversations on the significance of heritage languages to humanity, for issues of heritage languages do not only concern the ethnolinguistic minorities themselves. Rather, associated issues, discourses, ideologies, and practices impact on all society, for better or worse, and all society ought to be concerned about what transpires in this regard. I have collected some of the highlights of my thinking on this topic over the last two decades or so, which I hope, will at least inspire younger generations of thinkers and scholars of heritage languages and other interested individuals to pose new questions and revisit old ones.

Indeed, it is possible that new generations of scholars will rediscover questions that have been posed for decades and even view the work of figures such as

Fishman as sources of renewed inspiration. Some of them may even see Fishmanian sociolinguistics as a road map of sorts for the study of heritage languages. For instance, the questions that Fishman posed in his seminal article *Who Speaks What Language to Whom and When?* still resonate loudly today. The multitude of questions that can derive from the title alone can easily be linked in numerous ways to all the work on heritage languages that has been conducted since. Moreover, all the issues that are related to the many potential questions will no doubt speak to the work that will continue to be conducted in the decades to come. Given the need to conceptualize and analyze heritage languages using interdisciplinary approaches—which was so obvious to Fishman six decades ago—as it has become obvious to us in recent times, the implications of these questions are at least as relevant as ever.

To conclude, the discussion on heritage language studies I have undertaken in this book should be taken as a first gaze into a vast universe. Adapting an idea from Stephen Hawking's book *A Brief History of Time* (1988)—about the Big Bang and Black Holes—we still do not have a unified understanding of heritage language development and maintenance, but if we were to formulate such a theory, at least we know what some of its characteristics should be. In this book, I have attempted to uncover, illustrate, and discuss some of these features. Heritage language development is not only a linguistic phenomenon, but also a social, cultural, psychological, emotional, and political one. Thus, a complete understanding of its workings is bound to remain out of reach. Nevertheless, as a phenomenon interpermeated with issues of ideology, power, identity, and everything that these multidimensional concepts themselves entail, it is our collective responsibility, as global citizens, to leave none of these issues unexamined in our ongoing quest to understand and support heritage languages and their speakers.

References

Abdi, Klara. 2011. 'She really only speaks English': Positioning, language ideology, and heritage language learners. *The Canadian Modern Language Review* (67)2. 161–190.

Ahmed, Tasneem. 2016. *Language choices of Pakistani Canadians in the Peel Region*. Toronto, Canada: University of Toronto master's thesis.

Alim, H. Samy. 2010. Critical language awareness. In Nancy H. Hornberger & Sandra Lee McKay (eds.), *Sociolinguistics and language education*, 205–231. Bristol, UK: Multilingual Matters.

Andersen, Elaine S. 1986. The acquisition of register variation by Anglo-American children. In Bambi B. Schieffelin & Elinor Ochs (eds.), *Language socialization across cultures*, 153–164. Cambridge: Cambridge University Press.

Anderson, Benedict. 1983. *Imagined communities: Reflections on the origin and spread of nationalism*. London: Verso Editions.

Anderson, R. C., E. H. Hiebert, J. A. Scott & I. Wilkinson. 1985. Becoming a nation of readers: The report of the Commission on Reading. Washington, DC: The National Institute of Education.

Anzaldúa, Gloria. 1987. *Borderlands/La frontera: The new mestiza*. San Francisco: Aunt Lute Books.

Appiah, Kwame Anthony. 2006. *Cosmopolitanism: Ethics in a world of strangers*. New York: W. W. Norton & Co.

Arthur, Thomas. E. 2000. Issues in culturally competent mental health services for people of color. *Psychiatric Rehabilitation Skills* 4. 426–447.

Atkinson, Dwight. 2003. Language socialization and dys-socialization in a South India college. In Robert Bayley & Sandra R. Schecter (eds.), *Language socialization in bilingual and multilingual societies*, 147–162. Clevedon, UK: Multilingual Matters.

Austin, John. L. 1962. *How to do things with words*. Oxford: Oxford University Press.

Avni, Sharon. 2008. *Educating for continuity: An ethnography of multilingual language practices in Jewish day school education*. New York: New York University doctoral dissertation.

Baeza, Litzy. 2004. *"Voces del exilio": Testimonios orales del exilio chileno en Edmonton, Canadá ["Voices of exile": Oral testimonies of Chilean exile in Edmonton, Canada]*. Santiago, Chile: Universidad de Chile master's thesis.

Bakhtin, Mikhail. 1981. *The dialogic imagination*. Austin: University of Texas Press.

Bakhtin, Mikhail. 1986. *Speech genres and other late essays*. Austin: University of Texas Press.

Bale, Jeffrey. 2010. Arabic as a heritage language in the United States. *International Multilingual Research Journal* 4. 125–151.

Baquedano-Lopez, Patricia. 1997. Creating social identities through *doctrina* narratives. *Issues in Applied Linguistics* 8(1). 27–45.

Baquedano-Lopez, Patricia. 2000. Narrating community in doctrina classes. *Narrative Inquiry* 10(2). 429–452.

Baquedano-Lopez, Patricia & Shlomy Kattan. 2008. Language socialization in schools: An historical overview. In Patricia A. Duff & Nancy H. Hornberger (eds.), *Encyclopedia of language and education. Vol. 8: Language socialization*. Philadelphia/Heidelberg: Springer.

Barvosa, Edwina. 2008. *Wealth of selves: Multiple identities, Mestiza consciousness and the subject of politics*. College Station, TX: Texas A&M University Press.

Bauman, Richard & Charles L. Briggs. 1990. Poetics and performance as critical perspectives on language and social life. *Annual Review of Anthropology* 19. 59–88.

Bayley, Robert & Sandra R. Schecter (eds.). 2003. *Language socialization in bilingual and multilingual societies* (Bilingual education and bilingualism). Clevedon: Multilingual Matters.

Bayley, Robert & Sandra R. Schecter. 2004. Language socialization in theory and practice. *International Journal of Qualitative Studies in Education* 17(5). 605–625.

Bayley, Robert, Sandra R. Schecter & B. Torres-Ayala. 1996. Strategies for bilingual maintenance: Case studies of Mexican-origin families in Texas. *Linguistics and Education* 8. 389–408.

Becker, Ava. 2013. *Political ideology and heritage language development in a Chilean exile community: A multiple case study.* Edmonton, Canada: University of Alberta master's thesis.

Bell, Jill Sinclair. 2003. Back to school: Learning practices in a job retraining community. In Robert Bayley & Sandra R. Schecter (eds.), *Language socialization in bilingual and multilingual societies*, 251–268. Clevedon, UK: Multilingual Matters.

Bhola, Harbans. S. 1996. Family, literacy, development and culture: Interconnections, reconstructions. *Convergence* 29(1). 34–45.

Bjornson, Marnie. 2007. Speaking of citizenship: Language ideologies in Dutch citizenship regimes. *Focaal-European Journal of Anthropology* 49. 65–80.

Blommaert, Jan. 2005. *Discourse: A critical introduction.* Cambridge: Cambridge University Press.

Blum Kulka, Shoshana. 2008. Language socialization and family dinnertime discourse. In Patricia A. Duff & Nancy H. Hornberger (eds.), *Encyclopedia of language and education. Vol. 8: Language socialization*, 2nd edn, 87–99. Philadelphia/Heidelberg: Springer.

Bourdieu, Pierre. 1977. The economics of linguistic exchanges. *Social Science Information* 16(6). 645–668.

Bourdieu, Pierre. 1986. The forms of capital. In J. G. Richardson (ed.), *Handbook of theory and research for the sociology of education*, 241–258. Westport, CT: Greenwood.

Brain, Kevin & Ivan Reid. 2003. Constructing parental involvement in an Education Action Zone: Whose need is it meeting? *Educational Studies* 29(2/3). 291–305.

Braun, Andreas & Tony Cline. 2014. *Language strategies for trilingual families: Parents' perspectives.* Bristol, UK: Multilingual Matters.

Brennan, Timothy. 1997. *At Home in the world: Cosmopolitanism now.* Cambridge, MA: Harvard University Press.

Brooksbank, Joselyn. 2017. *Family language policy: Parental discourse strategies and child responses.* Ottawa, Canada: University of Ottawa master's thesis.

Bronson, Matthew C. & Karen Ann Watson-Gegeo. 2008. The critical moment: Language socialization and the (re)visioning of first and second language learning. In Patricia A. Duff & Nancy H. Hornberger (eds.), *Encyclopedia of language and education. Vol. 8: Language socialization*, 43–55. Philadelphia/Heidelberg: Springer.

Brown, Clara Lee. 2011. Maintaining heritage language: Perspectives of Korean parents. *Multicultural Education* 19(1). 31–37.

Brown, Gillian & George Yule. 1983. *Discourse analysis.* Cambridge: Cambridge University Press.

Brown, Sally Ann. 2007. *A critical discourse analysis of identity development and literacy practices: Latino English language learners at home and in the primary classroom.* Columbia, SC: University of South Carolina doctoral dissertation.

Canagarajah, A. Suresh. 1993. Critical ethnography of a Sri Lankan classroom: Ambiguities in opposition to reproduction through ESOL. *TESOL Quarterly* (27)4. 601–626.

Canagarajah, A. Suresh. 2004. Subversive identities, pedagogical safe houses, and critical learning. In B. Norton & K. Toohey (eds.), *Critical pedagogies and language learning*, 116–137. Cambridge: Cambridge University Press.

Carpenter, Helen, K. Seon Jeon, David MacGregor & Alison Mackey. 2006. Learners' interpretations of recasts. *Studies in Second Language Acquisition* 28. 209–236.

Carreira, Maria M. & Rey Rodríguez. 2011. Filling the void: Community Spanish language programs in Los Angeles serving to preserve the language. *Heritage Language Journal* 8(2). 1–16.

Cartwright, D. 1998. French language services in Ontario: A policy of "overly prudent gradualism"? In Thomas Ricento & Barbara Burnaby (eds.), *Language and politics in the United States and Canada*, 273–299. Mahwah, NJ: Lawrence Erlbaum Associates.

Cekaite, Asta. 2007. A child's development of interactional competence in a Swedish L2 classroom. *Modern Language Journal* 91(1). 45–62.

Cervantes, Christi A. 2002. Explanatory emotion talk in Mexican immigrant and Mexican American families. *Hispanic Journal of Behavioral Sciences* 24(2). 138–163.

Cho, Sunah Park. 2008. *Korean immigrants' social practice of heritage language acquisition and maintenance through technology*. Vancouver, Canada: University of British Columbia doctoral dissertation.

Chomsky, Noam. 1965. *Aspects of the theory of syntax*. Cambridge, MA: MIT Press.

Chumak-Horbatsch, Roma. 1999. Language change in the Ukrainian home: From transmission to maintenance to the beginnings of loss. *Canadian Ethnic Studies* 31(2). 61–75.

Clancy, Patricia M. 1986. The acquisition of communicative style in Japanese. In Bambi B. Schieffelin & Elinor Ochs (eds.), *Language socialization across cultures*. Cambridge: Cambridge University Press.

Clyne, Michael. 1996. *Inter-cultural communication at work: Cultural values in discourse*. Cambridge: Cambridge University Press.

Cole, KimMarie & Jane Zuengler. 2003. Engaging in an authentic science project: Appropriating, resisting, and denying "scientific" identities. In Robert Bayley & Sandra R. Schecter (eds.), *Language socialization in bilingual and multilingual societies*, 98–113. Clevedon, UK: Multilingual Matters.

Comanaru, Ruxandra & Kimberly A. Noels. 2009. Self-determination, motivation, and the learning of chinese as a heritage language. *Canadian Modern Language Review* 66(1). 131–158.

Constable, Nicole. 2005. Introduction: Cross-border marriages, gender mobility, and global hypergamy. In Nicole Constable (ed.), *Cross-border marriages*, 1–16. Philadelphia: University of Pennsylvania Press.

Cook, Guy. 2004. *Discourse*. Oxford: Oxford University Press.

Cope, Bill & Mary Kalantzis. 2000. Designs for social futures. In B. Cope & M. Kalantzis (eds.), *Multiliteracies: Literacy learning and designs of social futures*, 203–234. London: Routledge.

Cope, Lida. 2011. From ethnocultural pride to promoting the Texas Czech vernacular: Current maintenance efforts and unexplored possibilities. *Language and Education* 25(4). 361–383.

Crawford, James. 1992a. *Hold your tongue: Bilingualism and the politics of "English-only"*. Reading, MA: Addison-Wesley.

Crawford, James. (ed.) 1992b. *Language loyalties: A source book on the official English controversy*. Chicago: The University of Chicago Press.

Cummins, Jim. 1981. The role of primary language development in promoting educational success for language minority students. In California Department of Education (ed.), *Schooling and language minority students: A theoretical framework*, 16–62. Los Angeles: Evaluation, Dissemination and Assessment Center.

Cummins, Jim. 1984. *Bilingualism and special education: Issues in assessment and pedagogy*. Clevendon, UK: Multilingual Matters.
Cummins, Jim. 2000. *Language, power, and pedagogy: Bilingual children in the crossfire*. Buffalo, NY: Multilingual Matters.
Dagenais, Diane & C. Berron. 2001. Promoting multilingualism through French immersion and language maintenance in three immigrant families. *Language, Culture and Curriculum* 14(2). 142–155.
Dagenais, Diane & Elaine Day. 1999. Home language practices of trilingual children in French immersion. *Canadian Modern Language Review* 56(1). 99–123.
Davey, Beth. 1983. Think aloud: Modeling the cognitive processes of reading comprehension. *Journal of Reading* 27(1). 44–47.
de Courcy, Michèle 2007. Multilingualism, literacy and the acquisition of English as an additional language among Iraqi refugees in regional Victoria. *University of Sydney Papers in TESOL* 2. 1–31.
DeBruin-Parecki, Andrea & Scott G. Paris. 1997. Family literacy: Examining practice and issues of effectiveness. *Journal of Adolescent & Adult Literacy* 40(8). 596–605.
Decapua, Andrea & Ann C. Wintergerst. 2009. Second-generation language maintenance and identity: A case study. *Bilingual Research Journal* 32(1). 5–24.
del Pozo, José (ed.) 2006. *Exiliados, emigrados y retornados: Chilenos en América y Europa, 1973–2004*. Santiago de Chile: RIL Editores.
Delanty, Gerard. 2006. The cosmopolitan imagination: Critical cosmopolitanism and social theory. *The British Journal of Sociology* 57(1). 25–47.
Delgado, María Rocío. 2009. *Spanish heritage language socialization practices of a family of Mexican origin*. Tucson, AZ: University of Arizona Unpublished doctoral dissertation.
Demuth, Katherine. 1986. Prompting routines in the language socialization of Basotho children. In Bambi B. Schieffelin & Elinor Ochs (eds.), *Language socialization across cultures*, 51–79. Cambridge: Cambridge University Press.
Döpke, Susanne. 1992. *One parent one language: An interactional approach*. Amsterdam: John Benjamins Publishing.
Duff, Patricia A. 1995. An ethnography of communication in immersion classrooms in Hungary. *TESOL Quarterly* 29. 311–324.
Duff, Patricia A. 1996. Different languages, different practices: Socialization of discourse competence in dual-language school classrooms in Hungary. In K. Bailey & D. Nunan (eds.), *Voices from the language classroom: Qualitative research in second language education*, 407–433. New York: Cambridge University Press.
Duff, Patricia A. 2002. The discursive co-construction of knowledge, identity, and difference: An ethnography of communication in the high school mainstream. *Applied Linguistics* 23(3). 289–322.
Duff, Patricia A. 2003. New directions in second language socialization. *Korean Journal of English Language and Linguistics* 3(3). 309–339.
Duff, Patricia A. 2007a. Multilingualism in Canadian schools: Myths, realities, and possibilities. *Canadian Journal of Applied Linguistics* 10(2). 1001–1016.
Duff, Patricia A. 2007b. Problematising academic discourse socialisation. In H. Marriott, T. Moore & R. Spence-Brown (eds.), *Learning discourses and the discourses of learning*, 1.1–1.19. Melbourne: Monash University ePress.
Duff, Patricia A. 2007c. Second language socialization as sociocultural theory: Insights and issues. *Language Teaching* 40. 309–319.

Duff, Patricia A. 2012. Second language socialization. In Alessandro Duranti, Elinor Ochs & Bambi B. Schieffelin (eds.), *The handbook of language socialization*, 564–586. West Sussex, UK: Wiley-Blackwell.

Duff, Patricia A. & Nancy Hornberger (eds.). 2008. *Language socialization*, 2nd edn, vol. 8 (Encyclopedia of language and education. Vol. 8: Language socialization). Philadelphia/Heidelberg: Springer.

Duff, Patricia A. & Steven Talmy. 2011. Language socialization approaches to second language acquisition. In D. Atkinson (ed.), *Alternative approaches to second language acquisition*, 95–116. New York: Routledge.

Duff, Patricia A., Ping Wong & Margaret Early. 2000. Learning language for work and life: The linguistic socialization of immigrant Canadians seeking careers in healthcare. *Canadian Modern Language Review* 57(1). 9–57.

Duff, Patricia A. & Ava Becker-Zayas. 2017. Demographics and heritage languages in Canada: Policies, patterns, prospects. In Olga E. Kagan, Maria M. Carreira & Claire Hitchens Chik (eds.), *The Routledge handbook of heritage language education: From innovation to program building*, 57–67. New York: Routledge.

Duff, Patricia A. & May, Stephen (eds.). 2017. *Language socialization,* 3rd edn. Philadelphia/Heidelberg: Springer.

Duranti, Alessandro. 1997. *Linguistic anthropology* (Cambridge textbooks in linguistics). Cambridge: Cambridge University Press.

Duranti, Alessandro, Elinor Ochs & Bambi B. Schieffelin (eds.). 2012. *The handbook of language socialization*. West Sussex, UK: Wiley-Blackwell.

Eisenberg, Ann R. 1986. Teasing: Verbal play in two Mexicano homes. In Bambi B. Schieffelin & Elinor Ochs (eds.), *Language socialization across cultures*, 182–198. Cambridge: Cambridge University Press.

Eisenberg, Ann R. 2002. Maternal teaching talk within families of Mexican descent: Influences of task and socioeconomic status. *Hispanic Journal of Behavioral Sciences* 24(2). 206–224.

Ellis, Rod & Younghee Sheen. 2006. Reexamining the role of recasts in second language acquisition. *Studies in Second Language Acquisition* 28. 575–600.

Erikson, Erik H. 1950. *Childhood and society*. New York: Norton.

Fader, Ayala. 2001. Literacy, bilingualism, and gender in a Hasidic community. *Linguistics and Education* 12(3). 261–283.

Fail, Hellen, Jeff Thompson & George Walker. 2004. Belonging, identity and Third Culture Kids: Life histories of former international school students. *Journal of Research in International Education* 3(3). 319–338.

Fairclough, Norman. 1992. *Discourse and social change*. Cambridge: Polity Press.

Fairclough, Norman. 2001. *Language and power*. London: Longman.

Fairclough, Norman & Ruth Wodak. 2004. Discourse studies: A multidisciplinary introduction. In T. A. van Dijk (ed.), *Discourse as social interaction*. London: Sage Publications.

Faist, Thomas. 1998. Transnational social spaces out of international migration: Evolution, significance and future prospects. *Archives Européennes de Sociologie* 39(2). 215–247.

Farruggio, Pete. 2010. Latino immigrant parents' views of bilingual education as a vehicle for heritage preservation. *Journal of Latinos and Education* 9(1). 3–21.

Faulstich Orellana, Marjorie. 2009. *Translating childhoods: Immigrant youth, language and culture*. New Brunswick, NJ: Rutgers University Press.

Ferguson, Gibson Ronald. 2013. Language practices and language management in a UK Yemeni community. *Journal of Multilingual and Multicultural Development* 34(2). 121–135.

Field, Margaret. 2001. Triadic directives in Navajo language socialization. *Language in Society* 30(2). 249–263.
Fishman, Joshua A. 1965. Who speaks what language to whom and when? *La Linguistique* 2. 67–88.
Fishman, Joshua A. 1966. *Language loyalty in the United States*. The Hague: Mouton.
Fishman, Joshua A. (ed.) 1971. *Advances in the sociology of language*, vol. 1. The Hague: Mouton.
Fishman, Joshua A. (ed.) 1972. *Advances in the sociology of language*, vol. 2. The Hague: Mouton.
Fishman, Joshua A. 1991. *Reversing language shift: Theoretical and empirical foundations of assistance to threatened languages*. Clevedon, UK: Multilingual Matters.
Fishman, Joshua A. 1994. The truth about language and culture (and a note about its relevance to the Jewish case). *International Journal of the Sociology of Language* 109(1). 83–96.
Fishman, Joshua A. 1996a. *In praise of the beloved language: A comparative view of positive ethnolinguistic consciousness*. Berlin: Mouton de Gruyter.
Fishman, Joshua A. 1996b. What do you lose when you lose your language? In Gina Cantoni (ed.), *Stabilizing indigenous languages*, 80–91. Flagstaff, AZ: Center for Excellence in Education, Northern Arizona University.
Fishman, Joshua A. 1999. *Handbook of language and ethnic identity*. Toronto: Oxford University Press.
Fishman, Joshua A. (ed.) 2001. *Can threatened languages be saved?* Clevedon, UK: Multilingual Matters.
Fishman, Joshua A., Robert L. Cooper & Roxana Ma. 1971. *Bilingualism in the Barrio*. Bloomington, IN: Indiana University Press.
Fishman, Joshua A., Robert L. Cooper, Roxana Ma & et al. 1968. *Bilingualism in the Barrio*, vol. I. New York: Yeshiva University, Report to USOE under contract OEC-1-7-062817-0297.
Fogle, Lyn. 2013. Parental ethnotheories and family language policy in transnational adoptive families. *Language Policy* 12(1). 83–102.
Fogle, Lyn & Kendall A. King. 2013. Child agency and language policy in transnational families. *Issues in Applied Linguistics* 19. 1–25.
Fogle, Lyn & Kendall A. King. 2017. Bi- and multilingual family language socialization. In Patricia A. Duff & Stephen May (eds.), *Language socialization*, 1–17. Philadelphia/Heidelberg: Springer.
Foucault, Michel. 1965. *Madness and civilization: A history of insanity in the age of reason*. New York: Pantheon.
Foucault, Michel. 1972. *The archaeology of knowledge*. London: Tavistock Publications Limited.
Foucault, Michel. 1975. *Discipline and punish: The birth of the prison*. New York: Random House.
Foucault, Michel. 1980. *Power/knowledge: Selected interviews and other writings, 1972–77*. (ed. C. Gordon). New York: Pantheon Books.
Freud, Sigmund. 1923/1961. *The ego and the id*, translated by J. Riviere. New York: Norton.
Friedman, Debra. 2006. *(Re)imagining the nation: Language socialization in Ukrainian classrooms*. Los Angeles: University of California doctoral dissertation.
Gal, Susan. 1998. Multiplicity and contention among language ideologies: A commentary. In Bambi B. Schieffelin, Kathryn A. Woolard & Paul V. Kroskrity (eds.), *Language ideologies: Practice and theory*, 317–331. New York: Oxford University Press.
Galindo, René. 1997. Language wars: The ideological dimensions of the debates on bilingual education. *Bilingual Research Journal* 21(2–3). 163–201.

García, Ofelia. 1995. Spanish language loss as a determinant of income among Latinos in the United States: Implications for language policy in schools. In J. Tollefson (ed.), *Power and inequality in language education*, 142–160. New York: Cambridge University Press.

García, Ofelia & Harold Schiffman. 2006. Fishmanian sociolinguistics (1949 to the present). In Ofelia García et al. (eds.), *Language loyalty, continuity and change: Joshua A. Fishman's contributions to international sociolinguistics*, 3–68. Clevedon, UK: Multilingual Matters.

Gardner, Howard. 1993. *Frames of mind*. New York: Basic Books.

Garfinkel, Harold. 1967. *Studies in ethnomethodology*. Englewood Cliffs, NJ: Prentice Hall.

Garrett, Paul B. 2005. What a language is good for: Language socialization, language shift, and the persistence of code-specific genres in St. Lucia. *Language in Society* 34(3). 327–361.

Garrett, Paul B. & Patricia Baquedano-López. 2002. Language socialization: Reproduction and continuity, transformation and change. *Annual Review of Anthropology* 31. 339–361.

Gee, James P. 1999. *An introduction to discourse analysis*. New York: Routledge.

Gee, James P. 2005. *An introduction to discourse analysis: Theory and method*. New York: Routledge.

Germann Molz, Jennie 2005. Getting a "flexible eye": Round-the-world travel and scales of cosmopolitan citizenship. *Citizenship Studies* 9(5). 517–531.

Gibbons, John & Elizabeth Ramirez. 2004. Different beliefs: Beliefs and the maintenance of a minority language. *Journal of Language and Social Psychology* 23(1). 99–117.

Gilkes, Cheryl T. 1980. The black church as a therapeutic community: Suggested areas for research into the black religious experience. *Journal of the Interdenominational Theological Center* 8. 29–44.

Ginieniewicz, Jorge & Daniel Schugurensky (eds.). 2006. *Ruptures, continuities and re-learning: The political participation of Latin Americans in Canada*. Toronto, Ontario, Canada: Transformative Learning Centre, OISE, University of Toronto.

Giroux, Henry & Kostas Myrsiades (eds.). 2001. *Beyond the corporate university: Culture and pedagogy in the New Millenium*. Lanham: Rowman & Littlefield.

Goffman, Erving. 1967. *Interaction ritual*. New York: Pantheon.

Goldstein, Tara. 1997. *Two languages at work: Bilingual life on the production floor* (Contributions to the sociology of language). New York: Mouton de Gruyter.

Goodnow, Jacqueline J. 1997. Parenting and the 'transmission' and 'internalization' of values: From social-cultural perspectives to within-family analyses. In J. E. Grusec & L. Kuczynski (eds.), *Handbook of parenting and the transmission of values*, 333–361. New York: Wiley.

Gordon, Daryl. 2008. Gendered second language socialization. In Patricia A. Duff & Nancy H. Hornberger (eds.), *Encyclopedia of language and education. Vol. 8: Language socialization*, 231–242. Philadelphia/Heidelberg: Springer.

Gramsci, Antonio. 1971. *Selections from the prison notebooks*. New York: International Publishers.

Grancea, Liana. 2007. Conversation Analysis: Method, concepts, applications. *Cognition, Brain, Behavior* 11(2). 331–352.

Guardado, Martin. 2002. Loss and maintenance of first language skills: Case studies of Hispanic families in Vancouver. *Canadian Modern Language Review* 58(3). 341–363.

Guardado, Martin. 2006. Engaging language and cultural spaces: Latin American parents' reflections on language loss and maintenance in Vancouver. *Canadian Journal of Applied Linguistics* 9(1). 51–72.

Guardado, Martin. 2008a. *Language socialization in Canadian Hispanic communities: Ideologies and practices*. Vancouver, Canada: University of British Columbia doctoral dissertation.
Guardado, Martin. 2008b. Language, identity and cultural awareness in Spanish-speaking families. *Canadian Ethnic Studies* 40(3). 171–181.
Guardado, Martin. 2009. Speaking Spanish like a Boy Scout: Language socialization, resistance and reproduction in a heritage language Scout troop. *Canadian Modern Language Review* 66(1). 101–129.
Guardado, Martin. 2010. Heritage language development: Preserving a mythic past or envisioning the future of Canadian identity? *Journal of Language, Identity, and Education* 9(5). 329–346.
Guardado, Martin. 2011. Language and literacy socialization as resistance in Western Canada. In Kim Potowski & Jason Rothman (eds.), *Bilingual youth: Spanish in English-speaking societies*, 177–198. Amsterdam: John Benjamins.
Guardado, Martin. 2012. Toward a critical multilingualism in Canadian classrooms: Making local inroads to a cosmopolitan identity. *TESL Canada Journal* 30(1). 151–165.
Guardado, Martin. 2013a. The metapragmatic regimentation of heritage language use in Hispanic Canadian caregiver–child interactions. *International Multilingual Research Journal* 7(3). 230–247.
Guardado, Martin. 2013b. Parental regulation of heritage language use: A mapping of metapragmatic strategies. Paper presented at Canadian Association of Applied Linguistics Conference, Victoria, British Columbia.
Guardado, Martin. 2017. Heritage language development in interlingual families. In Peter. P. Trifonas & Themistoklis Aravossitas (eds.), *Handbook of research and practice in heritage language education*, 1–17. Philadelphia/Heidelberg: Springer.
Guardado, Martin & Ava Becker. 2013. Fostering heritage languages and diasporic identities: The role of grassroots initiatives in Alberta and British Columbia. In K. Arnett & C. Mady (eds.), *Minority populations in Canadian second language education: New perspectives on language and education*, 55–70. Bristol: Multilingual Matters.
Guilherme, Manuela. 2007. English as a Global Language and education for cosmopolitan citizenship. *Language and Intercultural Communication* 7(1). 72–90.
Gumperz, John Joseph & Dell H. Hymes. 1986. *Directions in sociolinguistics: The ethnography of communication*. New York: Blackwell.
Hackett, Steven C. & Michael C. Moore. 2011. *Enviromental and natural resources economics: Theory, policy, and the sustainable society*. Armonk, NY: M. E. Sharpe, Inc.
Hall, Suart & Paul Du Gay (eds.). 1996. *Questions of cultural identity*. London: Sage.
Halliday, Michael Alexander Kirkwood. 1978. *Language as social semiotic: The social interpretation of language and meaning*. Baltimore, MD: University Park Press.
Halliday, Michael Alexander Kirkwood & Christian M. I. M. Matthiessen. 2004. *An introduction to functional grammar*. London: Arnold.
Hannerz, Ulf. 1990. Cosmopolitans and locals in world culture. In Mike Featherstone (ed.), *Global culture: Nationalism, globalization, and modernity*, 237–252. London: Sage Publications.
Harklau, Linda. 2003. Representational practices and multi-modal communication in US high schools: Implications for adolescent immigrants. In Robert Bayley & Sandra R. Schecter (eds.), *Language socialization in bilingual and multilingual societies*, 83–97. Clevedon, UK: Multilingual Matters.

Hashimoto, Kumi & Jin Sook Lee. 2011. Heritage-language literacy practices: A case study of three Japanese American families. *Bilingual Research Journal* (34)2. 161–184.

Hawking, Stephen. 1988. *A brief history of time*. New York: Bantam Books.

He, Agnes Weiyun. 2001. The language of ambiguity: Practices in Chinese Heritage Language classes. *Discourse Studies* 3(1). 75–96.

He, Agnes Weiyun. 2003. Novices and their speech roles in Chinese heritage language classes. In Robert Bayley & Sandra R. Schecter (eds.), *Language socialization in bilingual and multilingual societies*, 128–146. Clevedon, UK: Multilingual Matters.

He, Agnes Weiyun. 2004. CA for SLA: Arguments from Chinese language classes. *The Modern Language Journal* 88(4). 568–582.

He, Agnes Weiyun. 2006. Toward an identity theory of the development of Chinese as a heritage language. *Heritage Language Journal* 4(1). 1–28.

He, Agnes Weiyun. 2008. Heritage language learning and socialization. In Patricia A. Duff & Nancy H. Hornberger (eds.), *Encyclopedia of language and education. Vol. 8: Language socialization*, 2nd edn, 201–213. Philadelphia/Heidelberg: Springer.

He, Agnes Weiyun. 2012. Heritage language socialization. In Alessandro Duranti, Elinor Ochs & Bambi B. Schieffelin (eds.), *The handbook of language socialization*, 587–609. West Sussex, UK: Wiley-Blackwell.

He, Agnes Weiyun. 2013. The wor(l)d is a collage: Multi-performance by Chinese heritage language speakers. *The Modern Language Journal* 97(2). 304–317.

He, Agnes Weiyun. 2016. Discursive roles and responsibilities: A study of interactions in Chinese immigrant households. *Journal of Multilingual and Multicultural Development* 37(7). 667–679.

Heath, Shirley Brice. 1983. *Ways with words: Language, life, and work in communities and classrooms*. Cambridge: Cambridge University Press.

Heller, Kenneth. 1989. Return to community. *American Journal of Community Psychology* 17(1). 1–15.

Heller, Monica & Laurette Levy. 1992. Mixed marriages: Life on the linguistic frontier. *Multilingua* 11(1). 11–43.

Heritage, John. 1984. A change-of-state token and aspects of its sequential placement. In J. M. Atkinson & John Heritage (eds.), *Structures of social action*, 299–345. Cambridge: Cambridge University Press.

Heritage, John & Steven Clayman. 2010. *Talk in action: Interactions, identities, and institutions*. Malden, MA: Wiley-Blackwell.

Hester, S. 1998. Describing 'deviance' in school: Recognisably educational psychological problems. In C. Antaki & S. Widdicombe (eds.), *Identities in talk*, 133–150. London: Sage Publications.

Hill, Jane H. 1985. The grammar of consciousness and the consciousness of grammar. *American Ethnologist* 12. 725–737.

Hill, Jane H. 1998. "Today there is no respect": Nostalgia, "respect," and oppositional discourse in Mexicano (Nahuatl) language ideology. In Bambi B. Schieffelin, Kathryn A. Woolard & Paul V. Kroskrity (eds.), *Language ideologies: Practice and theory*, 68–86. New York: Oxford University Press.

Holland, Dorothy & Jean Lave (eds.). 2001. *History in person: Enduring struggles, contentious practice, intimate identities*. Santa Fe, NM: School of American Research Press.

Hondagneu-Sotelo, Pierrette. 2001. *Domestica: Immigrant workers cleaning and caring in the shadows of affluence*. Berkeley: University of California Press.

hooks, bell. 1989. *Talking back: Thinking feminist, thinking Black*. Boston: South End Press.
Howard, Kathryn M. 2008. Language socialization and language shift among school-aged children. In Patricia A. Duff & Nancy H. Hornberger (eds.), *Encyclopedia of language and education. Vol. 8: Language socialization*, 2nd edn, 187–199. Philadelphia/Heidelberg: Springer.
Howarth, David & David R. Howarth. 2000. *Discourse*. Milton Keynes, UK: Open University Press.
Hurh, Won Moo. 1993. The 1.5 Generation phenomenon: A paragon of Korean-American pluralism. *Korean Culture* 14. 17–27.
Hymes, Dell 1974. *Foundations in sociolinguistics: An ethnographic approach*. Philadelphia: University of Pennsylvania Press.
Iqbal, Isabeau. 2005. Mother tongue and motherhood: Implications for French language maintenance in Canada. *The Canadian Modern Language Review* 61(3). 305–323.
Iyer, Radha. 2009. Entrepreneurial identities and the problematic of subjectivity in media-mediated discourses. *Discourse & Society* 20(2). 241–263.
Jackson, Lachlan. 2007. Talking tactics: Fathers' language work in bilingual childrearing in intermarried families in Japan. In R. Lougnane, C. Penry Williams & J. Verhoeven (eds.), *In between wor(l)ds: Transformation and translation*, 19–116. Melbourne, Australia: University of Melbourne.
Jackson, Lachlan. 2009. Language, power and identity in bilingual childrearing. *Crossroads* 3(2). 58–71.
Jaffe, Alexandra. 1999. *Ideologies in action: Language politics in Corsica*. Berlin: Mouton de Gruyter.
Jaffe, Alexandra. 2005. Collaborative literacy practices in French and Corsican: The ideological underpinnings of a bilingual education. *Crossroads of Language, Interaction, and Culture* 6. 3–28.
Jandt, Fred Edmund. 2006. *An introduction to intercultural communication: Identities in a global community*, 4th edn. Thousand Oaks, CA: Sage Publications.
Jaworski, Adam & Nikolas Coupland (eds.). 1999. *The discourse reader*. London: Routledge.
Jefferson, Gail. 1983. Issues in the transcription of naturally-occurring talk: Caricature versus capturing pronunciational particulars. The Netherlands: Tilburg University.
Jefferson, Gail. 1984. Transcript notation. In J. M. Atkinson & J. Heritage (eds.), *Structures of social action: Studies in conversation analysis*, ix–xvi. New York: Cambridge University Press.
Juan-Garau, Maria & Carmen Pérez-Vidal. 2001. Mixing and pragmatic parental strategies in early bilingual acquisition. *Journal of Child Language* 28. 59–86.
Kasper, Gabriele. 1985. Repair in foreign language teaching. *Studies in Second Language Acquisition* 7(2). 200–215.
Kastoryano, Riva. 2000. Global trends and issues: Settlement, transnational communities and citizenship. *International Social Science Journal* 52(165). 307–312.
Kim, Dongno. 1990. The transformation of familism in modern Korean society. *International Sociology* 5(4). 409–425.
Kim, Hye Yeong. 2011. Parents' perceptions, decisions, and influences: Korean immigrant parents look at language learning and their children's identities. *Multicultural Education* 18(2). 16–19.
Kim, Jean. 2008. *Negotiating multiple investments in language and identities: The language socialization of Generation 1.5 Korean-Canadian university students*. Vancouver, Canada: University of British Columbia doctoral dissertation.

King, Kendall A., Lyn Fogle & Aubrey Logan-Terry. 2008. Family language policy. *Language and Linguistics Compass* 2(5). 907–922.

Kipling, Rudyard. 1987. *The jungle book*. New York: Viking.

Knafo, Ariel & Neta Galansky. 2008. The influence of children on their parents' values. *Social and Personality Psychology Compass* (2)3. 1143–1161.

Kobayashi, Masaki. 2003. The role of peer support in ESL students' accomplishment of oral academic tasks. *The Canadian Modern Language Review* 59(3). 337–368.

Kopeliovich, Shulamit. 2010. Family language policy: A case study of a Russian-Hebrew bilingual family: Toward a theoretical framework. *Diaspora, Indigenous, and Minority Education* 4(3). 162–178.

Kormos, Judit. 1999. Monitoring and self-repair in L2. *Language Learning* 49(2). 303–342.

Kouritzin, Sandra G. 1999. *Face[t]s of first language loss*. Mahwah, NJ: Lawrence Erlbaum.

Kouritzin, Sandra G. 2006. Songs from taboo tongues: Experiencing first language loss. *Language and Literacy* 8(1). 1–28.

Krashen, Stephen D. 1996. *Under attack: The case against bilingual education*. Culver City, CA: Language Education Associates.

Kroskrity, Paul V. 1992. Arizona Tewa Kiva speech as a manifestation of linguistic ideology. *Pragmatics* 2(3). 297–309.

Kroskrity, Paul V. 2000a. Language ideologies in the expression and representation of Arizona Tewa ethnic identity. In Paul V. Kroskrity (ed.), *Regimes of language: Ideologies, polities, and identities*, 329–359. Santa Fe: School of American Research Press.

Kroskrity, Paul V. 2000b. Regimenting languages: Language ideological perspectives. In Paul V. Kroskrity (ed.), *Regimes of language: Ideologies, polities, and identities*, 1–34. Santa Fe: School of American Research Press.

Kroskrity, Paul V. (ed.) 2000c. *Regimes of language: Ideologies, polities, and identities*. Santa Fe: School of American Research Press.

Kroskrity, Paul V. 2010. Language ideologies-evolving perspectives. In Jürgen Jaspers, Jan-Ola Östman & Jef Verschueren (eds.), *Society and language use (Handbook of pragmatics highlights)*, 192–211. Amsterdam: John Benjamins.

Kulick, Don. 1992. *Language shift and cultural reproduction: Socialization, self and syncretism in a Papua New Guinean village*. Cambridge: Cambridge University Press.

Lam, Wan Shun Eva. 2008. Language socialization in online communities. In Patricia A. Duff & Nancy H. Hornberger (eds.), *Encyclopedia of language and education. Vol. 8: Language socialization*, 301–311. Philadelphia/Heidelberg: Springer.

Lambert, Wallace E. & Donald M. Taylor. 1996. Language in the lives of ethnic minorities: Cuban American families in Miami. *Applied Linguistics* 17. 477–500.

Landolt, Patricia, Luin Goldring & Judith K. Bernhard. 2009. Between grassroots politics and the ethnicizing imperative of the multicultural state: Latin American immigrant organizations in Toronto. *CERIS Working Paper* No. 73. 1–25.

Landry, Rodrigue, Real Allard & Jacques Henry. 1996. French in South Louisiana. *Journal of Multilingual and Multicultural Development* 17. 442–466.

Lanehart, Sonja L. 1999. African American Vernacular English. In Joshua A. Fishman (ed.), *The handbook of language and ethnic identity*, 211–225. New York: Oxford University Press.

Lanza, Elizabeth. 1992. Can bilingual two-year-olds code-switch? *Journal of Child Language* 19(3). 633–658.

Lanza, Elizabeth. 1997/2004. *Language mixing in infant bilingualism: A sociolinguistic perspective*. Oxford: Oxford University Press.

Lanza, Elizabeth. 2001. Bilingual language acquisition. A discourse perspective on language contact in parent–child interaction. In Jasone Cenoz & Fred Genesee (eds.), *Trends in bilingual acquisition*, 201–229. Amsterdam: John Benjamins.

Lanza, Elizabeth. 2007. Multilingualism and the family. In Peter Auer & Li Wei (eds.), *Handbook of multilingualism and multilingual communication*, 45–67. Berlin: Mouton de Gruyter.

Lanza, Elizabeth & Bente Ailin Svendsen. 2007. Tell me who your friends are and I might be able to tell you what language(s) you speak: Social network analysis, multilingualism, and identity. *International Journal of Bilingualism* 11(3). 275–300.

Lau, Siu-Kai. 1981. Chinese familism in an urban-industrial setting: The case of Hong Kong. *Journal of Marriage and the Family* 43. 977–992.

Lawson, Sarah & Itesh Sachdev. 2004. Identity, language use, and attitudes: Some Sylheti-Bangladeshi data from London, UK. *Journal of Language and Social Psychology* 23(1). 49–69.

Lessa, Iara. 2006. Discursive struggles within social welfare: Restaging teen motherhood. *British Journal of Social Work* 36(2). 283–298.

Levinson, Stephen C. 1983. Conversational implicature. In S. C. Levinson (ed.), *Pragmatics* 97–166. Cambridge: Cambridge University Press.

Lewis, Magda. 2008. Public good or private value: A critique of the commodification of knowledge in Higher Education—A Canadian perspective. In J. E. Canaan & W. Shumar (eds.), *Structure and agency in the neoliberal university*. New York: Routledge.

Li, Duanduan. 2008. Pragmatic socialization. In Patricia A. Duff & Nancy H. Hornberger (eds.), *Encyclopedia of language and education. Vol. 8: Language socialization*, 71–83. Philadelphia/Heidelberg: Springer.

Li, Guofang. 2006. Biliteracy and trilingual practices in the home context: Case studies of Chinese-Canadian children. *Journal of Early Childhood Literacy* 6(3). 355–381.

Li, Xiaoxia. 1999. How can language minority parents help their children become bilingual in familial context? A case study of a language minority mother and her daughter. *Bilingual Research Journal* 23(2/3). 211–223.

Liamputtong, Pranee. 1991. Motherhood and the challenge of immigrant mothers: A personal reflection. *Families in Society* 82(2). 195–201.

Liddicoat, Anthony J. 2007. *An introduction to Conversation Analysis*. New York: Continuum.

Lin, George. 2003. Identity, mobility, and the making of the Chinese diasporic landscape in Hong Kong. In L. J. C. Ma & C. Carter (eds.), *Space, place, mobility, and identity*, 141–161. New York: Rowman & Littlefield.

Lotherington, Heather. 2003. Multiliteracies in Springvale: Negotiating language, culture and identity in suburban Melbourne. In Robert Bayley & Sandra R. Schecter (eds.), *Language socialization in bilingual and multilingual societies*, 200–217. Clevedon: Multilingual Matters.

Luke, Allan. 2004. Teaching after the market: From commodity to cosmopolitan. *Teachers College Record* 106(7). 1422–1443.

Luke, Allan & Tara Goldstein. 2006. Building intercultural capital: A response to Rogers, Marshall, and Tyson. *Reading Research Quarterly* 41(2). 202–224.

Luke, Allan, Carmen Luke & Phil Graham. 2007. Globalization, corporatism, and critical language education. *International Multilingual Research Journal* 1(1). 1–13.

Luo, Shiow-Huey & Richard L. Wiseman. 2000. Ethnic language maintenance among Chinese immigrant children in the United States. *International Journal of Intercultural Relations* 24(3). 307–324.

Luykx, Aurolyn. 2003. Weaving languages together: Family language policy and gender socialization in bilingual Aymara households. In Robert Bayley & Sandra R. Schecter (eds.), *Language socialization in bilingual and multilingual societies*, 25–43. Clevedon, UK: Multilingual Matters.

Lyon, Jean. 1996. *Becoming bilingual: Language acquisition in a bilingual community*. Clevedon, UK: Multilingual Matters.

Lyotard, Jean-Francois. 1984. *The postmodern condition: A report on knowledge*. Minneapolis, MN: University of Minnesota Press.

Lyster, Roy. 1998. Recasts, repetition, and ambiguity in L2 classroom discourse. *Studies in Second Language Acquisition* 20(1). 51–81.

Lyster, Roy. 2001. Negotiation of form, recasts, and explicit correction in relation to error types and learner repair in immersion classrooms. *Language Learning* 51(1). 265–301.

Lyster, Roy & Leila Ranta. 1997. Corrective feedback and learner uptake: Negotiation of form in communicative classrooms. *SSLA* 20. 37–66.

MacDonald, V. & K. Monkman. 2005. Setting on context: Historical perspectives on Latino/a education. In P. Pedraza & M. Rivera (eds.), *Latino education: An agenda for community action research*, 47–74. Mahwah, NJ: Lawrence Erlbaum Associates.

MacPherson, Seonaigh & Dawa Bhuti Ghoso. 2008. Multilingualism in emerging diasporas: A Tibetan case study. *Diaspora, Indigenous, and Minority Education* 2(3). 188–216.

Maguire, Mary. 2005. Identity and agency in primary trilingual children's multiple cultural worlds: Third space and heritage languages. In James Cohen, Kara T. McAlister, Kellie Rolstad & Jeff MacSwan (eds.), *Proceedings of the 4th International Symposium on Bilingualism*, 1423–1445. Somerville, MA: Cascadilla.

Mankowski, Eric & Julian Rappaport. 1995. Stories, identity, and the psychological sense of community. In Robert S. Wyer Jr. (ed.), *Knowledge and memory: The real story*, 211–226. Hillsdale, NJ: Lawrence Erlbaum Associates.

Massey, Doreen. 1994. *Space, place, and gender*. Minneapolis, MN: University of Minnesota Press.

Mathews, Gordon. 2000. *Global culture / individual identity: Searching for home in the cultural supermarket*. London and New York: Routledge.

Matychuk, Paul. 2005. The role of child-directed speech in language acquisition: A case study. *Language Sciences* 27. 301–379.

Mays, Vickie. M. 1986. Identity development of Black Americans: The role of history and the importance of ethnicity. *American Journal of Psychotherapy* 40(4). 582–593.

McAdoo, Harriet P. 1995. African-American families: Strengths and realities. In H. I. McCubbin, E. A. Thompson, A. I. Thompson & J. A. Futrell (eds.), *Resiliency in African-American families*, 17–30. Thousand Oaks, CA: Sage.

McAll, Christopher. 2003. Language dynamics in the bi-and multilingual workplace. In Robert Bayley & Sandra R. Schecter (eds.), *Language socialization in bilingual and multilingual societies*, 235–250. Clevedon: Multilingual Matters.

McGroarty, Mary E. 2010. Language and ideologies. In Nancy H. Hornberger & Sandra Lee McKay (eds.), *Sociolinguistics and language education*, 3–39. Bristol, UK: Multilingual Matters.

McMillan, David W. & David M. Chavis. 1986. Sense of community: A definition and theory. *Journal of Community Psychology* 14(1). 6–23.

McRae, Mary B., Patricia M. L. Carey & Roxanna Anderson-Scott. 1998. Black churches as therapeutic systems: A group process perspective. *Journal of Health Education and Behavior* 25(6). 778–189.

Meek, Barbra A. 2007. Respecting the language of elders: Ideological shift and linguistic discontinuity in a Northern Athapascan Community. *Journal of Linguistic Anthropology* 17(1). 23–43.

Merino, Barbara. 1983. Language loss in bilingual Chicano children. *Journal of Applied Developmental Psychology* 4. 277–294.
Miles, Ann. 1994. Helping out at home: Gender socialization, moral development, and devil stories in Cuenca, Ecuador. *American Anthropological Association* 22(2). 132–157.
Miller, Peggy. 1982. *Amy, Wendy and Beth: Language learning in South Baltimore*. Austin: University of Texas Press.
Mills, Sara. 2004. *Discourse: The new critical idiom*. New York: Routledge.
Milroy, Lesley. 1980. Social network and language maintenance. In A. K. Pugh, V. J. Lee & J. Swann (eds.), *Language and language use*, 35–45. London: Heinemann Educational Books.
Minami, Shiho. 2013. *Voices within the Canadian mosaic: Japanese immigrant women and their children's heritage language socialization*. Vancouver, Canada: University of British Columbia master's thesis.
Moin, Victor, Mila Schwartz & Anna Breitkopf. 2011. Balancing between heritage and host languages in bilingual kindergarten: Viewpoints of Russian-speaking immigrant parents in Germany and in Israel. *European Early Childhood Education Research Journal* 19(4). 515–533.
Moore, Leslie C. 2012. Language socialization and repetition. In Alessandro Duranti, Elinor Ochs & Bambi B. Schieffelin (eds.), *The handbook of language socialization*, 209–226. West Sussex, UK: Wiley-Blackwell.
Morita, Naoko. 2000. Discourse socialization through oral classroom activities in a TESL graduate program. *TESOL Quarterly* 34(2). 279–310.
Morita, Naoko. 2004. Negotiating participation and identity in second language academic communities. *TESOL Quarterly* 38(4). 573–603.
Morris, Delyth & Kathryn Jones. 2008. Language socialization in the home for minority language revitalization in Europe. In Patricia A. Duff & Nancy H. Hornberger (eds.), *Encyclopedia of language and education. Vol. 8: Language socialization*, 127–143. Philadelphia/Heidelberg: Springer.
Muñiz, Nilsa M. 2009. *Young children's perception and experiences regarding their native language development*. New York: State University of New York unpublished doctoral dissertation.
Naidoo, Rajani & Ian Jamieson. 2005. Knowledge in the marketplace: The global commodification of teaching and learning in higher education. In P. Ninnes & M. Hellstén (eds.), *Internationalizing higher education: Critical explorations of pedagogy and policy*, 37–52. Dordrecht: Springer.
Nassaji, Hossein. 2007. Elicitation and reformulation and their relationship with learner repair in dyadic interaction. *Language Learning* 57(4). 511–548.
Nesteruk, Olena. 2010. Heritage language maintenance and loss among the children of Eastern European immigrants in the USA. *Journal of Multilingual and Multicultural Development* 31(3). 271–286.
Newport, Elissa L., Henry Gleitman & Lila A. Gleitman. 1977. Mother, I'd rather do it myself: Some effects and non-effects of maternal speech style. In C. Snow & C. A. Ferguson (eds.), *Talking to children: Language input and acquisition*, 109–149. Cambridge: Cambridge University Press.
Nicholas, Howard, Patsy M. Lightbown & Nina Spada. 2001. Recasts as feedback to language learners. *Language Learning* 51(4). 719–758.
Nicholas, Sheilah E. 2009. "I live Hopi, I just don't speak it"—The critical intersection of language, culture, and identity in the lives of contemporary Hopi youth. *Journal of Language, Identity, and Education* 8(5). 321–334.

Nieto, Sonia. 1999. *The light in their eyes: Creating multicultural learning communities*. New York: Teachers College Press.
Nieto, Sonia. 2001. *Why we teach*. New York: Teachers College Press.
Nonaka, Angela. 2004. The forgotten endangered languages: Lessons on the importance of remembering from Thailand's Ban Khor sign language. *Language in Society* 33(5). 737–767.
Noro, Hiroko. 2009. The role of Japanese as a heritage language in constructing ethnic identity among Hapa Japanese Canadian children. *Journal of Multilingual and Multicultural Development* 30(1). 1–18.
Norton, Bonny. 2000. *Identity and language learning: Gender, ethnicity, and educational change*. Harlow, UK: Pearson Education.
Ochs, Elinor. 1979. Transcription as theory. In Elinor Ochs & Bambi B. Schieffelin (eds.), *Developmental pragmatics*, 43–72. New York: Academic Press.
Ochs, Elinor. 1982. Talking to children in Western Samoa. *Language in Society* 11(1). 77–104.
Ochs, Elinor. 1986. Introduction. In Bambi B. Schieffelin & Elinor Ochs (eds.), *Language socialization across cultures*. Cambridge: Cambridge University Press.
Ochs, Elinor. 1988. *Culture and language development: Language acquisition and language socialization in a Samoan village* (Studies in the social and cultural foundations of language). Cambridge: Cambridge University Press.
Ochs, Elinor. 1991. Misunderstanding children. In Nikolas Coupland, Howard Giles & John M. Wiemann (eds.), *Miscommunication and problematic talk*, 44–60. Newbury Park, CA: Sage Publications.
Ochs, Elinor. 1993. Constructing social identity: A language socialization perspective. *Research on Language and Social Interaction* 26(3). 287–306.
Ochs, Elinor. 1996. Linguistic resources for socializing humanity. In J. Gumperz & S. Levinson (eds.), *Rethinking linguistic relativity*, 407–438. Cambridge: Cambridge University Press.
Ochs, Elinor. 2002. Becoming a speaker of culture. In C. Kramsch (ed.), *Language acquisition and language socialization*, 99–120. London: Continuum.
Ochs, Elinor & Bambi B. Schieffelin. 1995. The impact of language socialization on grammatical development. In P. Fletcher & B MacWhinney (eds.), *The handbook of child language*, 73–94. Oxford: Blackwell.
Ochs, Elinor & Bambi B. Schieffelin. 2008. Language socialization: An historical overview. In Patricia A. Duff & Nancy H. Hornberger (eds.), *Encyclopedia of language and education. Vol. 8: Language socialization*, 2nd edn, 3–15. Philadelphia/Heidelberg: Springer.
Ochs, Elinor & Bambi B. Schieffelin. 2012. The theory of language socialization. In Alessandro Duranti, Elinor Ochs & Bambi B. Schieffelin (eds.), *The handbook of language socialization*, 1–21. West Sussex, UK: Wiley-Blackwell.
Okita, Toshie. 2002. *Invisible work: Bilingualism, language choice, and childrearing in intermarried families*. Amsterdam: John Benjamins.
Oriyama, Kaya. 2010. Heritage language maintenance and Japanese identity formation: What role can schooling and ethnic community contact play? *Heritage Language Journal* 7(2). 76–111.
Oxford, Rebecca L. 1982. Research on language loss: A review with implications for foreign language teaching. *Modern Language Journal* 66(2). 160.
Pacini-Ketchabaw, Veronica, Judith K. Bernhard & Marlinda Freire. 2001. Struggling to preserve home language: The experiences of Latino students and families in the Canadian school system. *Bilingual Research Journal* 25(1/2).

Pahl, Kate. 2008. Language socialization and multimodality in multilingual urban homes. In Patricia A. Duff & Nancy H. Hornberger (eds.), *Encyclopedia of language and education. Vol. 8: Language socialization*, 115–126. Philadelphia/Heidelberg: Springer.

Palacios, Carolina. 2011. *Social movements as learning communities: Chilean exiles and knowledge production in and beyond the solidarity movement*. Vancouver, Canada: University of British Columbia doctoral dissertation.

Palys, Theodore S. 1997. *Research decisions: Quantitative and qualitative perspectives*, 2nd edn. Toronto: Harcourt Brace & Company Canada.

Pan, Barbara A. & Jean Berko-Gleason. 1986. The study of language loss: Models and hypotheses for an emerging discipline. *Applied Psycholinguistics* 7. 193–206.

Paredes, Alejandro. 2003. Las prácticas políticas de los exiliados chilenos en Mendoza y su incidencia en Chile (1970–1989) [The political practices of Chilean exiles in Mendoza and their impact in Chile (1970–1989)]. *Universum* 18. 133–146.

Park, Eunjin. 2006. Grandparents, grandchildren and heritage language use in Korean. In Kimi Kondo-Brown (ed.), *Heritage language development : Focus on East Asian immigrants*, 57–86. Amsterdam: John Benjamins Publishing.

Park, Kyeyoung. 1999. "I really do feel I'm 1.5": The construction of self and community by young Korean Americans. *Amerasia Journal* 25. 139–163.

Park, Seong Man & Mela Sarkar. 2007. Parents' attitudes toward heritage language maintenance for their children and their efforts to help their children maintain the heritage language: A case Study of Korean-Canadian immigrants. *Language, Culture and Curriculum* 20(3). 223–235.

Patrick, Donna. 2003. Language socialization and second language acquisition in a multilingual Arctic Quebec community. In Robert Bayley & Sandra R. Schecter (eds.), *Language socialization in bilingual and multilingual societies*, 165–181. Clevedon, UK: Multilingual Matters.

Patton, Michael Q. 1990. *Qualitative evaluation and research methods*, 2nd edn. Newbury Park, CA: Sage Publications.

Paugh, Amy. 2005. Learning about work at dinnertime: Language socialization in dual-earner American families. *Discourse & Society* 16(1). 55–78.

Pavlenko, Aneta. 2001. Bilingualism, gender, and ideology. *The International Journal of Bilingualism* 5(2). 117–151.

Pease-Alvarez, Lucinda. 2002. Moving beyond linear trajectories of language shift and bilingual language socialization. *Hispanic Journal of Behavioral Sciences* 24(2). 114–137.

Pease-Alvarez, Lucinda. 2003. Transforming perspectives on bilingual language socialization. In Robert Bayley & Sandra R. Schecter (eds.), *Language socialization in bilingual and multilingual societies*, 9–24.

Pemberton, Elizabeth F. & Ruth V. Watkins. 1987. Language facilitation through stories: Recasting and modelling. *First Language* 7. 79–89.

Pennycook, Alastair. 1994. *The cultural politics of English as an International Language*. London: Longman.

Pennycook, Alastair. 1998. *English and the discourses of colonialism*. London: Routledge.

Pennycook, Alastair. 2001. *Critical applied linguistics: A critical introduction*. Mahwah, NJ: Lawrence Erlbaum Associates.

Pesco, Diane & Martha Crago. 2008. Language socialization in Canadian aboriginal communities. In Patricia A. Duff & Nancy H. Hornberger (eds.), *Encyclopedia of language and education. Vol. 8: Language socialization*, 273–285. Philadelphia/Heidelberg: Springer.

Petri, Herbert. 1991. *Motivation: Theory, research and application*. Belmont, CA: Wadsworth.
Philips, Juliet. 1973. Syntax and vocabulary of mothers' speech to young children: Age and sex comparisons. *Child Development* 44(1). 182–185.
Philips, Susan U. 1998. Language ideologies in institutions of power: A commentary. In Bambi B. Schieffelin, Kathryn A. Woolard & Paul V. Kroskrity (eds.), *Language ideologies: Practice and theory*. New York/Oxford: Oxford University Press.
Phillipson, Robert & Tove Skutnabb-Kangas. 1996. English only worldwide or language ecology? *TESOL Quarterly* 30(3). 429–452.
Piller, Ingrid. 2001a. Linguistic intermarriage: Language choice and negotiation of identity. In A. Pavlenko, A. Blackledge, Ingrid Piller & M. Teutsch-Dwyer (eds.), *Multilingualism, second language learning, and gender*, 199–230. Berlin: Mouton de Gruyter.
Piller, Ingrid. 2001b. Private language planning: The best of both worlds? *Estudios de Sociolingüística* 2(1). 61–80.
Piller, Ingrid & Kimie Takahashi. 2006. A passion for English: Desire and the language market. In Aneta Pavlenko (ed.), *Bilingual minds: Emotional experience, expression and representation*. Clevedon,UK: Multilingual Matters.
Pomerantz, Anita. 1984. Agreeing and disagreeing with assessments: Some features of preferred/dispreferred turn shapes. In J. M. Atkinson & J. Heritage (eds.), *Structures of social action: Studies in Conversation Analysis*, 57–101. Cambridge: Cambridge University Press.
Pon, Gordon, Tara Goldstein & Sandra R. Schecter. 2003. Interrupted by silences: The contemporary education of Hong Kong-born Chinese Canadians. In Robert Bayley & Sandra R. Schecter (eds.), *Language socialization in bilingual and multilingual societies*, 114–127. Clevedon,UK: Multilingual Matters.
Poole, Deborah. 1992. Language socialization in the second language classroom. *Language Learning* 42. 593–616.
Popp, Richard K. 2006. Mass media and the linguistic marketplace: Media, language, and distinction. *Journal of Communication Inquiry* 30(1). 5–20.
Potts, Diane. 2005. Pedagogy, purpose, and the second language learner in on-line communities. *The Canadian Modern Language Review* 62(1). 137–160.
Pratt, Mary Louise. 1991. Arts of the Contact Zone. *Profession* 91. 33–40.
Preston, Dennis R. 1985. The Li'l Abner syndrome: Written representations of speech. *American Speech* 60(4). 328–336.
Rabain-Jamin, J. 1998. Polyadic language socialization strategy: The case of toddlers in Senegal. *Discourse Processes* 26. 43–65.
Ribeiro, Gustavo Lins. 2003. *Postimperialismo. Cultura y política en el mundo contemporáneo*. Barcelona/Buenos Aires: Gedisa.
Ricento, Thomas. 2005. Problems with the 'language-as-resource' discourse in the promotion of heritage languages in the U.S.A. *Journal of Sociolinguistics* 9(3). 348–368.
Robbins, Bruce. 1998. Introduction part I: Actually existing cosmopolitanism. In Pheng Cheah & Bruce Robbins (eds.), *Cosmopolitics: Thinking and feeling beyond the nation*, 1–19. Minneapolis, MN: University of Minnesota Press.
Roberge, Mark. 2002. California's Generation 1.5 immigrants: What experiences, characteristics, and needs do they bring to our English classes? *The CATESOL Journal* 14. 107–130.
Roberts, Celia. 1997. The politics of transcription—Transcribing talk: Issues of representation. *TESOL Quarterly* 31(1). 167–172.
Roca, Ana. 2005. Raising a bilingual child in Miami. In Ana Celia Zentella (ed.), *Building on strength: Language and literacy in Latino families and communities*, 110–118. New York: Teachers College Press.

Rodríguez, Richard. 1982. *Hunger of memory: The education of Richard Rodríguez*. Boston: Bantam Books.

Rodriguez, Terri L. 2007. *Language, culture, and resistance as resource: Case studies of bilingual/bicultural Latino prospective elementary teachers and the crafting of teaching practices*. Madison, WI: University of Wisconsin doctoral dissertation.

Ronjat, Jules. 1913. *Le développement du langage observé chez un enfant bilingue*. Paris, France: Champion.

Rothman, Jason & Mercedes Niño-Murcia. 2008. Multilingualism and identity: All in the family. In M. Niño-Murcia & J. Rothman (eds.), *Bilingualism and identity: Spanish at the crossroads with other languages*, 301–329. Amsterdam: John Benjamins.

Roudometof, Victor. 2005. Transnationalism, cosmopolitanism and glocalization. *Current Sociology* 53(1). 113–135.

Roy, Sylvie. 2003. Bilingualism and standardization in a Canadian call center: Challenges for a linguistic minority community. In Robert Bayley & Sandra R. Schecter (eds.), *Language socialization in bilingual and multilingual societies*, 269–285. Clevedon, UK: Multilingual Matters.

Ruiz, Richard. 1984. Orientations in language planning. *NABE Journal* 8(2). 15–34.

Rumbaut, Rubén G. & Kenji Ima. 1988. The adaptation of Southeast Asian refugee youth: A comparative study. Final report to the U.S. Department of Health and Human Services, Office of Refugee Resettlement. San Diego: San Diego State University (ERIC Document Reproduction Service No. ED 299372).

Ryu, Charles. 1991. 1.5 Generation. In J. F. J. Lee (ed.), *Asian American experiences in the United States: Oral histories of first to fourth generation of Americans from China, Philippines, Japan, India, the Pacific Islands, Vietnam and Cambodia*, 50–54. Jefferson, NC: McFarland & Company Inc.

Sabogal, Fabio, Gerardo Marin, Regina Otero-Sabogal, Barbara V. Marin & Eliseo J. Perez-Stable. 1987. Hispanic familism and acculturation: What changes and what doesn't? *Hispanic Journal of Behavioral Sciences* 9. 397–412.

Sacks, Harvey. 1973/1987. On the preferences for agreement and contiguity in sequences in conversation. In G. Button & J. R. Lee (eds.), *Talk and social organisation*, 54–69. Clevedon, UK: Multilingual Matters.

Sacks, Harvey, E. A. Schegloff & G. Jefferson. 1974. A simplest systematics for the organization of turn-taking for conversation. *Language* 50. 696–735.

Said, Edward W. 1978. *Orientalism: Western conceptions of the Orient*. New York: Pantheon Books.

Said, Edward W. 1993. *Culture and imperialism*. New York: Random House.

Sakamoto, Mitsuyo. 2000. *Raising bilingual and trilingual children: Japanese immigrant parents' child-rearing experiences*. Canada: Ontario Institute for Studies in Education, University of Toronto doctoral dissertation.

Sakamoto, Mitsuyo. 2001. Exploring societal support for L2 learning and L1 maintenance: A socio-cultural perspective. *ARAL* 24(2). 43–60.

Dare to Deliver 2011–2015: The Academic Plan for the University of Alberta http://www.president.ualberta.ca/~/media/University of Alberta/Administration/Office of the President/Documents/D2DAcademicPlan-2011-2015.pdf. Accessed September 25, 2011.

Saracho, Olivia N. 2002. Family literacy: Exploring family practices. *Early Child Development and Care* 172(2). 113–122.

Sarason, Seymour B. 1974. *The psychological sense of community: Prospects for a community psychology*. Oxford: Jossey-Bass.

Savignon, Sandra J. 1987. Communicative language teaching. *Theory into Practice* 26(4). 235–242.
Saville-Troike, Muriel. 2003. *The ethnography of communication: An introduction*, 3rd edn (Language in society 3). Malden, MA: Blackwell Publishing.
Schecter, Sandra R. & Robert Bayley. 1997. Language socialization practices and cultural identity: Case studies of Mexican-descent families in California and Texas. *TESOL Quarterly* 31(3). 513–541.
Schecter, Sandra R. & Robert Bayley. 2002. *Language as cultural practice: Mexicanos en El Norte*. Mahwah, NJ: Lawrence Erlbaum Associates.
Schecter, Sandra R., Diane Sharken-Taboada & Robert Bayley. 1996. Bilingual by choice: Latino parents' rationales and strategies for raising children with two languages. *Bilingual Research Journal* 20(2). 261–281.
Schegloff, Emanuel A. 2007. *Sequence organization in interaction: A primer in Conversation Analysis*. Cambridge: Cambridge University Press.
Schegloff, Emanuel A., G. Jefferson & H. Sacks. 1977. The preference for self-correction in the organization of repair in conversation. *Language and Education* 53. 361–382.
Schieffelin, Bambi B. 1986. Teasing and shaming in Kaluli children's interactions. In Bambi B. Schieffelin & Elinor Ochs (eds.), *Language socialization across cultures*. Cambridge: Cambridge University Press.
Schieffelin, Bambi B. 1990. *The give and take of everyday life: Language socialization of Kaluli children*. Cambridge: Cambridge University Press.
Schieffelin, Bambi B. & Elinor Ochs. 1986a. Language socialization. *Annual Review of Anthropology* 15. 163–191.
Schieffelin, Bambi B. & Elinor Ochs. 1986b. *Language socialization across cultures*. New York: Cambridge University Press.
Schieffelin, Bambi B., Kathryn A. Woolard & Paul V. Kroskrity (eds.). 1998. *Language ideologies: Practice and theory*. New York: Oxford University Press.
Schiff-Myers, Naomi B. 1992. Considering arrested language development and language loss in the assessment of second language learners. *Language, Speech, and Hearing Services in Schools* 23. 28–33.
Schiffrin, Deborah. 1994. *Approaches to discourse*. Oxford: Blackwell.
Schmidt, Richard. 1990. The role of consciousness in second language learning. *Applied Linguistics* 11. 129–158.
Seliger, Herbert W. & Robert M. Vago (eds.). 1991. *First language attrition*. New York: Cambridge University Press.
Séror, Jérémie. 2008. *Socialization in the margins: Second language writers and feedback practices in university content courses*. Vancouver, Canada: University of British Columbia doctoral dissertation.
Séror, Jérémie. 2009. Institutional forces and L2 writing feedback in higher dducation. *The Canadian Modern Language Review* 66(2). 203–232.
Shaw, Patricia A. 2001. Language and identity, language and the land. *BC Studies* 131. 39–55.
Shayne, Julie. 2009. *They used to call us witches: Chilean exiles, culture, and feminism*. Lanham, MD: Lexington Books.
Sheen, Younghee. 2004. Corrective feedback and learner uptake in communicative classrooms across instructional settings. *Language Teaching Research* 8. 263–300.
Sidnell, Jack. 2010. *Conversation Analysis: An introduction*. Malden, MA: Wiley-Blackwell.
Silva-Corvalán, C. 1991. Spanish language attrition in a contact situation with English. In H. Seliger & R. Vago (eds.), *First language attrition*, 151–171. Boston: Cambridge University Press.

Silverstein, Michael. 1979. Language structure and linguistic ideology. In Paul R. Clyne, William F. Hanks & Carol L. Hofbauer (eds.), *The elements: A parasession on linguistic units and levels*, 193–247. Chicago: Chicago Linguistics Society.

Simalchik, Joan. 2006. The material culture of Chilean exiles: A transnational dialogue. *Refuge* 23(2). 95–105.

Skutnabb-Kangas, Tove. 1999. Education of minorities. In J. A. Fishman (ed.), *Handbook of language and ethnic identity*, 42–59. New York & Oxford: Oxford University Press.

Slavik, Hannah. 2001. Language maintenance and language shift among Maltese migrants in Ontario and British Columbia. *International Journal of the Sociology of Language* 152. 131–152.

Smith, Elsie J. 1991. Ethnic identity development: Toward the development of a theory within the context of majority/minority status. *Journal of Counseling and Development* 70(1). 181–188.

Smith, William. 2007. Cosmopolitan citizenship: Virtue, irony and worldliness. *European Journal of Social Theory* 10(1). 37–52.

Smythe, Suzanne. 2006. *The good mother: A critical discourse analysis of literacy advice to mothers in the 20th century*. Vancouver, Canada: University of British Columbia doctoral dissertation.

Sodhi, Pavna. 2007. Respecting the East, embracing the West: A tribute to the women of the Maritime Sikh Society. *Journal of International Women's Studies* 9(1). 285–296.

Sommerer, Lotte. 2006. Language Acquisition revisited—a network-based approach. *Vienna English Working Papers* 15(1). 25–56.

Søndergaard, Bent & Catrin Norrby. 2006. Language maintenance and shift in the Danish community in Melbourne. *Journal of the Sociology of Language* 180. 105–121.

Sonn, Christopher & Adrian Fisher. 1996. Psychological sense of community in a politically constructed group. *Journal of Community Psychology* 24(4). 417–430.

Sonn, Christopher & Adrian Fisher. 1998. Sense of community: Community resilient responses to oppression and change. *Journal of Community Psychology* 26(5). 457–472.

Spolsky, Bernard. 2004. *Language policy*. Cambridge: Cambridge University Press.

Spolsky, Bernard. 2009. *Language management*. Cambridge: Cambridge University Press.

Starkey, Hugh. 2007. Language education, identities and citizenship: Developing cosmopolitan perspectives. *Language and Intercultural Communication* 7(1). 56–71.

Statistics Canada. 2011. 2011 Census: Mixed unions in Canada. https://www12.statcan.gc.ca/nhs-enm/2011/as-sa/99-010-x/99-010-x2011003_3-eng.cfm. Accessed 2016.

Statistics Canada: Income Statistics Division. 2004. Low income cutoffs from 1994—2003 and low income measures from 1992—2001. Ottawa: Minister of Industry.

Steuter, Erin & Deborah Wills. 2009. Discourses of dehumanization: Enemy construction and Canadian media complicity in the framing of the war on terror. *Global Media Journal— Canadian Edition* 2(2). 7–24.

Suarez, Debra. 2007. Second and third generation heritage language speakers: HL scholarship's relevance to the research needs and future directions of TESOL. *Heritage Language Journal* 1(5). 27–49.

Suárez-Orozco, Carola Elizabeth. 1993. *Generational discontinuities: A cross-culture study of familism and achievement motivation in Mexican, Mexican immigrant, Mexican American, and white non-Hispanic adolescents*. San Diego, California: California School of Professional Psychology.

Szecsi, Tunde & Janka Szilagyi. 2012. Immigrant Hungarian families' perceptions of new media technologies in the transmission of heritage language and culture. *Language, Culture and Curriculum* 25(3). 265–281.

Tahan, Malba. 1972. *El hombre que calculaba*. Barcelona: Editorial Verón.
Talmy, Steven. 2005. *Lifers and FOBs, rocks and resistance: Generation 1.5, identity, and the cultural productions of ESL in a high school*. Honolulu, HI: University of Hawai'i at Mānoa doctoral dissertation.
Talmy, Steven. 2008. The cultural productions of the ESL student at Tradewinds High: Contingency, multidirectionality, and identity in L2 socialization. *Applied Linguistics* 29(4). 619–644.
Talmy, Steven. 2009. A very important lesson: Respect and the socialization of order(s) in high school ESL. *Linguistics and Education* 20. 235–253.
Talmy, Steven. 2010. Qualitative interviews in applied linguistics: From research instrument to social practice. *Annual Review of Applied Linguistics* 30. 128–148.
Talmy, Steven. 2015. A language socialization perspective on identity work of ESL youth in a superdiverse high school classroom. In Numa Markee (ed.), *The handbook of classroom discourse and interaction*, 353–369. Oxford, UK: John Wiley & Sons.
Talmy, Steven & Keith Richards. 2010. Theorizing qualitative research interviews in applied linguistics. *Applied Linguistics* 32(1). 1–5.
Tamura, Eileen H. 1996. Power, status, and Hawai'i Creole English: An example of linguistic intolerance in American history. *The Pacific Historical Review* 65(3). 431–454.
Tannenbaum, Michal. 2005. Viewing family relations through a linguistic lens: Symbolic aspects of language maintenance in immigrant families. *Journal of Family Communication* 5(3). 229–252.
Tannenbaum, Michal & Marina Berkovich. 2005. Family relations and language maintenance: Implications for language educational policies. *Language Policy* 4. 287–309.
Tannenbaum, Michal & Pauline Howie. 2002. The association between language maintenance and family relations: Chinese immigrant children in Australia. *Journal of Multilingual and Multicultural Development* 23. 408–424.
Teale, William H. & E. Sulzby. 1986. Home background and young children's literacy development. In W. H. Teale & E. Sulzby (eds.), *Emerging literacy: Writing and reading*, vii-xxv. Norwood, NJ: Ablex Publishing Corporation.
ten Have, Paul. 2001. Applied conversation analysis. In McHoul A & Rapley M (eds.), *How to analyze talk in institutional settings: A casebook of methods*, 3–11. London: Continuum.
ten Have, Paul. 2007. *Doing Conversation Analysis: A practical guide*. Thousand Oaks, CA: Sage.
Thomas, Lee & Linh Cao. 1999. Language use in family and in society. *English Journal* 89. 107–113.
Tigchelaar, Marianne. 2003. *Language loss and language maintenance: Life history accounts of selected members of the Sikh community*. Winnipeg, Manitoba: University of Manitoba master's thesis.
Ting-Toomey, Stella & Leeva C. Chung. 2007. *Understanding intercultural communication*. New York: Oxford University Press.
Torres, Ana. 2006. *Family, ethnic identity and education in relation to generational heritage language maintenance and shift among Chicanos of the South Plains*. Lubbock, TX: Texas Tech University doctoral dissertation.
Tsushima, Rika & Martin Guardado. 2015. Japanese mothers in interlingual families: Mobilizing family-generated knowledge through community workshops. Paper presented at Joint Conference American Association for Applied Linguistics & Canadian Association of Applied Linguistics, Toronto, Ontario, Canada.

Tsushima, Rika & Martin Guardado. in press. "Rules ... I want someone to make them clear": Japanese mothers in Montreal talk about multilingual parenting. *Journal of Language, Identity, and Education*.

Place and Promise: The UBC Plan http://strategicplan.ubc.ca/files/2009/11/UBCStrategicPlan.pdf. Accessed December 12, 2011.

Towards 2030: Planning for a third century of excellence at the University of Toronto http://www.towards2030.utoronto.ca/files/2030_REDUXv7.pdf. Accessed December 12, 2011.

Useem, John, Ruth Useem & John Donoghue. 1963. Men in the middle of the third culture: The roles of American and non-Western people in cross-cultural administration. *Human Organization* 22(3). 169–179.

Valdés, Guadalupe. 1996. *Con respeto: Bridging the distances between culturally diverse families and schools*. New York: Teachers College Press.

van Dijk, Teun A. 1993. *Elite discourse and racism*. London: Sage.

van Dijk, Teun A. 2008. *Society and discourse: How social contexts control text and talk*. Cambridge: Cambridge University Press.

Von Staden, Anna & Andrea Sterzuk. 2017. "Un-frenching" des Canadiennes françaises: Histoires des Fransaskoises en situation linguistique minoritaire ["Un-frenching" francophone Canadians: The histories of Fransaskatchewanians in a linguistic minority situation]. *Canadian Journal of Applied Linguistics* 20(1). 98–114.

Vygotsky, Lev S. 1978. *Mind in society: The development of higher psychological processes*. Cambridge, MA: Harvard University Press.

Waas, Margit. 1993. Loss of first language skills in the community: Intermediate stage. *Language Problems and Language Planning* 17. 225–237.

Waas, Margit. 1997. First language loss: Reflex responses, repartee and sound symbolism. *Language Problems and Language Planning* 21. 119–131.

Watson-Gegeo, Karen Ann & David W. Gegeo. 1986. Calling-out and repeating routines in Kware'ae chidlren's language socialization. In Bambi B. Schieffelin & Elinor Ochs (eds.), *Language socialization across cultures*. Cambridge: Cambridge University Press.

Wei, Li. 1994. *Three generations, two languages, one family: Language choice and language shift in a Chinese community in Britain*. Clevedon, UK: Multilingual Matters.

Wei, Li (ed.) 2000. *The bilingualism reader*. New York: Routledge.

Weise, Elizabeth. 2007. As China booms, so does Mandarin in US schools. USA Today. http://www. usatoday. com/news/education/2007-11-19-mandarincover_n.htm.

Wiley, Terrence & Marguerite Lukes. 1996. English-only and Standard English ideologies in the U.S. *TESOL Quarterly* 30(3). 120–144.

Willett, Jerri. 1995. Becoming first graders in an L2: An ethnographic study of L2 socialization. *TESOL Quarterly* 29(3). 473–503.

Wodak, Ruth, Rudolf de Cillia, Martin Reisigl & Karin Liebhart. 1999. *The discursive construction of national identity*, translated by Angelika Hirsch & Richard Mitten. Edinburgh: Edinburgh University Press.

Wodak, Ruth & Michael Meyer. 2009. Critical discourse analysis: History, agenda, theory, and methodology. In Ruth Wodak & Michael Meyer (eds.), *Methods of critical discourse analysis*, 1–33. Los Angeles: SAGE.

Wong Fillmore, Lilly. 1991. When learning a second language means losing the first. *Early Childhood Research Quarterly* 6. 323–346.

Wooffitt, R. 2001. Researching psychic practitioners: Conversation analysis. In M. Wetherell, S. Taylor & S. J. Yates (eds.), *Discourse as data: A guide for analysis*, 49–92. London: The Open University/Sage.

Woolard, Kathryn A. 1998. Introduction: Language ideology as a field of inquiry. In Bambi B. Schieffelin, Kathryn A. Woolard & Paul V. Kroskrity (eds.), *Language ideologies: Practice and theory*, 3–47. New York: Oxford University Press.
Woolard, Kathryn A. & Bambi B. Schieffelin. 1994. Language ideology. *Annual Review of Anthropology* 23. 55–82.
Wortham, Stanton. 2005. Socialization beyond the speech event. *Journal of Linguistic Anthropology* 15(1). 95–112.
Wortham, Stanton. 2012. Introduction to the special issue: Beyond macro and micro in the linguistic anthropology of education. *Anthropology & Education Quarterly* 43(2). 128–137.
Worthy, Jo & Alejandra Rodríguez-Galindo. 2006. "*Mi hija vale dos personas*": Latino immigrant parents' perspectives about their children's bilingualism. *Bilingual Research Journal* 30(2). 579–601.
Wright, Wayne E. 2010. Khmer as a heritage language in the United States: Historical sketch, current realities, and future prospects. *Heritage Language Journal* 7(1). 117–147.
Xiao, Hong. 1998. Chinese language maintenance in Winnipeg. *Canadian Ethnic Studies* 30(1). 86–96.
Xie, Mianmian. 2010. *First language maintenance and attrition among young Chinese adult immigrants: A multi-case study*. Edmonton, Canada: University of Alberta Unpublished doctoral dissertation.
Yamamoto, Masayo. 2001. *Language use in interlingual families: A Japanese-English sociolinguistic study*. Clevedon, UK: Multilingual Matters.
Yamamoto, Masayo. 2005. What makes who choose what languages to whom?: Language use in Japanese–Filipino interlingual families in Japan. *International Journal of Bilingual Education and Bilingualism* 8(6). 588–606.
Yim, Yoon-kyung Kecia. 2011. Second language students' discourse socialization in academic online communities. *The Canadian Modern Language Review* 67(1). 1–27.
Yin, Robert K. 1994. *Case study research: Design and methods*, 2nd edn. Thousand Oaks, CA: Sage.
Zappa-Hollman, Sandra. 2007. Academic presentations across post-secondary contexts: The discourse socialization of non-native English speakers. *The Canadian Modern Language Review* 63(4). 455–485.
Zentella, Ana Celia. 1996. The "chiquitafication" of U.S. Latinos and their language, or why we need a politically applied Applied Linguistics. Paper presented at Plenary address to the American Association for Applied Linguistics Annual Meeting, Chicago, IL.
Zentella, Ana Celia. 1997. *Growing up bilingual: Puerto Rican children in New York*. Oxford: Blackwell.
Zentella, Ana Celia (ed.) 2005. *Building on strength: Language and literacy in Latino families and communities*. New York: Teachers College Press.
Zhang, Donghui. 2005. *Home language maintenance and acculturation among second-generation Chinese children*. Philadelphia: University of Pennsylvania Unpublished doctoral dissertation.
Zhou, Yali & Enrique T. Trueba (eds.). 1998. *Ethnic identity and power: Cultural contexts of political action in school and society*. New York: SUNY Press.

A note on the texts

Permission to reproduce texts is acknowledged here as follows:

Chapter 6: An earlier version appeared as (2014) 'The Discourses of Heritage Language Development: Engaging Ideologies in Canadian Hispanic Communities', by Martin Guardado, *Heritage Language Journal*, 11(1), 1–28.

Chapter 12: An earlier version appeared as (2013) 'The Metapragmatic Regimentation of Language Use in Hispanic Canadian Caregiver-Child Interactions', by Martin Guardado, *International Multilingual Research Journal*, 7(3), 230–247.

Chapter 13: An earlier version appeared as (2010) 'Heritage Language Development: Preserving a Mythic Past or Envisioning the Future of Canadian Identity?', by Martin Guardado, *Journal of Language, Identity, and Education*, 9(5), 329–346.

Chapter 14: An earlier version appeared as (2012) 'Toward a Critical Multilingualism in Canadian Classrooms: Making Local Inroads into a Cosmopolitan Identity', by Martin Guardado, *TESL Canada Journal*, 30(1), 151–165.

Subject index

adjacency pair 175
   see also conversation analysis
Afghanistan 75, 85
Africa 38, 126, 182
   see also Black community
agency 2, 5, 46, 52–53, 69, 89, 129, 140, 202
Alberta 60, 109, 134, 223, 225, 234, 143
   see also University of Alberta
analysis
– critical discourse analysis 70–72, 74–79
– conversation analysis v, 2, 9, 15, 166, 171–175, 177–180, 183, 186–187, 191, 193–197, 199–202
– folk analysis 67, 99
– of interaction 13, 39, 62, 78, 166, 170, 172, 176, 182, 187–188, 200–201
– language socialization analysis 35, 43–44, 54–55, 63
– linguistic analysis v
– meta analysis 14, 101–114, 233
– thematic analysis v, 9, 13, 81–83, 86, 91–92, 96, 119–121, 176–177, 186–187, 201, 233
– unit of analysis 125, 145
Appalachian English 59
Argentina 95, 210
assimilation, assimilative forces 33, 93–94, 112, 117, 129, 139, 143, 147, 149, 163, 188, 211, 227
attitudes
   see language ideologies
Australia 39

baby–talk
   see motherese
Baghdad 162
belonging 104, 109, 117, 125–127, 134, 137–138, 143, 207, 214, 218, 221, 228, 234
   see also community membership
   see also identity
Big Bang 238
   see also black holes

bilingual, bilingually, bilingualism, multilingual, multilingualism 1, 4–5, 11–12, 27–28, 34, 39, 43, 45–49, 52, 54, 57–58, 62, 66, 68, 81, 92, 94, 96, 104, 117, 166, 170, 173, 178, 201, 207, 209–210, 214, 216–217, 219–220, 226–229, 234–236
biliteracy 4, 168
British Columbia 10, 128–129, 136, 143, 223, 225, 234
   see also University of British Columbia

Canada 9–10, 12, 23–24, 26, 28, 39, 43, 49–51, 58–61, 63, 67, 85, 97, 101, 109–110, 120, 129, 132, 134–136, 138, 141–143, 147, 152, 156, 159, 169, 184, 208, 211–212, 214, 216, 220, 222–227, 229
Canadian
– culture 162
– identity 139, 213–214, 218, 220, 227, 229
capital
– inguistic, cultural, symbolic, social, economic capital 27–28, 33, 66, 84, 89, 96, 109, 140, 224, 226
change-of-state token 198–199
CHILDES (Child Language Data Exchange System) 201
Chile 134–135
Chilean
– culture 135
– population 60, 67, 134–135
– Spanish 61
Chinese
– as a heritage language 30–31, 58, 109, 173
– as a second language 225
– community 23, 29, 32, 61, 112, 128, 169, 209, 213
Christmas 130, 159
citizen of the world 97, 100, 207, 214, 221
   see also global citizenship
   see also global citizen
   see also cosmopolitan, cosmopolitanism
   see also identity

https://doi.org/10.1515/9781614513841-017

clarification requests 184–185, 195–196, 200–201
  see also commands
  see also cross-code recasts, CCRs
  see also metapragmatic strategies
code-mix, code-mixing 92, 178, 181, 198
code-switch, code-switching, code-shift, code-shifting 8, 36, 44–45, 92, 111, 170–173, 178–179, 181, 184, 191, 201
coding (data) 13, 82, 110, 187–188
  see also analysis
Colombia 85, 93–94, 150, 152
commands 91, 182, 190, 193–194, 196–197, 199, 201–202
  see also clarification requests
  see also cross-code recasts, CCRs
  see also metapragmatic strategies
Common Curriculum Framework for International Languages, Kindergarten to Grade 12, *225*
community 8, 48, 97, 125–126, 144
 – Black community 37, 59, 127–128, 143, 145
  see also Africa
 – cohesive community 7
 – culture 14
 – engagement 223, 234, 236
 – ethnic community 1
 – groups 104, 125, 128
 – minority community 58
 – language 37
 – leaders 7, 237
 – membership 1, 3, 14, 24, 30–31, 33–34, 36–41, 43, 44–45, 48–49, 52–54, 56, 61–62, 67–68, 77, 97–98, 101, 104, 118, 120, 125–128, 142–143, 148, 172, 206–207, 209, 218, 221–224, 228, 231, 233–234
  see also belonging
 – role of community 25, 125
 – organizations 12
 – sense of community 125–126, 132, 138, 142, 144–145
 – service 130, 136, 143
 – Spanish-speaking community 8
 – Speech community 12, 31, 36, 39–41, 44–45, 54
  see also grassroots groups

contact zones 94, 137–138
corrective feedback 63, 180–183, 192
  see also cross-code recasts, CCRs
  see also metapragmatic strategies
cosmopolitan, cosmopolitanism 15, 23, 32, 61, 81, 96–99, 104, 106, 112–113, 117–118, 162, 205, 206, 207, 208, 212–229, 235
critical
 – discourse analysis 1, 14, 70–78, 118, 163
 – theory 1, 2, 14, 16, 70–72, 74, 76–78, 94, 118, 220, 224, 227, 230
 – discourse studies
  see critical discourse analysis
 – pedagogy
  see critical theory
cross-code recasts 92, 183–184, 191–193, 199–200, 202
  see also corrective feedback
  see also metapragmatic strategies
cross-linguistic/cross-cultural marriages
  see interlingual families
cultural
 – affirmation 90
 – ambivalence 126
 – contact 39, 47
 – hegemony 117, 161
 – identity 27, 33, 89, 93, 96, 108, 126, 154, 163, 213
 – tension 137
culture(s), Hispanic and others 3, 11, 14, 23, 36, 38, 58, 75, 86–87, 93, 95–96, 110, 118, 121, 128, 130, 135–136, 138–139, 143–144, 151–152, 158, 160, 202, 206–207, 210214, 217–218, 224, 233–234
 – marginal culture 137, 141
 – subversive culture 139
 – valuing 58, 97
Cynics 221

Danish language 169
data
 – analysis
  see analysis
 – collection 9, 13, 82–83, 121
 – sources v 9–13

diaspora 109, 126, 128, 134–135, 142, 207, 218, 234
diasporic
– familism 142, 144–145, 152
– identities 135
  see also familism
Diogenes 221
directives 167
discourse
– definition 70–71
– origin 71–74
discourses of
– access 110
– affect 86, 110
– coercion 72, 168, 201, 234
– cohesiveness 85, 98, 106, 108
– correctness 91
– cosmopolitanism 96–98, 216
– dehumanization 75
– domination 75
– exclusion 77
– global citizenship 222
– heritage language development 81
– heritage languages 1, 14, 81, 83, 85, 94, 98, 101, 105, 108, 113–114, 116, 118–121, 146, 216, 232–233
– identity 108
– inclusion 77
– opposition 111, 163
– patriarchy 76
– Spanish as a heritage language 83, 94
– terrorism 222
– validation 89–91
diversity 8, 12–13, 50, 95, 97, 131, 139, 146, 207–208, 210, 214, 220–221, 224, 227–228
dominant
– language 8
– culture 45, 93, 99, 103, 112, 125, 137
– discourses 147
Dora the Explorer 224

Edmonton 60, 120, 134–135, 137, 140, 143, 145
El Barrio (New York) 7–8, 22, 44, 172,
El Centro de Cultura 13, 87, 90, 95, 131, 135, 138, 140, 181, 191, 193, 209–210

  see also grassroots groups
El Grupo Scout Vistas 13, 63–64, 129, 136, 143, 188, 197
  see also grassroots groups
El Salvador 148, 164
ethnography 8–12, 14, 21, 33, 36–37, 39, 41–42, 44, 81, 102, 139, 152, 181, 208
ethnography of communication v, 12, 21, 36, 39
ethnolinguistic
– community 22, 39, 108, 151, 234
– identity 196
expressed guess strategies 171, 185, 200
  see also minimal grasp strategies
  see also clarification requests
  see also metapragmatic strategies
eye dialect 178

familism 128–129, 138, 141–142, 145, 234
family
– as community 145, 147, 236
– language policy 51, 65, 163, 166–167, 181, 185–186, 192, 236
– literacy 156, 159–160, 162–163
First Nations/Indigenous
– communities 43
– languages 61, 102
French 26, 57, 61, 73, 84, 95, 181, 184, 209, 225–226
– immersion 184, 209, 225–226

Generation 1.5 43, 205–207, 212, 216, 218
  see also Third Culture Kids
German 7, 110
Germany 110, 222
global
– citizen 213
– citizenship 214, 217, 222–225, 228
  see also citizen of the world
  see also identity
globalization 39, 220, 222, 228, 235
  see also cosmopolitan, cosmopolitanism
  see also internationalization
  see also transnationalism
grassroots groups 2, 13–14, 32, 59, 90–91, 99, 101, 125, 127–129, 134–135, 137, 139–146, 148, 165, 185, 187, 191–192, 197–198, 202, 208–209, 219, 233–235, 237

– role of 125, 128, 134, 136–137, 141,
    144–145, 233
– as primary communities 144–145
Great Britain
    see United Kingdom
Greek Stoics 221
Guatemala 95, 97, 129, 159–160, 208, 210, 214

Hawaii 38
heritage language
– community 31
– culture 35, 48–49, 100, 104, 112, 137,
    146–147, 164, 169, 190, 214, 234
    see also culture
– development v, 1, 8–10, 12, 15–16, 19–20,
    22–23, 25, 27–33, 51, 54, 56–58, 62–63,
    77–78, 60, 62, 69, 71, 77, 81, 83–87,
    9195, 97–99, 101–105, 108, 110–121, 125,
    128, 133–134, 143, 145–148, 150–151,
    153–154, 160, 163–165, 168–170, 172,
    179, 186–187, 200–202, 205, 207, 209,
    210, 213, 215–218, 233–236, 238
– identity 22, 27, 48, 116, 158–159, 173,
    217–218
– ideology *see* language ideologies
– socialization v, vi, 2, 4–6, 11, 19, 21, 30, 34,
    46–51, 58, 145, 159, 165, 167, 172–173,
    186, 205, 214, 231, 233, 235–237
– and self-esteem 24, 86–87, 98, 117, 137,
    144, 219
Hispanic
– community 84, 98, 128–129, 136, 146
– culture 87, 128, 130, 136, 143, 164, 224
    – *see* also culture
– families 11, 23–24, 32, 43, 58–59, 81, 101,
    139, 144, 159, 168, 224, 226
– identity 86, 208, 217
    see also identity
– population 10, 12, 32, 58, 63, 89, 120, 128,
    136, 140–143, 147, 149, 165, 234, 216
hybrid
– cultures 109, 207, 215, 221
– identities 97, 110, 187, 212, 214, 222
    see also syncretic identity

identity
– affirmation 201–202
– ambivalence 28
– and agency 53
– complex identities 58, 205–206,
    209, 215, 217
– cosmopolitan identities 23, 97, 104, 118,
    205–209, 212–218, 221–222, 227, 235
– discourse and identity 71–72
– discourses of identity 85–86, 98, 102–103,
    108–109 111, 117
– ethnic identities 57
– formation 1, 5, 44–45, 48, 62, 67–68, 74,
    96, 103, 127, 133, 144, 147, 152, 164,
    205–206, 213–214, 217, 228
– ideology 5, 55–57, 66, 224
– imposed identities 64
– local identities 135
– linguistic identities 21, 44
– multilingual identities 92, 94
– multiple identities 43, 162
– national identities 74, 208
– negotiation 45
– pan-ethnic identities 23, 208–209, 215
– politics of identity 94
– religious identities 58
– resistance and identity 99, 201
– role of identity 23, 98
– syncretic identity 212–213, 217
– social identity 38, 42, 44
– and socialization 168
– theory of identity 30
– validation 93
implicature 196
insisting strategies 167
    see also metapragmatic strategies
    see also parental discourse strategies
    see also commands
    see also cross-code recasts, CCRs
    see also clarification requests
intercultural couples
    see interlingual families
intergenerational
– communication 28–29, 85, 98, 128, 167
– unity 142
interlingual families 49–51, 54, 136,
    168, 236
intermarried couples
    see interlingual families
international community 15
internationalization 220, 222–223, 225

interview, interviewing 10–13, 67, 81–83, 88, 95–96, 131, 134, 153, 159–160, 168–170, 172–173, 176, 178, 186, 195, 200, 214
see also analysis
Israel 169

Japan 38, 50
Japanese
– as a heritage language 26, 109, 111–112
– community 26, 28–29, 42, 50, 51, 109, 213,
– language 26, 38, 109
– Saturday School 28

K–12 9, 26, 220, 225
Kaluli 37
Kant, Immanuel 221–222
Korean
– community 43, 62
– language 43, 111, 168–169
– population 128, 169
kosmopolitês 207, 222
see also cosmopolitan, cosmopolitanism

language ideologies 2–6, 11, 14, 21, 23, 25, 27, 32–33, 46, 48, 55–69, 75–78, 84–85, 98, 103, 117–118, 120, 128, 150, 167, 173, 178, 182, 186, 201, 216–217, 230–233, 235–238
– definition 55–56, 62, 67–68, 231–232
– origin 55–56
language socialization
– defensive language socialization 188–191, 201–202
– definition 34–36
– heritage language socialization see heritage language socialization,
– origin and contexts 37–46
L1
– community 151
– definition of 5–6
– loss 5, 7–8, 10, 19, 22–25, 27–29, 32–33, 60–62, 81, 98, 106–108, 115, 147, 159, 169, 201, 224
– maintenance, HL maintenance 1, 3, 5–8, 10–11, 14–16, 19, 21–25, 27, 29, 32–33, 44, 48, 55–58, 60, 62, 68–69, 78, 81, 83–87, 94, 96–99, 101–102, 108, 110, 115, 118, 134, 141–142, 144, 147–148, 150–152, 154–155, 159, 163–164, 169, 171–172, 186, 210, 213–218, 227, 235, 238
– research methods in 6–9
La Casa Amistad 13, 87, 90, 132–133, 135, 138, 140–142, 182, 208
see also grassroots groups
language
– and culture 1, 6, 15, 24, 29, 30, 34–35, 37, 45, 47, 53, 86, 90–91, 96–97, 100, 125, 129, 133–134, 136, 138, 140–142, 147, 151, 162, 209, 214, 217, 219, 228
– management 169, 191
– planning 21, 166–168, 201, 234, 236
– policy
see family language policy
– heritage language policy
see family language policy
– regulation 166–169, 172, 180, 185, 187, 193, 196, 199, 202
Latin America 74, 151, 209
Latin American
– countries 74, 150, 160
– culture 93, 136, 139, 151–152, 158
see also culture
– families 108
– identity 97, 139, 152, 154, 208, 213–214, 217
– people 151
– Spanish 191
linguistic
– community 1, 31, 34
– exogamy
see interlingual families
– minority 28
– strategies 2, 171, 186
literacy 4, 6, 15, 30, 37–38, 42, 46, 58, 65, 76, 103, 130, 133, 146–147, 149–150, 153, 155–158, 160–163, 165
locutionary, illocutionary, perlocutionary 191, 194, 200
London 50

Manitoba 225
Maya, Mayan 208
meta

– discourses 117
– language 49, 69, 184, 194, 199, 201–202, 234
– linguistic strategies
  see metapragmatic strategies
metapragmatic strategies 69, 199–200, 202
  see also commands
  see also cross-code recasts, CCRs
  see also clarification requests
  see also expressed guess strategies
  see also insisting strategies
  see also minimal grasp strategies
  see also parental discourse strategies
Mexican 8, 27, 45, 58–59, 97, 111, 171, 208, 213–214
Mexico 57, 95, 97, 132–133, 140, 142, 152–155, 195, 208–210, 212
Miami 151, 152
micro/macro scale v, 1–4, 11, 16, 21, 32, 35, 40–42, 48, 54, 92, 105, 115, 121, 172
Middle East 160, 162
minimal grasp strategies 171, 185, 196, 200
  see also expressed guess strategies
  see also clarification requests
  see also metapragmatic strategies
monolingual, monolingualism 4, 12, 26, 38, 44, 49, 54, 182–183, 200, 218, 229, 231, 235
mixed unions
  see interlingual families
Montreal 24, 26, 51, 151–152, 184
motherese 44, 181, 182
multicultural, multiculturalism 12, 15, 39, 43, 45, 60, 94, 97, 104, 206–207, 211–212, 214, 217, 220, 223, 226–229
multiculturality 219
multilingual couples
  see interlingual families
multilingual identities
  see identity
multilingually 4
multiple identities
  see identity

national identity
  see identity
New York 7, 8, 22, 44, 50, 169, 172
  see also El Barrio
noticing 176, 181, 183–184, 192–193

NUD*IST 82
NVivo 82

Obama, Barack 222
official
– bilingualism and culture 226
– multiculturalism 60
ontology v
oracy 156–157

pan-ethnic identity
  see identity
Papua New Guinea 37
parental discourse strategies 167, 170, 173, 200
  see also metapragmatic strategies
  see also commands
  see also cross-code recasts, CCRs
  see also clarification requests
  see also insisting strategies
  see also expressed guess strategies
  see also minimal grasp strategies
parentese
  see motherese
Persian 85
Peru 156, 158–159
pop culture 150
post-
– globalization 32
– modernism 119
– structuralism 205
Prairie Provinces, Canada 225
preference organization 174–175
primary community 144
prompting 38, 92, 167, 182–184, 191–193, 196, 198
prosody 174, 182, 196, 198
Pueblo Indian 57
Puerto Rican 7–8, 44, 172

qualitative research v, 10, 19, 29, 60, 82, 148
  see also analysis
Quebec 26, 61, 110

recasts 63, 182–184, 191–192
  see also cross-code recasts, CCRs
religious identities
  see identity

repair, self-repair, other repair 63, 171, 173–174, 176–177, 180–181, 196
REPARA (Recordar para Actuar) 135
  see also Co-Op
  see also grassroots groups
requests 132, 169, 172, 193, 199, 200, 201
  see also clarification requests
reversing language shift 28
Russian
 – community, language 169

safe houses 90, 110, 129, 137–140, 143
  see also grassroots groups
Samoa 37–38
Saskatchewan 225
Scouts, Scout Movement 59, 63–68, 87–89, 93, 95, 97, 129–131, 136, 143, 159–162, 170, 185, 188, 190, 197, 202
Senegal 182
sense of community
  see community
social identity
  see identity
socializing strategies 15, 45, 47, 63, 69, 93, 125, 132, 147–148, 157, 160, 163, 165–166, 171–173, 182, 185–186, 193, 199–202, 233
sociolinguistics 3, 19–21, 34, 36–37, 115, 167, 238
sociology of language vi, 3, 20–21, 33
Solomon Islands 38
Spain, España 59, 74, 85, 95, 191, 208, 209, 210
Spanish
 – community 26, 46, 135–136, 142, 191, 208–209
 – culture see culture
 – language 8, 12, 61, 66–67, 84, 86, 90, 112, 132–133, 143, 149, 152–155, 165, 171, 191, 210, 212, 224, 234
speech act 38, 182
speech community
  see community
subversive cultures
  see culture
surrogate extended families 134, 142, 234
  see also grassroots groups
Sydney 50
syncretic identity
  see identity
systemic functional linguistics v, 56, 74

Tewa 57
The Co-Op 134, 137
  see also grassroots groups
  see also REPARA (Recordar para Actuar)
theory of identity
  see identity
think-aloud 192
Third Culture Kids 205–207, 212, 216–218
Tiergarten, Berlin 222
Toronto 60, 62, 223, 224
  see also University of Toronto
transcription v, 9, 13, 64, 81–82, 166, 173, 176–179, 187–188
  see also analysis
transnational, transnationalism 152, 156, 164, 206–207, 215, 217–218, 221, 227, 233, 235
  see also cosmopolitan, cosmopolitanism
turn-taking 42, 174–175, 177
  see also conversation analysis

United Kingdom 29, 50
United States 7, 23–24, 30, 37–39, 41, 43–46, 50, 57, 59, 75, 126–128, 143, 145, 182, 225
University of
 – Alberta vii, 223
 – British Columbia vii, 10, 223
 – Toronto 223–224

Vancouver 9–14, 24, 58, 63, 81, 90, 99, 102, 129, 131, 136, 140–141, 143, 145–146, 148–152, 154, 165, 168–169

Western
 – Canada 59, 225
 – Canadian Protocol for Collaboration in Basic Education 225
 – dominance 163
 – education 42
 – interactional style 41
 – world 38, 163
White community 37, 18
worldview 1, 23, 34, 37, 97, 104, 161–162, 212–214, 216–218, 225–226, 228

Yukon 225

www.ingramcontent.com/pod-product-compliance
Lightning Source LLC
Chambersburg PA
CBHW031724230426
43669CB00007B/239